Palgrave Studies in L

Series Editors
Clare Brant
Department of English
King's College London
London, UK

Max Saunders
Department of English
King's College London
London, UK

This series features books that address key concepts and subjects in life writing, with an emphasis on new and emergent approaches. It offers specialist but accessible studies of contemporary and historical topics, with a focus on connecting life writing to themes with cross-disciplinary appeal. The series aims to be the place to go to for current and fresh research for scholars and students looking for clear and original discussion of specific subjects and forms; it is also a home for experimental approaches that take creative risks with potent materials.

The term 'Life Writing' is taken broadly so as to reflect its academic, public, digital and international reach, and to continue and promote its democratic tradition. The series seeks contributions that address global contexts beyond traditional territories, and which engage with diversity of race, gender and class. It welcomes volumes on topics of everyday life and culture with which life writing scholarship can engage in transformative and original ways; it also aims to further the political engagement of life writing in relation to human rights, migration, trauma and repression, and the processes and effects of the Anthropocene, including environmental subjects where lives may be non-human. The series looks for work that challenges and extends how life writing is understood and practised, especially in a world of rapidly changing digital media; that deepens and diversifies knowledge and perspectives on the subject; and which contributes to the intellectual excitement and the world relevance of life writing.

More information about this series at
http://www.palgrave.com/gp/series/15200

Alexandra Effe • Hannie Lawlor
Editors

The Autofictional

Approaches, Affordances, Forms

Editors
Alexandra Effe
University of Oslo
Oslo, Norway

Hannie Lawlor
University of Oxford
Oxford, UK

ISSN 2730-9185 ISSN 2730-9193 (electronic)
Palgrave Studies in Life Writing
ISBN 978-3-030-78442-3 ISBN 978-3-030-78440-9 (eBook)
https://doi.org/10.1007/978-3-030-78440-9

© The Editor(s) (if applicable) and The Author(s) 2022. This book is an open access publication.

Open Access This book is licensed under the terms of the Creative Commons Attribution 4.0 International License (http://creativecommons.org/licenses/by/4.0/), which permits use, sharing, adaptation, distribution and reproduction in any medium or format, as long as you give appropriate credit to the original author(s) and the source, provide a link to the Creative Commons licence and indicate if changes were made.

The images or other third party material in this book are included in the book's Creative Commons licence, unless indicated otherwise in a credit line to the material. If material is not included in the book's Creative Commons licence and your intended use is not permitted by statutory regulation or exceeds the permitted use, you will need to obtain permission directly from the copyright holder.

The use of general descriptive names, registered names, trademarks, service marks, etc. in this publication does not imply, even in the absence of a specific statement, that such names are exempt from the relevant protective laws and regulations and therefore free for general use.

The publisher, the authors and the editors are safe to assume that the advice and information in this book are believed to be true and accurate at the date of publication. Neither the publisher nor the authors or the editors give a warranty, expressed or implied, with respect to the material contained herein or for any errors or omissions that may have been made. The publisher remains neutral with regard to jurisdictional claims in published maps and institutional affiliations.

Cover image © Guy Lambrechts, Image ID: 992782718

This Palgrave Macmillan imprint is published by the registered company Springer Nature Switzerland AG.
The registered company address is: Gewerbestrasse 11, 6330 Cham, Switzerland

ACKNOWLEDGEMENTS

This volume is the outcome of extensive collaboration with individuals and institutions to whom and to which we wish to express our gratitude. We owe special thanks to the Friedrich Schlegel Graduate School in Berlin and to the Oxford Centre for Life-Writing, and within them, to Professor Dr. Jutta Müller Tamm, Prof. Dr. Elleke Boehmer, and Dr. Kate Kennedy, for helping the project come into being through institutional support, intellectual input, and personal encouragement. We also thank the project "Literature, Cognition and Emotions" at the University of Oslo, and its convenor, Professor Dr. Karin Kukkonen, for providing funding for an editorial assistant and for help in the early planning stages of the publication. Funding from the University of Oxford and the Berlin University Alliance (the VC Diversity Fund and Andrew W. Mellon Foundation [2019] and the Oxford-Berlin Partnership Seed Funding [2019–2021]) has allowed us to organize an international conference during which some first thoughts for this book were sparked, to finance proof-reading, and to make the research presented here widely available as an open-access publication. For their thorough proof-reading and invaluable help in the editing process, we thank Andrea Dale Wefring and Dr. Sam Ferguson. We also owe our thanks to Dr. Marie Lindskov Hansen, for her conceptual and organizational help in the early stages of the project. Thanks are due lastly, and most importantly, to our contributors for their commitment to and enthusiasm for the project. We are grateful to them for taking us on a journey from autofiction to the autofictional.

Contents

1 Introduction: From Autofiction to the Autofictional 1
Alexandra Effe and Hannie Lawlor

Part I Approaches 19

2 Of Strange Loops and Real Effects: Five Theses on
Autofiction/the Autofictional 21
Martina Wagner-Egelhaaf

3 The Fictional in Autofiction 41
Alison James

4 A Cognitive Perspective on Autofictional Writing, Texts,
and Reading 61
Alexandra Effe and Alison Gibbons

5 "The Pragmatics of Autofiction" 83
Arnaud Schmitt

6 The Autofictional in Serial, Literary Works 101
Ricarda Menn and Melissa Schuh

Part II   Affordances 119

7   Metanarrative Autofiction: Critical Engagement with
    Cultural Narrative Models 121
    Hanna Meretoja

8   Multilingual Autofiction: Mobilizing Language(s)? 141
    Helle Egendal

9   Visual Autofiction: A Strategy for Cultural Inclusion 161
    Karen Ferreira-Meyers and Bontle Tau

10 Autofiction, Post-conflict Narratives, and New Memory
    Cultures 185
    Hywel Dix

11 Autofiction as a Lens for Reading Contemporary
    Egyptian Writing 205
    Hala Kamal, Zainab Magdy, and Fatma Massoud

Part III   Forms 225

12 Autofiction and Film: Archival Practices in Post-
    millennial Documentary Cinema in Argentina and Spain 227
    Anna Forné and Patricia López-Gay

13 Autofiction and *Shishōsetsu*: Women Writers and
    Reinventing the Self 247
    Justyna Weronika Kasza

14 Autofiction and the Diary: The Radicalization of
    Autofiction in Works by Hervé Guibert and Christine
    Angot 267
    Sam Ferguson

15 Autofiction and Self-Portraiture: Jenny Diski and Claude
    Cahun   287
    Ben Grant

16 Autofiction and Photography: "The Split of the Mirror"   309
    Laura Marcus

Index   327

Notes on Contributors

Hywel Dix is Principal Academic in English and Communication at Bournemouth University. He has published on Raymond Williams, British postmodern fiction, multicultural narratives, and autofiction. He is the editor of *Autofiction in English* (Palgrave, 2018).

Alexandra Effe is a postdoctoral fellow at the Department of Literature, Area Studies and European Languages, University of Oslo. Her research focuses on narrative theory, life writing, autofiction, and cognitive literary studies. As visiting scholar at the Oxford Centre for Life-Writing, she co-runs the project "Autofiction in Global Perspective." She is the author of *J. M. Coetzee and the Ethics of Narrative Transgression: A Reconsideration of Metalepsis* (Palgrave, 2017).

Helle Egendal is Lecturer in Danish at the University of Freiburg, Germany. Her research focuses on multiculturalism and multilingualism in Scandinavian literature. She is pursuing a doctoral thesis at the University of Freiburg entitled "Multilingual Autofictional Mode in Literature: Studies of Aesthetic Expressions and Political Impacts in Three Multilingual and Transcultural Literary Works." She is the author of two textbooks on language acquisition.

Sam Ferguson is an independent scholar and freelance academic translator. He is a specialist in life writing, particularly the diary, as well as the work of André Gide and Roland Barthes. In 2018 he published *Diaries Real and Fictional in Twentieth-Century French Writing*. He previously completed a doctorate in French literature at the University of Oxford in 2014 and was a junior research fellow at Christ Church, Oxford, from 2014 to 2018.

Karen Ferreira-Meyers is Associate Professor and Coordinator Linguistics and Modern Languages at the Institute of Distance Education, University of Eswatini (UNESWA), Kwaluseni, Swaziland. She holds a PhD in French and four Master's degrees. Her research fields include French and Francophone autofiction and autobiography, crime and detective fiction, the teaching and learning of languages, and distance and e-learning. She publishes regularly and widely, often speaks at international conferences, edits and proofreads for various academic journals, and is a keen translator and interpreter (French-English).

Anna Forné is Associate Professor of Hispanic Literature and Cultures at the University of Gothenburg. Her research projects include "The Politics of Poetics: The Testimonial Genre and the Literary Prize of Casa de las Américas (1970–2011)" and "Archival Autofiction in Post-dictatorship Argentina."

Alison Gibbons is Reader of Contemporary Stylistics at Sheffield Hallam University. She researches autofiction and contemporary experimental literature, often taking a cognitive approach. She is the author of *Multimodality, Cognition, and Experimental Literature* (2012) and has edited several books: *Mark Z. Danielewski* (2011), *Routledge Companion to Experimental Literature* (2021), *Metamodernism: Historicity, Affect, and Depth after Postmodernism* (2017), *Pronouns in Literature: Positions and Perspectives in Language* (Palgrave Macmillan, 2018), and *Style and Reader Response: Minds, Media, Methods* (2021).

Ben Grant is a Departmental Lecturer in English Literature at the Department for Continuing Education, University of Oxford. His research interests include postcolonial and world literature, the theory and practice of the aphorism, travel literature, psychoanalysis, and translation studies. He is the author of *Postcolonialism, Psychoanalysis and Burton: Power Play of Empire* (2009) and *The Aphorism and Other Short Forms* (2016).

Alison James is Professor of French at The University of Chicago. Her research interests include the Oulipo group, the contemporary novel, theories and representations of everyday life, and documentary narrative. She is the author of *Constraining Chance: Georges Perec and the Oulipo* (2009) and *The Documentary Imagination in Twentieth-Century French Literature: Writing with Facts* (2020). She has also edited or co-edited volumes and journal issues on literary formalism, fieldwork literatures, and nonfiction across media.

Hala Kamal is Professor of Gender Studies in the Department of English Language and Literature, Faculty of Arts, Cairo University. She was educated at the University of Leeds, Smith College, and Cairo University. Her research interests and publications, in Arabic and English, lie in the areas of autobiography studies, women and gender studies, and the history of the Egyptian feminist movement. Her latest publications include "Trends in Autobiography Theory and Writing," *Philological Studies* (Kielce, Poland 2020), and "Virginia Woolf in Arabic," *The Edinburgh Companion to Virginia Woolf and Contemporary Global Literature*, ed. Jeanne Dubino et al. (Edinburgh University Press, 2021).

Justyna Weronika Kasza is Associate Professor at Seinan Gakuin University in Fukuoka, Japan. She has taught courses in the Japanese language, literature, and translation at universities in England and Poland. She is the recipient of the Japan Foundation Fellowship. Her research interests include the works of Endō Shūsaku, life-writing narratives in Japan, world literature, and translation theories. She is the author of two monographs: *Hermeneutics of Evil in the Works of Endō Shūsaku: Between Reading and Writing* (2016) and *The "I" in the Making: Rethinking the Japanese Shishōsetsu in a Global Age* (2020).

Hannie Lawlor is Lecturer in Spanish at Exeter and Keble College, University of Oxford. She holds a PhD in Contemporary French and Spanish Women's Life-Writing, under the supervision of Professor Marie-Chantal Killeen and Dr Daniela Omlor and funded by the Arts and Humanities Research Council and the Oxford Centre for Life-Writing. Her doctoral thesis, "Balancing Acts? Relational Responses to Trauma in Twenty-First Century French and Spanish Women's Writing," puts questions to long-standing expectations of how writers should navigate and represent the multiple, interlocking stories in a family history.

Patricia López-Gay is Professor of Spanish and Portuguese Languages and Literatures at Bard College, New York, where she directs the Latin American and Iberian Studies program. Her latest book, *True Fictions: Life-Writing and the Archive* [*Ficciones de verdad: archivo y narrativas de* *vida*] (Iberoamericana/Vervuert, 2020), focuses on archive fever and autofictional writing through traditional and digital media. She is part of the international research group on autofiction based at the University of Alcalá de Henares in Madrid. In addition to her teaching and research, López-Gay is a member of the North American Academy of the Spanish Language.

Zainab Magdy holds an MA in Performance Studies and American Studies from the Department of English Language and Literature, Cairo University, where she teaches. Magdy is an actor, writer, and theater maker, based in Cairo. Her interest in the autobiographical started in performance with her piece *Ordinary People* (2016, Berlin, Cairo). She further explored her interest in self-narratives between writing and performance in 2017 by facilitating a performative writing workshop at the Contemporary Image Collective: "Geography for Beaten Heroes." This led to her research in life-writing genres and the performative in Waguih Ghali's body of work for her PhD.

Laura Marcus is Goldsmiths' Professor of English Literature at the University of Oxford. Her research interests include life writing, modernism, Virginia Woolf, and Bloomsbury culture. She is the author of *Auto/biographical Discourses: Theory, Criticism, Practice* (1994), *Virginia Woolf: Writers and Their Work* (1997/2004), and *The Tenth Muse: Writing About Cinema in the Modernist Period* (2007) and the co-editor of *The Cambridge History of Twentieth-Century English Literature* (2004), among other works.

Fatma Massoud is an assistant lecturer in the British University in Egypt (BUE). She holds an MA from the American University in Cairo, where she wrote a thesis titled "The Ivory Tower Exposed: The University in Ashour's *Specters* and Coetzee's *Disgrace*." She is working on her PhD degree at the Department of English Language and Literature in Cairo University, with a thesis on "Autofiction in Selected Works by Radwa Ashour and Doris Lessing." Her research interests include autobiography studies, modern Arabic literature, comparative literature, and women's literary production.

Ricarda Menn is a research assistant at the Institute for Advanced Study in the Humanities (KWI) in Essen. She holds an MA in American Studies as well as in Anglophone Literatures, Cultures and Medias from Goethe University Frankfurt. She recently submitted her dissertation titled

"Constellations of Serial Life Writing." In 2018, she published "Unpicked and Remade: Creative Imperatives in John Burnside's Autofictions" in *Autofiction in English*, ed. Hywel Dix. Her research interests include, but are not limited to, contemporary literature, life writing and autofiction, narrative theory, and book studies.

Hanna Meretoja is Professor of Comparative Literature and Director of *SELMA: Centre for the Study of Storytelling, Experientiality and Memory* at the University of Turku (Finland). Her research is mainly in the field of interdisciplinary narrative studies. Her monographs include *The Ethics of Storytelling: Narrative Hermeneutics, History, and the Possible* (2018) and *The Narrative Turn in Fiction and Theory* (2014, Palgrave Macmillan), and she has co-edited the *Memory Studies* special issue "Cultural Memorial Forms" (2021), *The Routledge Companion to Literature and Trauma* (2020), and *Storytelling and Ethics: Literature, Visual Arts and the Power of Narrative* (2018).

Arnaud Schmitt is Professor of American Studies at the University of Bordeaux. He works on American literature and on the concepts of "autofiction" and "self-narration." He recently published *The Phenomenology of Autobiography: Making It Real* (2017).

Melissa Schuh is Lecturer in English Literature at Christian-Albrechts-University Kiel. She holds a PhD (2019) from the English department at Queen Mary University of London, with a thesis titled "The (Un-)Making of the Novelist's Identity." She is a deputy editor for *C21 Literature: Journal of 21st Century Writings*. Her research interests include English and German contemporary fiction, autobiography and life writing, and Brexit in literature as well as seriality and Modernism. Recent publications include an article on "Lateness, Memory, and Imagination in Literary Autobiography" (2020) in *The European Journal of Life Writing*.

Bontle Tau is a visual artist, researcher, and curator based in Bloemfontein, South Africa. She holds her BA Fine Arts degree (2018) from the University of the Free State and is completing her MA in Fine Arts from the same university. Tau is a lecturer at the Central University of Technology. As an emerging artist, she is a member of the Free State Art Collective and has participated in group exhibitions at the Turbine Art Fair, Oliewenhuis art museum in South Africa, and Galerie L'App'Art in Périgueux, France.

Martina Wagner-Egelhaaf is Professor of German literature at the University of Münster. She is the author of *Autobiographie* (Stuttgart and Weimar 2000; second edition 2005) and she edited the three-volume *Handbook of Autobiography/Autofiction* (2019).

List of Figures

Fig. 9.1	"The Look of Reading (After Garret Stewart)," 2018. Digital Self-Portrait Photograph	166
Fig. 9.2	"L'Inscription," 2018. Digital Self-Portrait photograph	167
Fig. 9.3	"Je t'attends là, je t'attends là pendant toute ma vie," 2020. Digital Self-Portrait	169
Fig. 9.4	"En regardant mes peuples," 2020. Digital Self-Portrait	170
Fig. 9.5	"Of Another Time When I Existed," 2020. Self-portrait drawn in smoke and charcoal on paper	172
Fig. 9.6	"I knew who I was this morning, but I've changed a few times since then" (After Lewis Carroll), 2020. Digital Self-Portrait	175
Fig. 9.7	"Portrait de Madeleine" (formerly known as Portrait d'une négresse), Marie-Guillemine Benoist, 1800. Louvre Museum, Paris. Picture in public domain	178
Fig. 9.8	"Amour non partagé" (Unrequited Love), 2020. Digital Self-Portrait	179
Fig. 12.1	Albertina Carri, *Several parallel but thematically disconnected screens of found footage in Cuatreros*	232
Fig. 12.2	Víctor Erice, *Workers from the Vizela Factory: Close-up of Photograph in Vidros partidos*	236
Fig. 15.1	Photomontage at the beginning of chapter IX, entitled I.O.U., of Cahun's *Aveux non avenus*. Courtesy of the Jersey Heritage Collections	294
Fig. 15.2	Photomontage at the beginning of chapter I, entitled R.C.S., of Cahun's *Aveux non avenus*. Courtesy of the Jersey Heritage Collections	305

CHAPTER 1

Introduction: From Autofiction to the Autofictional

Alexandra Effe and Hannie Lawlor

The apparent simplicity of the etymology of "autofiction"—designating texts that have something to do with the self and with fiction—is belied by the proliferation of meanings and practices with which it is associated. Critical writing on autofiction will usually mention one or more of the following characteristics, all of which can characterize autofictional texts, but none of which is unique or defining: a combination of real and invented elements; onomastic correspondence between author and character or narrator; and stylistic and linguistic experimentation. Where critics or theorists focus more on the context of production and reception, we also find references to a double pact—autobiographical and fictional—or to a combination of, or oscillation between, reading modes. Perhaps the only thing on which everyone can agree is indeed that basic etymological claim: autofiction has something to do with the self and with fiction. But even this

A. Effe (✉)
University of Oslo, Oslo, Norway
e-mail: alexandra.effe@ilos.uio.no

H. Lawlor
Exeter College, Oxford, UK
e-mail: hannie.lawlor@exeter.ox.ac.uk

© The Author(s) 2022
A. Effe, H. Lawlor (eds.), *The Autofictional*, Palgrave Studies in Life Writing, https://doi.org/10.1007/978-3-030-78440-9_1

seems to be up for debate, as several recent autofictional practitioners have proclaimed a turn away from fiction. Sheila Heti, for example, has said that she is "[i]ncreasingly [...] less interested in writing about fictional people, because it seems so tiresome to make up a fake person and put them through the paces of a fake story" (Heti 2007). Heti's lack of interest in invented people does not equate to a rejection of any form of fictionality, of course, but it nonetheless puts strain on the term "autofiction." So too does Rachel Cusk's comment, in a review essay on Yiyun Li's work, that, while the denominator "novel" has become a norm for autofictional texts, this is difficult to justify, "especially when the work cannot be understood without its autobiographical basis" (2019).

The impossibility of reaching a satisfactory consensus on the definition of autofiction prompts arguments that it is best to dispose of the term altogether, to replace it with "life writing," perhaps with the addition of a modifier such as "experimental" or "hybrid." It quickly becomes apparent, however, that such labels do little to delineate the specific kinds of hybridity and experimentalism we find in autofictional texts, and would hence lose the conceptual focus that "autofiction" provides. The term is clearly problematic, possibly flawed, which may have to do with Serge Doubrovsky's coining it in passing to describe one particular book, *Fils* (1977). Doubrovsky himself clearly felt that it needed further development, having proposed various descriptions of autofiction in the course of his career (see, e.g., Dix 2018, 2–5; and Wagner-Egelhaaf, this volume). Many other writers, critics, and theorists have since contributed to revising, fine-tuning, and often also challenging autofiction as a concept—a process that began in French criticism and then spread more widely. The term and concept are now firmly established in German-language, Anglophone, and Scandinavian criticism (for an overview of the term's development, see, for instance, Jones 2010; Ferreira-Meyers 2018), but has not yet caught on globally, as we will see in the discussion of Egyptian literature and literary criticism in this volume (Chap. 11). Autofiction, it seems, requires continuous reconsideration in order to accommodate the variety of texts that writers, critics, and readers feel should be discussed under the label. Despite this, or perhaps because of it, autofiction as term, concept, and literary practice persists and is thriving more than ever.

A recent issue of *The Times Literary Supplement* speaks of a current "fashion for autofiction" and features an article by Alice Attlee, in which she acknowledges the "booming popularity of autofiction," as well as the difficulty of defining it as a genre, claiming that "it requires if not a new, then a reconsidered, critical response" (2019). Armine Kotin Mortimer (2009, 22) proclaimed over ten years ago that a "consensus definition has become impossible," and perceives "a collective will to blur the boundaries of the genre as much as possible: the more fluid the definition, the happier the collective thinking is." Hywel Dix, too, begins his 2018 edited volume on *Autofiction in English* by stressing "that there is no single definition of autofiction either in English or in French" (2). Dix also reminds us, however, in a comparison with the history of the concept of intertextuality, that the development and extension of applications of a term need not mean loss of meaning or imprecision. Rather, they can be taken positively as "symptoms of a rich, vibrant and expanding field" (9). The introductory text to the website autofiction.org, dedicated to the discussion of the concept and of autofictional texts, offers a similarly optimistic description of autofiction's indefinability:

> Autofiction has established itself as one of the most open and lively fields in contemporary literature. It is a complex notion to define, connected to the author's defiance with regard to autobiography, *romans à clef*, the constraints or illusions of transparency; a notion that is enhanced by its many extensions even as it robustly resists the incessant attacks to which it is subjected. (autofiction.org, n.d.; our translation)

This volume embraces the openness of autofiction as a concept, as well as the critical dialogue it has inspired. The chapters, both individually and collectively, offer innovative responses to a continuously flourishing literary phenomenon. These responses include reflections from several critics who have contributed substantially to shaping our understanding of autofiction in recent years, and who offer new perspectives here, as well as contributions from new voices that expand on and challenge established approaches.

The shift from the noun and genre-descriptor "autofiction" to the adjective "autofictional," in this study's title, creates the necessary flexibility for extending and revising our understanding of the concept. While some individual chapters do propose possible definitions of autofiction, including new subcategories of autofictional texts, the volume as a whole does not aim to arrive at a uniform definition, and much less to impose one. Instead, it expressly extends the texts and phenomena that can be considered autofictional and fosters a dialogue between a range of different approaches and case studies in order to foreground the diversity of autofictional practice and criticism. It explores the autofictional as a mode, moment, and strategy that can appear in a variety of texts across time. As part of this cross-disciplinary approach, the volume considers how autofictional strategies relate to, work in, and work with different text types and media, such as photography, film, the diary, and the self-portrait. There is a strong focus, moreover, on the effects, or potential effects, of autofictional techniques, signals, and structures within a given literary work, as well as on its context of production and reception.

This approach allows us to bring into view texts, forms, and media that have not traditionally been considered in the light of their autofictional dimensions, to illustrate the many affordances of autofiction as theoretical lens and aesthetic strategy, and to propose new ways of exploring autofictional writing and its surrounding structures. Authors in this study do speak of autofiction as a genre but also of modes of autofictional writing and modes of autofictional reading, of an autofictional sense of self and of an autofictional approach to self-presentation, of how texts create and enhance a sense of the autofictional, and of degrees of autofictionality. The different chapters feature many major names that commonly arise in discussions of autofiction (including Doubrovsky, Annie Ernaux, Hervé Guibert, Christine Angot, Felicitas Hoppe, Jenny Diski, Philip Roth, Cusk, Olivia Laing, Siri Hustvedt, Ben Lerner, and Karl Ove Knausgaard) but also draw our attention to the autofictional dimensions of texts which have barely featured, if at all, in the conversation to date. The latter include precursors—writers who developed autofictional techniques before Doubrovsky's coinage of the term, including Johann Wolfgang von Goethe, Dorothy Richardson, Virginia Woolf, Claude Cahun, and Doris Lessing—and contemporary authors who are more typically discussed under headings such as postcolonialism or cosmopolitanism rather than autofiction, including Chimamanda Ngozi Adichie and Justin Cartwright.

Certainly, this volume's extension of the concept of autofiction means a broad application, perhaps too broad for the likings of some, but the chapters assembled here demonstrate what is gained from an encompassing approach of this kind. It sparks a productive discussion of the phenomena that cluster around a certain kind of text, one that remains difficult to pin down not least because a dominant (but again, by no means defining) characteristic of autofictional writing is that it challenges conventions, resisting traditional autobiographical and novelistic modes but also constantly reinventing itself.

It is through the volume's broadening of the parameters of the term and concept that the diversity and global range of autofictional practice becomes apparent. As the conversation on autofiction thus far has taken place principally in Western Europe and North America, the case studies that typically take center stage are from these same traditions. French, Anglophone, German, and Scandinavian texts make up the most iconic examples, as critics and authors reflect on, and clash over, the application of "autofiction" as a genre label; works by Knausgaard, Angot, and Hoppe have triggered some of the more public and virulent of these debates. In each of these contexts, autofictional practice has proliferated together with the term's increasing embeddedness in critical discourse. The state of the field elsewhere in Europe, however, and indeed globally, varies considerably. Despite Spain's geographical and cultural proximity to France, Spanish texts have featured very infrequently to date in international discussions on the autofictional (see, e.g., Manuel Alberca 2007). Likewise, in Italy, while Elena Ferrante's "Neapolitan Novels" have recently received attention as an example of "autofiction," there is certainly a need for further investigation of Italian autofictional works. Lucia Boldrini and Julia Novak, in their volume *Experiments in Autobiography: Intersections of Auto/Biography and Fiction* (2017), make strides in including case studies from European countries that are typically underrepresented in discussions of life writing, referring to Spanish, Italian, and Austrian literature, although only Spanish Mexican author Jordi Soler's work is discussed explicitly as an autofictional experiment. An important body of work is slowly emerging on autofictional practices in other European countries (to give two examples, Lut Missinne discusses Dutch autofictional works [2013, 2019] and Stavrini Ioannidou's doctoral thesis has put forward a case for the existence of autofiction in Greek literature even before the emergence of the term [2013]). The website autofiction.org provides helpful, albeit inevitably selective and incomplete, lists of autofictional works from Latin America, the Caribbean, the Arab world, and Africa. Although these are important steps toward broadening our perception of autofictional texts, they also show that there is clearly still much need for a more inclusive perspective and much room for future research.

In *The Autofictional*, we take a further step toward a more global perspective by shining a light on select underrepresented practices, traditions, and cultures, both within and outside of Europe, and by putting these into dialogue with the more established traditions. This volume does not only establish the presence of the autofictional in other cultures, forms, and media but also demonstrates how the inclusion of these diverse examples challenges and develops current conceptions of the autofictional. The *Handbook of Autobiography/Autofiction* (2019), edited by Martina Wagner-Egelhaaf, is pioneering in providing an overview of autobiographical practices across the globe and in different media. The present volume instigates a dialogue between several case studies and forms that the handbook brings into view, with a specific focus on the autofictional, rather than on autobiographical life-writing practices more generally. It addresses, for example, the correspondences between autofiction and the Japanese tradition of the I-novel, the function of the autofictional in documentary cinema and that of the diary in the autofictional, and vice versa. The volume considers the affordance of autofictional techniques in contemporary South African self-portraiture and the potential role that the incorporation of the term could play in the reception of life writing in the Arabic tradition. As well as establishing possible connections between these cultures, forms, and media, this dialogue also testifies to the very different ways in which the autofictional functions across different places and times.

To date, few studies on autofiction have attempted to start this kind of conversation. Dix's *Autofiction in English* addresses cultural specificities, asking whether the concept is applied in the same way in Anglophone works as it is in the French context, or whether the concept itself changes and evolves upon entering new cultural contexts (2018, 9). He concludes that certain characteristics play a more conspicuous role in the British tradition than they do in the French: these include intersubjectivity, seriality, metafiction, and intertextuality, as well as attention to the therapeutic possibilities of the act of writing. Karen Ferreira-Meyers notes in addition that, in the Anglophone world, autofiction is perceived primarily as a mode rather than as a genre (2018, 41). Laura Marcus's contribution to the present volume further develops such comparisons by demonstrating that French autofictional works exhibit features that are not as prevalent in British ones, particularly the prominent intersection of photography and narrative. In this volume, the French tradition remains a crucial part of the discussion and an important reference point in many of the chapters, but it is brought into dialogue with a broad range of traditions, with the effect of reshaping, expanding, and enriching our understanding of the autofictional.

* * *

In light of the recognition that "autofiction" as a term is problematic and that a consensus definition is neither attainable nor necessarily desirable, Part I of this study considers how we might find new, productive ways of approaching autofiction and the autofictional. Wagner-Egelhaaf opens with "Five Theses on Autofiction/the Autofictional," and her first thesis is one on which this volume's overall approach is based; namely, that we still need the term and that the critical discussion which surrounds it is of value for how it continuously challenges us to reconsider the concept and the texts we discuss in relation to it. She shows the advantages of an open and flexible understanding of the autofictional as a conceptual matrix with scalable parameters. From this perspective we see the autofictional as a latent dimension of autobiographical writing in general (her second thesis) and understand that imagined and supernatural elements can support autobiographical reference (her third thesis) and that there is an oscillation between fictionality and factuality in autofictional texts (her fifth thesis). Her approach is rooted in a performative understanding of writing, which becomes most evident in her fourth thesis when she elaborates on the "Strange Loops and Real Effects" of her chapter's title: she considers how art and life cross-influence one another insofar as the fictional affects our perception of the real, and shows this to be true not only for her contemporary examples (Doubrovsky, Knausgaard, Hoppe, and Thomas Glavinic) but also for Goethe in the late eighteenth and early nineteenth centuries.

In an important response to the problematics inherent in the combination of the constituents "auto" and "fiction," Alison James asks what exactly is "The Fictional in Autofiction." She shows in a discussion of works by Ernaux, Cusk, Laing, Knausgaard, Christophe Boltanski, and Camille Laurens how narratological and rhetorical theories of fictionality can help discern different forms and degrees of fictionality in autofictional texts, thus enabling us to better understand the workings of this type of writing, and how autofictional practice in turn helps refine theories of fiction and fictionality. James proposes, for example, the important distinction between fictionality and fictionalization, the latter term describing the transposition of real-life elements into fictional form. Finally, her approach brings to light the various effects that distinct configurations of the interplay of fact and fiction in autofictional texts can create, a dimension subsequently explored in more detail in the chapters by Alexandra Effe and Alison Gibbons, and by Arnaud Schmitt, as well as throughout Part II of this volume.

Effe and Gibbons offer a "Cognitive Perspective on Autofictional Writing, Texts, and Reading." They argue for the necessity of considering textual signposts in combination with the cognitive-affective dynamics of production and reception of a given text. They note that existing accounts of autofictional writing and reading rely primarily on the conjectures of individual critics, and propose that we should consider instead how authors themselves describe their acts of autofictionalization, and what we can surmise about readers' responses on the basis of empirical research into textual processing. Effe and Gibbons approach the three constituents of their holistic approach through data from self-reports by the three authors of their case studies (Roth, Laing, and Lerner), through empirical, psychological studies into differences between fictional and factual reading modes, and through close textual analysis of the formal makeup of *The Facts* (1988), *Crudo* (2018), and *10:04* (2014). They simultaneously extend and fine-tune definitions of autofiction by offering definitions of autofictional modes of writing and autofictional modes of reading. Their focus on both author and reader, and on psychological motivations and cognitive effects, allows them to show potential affordances and effects of autofictional modes, thus looking ahead to those illustrated in Part II.

Schmitt suggests moving away from trying to define what autofiction is and toward describing how it works, that is, toward "The Pragmatics of Autofiction." Taking up an example from the previous chapter—Lerner's *10:04*—and adding Siri Hustvedt's *Memories of the Future* (2019), he provides us with helpful terminological distinctions for approaching the workings of autofictional texts with more precision, specifically for describing which textual and paratextual elements invite an autofictional reading. He distinguishes between primary, necessary characteristics and secondary, supplementary ones. Without onomastic correspondence—which in autofictional texts often takes the form of a first name or initials, thus simultaneously inviting and resisting the identification of author and character—autofiction, in his understanding of the term, cannot exist. Recognizing that, while this criterion may be necessary, it is not sufficient in and of itself as autofiction ultimately depends on the reader, Schmitt argues that autofiction really only exists if readers make the connections between author and character that the text offers and find them fruitful. Other characteristics such as metafictional elements, the foregrounding of the fallibility of memory (thematically and through narrative strategies), and apostrophic addresses to readers are not absolutely necessary but enhance the sense of the autofictional (hence his designation of them as "enhancers"). Overall, the chapter foregrounds the importance of peritextual but also epitextual material in the reception of texts as autofictional. The latter becomes crucial in particular for the application of the concept to texts not previously or usually discussed under the label of "autofiction," such as the postcolonial and Egyptian texts in Chaps. 10 and 11.

Part I closes with Ricarda Menn and Melissa Schuh's chapter on how to approach "The Autofictional in Serial, Literary Works." They take up Doubrovsky's focus (in his initial definition of the term "autofiction") on the fragmentation of the self in order to pay more attention to the incompleteness that is characteristic of autofictional projects. Menn and Schuh therefore invite us to consider how this takes form in serialized publications and show what it means to consider an author's entire oeuvre or a series of works as a dynamic site of self-expression and as an autofictional act. They propose considering serial, literary autofiction as a distinct subcategory of autofictional texts, and distinguish between different forms of seriality. With reference to texts ranging from the early twentieth to the twenty-first century—Richardson's *Pilgrimage* (1915–1938), Lessing's autobiographical, fictional, and hybrid works, and Cusk's *Outline* trilogy (2014–2018)—they show how serial publications and structures challenge autobiographical unity and coherence, and how, in so doing, they productively interconnect with, and enhance, these thematic and representational concerns in autofictional texts. They argue that autofictional and serialized forms of self-writing present a discontinuous, non-linear, contingent, and multi-faceted sense of self—what we might, in other words, call an autofictional sense of self.

Each of the five chapters in Part I offers a distinct, and distinctly new, way of approaching the autofictional. The connections and variations between them come to light in the overlaps in the selection of authors and texts discussed. For instance, we see Lerner's *10:04* approached with a cognitive perspective on autofictional modes of writing and reading, and with a focus on pragmatic ways of signaling ambiguity over the proximity between author and character. We consider Cusk's *Outline* trilogy with regard to the question of what precisely is fictional and fictionalized in this work, and from the angle of her serial form of self-presentation; and we are invited to think about what kind of fact/fiction configuration is at play in Laing's *Crudo*, as well as about the potential cognitive affordances her act of autofictionalization has for her and for her readers. By rethinking the theoretical and methodological bounds of what is autofictional and how we can study it, this part of the volume opens up the discussion to the wide spectrum of forms and contexts of the autofictional that are explored in the remainder of the volume.

Part II considers the affordances and effects of autofiction as a literary strategy. Examining the autofictional as both a writing and reading technique, the chapters focus on what is gained from the application and extension of the term, and from the adoption of autofictional practices. Hanna Meretoja shows, under the title of "Metanarrative Autofiction," how what she views as a new twenty-first-century subgenre of autofictional texts affords new perspectives on, and has the potential to heighten, the collective narrative agency of readers and writers. She understands by "metanarrativity" a kind of self-reflexive storytelling that critically engages with larger cultural narrative templates and their role in how we make sense of our lives. Using the examples of Ernaux's *Les Années (The Years)* (2008), Knausgaard's *Min kamp (My Struggle)* (2009–2011), and Finnish singer-songwriter Astrid Swan's *Viimeinen kirjani* (2019, *My Last Book*), Meretoja illustrates how the texts comment on and offer alternatives to existing master-narratives about aging, illness, masculinity, or fatherhood. Autofictional texts, she shows, are particularly well placed to alert us to the ways in which our lives and our self-understanding are determined by dominant and normative cultural narrative models. They also help us to challenge these narratives, and to actively choose the ones we use to interpret our lives and selves because autofiction often pivots on the relation between what is real and what is imaginary, and on the relation between our lives and their narrativization.

Helle Egendal continues the exploration of the affordance of the autofictional for exposing normative social models in "Multilingual Autofiction: Mobilizing Language(s)." She argues that in post-migrant literature published since the 1990s, a new mode, multilingual autofiction, has emerged that highlights and resists the monocultural assumptions shaping the social and political context in which the respective texts are published. Her three case studies, written by German-Turkish, Swedish-Tunisian, and Danish-Palestinian authors, demonstrate that this mode transverses different countries and cultures. Egendal considers both the aesthetic scope and the political potential of this autofictional mode, in which the authors use polyphony and polyglossia to express and negotiate their multilingual identities. The flexibility and diversity that the autofictional affords in this respect is further mobilized in these texts to penetrate political discourses on migration, transculturality, and racism. By considering the reception of these texts and the public engagement of their authors, Egendal directs our focus to the political and social affordances of the autofictional.

Turning our attention to the autofictional in the visual arts, Ferreira-Meyers and Bontle Tau continue the discussion of social affordances in "Visual Autofiction: A Strategy for Cultural Inclusion." They argue that the autofictional is being employed in the creative practice of contemporary South African artists to initiate cultural inclusion within a field that has historically favored European visual narratives and excluded many others. Focusing on Tau's self-portrait photography, they explore the ways in which the autofictional enables a practice of self-narration which is ever-changing in terms of the viewpoints adopted and offered. The role-playing and constant repositioning of selves and stories that autofictional techniques afford offers a means through which artists can figuratively insert themselves into the Western tradition of portraiture: Tau assumes the classical postures in which white, Western women have typically been represented, and in so doing highlights the virtual absence of black protagonists in the canon. Ferreira-Meyers and Tau consider how autofictional self-portraiture highlights the skewed nature of representation in this tradition, and how it might better accommodate the diversity of selves and stories of creative practitioners.

Dix's chapter "Autofiction, Post-conflict Narratives, and New Memory Cultures" demonstrates the affordance of autofictional techniques for creating new forms of public commemoration. This affordance is utilized in particular, he argues, by contemporary postcolonial writers in post-conflict societies. Focusing on Adichie's *Half of a Yellow Sun* (2006) and Cartwright's *Up Against the Night* (2015), Dix shows how both texts use autofictional structures and techniques to forge a form of cultural memory of the Nigerian Biafran War of 1967–1970 and of the massacre of Zulus by Boers in 1838, respectively. In both cases, this form of cultural memory is simultaneously individual (albeit concerning events before the authors' lifetime) and collective, and aspires to post-conflict reconciliation. Dix's analysis foregrounds the importance of the context of reception and of the paratextual and intertextual signals that invite autofictional readings in the absence of onomastic correspondence. His analysis of Adichie's and Cartwright's works through an autofictional lens enables an enriched understanding of their effects and of how these are engendered—an understanding achieved through his extension of the term.

Hala Kamal, Fatma Atef Massoud, and Zainab Magdy subsequently explore this extension of the term in "Autofiction as a Lens for Reading

Contemporary Egyptian Writing." In a literary tradition where "autofiction" has not yet entered into the critical discourse and life writing is typically situated within the domain of biographical and historical studies, the authors demonstrate the affordances of autofiction as a strategy for writing and reading Egyptian texts. Using three different case studies, Waguih Ghali's *Beer in the Snooker Club* (1964), Radwa Ashour's *Atiaf* (*Specters*) (1999), and Miral al-Tahawy's *Brooklyn Heights* (2010), they consider evidence of autofictional readings in the texts' reception, how the authors themselves invite autofictional readings through the use of paratextual material and self-reflexive commentary, and how the concept of the autofictional might resist the dominant trend in critical reception of reading women's writing as being straightforwardly autobiographical. Their readings highlight the insights that adopting the autofictional as a critical lens can provide into constructions of identity, memory, and experience at the intersections of reality and the imagination in Egyptian literature.

Together, the chapters in Part II testify to the value of extending the concept of the autofictional to encompass a variety of texts, traditions, and cultures. Inviting new kinds of examples and new voices into the discussion brings to light the many dimensions of the autofictional and the reach of its engagement with narratives of identity beyond the bounds of the text. The social, political, and literary affordances of autofictional techniques and readings emerge powerfully in these chapters and, as we have seen, are centrally linked to form. The final section explores in depth the manifold forms that the autofictional can take and with which it engages, and some of the diverse media in which it can be found.

Part III of the volume discusses how the autofictional functions in different forms and media (the diary, the Japanese I-novel, the literary self-portrait, film, and photography), and how these forms and media work in turn in autofictional texts. Through the lens of this range of case studies, the section demonstrates the insights that are gained from the inclusion of diverse socio-historical, cultural, and political contexts in conversations on the autofictional. Anna Forné and Patricia López-Gay explore the affordances of autofiction as they emerge in a different medium in "Autofiction and Film: Archival Practices in Post-Millennial Documentary Cinema in Argentina and Spain." Focusing on films that respond to two different crises, they approach the autofictional as a contemporary cinematic mode that can unsettle the paradigm of the archive as static evidence of a given reality. The first part of the chapter engages with the documentary trilogy *Los rubios* (*The Blonds*) (2003), *Restos* (*Remains*) (2010), and *Cuatreros*

(*Rustlers*) (2016), directed by Albertina Carri. Carri's parents were among the 30,000 people "disappeared" by the military during the last dictatorship in Argentina, and the trilogy reflects on the resulting crisis of memory construction for the second generation. The second part discusses the self-reflexive responses of Spanish filmmakers to the Iberian financial crisis in Mercedes Álvarez's *Mercado de futuros* (*Futures Market*) (2011) and Víctor Erice's *Vidros partidos: Testes para um filme em Portugal* (*Broken Windows: Tests for a Film in Portugal*) (2012). In exploring what they describe as the aesthetics of ambiguity that underpins these films, Forné and López-Gay demonstrate the ways in which the autofictional reveals and challenges the generic limits of documentary film, and invites new reflections on processes of memory construction.

Justyna Kasza turns to a very different cultural context in "Autofiction and *Shishōsetsu*: Women Writers and Reinventing the Self" to draw out the relationship between autofiction and another form with which it has not traditionally been linked: the Japanese I-novel. Kasza notes that the link between language and the reinvention of the self in literature comes to the fore in *shishōsetsu*, a form which originates in the lack of a fixed and stable first-person pronoun in Japanese. Yet, despite the seeming cultural specificity of this form, *shishōsetsu* has much in common with the autofictional in its scope for modifying, creating, and re-creating the supposedly unitary self, as well as with the debates that surround the label. Both concepts prove elusive in attempts to establish a fixed definition, and both labels are as often rejected as they are accepted by the authors to whose work they are applied. Kasza investigates this relationship in depth in relation to three contemporary women writers: Kanai Mieko, Sagisawa Megumu, and Mizumura Minae, who use the form to negotiate national, lingual, and gender identities and to redefine the self. By putting the two forms into conversation, she shows that *shishōsetsu* exceeds the borders of national literature and expands the scope of discussions of the autofictional, which rarely feature Japanese works.

Sam Ferguson proposes that there is also an important, and largely unexplored, relationship between "Autofiction and the Diary." He argues that the diary, a form often perceived as "antifictional," has in fact played a key role in shaping the practices of the generation of French autofictional writers that emerged in the 1990s. Ferguson proposes that there is a shift in autofiction from its orientation toward autobiographical modes of writing in the previous generation, visible in Doubrovsky's work as well as the work of writers including Roland Barthes, Alain Robbe-Grillet, and

Marguerite Duras, toward a diaristic mode of writing. He takes Guibert and Angot to be the key proponents in this reorientation, and through close analysis of their experimental writing projects in *Voyage avec deux enfants* (*Journey with Two Children*, 1982) and *Léonore, toujours* (*Léonore, Always*, 1993), respectively, he shows how the diary serves as the basis from which the authors challenge established literary forms and forge new approaches to writing the self. The dialogue he uncovers between the diary and the autofictional complicates the modalities of truth, fiction, and self-representation in both forms.

The final two chapters focus on different forms in the French context, drawing them into dialogue with British literature. Ben Grant reflects on the relationship between "Autofiction and Self-Portraiture" in the literary tradition, as it is defined by Michel Beaujour. The two are united, Grant argues, in opposing autobiography's claim to giving a "truthful" account of its subject, but while autofiction does so primarily by emphasizing fictional constructions of the self, self-portraiture primarily foregrounds the self's fragmentary nature. Grant proposes that we should regard self-portraiture and autofiction as two poles in life writing, which represent two different conceptions of the self, but which can coexist with varying degrees of visibility. He explores this coexistence in the work of British writer Diski and French author and photographer Cahun, arguing that while both their oeuvres invite autofictional readings, they should be seen first and foremost as self-portraitists. Starting from the very different relationship between narcissism and creativity that emerges in self-portraiture compared to in autobiographical writing, Grant analyzes the points of intersection and divergence the two traditions self-portraiture and autofiction.

Remaining in the field of visual self-representation, Laura Marcus's chapter traces the relationship she discerns between "Autofiction and Photography." Rather than representing the reflected self, she observes, visual artist and literary autobiographer alike turn inward to find their self-image. Marcus analyzes the ways in which photography has intensified and reshaped the relationship between memory, image, and text in literary self-representation. She argues that the connections between life writing, memory, and photography are at their most prominent in autofictional works, in which photographs become an important site for their play with the porous boundary between autobiography and fiction. Her comparative study explores the role that photographs play in negotiating shifting identities, with a specific focus on images of seeing and mirroring. She turns first to transsexual life-writing texts by Anglophone authors, in which she sees a striking incidence between photographs and self-representation, before considering the relationship between photography and/as absence in the work of Ernaux. Marcus demonstrates that there is a compelling link between the intersections of the visual and verbal, photography and narrative, in these texts and those of the autofictional mode, and explores the prevalence of this phenomenon in French literature compared with its British counterpart.

As a whole, Part III demonstrates how a comparison of the autofictional across different forms, media, and cultures reveals its diversity, range, and global reach, and the many shapes it can assume at different times and in different contexts. The connections uncovered in these comparisons offer insight into the function of the autofictional in these literary and visual forms and media, and into how these work in turn in autofictional texts. Perhaps most importantly, these chapters show, as does the volume overall, how our understanding of the autofictional, and of its different forms and affordances, is enhanced when they are approached from diverse angles and drawn into dialogue.

This dialogue takes place within chapters, within sections, and across them. Schmitt's, Effe and Gibbons's, and Dix's chapters all underscore the importance of considering how exactly autofictional texts trigger a certain kind of reading, and to what effect. Menn and Schuh investigate how these effects can be created across a series of works, and this serial staging of the self in autofictional writing resonates with the visual staging of the self in different guises and across time that Ferreira-Meyers and Tau explore. Their contribution on self-portrait photography speaks to Grant's chapter on literary self-portraiture, and together the visual and the literary tradition serve as the starting point for Marcus's analysis of the role of photographs in autofictional texts. Ferguson draws a parallel between the symbolic attachment to the truth that the photograph represents and the role of the diary in developing this French autofictional practice. The productive, yet paradoxical, relationship that transpires between these two forms invites comparison, too, with Kasza's exploration of autofiction and *shishōsetsu*, a form considered to be rooted in the specifics of the Japanese language, but whose scope is shown through this comparison to be much wider.

That the dialogue between autofiction and *shishōsetsu* invites us to rethink our understanding of both forms testifies to the gains of an expanded concept of autofiction and the autofictional for critical readings. The new insights that autofiction as a critical lens affords are prominent in Kamal, Massoud, and Magdy's discussion of Egyptian life writing. An important insight gained in their application of autofiction as a concept to Arab literature is that autofiction's affordances are not only literary and critical but also political and social, a perspective that emerges powerfully in Egendal's study of transcultural autobiographical literature, in Dix's discussion of postcolonial texts in post-conflict societies, and in Forné and López-Gay's exploration of Argentinian and Spanish documentary cinema. All three of these chapters illustrate the potential that Meretoja describes for the autofictional to challenge dominant cultural narrative models. This grounds the practice's real-world relevance, which comes to the fore in Wagner-Egelhaaf's discussion of Doubrovsky's autofictional works. Effe and Gibbons's holistic and cognitive approach to autofictional texts, and modes of writing and reading, offers a new way of substantiating our critical hypotheses on such real-life effects. In the volume's various extensions and modifications of term and concept, James's chapter helps us to differentiate between the kinds of fictionalization and modes of fictionality we find in different autofictional texts.

* * *

Across the chapters, we see autofictional practice and criticism take many different shapes, and it is on these differences as much as on the intersections between chapters and approaches that this volume's contribution is based. The volume sets out to expand the concept with a view to creating a heterogeneous, malleable, and ongoing discourse on the autofictional. Our hope is that, in the reading of this volume, many more connections and comparisons will be made, and many more conversations on the autofictional will take place. Overall, the volume offers the kind of "reconsidered, critical response" that Attlee calls for in her recent article on autofiction. Perhaps, as the conversation develops, we will turn more toward the pragmatics of autofiction, and adopt a holistic and cognitive perspective, focusing on how, why, and in which contexts authors write texts that readers perceive as autofictional. Perhaps we will pay more attention to autofictional strategies and structures as they emerge across an author's oeuvre, or in intertextual relations between parts of a series. Perhaps we will be more open to recognizing autofictional moments in works that do not seem to fit the generic category, as well as in media other than literature: visual art, photography, painting, and film, to name but a few. Perhaps, in adopting this more encompassing approach, we will be receptive to the ways in which our understanding of texts from countries and literary traditions where autofiction does not (yet) exist as a concept changes if we approach them through an autofictional lens, and to how such texts can, in turn, enrich and transform our understanding of autofiction and the autofictional.

WORKS CITED

Alberca, Manuel. 2007. *El pacto ambiguo: De la novela autobiográfica a la autoficción*. Colección Estudios Críticos de Literatura 30. Madrid: Biblioteca Nueva.
Attlee, Alice. 2019. Fiction of Facts. *Times Literary Supplement*, May 9, 2019. https://www.the-tls.co.uk/articles/autofiction-fiction-of-facts/. Accessed 5 Apr 2021.
autofiction.org. n.d. Présentation. https://www.autofiction.org/index.php?category/Accueil. Accessed 5 Apr 2021.
Boldrini, Lucia, and Julia Novak, eds. 2017. *Experiments in Life-Writing: Intersections of Auto/Biography and Fiction*. Basingstoke: Palgrave Macmillan.
Cusk, Rachel. 2019. "The Case of Yiyun Li." Review of Dear Friend, from My Life I Write to You in your Life and When Reasons End. *New York Review of Books*, July 18, 2019.
Dix, Hywel. 2018. Introduction: Autofiction in English: The Story So Far. In *Autofiction in English*, ed. Hywel Dix, 1–23. Cham: Palgrave Macmillan.
Ferreira-Meyers, Karen. 2018. Does Autofiction Belong to French or Francophone Authors and Readers Only? In *Autofiction in English*, ed. Hywel Dix, 27–48. Cham: Palgrave Macmillan.
Heti, Sheila. 2007. "Interview with David Hickey." Interview by Sheila Heti. *The Believer*, November 1, 2007. https://believermag.com/an-interview-with-dave-hickey/. Accessed 5 Apr 2021.
Ioannidou, Stavrini. 2013. Autofiction à la grecque: Greek Autobiographical Fiction (1971–1995), PhD diss., King's College, University of London. https://kclpure.kcl.ac.uk/portal/files/12691039/Studentthesis-Stavrini_Ioannidou_2013.pdf. Accessed 7 Apr 2021.
Jones, Elizabeth H. 2010. Autofiction: A Brief History of a Neologism. In *Life Writing: Essays on Autobiography, Biography and Literature*, ed. Richard Bradford, 174–184. Houndmills: Palgrave Macmillan.
Missinne, Lut. 2013. *Oprecht gelogen: Autobiografische romans en autofictie in de Nederlandse literatuur na 1985*. Vantilt: Nijmegen.

Missinne, Lut. 2019. "Jeroen Brouwers: Bezonken Rood (1981) [Sunken Red]." In *Autobiography/Autofiction: An International and Interdisciplinary Handbook*, edited by Martina Wagner-Egelhaaf, 1930–1945. Berlin: De Gruyter.

Mortimer, Armine Kotin. 2009. Autofiction as Allofiction: Doubrovsky's 'L'Après-vivre.'. *L'Esprit Créateur* 49 (3): 22–35.

Wagner-Egelhaaf, Martina, ed. 2019. *Handbook of Autobiography/Autofiction*. Vol. 3. Berlin: De Gruyter.

Open Access This chapter is licensed under the terms of the Creative Commons Attribution 4.0 International License (http://creativecommons.org/licenses/by/4.0/), which permits use, sharing, adaptation, distribution and reproduction in any medium or format, as long as you give appropriate credit to the original author(s) and the source, provide a link to the Creative Commons licence and indicate if changes were made.

The images or other third party material in this chapter are included in the chapter's Creative Commons licence, unless indicated otherwise in a credit line to the material. If material is not included in the chapter's Creative Commons licence and your intended use is not permitted by statutory regulation or exceeds the permitted use, you will need to obtain permission directly from the copyright holder.

PART I

Approaches

CHAPTER 2

Of Strange Loops and Real Effects: Five Theses on Autofiction/the Autofictional

Martina Wagner-Egelhaaf

Critical thinking works productively by perpetually reconsidering terms and concepts. This is evident, for example, in the case of Sigmund Freud's concept of narcissism and Michel Foucault's notion of discourse. Both of these terms have prompted a range of interpretations and revisions, by these theorists themselves as well as by other critics. One could say that the more flexible and contested a term, the more lively and stimulating the critical debate about it. In this chapter, it will become evident that the debate around and criticism of autofiction should, in fact, be considered evidence of the strength of the concept, at least as long as one is open to a flexible mode of thinking.

Since its 1977 appearance on the cover of Serge Doubrovsky's *Fils* in its oft-quoted, but somewhat enigmatic, description "Fiction, of strictly real events and facts; *autofiction* if you like"[1] (Groneman 2019a, 241), the term "autofiction" has seen a lively reception in literary studies, especially in research on the genre of autobiography. The term's—or rather the

---

M. Wagner-Egelhaaf (✉)
Germanistisches Institut, University of Münster, Münster, Germany
e-mail: sekretariat.wagner-egelhaaf@uni-muenster.de

© The Author(s) 2022
A. Effe, H. Lawlor (eds.), *The Autofictional*, Palgrave Studies in Life Writing, https://doi.org/10.1007/978-3-030-78440-9_2

concept's—career started in France where, in the following years, writers and critics such as Jacques Lecarme, Vincent Colonna, Marie Darrieussecq, and Philippe Gasparini picked up, deepened, and diversified the discussion (Doubrovsky, Lecarme, and Lejeune 1993; Darrieussecq 1996; Colonna 1989, 2004; Gasparini 2008; Grell 2014; autofiction.org, n.d.). Doubrovsky's term soon made its way into other European academic contexts (Groneman 1999; Wagner-Egelhaaf 2013; Casas 2012). The English-speaking world remained reluctant for a long time, perhaps because in the Anglophone context the common umbrella term "life writing" already encompasses modes between fact and fiction. Whereas many scholars, mostly of the younger generation, quickly picked up the term "autofiction," others have remained skeptical. For instance, Beatrice Sandberg, who wrote on Karl Ove Knausgaard's autobiographical book project *Min kamp* (*My Struggle*) in 2013, well before the international Knausgaard hype started, declared that we do not need the term "autofiction" as we have "autobiographical writing" (or "autobiographisches Schreiben" in German) to describe texts that practice a less traditional form of autobiographical writing (Sandberg 2013, 374–375; see also Schmitt 2010). Indeed, one can easily argue that there is no need for the term "autofiction" on the basis that we have the terms "life writing" and "autobiographical writing." These terms are, without a doubt, useful umbrella terms that cover different forms of (auto)biographical testimony. However, when it comes to differentiating and specifying these forms, a more systematic and refined terminology is needed.

What has furthermore made critics skeptical about the term "autofiction" is that, from the beginning, critics have appropriated the concept in their own way, interpreting it according to their own needs and critical background. Certainly, there is a difference between conceiving autofiction as, for instance, a "linguistic adventure" (Doubrovsky 1993, 207; my translation) and as self-fictionalization (see Genette 1982, 293). The German critic Frank Zipfel has differentiated three definitions of autofiction in one and the same essay. First, Zipfel argues, autofiction can designate the constructive mode of every autobiography; second, texts where the author and the protagonist share the same name in combination with an index of fictionality; and, third, texts in which we find an oscillation between the autobiographical and the novelistic pact, as they have been conceived of by Philippe Lejeune (Zipfel 2009, 284–314, 299). Doubrovsky himself has, in the course of the debate on autofiction, stressed various aspects or elements that are crucial to the concept in his opinion: the autobiographer presents himself or herself as an ordinary person and makes the self interesting by means of writing, the autobiographical and novelistic (or fictional) pacts are both subscribed to at the same time, self-invention happens through the process of remembering, there occurs an assembling/putting together of the self, there is an adventure of language, and the autofictional has an effect on the real life of the author, just to mention the most important ones for the discussion to follow (Doubrovsky 1993, 207–217). For purists looking for unambiguous terms and definitions, the fact that Doubrovsky himself named different aspects in his definition of autofiction must appear as deeply frivolous, whereas less dogmatic minds may acknowledge the multi-faceted potentiality and creativity of more positively open notions.

This chapter does not, as some critics have tried to do, attempt to define "autofiction" as a distinct genre that should be clearly separated from either autobiography or the novel. Rather, it proposes conceiving of autofiction or—perhaps better—"the autofictional" as a conceptual matrix with scalable and interactive dimensions. This open and flexible understanding of autofiction is in line with the present volume's overall approach. In the following, five theses will be put forward in order to further elaborate upon the concept of autofiction and the autofictional as flexible, critical tools. These theses will be substantiated through examples from different languages, cultures, and periods in order to acknowledge the diversity and range of autofiction/the autofictional.

There Is a Need for the Term "Autofiction"

The first thesis is that we need the term "autofiction." A great number of scholars have sought to define and work with the term. This demonstrates that there has been, and still is, an obvious need in literary studies, especially in the field of autobiographical research, to grasp the vibrant interrelation between life and text, fiction and real, and for which there is no appropriate alternative concept. This perceptible need alone justifies the term's existence, but certainly not its sloppy use. The various definitions of autofiction should be understood as both drawing attention to and manifesting the great diversity of literary forms of self-presentation between fact and fiction. Nevertheless, scholars who use the term "autofiction" should clearly state how they understand it. Simply dropping in the word without further explanation raises questions and leads to suspicion that the popular term has been used uncritically and unthinkingly.

THE AUTOFICTIONAL IS A SCALABLE AND LATENT DIMENSION IN ALL AUTOBIOGRAPHICAL WRITING

This chapter's second thesis maintains that the autofictional is an intrinsic mode within the autobiographical that can be performed in various ways and with changing intensity. Johann Wolfgang Goethe, for instance, called his autobiography, published in four volumes between 1811 and 1833, *Dichtung und Wahrheit*, thereby already drawing attention in the title to the poetic or fictional element. Robert R. Heitner, in 1987, translated the title as *Poetry and Truth*, whereas John Oxenford, in 1882, chose *Fiction and Truth*. These two different translations reflect the variable understanding of the word "Dichtung." In contemporary German one would read "Dichtung" as "poetry," in the sense of verse. While *Dichtung und Wahrheit* does indeed include some poems, in this instance, "Dichtung" can by no means be reduced to poetry. When Goethe composed this text, "Dichtung" would have been understood to designate a literary mode more generally. Goethe's *Dichtung und Wahrheit* has played a dominant part in the scholarly reflection on the genre of autobiography, at least in the German tradition (Dilthey 1981, 244–246; Wagner-Egelhaaf 2005, 166–174). *Dichtung und Wahrheit* implicitly presents its own autobiographical theory, as do Goethe's letters, and in his talks with Johann Peter Eckermann, Goethe's interlocutor in later years, we find statements clarifying Goethe's ideas about the autobiographical. He explains to Eckermann that the use of the symbolic is the main characteristic of what he refers to as "poetry," leading one to wonder whether he would have used the term "autofiction" had it existed in his time.

As the title of his autobiography indicates, Goethe attributed an important role to the poetical in autobiographical writing. He makes this explicit in a letter to King Ludwig of Bavaria, dated December 17 and 27, 1829:

> As far as the somewhat paradoxical title of the confidences from my life, Truth and Poetry, is concerned, it was inspired by the experience that the public always has some doubts about the truthfulness of such biographical attempts. To counter this, I confessed to a kind of fiction, driven, as it were, without necessity, by a certain spirit of contradiction, for it was my most serious endeavor to represent and express, as far as possible, the actual fundamental truth, which, as far as I understood it, had prevailed in my life. However, if such a thing is not possible in subsequent years without letting recollection, and hence imagination, work and one always falls into the trap of exercising the poetic capacity, so to speak, then it is clear that one will lay

out and emphasize the results and our current perceptions of the past more than the details as they occurred at the time. (Goethe 1993, 209; my translation)[2]

Tellingly enough, Goethe uses the word "fiction" and he refers to "imagination," which he identifies as "the poetic capacity," in his search for what he calls the "fundamental truth" in autobiography. This fundamental truth is not composed of empirical facts but is brought forth by the poetic capacity. For this reason, he included elements such as the fairy tale "The New Paris" in *Poetry and Truth*, which, he reports, he told to other children when he was a boy; Goethe actually composed the fairy tale much later. In the form in which it appears in *Poetry and Truth*, it is an artfully composed tale from the pen of a mature Goethe. However, this dreamlike story, full of fancy, conveys what Goethe wanted to present as the truth about a certain phase of his life. Furthermore, he invented love affairs for his younger years that did not actually take place, at least based on what we know. There is one episode, for instance, where the narrator recounts a relationship the young Goethe had as a student in Strasbourg. According to the narration, Goethe made friends with his dance instructor's two daughters. He fell in love with the younger, Emily, while the elder, Lucinde, fell in love with him. The situation became complicated and Goethe decided to leave the dance master's house. In the moment of parting, Lucinde suddenly kisses him but curses him with the kiss so that the next girl that Goethe kisses would be forever unlucky. Of course, Lucinde's intention is to prevent Goethe from kissing her sister. The autobiographical narrator indeed takes the curse very seriously, reporting that he did not dare to kiss Friederike, a girl with whom Goethe had a real relationship as a student in Strasbourg, for a long time and he even uses this fictive and fictional cursed kiss as a motif when describing the end of his affair with Friederike, whom he eventually left (Wagner-Egelhaaf 2020, 109–126). This motif of the cursed kiss illustrates that there is an intricate interweaving of fiction and life. Goethe, who, in the German tradition of life writing, is considered a canonical autobiographer, changed the chronological order of life events for the sake of a more rounded narrative. For example, in reality, the drama *Clavigo* was written earlier than *Werther*, whereas in the autobiography, it seems to be the other way round. Goethe might have argued for an autofictional mode on the basis that he considered poetry and fiction to be more adequate producers of autobiographical truth than mere facts could be. Where Zipfel's first definition acknowledges the necessarily constructive dimension of every autobiography as autofictional (2009, 299), the position taken in this chapter conceives of the fictional element in autobiography as deliberately introduced and artistically handled.

Researchers have discussed autofiction as a separate genre, distinct from autobiography, novel, and autobiographical novel. Against the backdrop of Goethe's *Dichtung und Wahrheit*, it seems more appropriate to conceptualize the autofictional as an inherent dimension of autobiographical writing, that is, as a latent force that can be activated in different ways and to different degrees. The autofictional is scalable. There may be more factuality as in Annie Ernaux's *Les Années* (2008) or in Salman Rushdie's *Joseph Anton* (2012), texts which refer to a plenitude of historical events that the reader likely also remembers, or there may be much more fictionality as in Felicitas Hoppe's *Hoppe* (2012), discussed below. However, there is no factuality without fictionality if one takes into account that even the order in which facts are presented creates somewhat fictional relations. This is certainly not an argument for panfictionalism, as panfictionalism claims that everything is fictional and considers the fictional as opposite to the factual. The argument brought forward here is that fictional elements shape the perception of the factual. The title of Goethe's *Dichtung und Wahrheit* suggests that "poetry" and "truth" are equally involved in the narrative of Goethe's life. However, the crucial point of Goethe's concept is that he takes poetry as the driving force of truth. In this sense, the structural make-up of *Dichtung und Wahrheit* remains in a sort of balance between factuality and fictionality, although, of course, it is impossible to differentiate between how much is real and factual, and how much is fiction within the text. Such differentiation would not even be especially fruitful for critical discussion.

IMAGINATION SUPPORTS AUTOBIOGRAPHICAL REFERENCE

The third thesis of this chapter highlights the constructive role of imagination and invention in the autofictional. One can observe that quite a lot of texts in contemporary literature demonstratively combine elements from their author's real life with the supernatural. One prominent example from the field of German literature is Felicitas Hoppe's *Hoppe* (2012), which has received much critical attention and acclaim because of its sophisticated autofictional form. The title enacts one of Lejeune's criteria for autobiography, the identification of the name of the protagonist with the name of the author, yet there is something disconcerting about the plain and somewhat brutal title of just *Hoppe*.

Hoppe is the story of a girl named Felicitas Hoppe who was born in Hameln, a town in Lower Saxony. Felicitas grows up with her father in Canada and Australia and later lives in the United States. Many aspects of this book are absolutely fantastical, yet the fantastical is combined with facts and figures from the author's life. Thus, the back cover of the book tells the reader that *Hoppe* is "Hoppe's dream biography." On the one hand, this indicates invention comparable in nature to Goethe's invented episodes and fantasies, such as the fairy tale "The New Paris." On the other hand, it takes account of the idea that desires and dreams are an intrinsic element of a person's existence and perhaps disclose more, and different, things about a person than mere biographical data in chronological order. The way in which *Hoppe* links the factual and the fictional, by integrating real-life details into fantastical accounts and insisting on the truth of the fantastical, creates a delightful play with factual and invented information. There are also episodes in the text that appear entirely unbelievable and foreground their fantastical character, for instance, when the narrator tells us that Hoppe can understand and speak any language without ever having learned it. The fact that Felicitas presents herself as a linguistic miracle can be read as a reflection of the autofictional potentiality of language (Egendal, this volume). The choice and combination of words, as well as the different tones adopted, may also produce autofictional effects, for instance, when the narrator of *Hoppe* imitates scholarly discourse and thus puts the protagonist, Hoppe, at a playful ironic distance. This dimension may be related to what Doubrovsky called "the adventure of language" (1993, 213; my translation) and, indeed, *Hoppe* mimics not only academic discourse but also the genre of the adventure novel when Felicitas is presented as the hero of odd and unbelievable adventures. *Hoppe*'s narrated adventures are, however, a mere "pleasure of the text" in Roland Barthes's sense of directing attention to the play of words rather than the meaning of a text (Barthes 1973).

Combining the fantastical and the factual is also characteristic of the Austrian writer Thomas Glavinic's so-called Jonas novels. Glavinic has published a series of books centered on a protagonist called Jonas: *Die Arbeit der Nacht* (2006), *Das Leben der Wünsche*, published (2009), *Das größere Wunder* (2013), and, finally, *Der Jonas-Komplex* (2016). The character Jonas seems to be the same person in all of the books, but although there are episodes that reappear in all books, the story worlds are different and do not form a traditionally serial autofictional work (Schuh and Menn, this volume). Furthermore, Jonas shares biographical features with the author and there are strange, fairytale-like events. For example, one morning the protagonist gets up and finds the world completely empty of people and is seemingly the only person left. On other occasions, he finds that all his wishes are being miraculously fulfilled. Yet, the persistent use of the name Jonas and the interweaving of the four Jonas-lives create a specific effect of real-world reference. For the reader who has read all of the books, the individual texts seem to refer to a shared story world, but one cannot be sure whether Jonas is the same character in all of them. There seems to be a world beyond the text. However, this world beyond is, first and foremost, another text. Jonas's persistent, ghostly reappearance in the different texts and the reader's memory of what they have already read about his life in the different texts create the impression of a powerful fictional persona driven by an intense (auto-)biographical energy behind the texts. This effect is produced by the work's strategic and artfully staged intertextuality.

Norwegian writer Karl Ove Knausgaard's six-volume autobiographical project *Min kamp* (*My Struggle*) (2009–2011) has frequently been referred to as autofictional, and even as a paradigm of autofictionality. Knausgaard's claim that he has written his life exactly as it was rather than producing an artful autobiography invokes Doubrovsky's argument that autobiography is for great men while autofiction can be practiced by everybody. Autofiction, Doubrovsky says, should tell everything, a claim previously made by Jean-Jacques Rousseau in his *Confessions* (published 1782/1789). For Doubrovsky, therefore, autofiction is more realistic than autobiography. The enormous international success of Knausgaard's work seems to reflect a new need for the real as he narrates seemingly everything about his life in great detail, even the most boring and unspectacular events (see also Schmitt 2017). This is consistent with Knausgaard's claim that he has abandoned the sophisticated artistic form, and with his use of a language that, in contrast to Doubrovsky, renounces linguistic experimentation. It is the hyperrealism, among other characteristics, of Knausgaard's writing that has caused critics to perceive *Min kamp* as autofiction, as the hyperrealistic mode of his narration shines a bright spotlight on details that may thus appear artificial. Attempts to play off an allegedly traditional poststructuralist paradigm of the autofictional against a new need for the real fall short, as reality is, of course, always mediated. The opening of the first volume of

A Death in the Family demonstrates, quite vividly, the fictional character of Knausgaard's reality effects:

> FOR THE HEART, life is simple: it beats for as long as it can. Then it stops. Sooner or later, one day, this pounding action will cease of its own accord, and the blood will begin to run towards the body's lowest point, where it will collect in a small pool, visible from the outside as a dark, soft patch on ever whiter skin, as the temperature sinks, the limbs stiffen and the intestines drain. These changes in the first hours occur so slowly and take place with such inexorability that there is something almost ritualistic about them, as though life capitulates according to specific rules, a kind of gentleman's agreement, to which the representatives of death also adhere, inasmuch as they always wait until life has retreated before they launch their invasion of the new landscape. By which point, however, the invasion is irrevocable. The enormous hordes of bacteria that begin to infiltrate the body's innards cannot be halted. Had they but tried a few hours earlier, they would have met with immediate resistance; however, everything around them is quiet now, as they delve deeper and deeper into the moist darkness. They advance on the Haversian canals, the crypts of Lieberkühn, the islets of Langerhans. They proceed to Bowman's capsule in the kidneys, Clark's column in the Spinalis, the black substance in the mesencephalon. And they arrive at the heart. As yet, it is intact, but deprived of the activity to which end its whole construction has been designed, there is something strangely desolate about it, like a production plant, that workers have been forced to flee in haste, or so it appears, the stationary vehicles shining yellow against the darkness of the forest, the huts deserted, a line of fully loaded cable buckets stretching up the hillside. (2012, 3)

This passage almost makes the blood freeze in the veins as the apparently factual and unemotional description of the process of bodily decay, reaching as deep as the microscopic level and seemingly based on scientific medical knowledge, appears excessively sharp and hyperrealistic. At the same time, the image presented is a product of the imagination, especially given that the biological process of decay is depicted through the use of metaphors such as "a small pool," "gentleman's agreement," "invasion," or "landscape." At the end of the book, it is the protagonist's father who dies, and thus the opening passage, which seemingly describes a general phenomenon of human life, that is, death, becomes personal. Strikingly, both the beginning and end of this autobiographical narrative are about life, as well as about death. This connective literary frame is certainly a sophisticated fictional technique. The passage quoted is a paradigm of how referential description within a text and the fictional mode consistently tilt into one another. The example of Knausgaard supports this chapter's third thesis that imagination by no means contradicts autobiographical reference but may even fundamentally support it. The same holds true for what has been said on Goethe's *Dichtung und Wahrheit*. Imagination, and even the use of fantastical elements, may highlight the claim of truth in life writing by giving emphasis to what is related and attracting the reader's attention, as has been shown by the example of the fairy tale in Goethe's autobiography.

Autofiction Produces Real-Life Effects

This chapter's fourth thesis highlights a dimension hinted at by Serge Doubrovsky, but largely neglected or overlooked in the critical debate on autofiction: the fact that autofiction produces real-life effects and should, therefore, be considered fundamentally performative. In *Le Livre brisé*, published in 1989, Doubrovsky writes about his marriage and his wife Inge's alcoholism. As the reader is informed at the end of the book, the author worked on the manuscript between May 1985 and May 1988 (1991, 612) and during this period, in November 1987, Ilse died of an alcohol overdose (1993, 216). In the text, Doubrovsky discloses that the couple had worked on the book together. While autobiography, he explains, is a retrospective genre in the face of death, his wife wanted them to tell "a story of life" (1991, 452).[3] Ilse's death causes the book to break, indicated by the participle *brisé* in the title. Her death, imagined as possibly suicide by the author himself (Gronemann 2019b),[4] can be seen as the fulfillment of what was already laid out in the book. The autofiction "in a stroke" (Doubrovsky 1993, 217; my translation) turned into an autobiography he resumes. What he experienced in his life as a dreadful shock of the unexpected, which crushed him, namely Ilse's death, he tells us, seems to be presented in his text as the progression of the inevitable. The retrospectively reported problems of this marriage actually became, after the death of Ilse, forward-looking signs.[5] Doubrovsky explains that he continued to write his autofiction until he completely lost control of the project. The real was assassinated in the games of fiction that were telling the truth even though the author was not aware of it (1993, 207). This analysis by Doubrovsky himself of what happened to him upon the death of his wife can be taken as proof that autofiction is not merely a postmodern joke or sliding effect of linguistic signs, as some critics have claimed. Rather, autofiction, as Doubrovsky's case demonstrates, may have a very serious background indeed, as well as disquieting consequences for the author's life.[6]

The idea that autobiographers not only aim to represent their lives by writing about them truthfully, albeit in a more or less fictional mode, but that their autobiographical project has a real effect on their life was not a completely new insight offered by Doubrovsky. In his seminal text on "Autobiography as De-facement" from 1979, Paul de Man put forward the view that autobiographical writing, first and foremost, produces the life which it depicts. "We assume that life *produces* the autobiography as an act produces its consequences," de Man writes, but then asks whether we cannot "suggest, with equal justice, that the autobiographical project may itself produce and determine the life and that whatever the writer *does* is in fact governed by the technical demands of self-portraiture and thus determined, in all its aspects, by the resources of his medium?" (1979, 920). This statement draws attention to the fact that writing one's autobiography is not to be considered a divide between life and text but that the act of writing itself is part of the life that is autobiographically represented. Hence, the act of autobiographical writing is the crucial point where life and writing merge.

This real-life effect, with its potentiality to merge life and writing, as a crucial feature of autofiction triggers the thought that we can visualize the performative text/life relation using the strange loop figure also known as the Möbius strip. This has already been suggested in an earlier article that demonstrates the theoretical productivity of the strange loop figure (see Wagner-Egelhaaf 2015). The Möbius strip, ingeniously used as the core device in drawings by the Dutch artist M. E. Escher (1898–1972), permanently twists outside and inside so that it becomes impossible to determine where one ends and the other begins. Douglas R. Hofstadter discussed the Möbius strip as a recurrent structural pattern in cultural production in his famous book *Gödel, Escher, Bach: An Eternal Golden Braid* (1979). In his view, it has proven eminently productive in various cultural constellations that struggle to overcome dichotomous explanations. When applied to the discussion of autofiction, the strip can be viewed as both subject and object, life and writing, twisting into each other, and thus as deconstructing the oppositions.[7] However, to function as a successful conceptualization of autofiction, this strange loop must be understood as being in continuous motion, as a dynamic process. If a person contemplates their life, the contemplation, in the very moment it takes place, turns into an element of the life that the person is reflecting on. For autofiction, this permanently twisting movement forms a constitutive principle that renders the text performative.

AUTOFICTION OSCILLATES BETWEEN FICTIONALITY AND FACTUALITY

While the fourth thesis focuses on the author and the effects of the text on their life, the fifth considers the effects that autofictional texts have on the reader. Drawing on Philippe Lejeune's notion of the "autobiographical pact" (1975),[8] Doubrovsky called his books "neither autobiographies nor completely novels, caught in the turnstile, the in-between of the genres, subscribing at the same time and contradictorily to the autobiographical pact and the novelistic pact, perhaps in order to abolish their limits or limitations" (1993, 210; my translation).[9]

The turnstile imagery is reminiscent of Paul de Man's image of the revolving door, which he uses to describe the rhetoricity of language. People enter revolving doors when they want to get inside a building or a closed area. However, the revolving door, at the same time and in the same movement, guides them outward again (De Man 1979, 921). Some critics doubt that one can subscribe to the autobiographical and the fictional pact at the same time; Arnaud Schmitt, for example, asks, "Can one really understand a textual segment as being both referential and fictional?" (2010, 128). Schmitt answers that it would be cognitively impossible to adhere to the autofictional and the fictional pact simultaneously. With reference to Philippe Gasparini, who struggled with the same problem, he contemplates that "simultaneous" could probably be understood as "ceaselessly alternating" between referential and fictional readings (Schmitt 2010, 128; see also Gasparini 2004, 13, who speaks of "a simultaneous double reading"; my translation), yet he doubts the practicality of this ceaseless movement in the concrete act of reading. However, he also concedes that this confused state between autobiography and fiction could be received as an aesthetic pleasure. Zipfel, in his third definition of autofiction, allows the two Lejeunian pacts to oscillate. One can conceive how, in the practical act of reading, this may indeed be a challenge that results in the reader's confusion and/or aesthetic pleasure. Seen as a model of autofiction, however, it gets right to the heart of the matter, namely, the being in-between or, alternatively, both autobiographical and fictional.

This intriguing oscillatory movement is compatible with the strange loop figure introduced in the previous section; the oscillation between fact and fiction imperceptibly twists the real and the fictional. Thus, slippery autofiction presents itself as a dynamic and versatile mental concept which alternately brings one or the other dimension into the foreground while still allowing the other to permanently resonate.

In German-language literature, authors from the first decade of this millennium have made extensive use of this principle of oscillation. Thomas Glavinic's *Das bin doch ich* (translatable—albeit inadequately—as "That's me, isn't it?"), published in 2007, tells the story of an Austrian author named Thomas Glavinic, who wrote a book titled *Die Arbeit der Nacht* which had come out the previous year. *Das bin doch ich* deals with, among other topics, the marketing process of *Die Arbeit der Nacht*. The book is a somewhat satirical depiction of the literary market. The title, *Das bin doch ich*, refers to an episode in the text where the protagonist reads a feuilleton review. The author of this review praises Daniel Kehlmann, a very successful German writer who has won many literary prizes, as "Germany's best writer of his generation." "Das bin doch ich" (41)—alternatively translated as "What? No, that's me!"—is the spontaneous and indignant reaction of Glavinic's protagonist, who is a good friend of Daniel Kehlmann's in both the book and in reality (Jensen and Tamm 2013). The bemusing autofictional clou is located in the seemingly harmless colloquial wording of the title: *Das bin doch ich*, with *doch* being virtually untranslatable into English. It indicates the speaker's defiant and indignant claim that, surely, nobody other than himself could be Germany's best writer of his generation. At the same time, the wording of "Das bin doch ich" performs an act of comic self-identification or self-assertion as a reaction to an obvious feeling about the protagonist's uncertainty about who or what he is. Thus, this is a simultaneously funny and serious reflection of the first-person speaker's hybrid autofictional status; readers may ask themselves whether Glavinic's book is an autobiographical confession or a fictional joke.

Glavinic's book has been labeled "metafiction," which, of course, it is. However, "metafiction" as a label is not precise enough. It does not address the fact that the protagonist seems to be recognizable as the author, that he bears the same name as the author, and that he has written the same book as the author. These parallels do offer an autobiographical pact according to Lejeune. There are other characters in the book who seem to be real-world persons, too. In addition to the aforementioned Kehlmann, real-life author Jonathan Safran Foer makes an appearance at the beginning of the book when the protagonist attends a reading by him. Therefore, the question of how autobiographical the book is arises again and again—and yet the reader continually doubts. The narrator's somewhat mocking tone and the all too frank disclosure of politically incorrect thoughts and embarrassing personal weaknesses arouse suspicion. On the one hand, these features of the book connect with confession and self-exploration as traditional characteristics of the genre of autobiography, and on the other hand, they ironically counteract these exact same genre features.

Another example that demonstrates the oscillation of pacts is Felicitas Hoppe's previously mentioned *Hoppe*. In *Hoppe*, two telling paratexts attract attention right at the beginning of the book. The reminder "The spoken word holds for family members!"[10] is inserted between the main title and the table of contents. Yet, no matter how one reads this sentence, whether as the author distancing herself from the written text or merely from its fictitious factuality, it seems to refer to binding extratextual oral conversations with family members. As only the text is accessible for literary analysis, this preamble, which sounds authentically personal, places the book in a hard to define, but clearly marked, relationship with the biography of the author. Immediately after the table of contents, the reader finds as chapter "0. Felicitas Hoppe, *22.12.1960 in Hameln, is a German writer. *Wikipedia.*" *Wikipedia* is often used to find information quickly, although it is not generally held to be an entirely reliable source. Furthermore, it is equally clear that many personal entries in *Wikipedia* are authored by the persons whose lives and achievements are presented themselves—which makes the *Wikipedia* entries in question autobiographical texts. This is, however, not the case with the entry for Felicitas Hoppe (personal communication, April 8, 2020).[11] Surely, the *Wikipedia* reference is an ironic comment on which sources people consult and the questionable reliability of these sources. Thus, the fact that the book cites the *Wikipedia* entry constitutes a play with the relationship between fiction and facts. *Hoppe* not only incorporates the so-called factual into the text, but, by doing so, extends the textual story world into the realm of the factual—even if *Wikipedia* is an ambivalent source for facts, whatever we consider *facts* to be.

Included right at the beginning of the book, these two paratexts signal real-world referentiality which they question at the same time. The first two sentences of the current German *Wikipedia* entry are as follows: "Felicitas Hoppe (* 22. Dezember 1960 in Hameln) ist eine deutsche

Schriftstellerin. Sie ist Trägerin des Georg-Büchner-Preises 2012" ("Felicitas Hoppe [* 22 December 1960 in Hameln] is a German writer. She is the winner of the Georg Büchner Prize 2012"; my translation). The entry further reports that Hoppe was born the third of five children in Hameln, where she also went to school. This could mean that the four brothers and sisters mentioned in the book do actually exist in Hoppe's real life, even though the book confronts us with the sentence "The Hameln childhood is pure invention" (Hoppe 2012, 14; my translation). Incidentally, the English version of *Wikipedia* does not mention the siblings. It begins with the information that "Felicitas Hoppe (born 22 December 1960 in Hamelin, Lower Saxony) is a German writer" and that she "was born in Hamelin, Lower Saxony, and grew up there." Certainly, the text is not simply to be read in terms of what is factual and what is fictional—yet *Hoppe* provokes this reading in order to make fun of it at the same time (Wagner-Egelhaaf 2018). By mixing factual and invented information, *Hoppe* makes the factual appear fictional and the fictional appear factual and makes the reader oscillate between the two modes.

* * *

Five theses on autofiction—are they just isolated observations or is there a deeper connection between them? The first thesis justifies the term "autofiction": its frequent and ongoing use indicates an obvious epistemological need. The term is most useful, this chapter claims, not as a strict genre denominator but as a flexible concept with scalable parameters. The second thesis recognizes that autofiction is an inherent dimension of autobiography in general and argues against autofiction as a separate genre. Thesis three highlights imagination and even the supernatural as a potential feature of autofiction that in no ways speaks against (auto-)biographical relevance. Thesis four reinforces this point through the claim that the fictional element (which may include imagination, the fantastical, and the supernatural) has real-life effects and may produce what it narrates. Finally, the fifth thesis argues for understanding autofiction as oscillating between fictionality and factuality, that is, for a dynamic mode, in order to reflect on the fictionality of the factual and the factuality of fiction. In how the autofictional is conceptualized in this chapter, these five aspects work together. Autofiction may flexibly bring one or other aspect to the foreground while all of them, to varying extents, resonate together in texts that can be qualified as autofictional.

Notes

1. "Fiction, d'événements et de faits strictement réels; si l'on veut *autofiction*."
2. "Was den freilich einigermaßen paradoxen Titel der Vertraulichkeiten aus meinem Leben Wahrheit und Dichtung betrifft, so ward derselbige durch die Erfahrung veranlaßt, daß das Publikum immer an der Wahrhaftigkeit solcher biographischen Versuche einigen Zweifel hege. Diesem zu begegnen, bekannte ich mich zu einer Art von Fiktion, gewissermaßen ohne Not, durch einen gewissen Widerspruchs-Geist getrieben, denn es war mein ernstestes Bestreben das eigentliche Grundwahre, das, insofern ich es einsah, in meinem Leben obgewaltet hatte, möglichst darzustellen und auszudrücken. Wenn aber ein solches in späteren Jahren nicht möglich ist, ohne die Rückerinnerung und also die Einbildungskraft wirken zu lassen, und man also immer in den Fall kommt gewissermaßen das dichterische Vermögen auszuüben, so ist es klar daß man mehr die Resultate und, wie wir uns das Vergangene jetzt denken, als die Einzelheiten, wie sie sich damals ereigneten, aufstellen und hervorheben werde."
3. See Doubrovsky 1991, 452: "L'autobiographie est un genre posthume. Elle voulait de nous un récit à vif." "À vif" is usually translated as "raw," but in the context in question, it refers to "unsophisticated life."
4. In "Textes en main," Doubrovsky says that his wife's death was an accident. However, he also says in *Le livre brisé* that he had called her "suicide wife, kamikaze woman" and that he had written that he would kill a woman with every book (see Doubrovsky 1993, 132; my translation).
5. "L'autofiction est devenue d'un seul coup autobiographie. De rétrospective, elle s'est faite prospective. Ce que j'ai ressenti dan[s] ma vie comme le choc effroyable de l'imprévu, qui m'a écrasé, le livre semble le présenter comme la progression d'un inéluctable" (Doubrovsky 1993, 217).
6. This aspect has been further developed on the basis of Foucault's concept of "subjectivation" by Innokentij Kreknin (2014).
7. Significantly, Douglas R. Hofstadter has also published an autobiography under the symbol of the strange loop; see Hofstadter (2007). The discussion of this very special case of autobiography/autofiction will have to take place elsewhere.
8. Lejeune's concept of "the autobiographical pact" has been, for good reasons, extremely influential in the scholarship of autobiography. However, it has also been criticized, especially by poststructuralist critics who objected that the autobiographical "I" is far from a stable and recognizable entity and that an author, a narrator, and a protagonist could never be identified. This is true from a poststructuralist, or better deconstructive, perspective, but from a deconstructive perspective nothing can ever be identified.

Lejeune's idea of the autobiographical pact is to be seen in the vein of reception theory, the heyday of which fell exactly in the time when Lejeune elaborated on this concept. Viewed from this perspective, the autobiographical pact maintains that a reader who realizes that author, narrator, and protagonist share the same name, and who reads on the book cover a subtitle such as "My Life" or "Autobiography," is inclined to read the book as an autobiography. On the basis of this pragmatic reading, the concept of the autobiographical pact is an appropriate auxiliary concept for the conceptualization of autofiction.

9. "Ni autobiographies, ni totalement romans, pris dans le tourniquet, l'entre-deux des genres, souscrivant à la fois et contradictoirement au pacte autobiographique et au pacte Romanesque, peut-d'être pour en abolir les limites ou limitations."
10. "Für Familienmitglieder gilt das gesprochene Wort!"
11. Thanks to Stefan Neuhaus for establishing the contact and thanks to Felicitas Hoppe for her immediate and open reply.

Works Cited

Barthes, Roland. 1973. *The Pleasure of the Text*. Translated by Richard Miller. New York: Hill & Wang.
Casas, Ana, ed. 2012. *La autoficción: Reflexiones teóricas*. Madrid: Arco/Libros.
Colonna, Vincent. 1989. L'Autofiction, essai sur la fictionalisation de soi en littérature. PhD diss., École des Hautes Études en Sciences Sociales.
———. 2004. *Autofiction et autres mythomanies littéraires*. Paris: Tristram.
Darrieussecq, Marie. 1996. L'autofiction, un genre pas sérieux. *Poétique* 107: 367–380.
De Man, Paul. 1979. Autobiography as De-facement. *Modern Language Notes* 94 (5): 919–930.
Dilthey, Wilhelm. 1981. *Der Aufbau der geschichtlichen Welt in den Geisteswissenschaften*. Frankfurt a. M.: Suhrkamp.
Doubrovsky, Serge. 1991. *Le livre brisé*. Paris: Gallimard.
———. 1993. Textes en main. In *Autofiction & Cie*, ed. Serge Doubrovsky, Jacques Lecarme, and Philippe Lejeune, 207–217. Nanterre: Université Paris X.
Doubrovsky, Serge, Jacques Lecarme, and Philippe Lejeune, eds. 1993. *Autofiction & Cie*. Nanterre: Université Paris X.
Ernaux, Annie. 2008. *Les Années*. Paris: Gallimard.
Gasparini, Philippe. 2004. *Est-il je? Roman autobiographique et autofiction*. Paris: Éditions du Seuil.
———. 2008. *Autofiction: Une aventure du langage*. Paris: Éditions du Seuil.
Genette, Gérard. 1982. *Palimpsestes: La littérature au second degré*. Paris: Éditions du Seuil.

Glavinic, Thomas. 2006. *Die Arbeit der Nacht.* München: Hanser.
———. 2007. *Das bin doch ich.* München: Hanser.
———. 2009. *Das Leben der Wünsche.* München: Hanser.
———. 2013. *Das größere Wunder.* München: Hanser.
———. 2016. *Der Jonas-Komplex.* Frankfurt a. M.: Fischer.
Goethe, Johann Wolfgang von. 1882. *Truth and Fiction: Relating my Life.* Translated by John Oxenford. New York: John D. Williams.
———. 1987. *From My Life: Poetry and Truth.* Translated by Robert R. Heitner. In *Goethe's Collected Works,* ed. Thomas P. Saine and Jeffrey L. Sammons, vols. 4 and 5. New York: Princeton University Press.
———. 1993. *Die letzten Jahre: Briefe, Tagebücher und Gespräche von 1823 bis zu Goethes Tod, Teil II: Vom Dornburger Aufenthalt 1828 bis zum Tode.* In *Sämtliche Werke, 40 Bde., Bd. II/11,* ed. Horst Fleig. Frankfurt a. M.: Deutscher Klassiker Verlag.
Grell, Isabelle. 2014. *L'Autofiction.* Paris: Armand Colin.
Gronemann, Claudia. 1999. Autofiction und das Ich in der Signifikantenkette: Zur literarischen Konstitution des autobiographischen Subjekts bei Serge Doubrovsky. *Poetica. Zeitschrift für Sprach- und Literaturwissenschaft* 31 (1-2): 237–262.
———. 2019a. Autofiction. In *Handbook of Autobiography/Autofiction,* ed. Martina Wagner-Egelhaaf, vol. 1, 241–246. Berlin: De Gruyter.
———. 2019b. Serge Doubrovsky: *Le Livre Brisé* (1989) [*The Broken Book*]. In *Handbook of Autobiography/Autofiction,* ed. Martina Wagner-Egelhaaf, vol. 3, 1977–1988. Berlin: De Gruyter.
Hofstadter, Douglas R. 1979. *Gödel, Escher, Bach: An Eternal Golden Braid: A Metaphorical Fugue on Minds and Machines in the Spirit of Lewis Carroll.* New York: Basic Books.
———. 2007. *I Am a Strange Loop.* New York: Basic Books.
Hoppe, Felicitas. 2012. *Hoppe.* Frankfurt a. M.: Fischer.
Jensen, Annika, and Jutta Müller Tamm. 2013. Echte Wiener und falsche Inder: Strategien und Effekte autofiktionalen Schreibens in der Gegenwartsliteratur. In *Auto(r)fiktion,* ed. Martina Wagner-Egelhaaf, 315–328. Bielefeld: Aisthesis.
Knausgaard, Karl Ove. 2012. *A Death in the Family.* Translated by Don Bartlett. London: Harvill Secker.
Kreknin, Innokentij. 2014. *Poetiken des Selbst: Identität, Autorschaft und Autofiktion am Beispiel von Rainald Goetz, Joachim Lottmann und Alban Nikolai Herbst.* Berlin: De Gruyter.
Lejeune, Philippe. 1975. Le pacte autobiographique. In *Le pacte autobiographique,* 13–46. Paris: Éditions du Seuil.
Sandberg, Beatrice. 2013. Unter Einschluss der Öffentlichkeit oder das Vorrecht des Privaten. In *Auto(r)fiktion: Literarische Verfahren der Selbstkonstruktion,* ed. Martina Wagner-Egelhaaf, 355–377. Bielefeld: Aisthesis.

Schmitt, Arnaud. 2010. Making the Case for Self-Narration. Against Autofiction. *a/b. Auto/Biography Studies* 25 (1): 122–137.
———. 2017. *The Phenomenology of Autobiography: Making it Real*. New York: Routledge.
Rushdie, Salman. 2012. *Joseph Anton. A Memoir*. New York: Random House.
Wagner-Egelhaaf, Martina. 2005. *Autobiographie*. Stuttgart/Weimar: J. B. Metzler.
———, ed. 2013. *Auto(r)fiktion: Literarische Verfahren der Selbstkonstruktion*. Bielefeld: Aisthesis.
———. 2015. Literaturtheorie als Theorie der Gesellschaft. In *Literatur, Macht, Gesellschaft: Neue Beiträge zur theoretischen Modellierung des Verhältnisses von Literatur und Gesellschaft*, ed. Promotionskolleg Literaturtheorie als Theorie der Gesellschaft, 17–38. Heidelberg: Winter.
———. 2018. Autofiktion? Zur Brauchbarkeit einer Kategorie. In *Akten des XIII. Kongresses der Internationalen Vereinigung für Germanistik Shanghai 2015. Germanistik zwischen Tradition und Innovation*, ed. Jianhua Zhu, Jin Zhao, and Michael Szurawitzki, vol. 11, 295–299. Frankfurt a. M.: Peter Lang.
———. 2020. *Sich entscheiden: Momente der Autobiographie bei Goethe*. Göttingen: Wallstein.
Wikipedia. 2020a. *Felicitas Hoppe*. https://de.wikipedia.org/wiki/Felicitas_Hoppe. Accessed 20 Oct 2020.
———. 2020b. *Felicitas Hoppe*. https://en.wikipedia.org/wiki/Felicitas_Hoppe. Accessed 11 Sept 2020.
Zipfel, Frank. 2009. Autofiktion: Zwischen den Grenzen von Faktualität, Fiktionalität und Literarität? In *Grenzen der Literatur: Zu Begriff und Phänomen des Literarischen*, ed. Simone Winko, Fotis Jannidis, and Gerhard Lauer, 284–314. Berlin: De Gruyter.

Open Access This chapter is licensed under the terms of the Creative Commons Attribution 4.0 International License (http://creativecommons.org/licenses/by/4.0/), which permits use, sharing, adaptation, distribution and reproduction in any medium or format, as long as you give appropriate credit to the original author(s) and the source, provide a link to the Creative Commons licence and indicate if changes were made.

The images or other third party material in this chapter are included in the chapter's Creative Commons licence, unless indicated otherwise in a credit line to the material. If material is not included in the chapter's Creative Commons licence and your intended use is not permitted by statutory regulation or exceeds the permitted use, you will need to obtain permission directly from the copyright holder.

CHAPTER 3

The Fictional in Autofiction

Alison James

At first glance, autofiction seems to be at odds with theories of fiction and fictionality. Serge Doubrovsky's inaugural definition of autofiction, on the back cover of *Fils* (1977), arguably capitalizes on a broadly postmodern or poststructuralist consensus around the fictional status of self-narration: even if the events and facts recounted are "strictly real," the "adventure" of language produces a fiction.[1] By contrast, both semantic and pragmatic theories of fiction and fictionality, especially as they have developed since the 1990s, have tended to reaffirm the fundamental distinction between fictional and nonfictional narratives, aiming to specify the borders, the autonomy—the "distinction" as Dorrit Cohn (1999) puts it—of fiction. Although this ostensible opposition between autofiction and theories of fiction requires some qualification (as we shall see), it no doubt accounts for the misunderstandings that arise in debates around autofiction, autobiography, and autobiographical fiction. For those who wish to maintain a clear distinction between fact and fiction, autofiction must appear

A. James (✉)
Department of Romance Languages and Literatures, University of Chicago, Chicago, IL, USA
e-mail: asj@uchicago.edu

© The Author(s) 2022
A. Effe, H. Lawlor (eds.), *The Autofictional*, Palgrave Studies in Life Writing, https://doi.org/10.1007/978-3-030-78440-9_3

defective: a narcissistic failure of imagination, in the eyes of the partisans of fiction (e.g., Petit 1999); an excuse for carelessness with the truth, for those who defend the specific referential claims of factual literature (e.g., Lejeune 2007, 3). At first glance, the same characteristics that have allowed autofiction to become a broad, fluid, almost infinitely extensible term also make it the object of an impasse—amenable to sociological study, perhaps, as Jean-Louis Jeannelle has argued, but resistant to literary-theoretical investigation (2013, 226).

Attempting to move beyond this theoretical deadlock, I will posit here that theories of fiction and fictionality can indeed shed light on autofiction, and vice versa. I will first examine how accounts of autofiction engage with theoretical approaches to both autobiography and fiction, before asking whether autofiction can be reconciled with existing definitions of fictionality. Drawing on pragmatic, narratological, and rhetorical theories of fictionality, I will then aim to locate factual and fictional modes at work within texts, showing how they operate at the level of formal devices or narrative frames to foreground either referential force or the work of fictionalization. This chapter thus aims to bring some precision to our understanding of the fictional in autofiction, while also accounting for ambiguities in reception. Ultimately, we will see that autofictional texts allow for a range of configurations of the fact/fiction relationship, while theory can help us locate sites and signposts of fictionality or factuality within works. Conversely, due to the very ambiguity and hybridity of autofictional texts, they can serve as a useful empirical testing ground for theories of fiction, which have traditionally based their arguments on narratives and entities already established as generically fictional (the exception here are rhetorical theories of fictionality, discussed later, which identify local uses of fictionality within nonfictional discourse [Walsh 2007; Nielsen, Phelan, and Walsh 2014]). This dialectical approach takes theories of fiction out of their comfort zone in the novel, while also attempting to bring some clarity to the debates about autofiction.

The Theoretical Adventures of Autofiction

Autofictional texts bring to light disjunctions between theory and practice, as well as divergent understandings of the fact/fiction divide. Doubrovsky's initial coining of the genre descriptor responds in large part to renewed scholarly interest in the genre of autobiography, in particular Philippe Lejeune's influential work—as Doubrovsky himself confirms in a letter to Lejeune, mentioning his desire to fill the "empty square" in the latter's analysis (cited in Lejeune 1986, 63). In 1975, Lejeune had posited the identity of author, narrator, and character as the fundamental condition for autobiography. This identity may or may not be backed up by an explicit "autobiographical pact" that affirms it within the text (Lejeune [1975] 1996, 26). Aside from the classic case where we find both a proper name and an explicit pact (the canonical model of Rousseau's *Confessions*, Lejeune's case 3b), it is possible, within Lejeune's schema, to find "indeterminate" cases where no proper name or pact allows generic identification (case 2b); to find an autobiographical pact without mention of a proper name (case 2c); or to observe an identity of proper names without a direct autobiographical pact (case 3a) (Lejeune [1975] 1996, 28–30). What does not seem possible, however, is an explicit divergence of identity and pact, hence the two empty squares in Lejeune's chart of autodiegetic narratives (28). The difficulty is not just empirical (even if Lejeune initially presents it as such, mentioning a lack of examples) but also logical, for it is precisely the identity of author, narrator, and character that grounds the autobiographical pact for Lejeune. Yet, Doubrovsky insists on this divergence in *Fils*. On the one hand, the narrator is clearly named "Serge Doubrovsky" and is a university professor in the United States; on the other, in addition to the famous sentence on "autofiction" on the back cover, the front cover bears the designation "novel" ("roman"). The notion of autofiction thus originates as a curious and contradictory theoretical experiment, one that simultaneously occupies one of the empty squares in Philippe Lejeune's chart and undermines the pragmatic basis of Lejeune's distinctions.

At the same time, Doubrovsky's aim is not to define a genre but to describe a particular literary practice—his own, which leans toward the *auto* rather than the *fictional*. As Arnaud Schmitt notes (2010, 126), Doubrovsky's term is flawed "since autofiction as a substantive lays stress on the non-referential part of the personal discourse, whereas Doubrovsky's textual practice went rather in the opposite direction." Frank Zipfel observes that Doubrovsky seems to use "fiction" merely to designate a specific form of non-chronological and associative construction, which, strictly speaking, does not make his narrative fictional (2009, 299). Doubrovsky's own conception of autofiction as a "fiction based on strictly real events and facts" thus remains close to autobiography, while incorporating (at least in its initial form) a psychoanalytic dimension and a focus on linguistic "adventure" (see Gasparini 2008, 19–31). In practice, of course, readers may not know in which respects exactly the author "strictly" adheres to the facts. Other theorists' definitions, taking seriously the *fiction* component of the term, demand an overt "self-fictionalization process" or "autofabulation" (Colonna 2004, 75), which combines onomastic identity with avowed fictionality. But autofiction has also been seen as a category of "undecidable" texts (Bersani, Lecarme, and Vercier 1982, 150–165) or even as a way of erasing the distinction between reality and fiction altogether (Vilain 2005, 124–125).

Autofiction owes much of its success, but also its ambiguity, to the semantic fuzziness of the term *fiction*, which (in both English and French) is sometimes conflated with narrative emplotment in general or else with literariness as such. This ambiguity may also be cultivated to express suspicion of referential discourse. Doubrovsky acknowledges as much in a 2005 interview, where he describes "autofiction" as a postmodern variant of autobiography, suited to a moment that no longer believes in the literal truth of historical narrative (2005, 212). Other practitioners of autofiction make similar claims, sometimes in rather contradictory terms. For instance, Catherine Cusset distinguishes between strict factual accuracy and the writer's quest for truth, while claiming that "the only fiction in autofiction is the work on the language" (2012). While the recognition of the gap between life and stories might seem innocuous enough, it can be identified with a broader skepticism that rejects the notions of unitary selfhood and transparent self-discovery (see Zipfel 2009, 308), and even the possibility of referential language. This skeptical position risks extending the notion of fiction to the point of meaninglessness, subsuming all utterances into this category in line with what Marie-Laure Ryan (1997) calls the "doctrine of panfictionality."

Fictionality and Hybridity

Theories of fiction, by contrast, have aimed to develop precise accounts of fiction and fictionality, even as they offer different approaches to the relationship between fictional and referential narrative. For semantic theories of fiction, for instance, fiction depends on structures of reference and the ontological status of named entities, not on stylistic factors or elements of narrative construction. In philosophical debates on nonexistent entities, the proper names of fictional characters serve as paradigmatic cases—notably Odysseus (Frege [1892] 1948), Mr. Pickwick (Ryle 1933), and Sherlock Holmes (Kripke 1972; Lewis 1978)—whether it is to conclude that these names have sense but no reference (Frege), to allow reference to pertain in some possible world (Lewis), or to argue for the "discursive unity" of fictional worlds beyond the propositional content of their components (Pavel 1986, 16).

While the fictional status of Sherlock Holmes or Mr. Pickwick is not in doubt, the semantic or ontological issue at stake in autofictional writing is the referential force (or lack thereof) of the autodiegetic "I" and the associated proper name. We should note here that several definitions of fiction rely precisely on the status of the speaker or subject. This is the case for Käte Hamburger's distinction in *The Logic of Literature* between reality statements that originate with a real "I-Origo"—that is, a genuine statement subject at the center of a "system of temporal and spatial coordinates" (1973, 67)—and statements that refer what is narrated to fictive "I-Origines" (73). On this basis, Hamburger goes so far as to exclude all first-person narratives from the category of fiction proper: because of their autobiographical origins in the statement system (213), first-person narratives can only be "feigned" reality statements (rather than fictive figurations), while their "degree of feint is subject to variation" (328).[2] It is also from the point of view of the speaker's relationship to his/her speech acts that later philosophers and narratologists will distinguish fact from fiction, albeit without following Hamburger's distinction between I-Origo and I-Origines. John Searle separates fictional utterances from truth claims via an account of "pretended illocutions" (1975, 326)—operating according to conventions that suspend the speaker's normal commitments to the truth of propositions (the question, then, is not who speaks, but whether the speaker is pretending to make assertions). In *Fiction and Diction*, Gérard Genette refers to both Lejeune and Searle in basing his definition of fiction on the relationship between author and narrator: while their "rigorous identification [...] defines factual narrative," "their dissociation [...] defines fiction, that is, a type of narrative whose veracity is not seriously assumed by the author" (1993, 70). The question hinges, as with Lejeune, on establishing the identity or nonidentity of author and narrator. Autofiction, in this perspective, can only be a logical and pragmatic contradiction, amounting to the statement "It is I and it is not I" (Genette 1993, 77).

Dorrit Cohn, who defines fiction as "literary nonreferential narrative" (1999, 12), differs from Genette in positing the existence of formal "signposts of fictionality" that mark the unique domain of fiction: the "synchronic bi-level" model of narrative (that is, the division into story and discourse), certain narrative modes free of referential constraints (for instance, techniques for the presentation of consciousness), and the "doubling of the narrative instance into author and narrator" (130). This last criterion coincides with Genette's distinction and serves to define nonfiction in terms of the identity of author and narrator. Cohn groups autofiction, mentioned only in passing, with other "crossbreeds" that "adopt the contradictory practice of naming their fictional self-narrators after their authors, thereby effectively ambiguating the distinction between fiction and nonfiction for self-narrated lives" (1999, 94). Cohn's account, like Genette's, is consistent with Lejeune's view of the autobiographical pact—or what he will later call the "truth pact"—as an all or nothing proposition, with respect to which the term "autofiction" can only generate perplexity (Lejeune 2005, 25–26).

We fall back, then, on the impasse already outlined above, which seems to make the notion of autofiction incompatible with any serious account of fictionality. The same seems to hold for Kendall Walton's definition of fiction as "make-believe" (1990), or Jean-Marie Schaeffer's "shared ludic feint" (2010, 138–139). In its Aristotelian argument for the distinction between reality and its mimetic representation, and its insistence on the pragmatic framing that creates the conditions of make-believe or ludic feint, Schaeffer's account can be partially aligned with Searle's account of "pretense" and, by extension, with Lejeune's reading pact; thus, Schaeffer speaks of a "pragmatic contract," by which a fiction announces itself as such (2010, 137). As for Olivier Caïra's extension of the category of fiction to incorporate non-mimetic, "axiomatic" fictions (such as rule-based games), it still rests on a basic distinction between "documentary" and "fictional" communication, established via pragmatic "framing operations" (2011, 75).

To compound the problem, these approaches to fiction often have difficulty accounting for literary nonfiction. Genette is most explicit about this issue, asserting that fictions are "constitutively" literary, while the status of factual narratives depends on the "conditional" criterion of "diction"—that is, on formal features or a subjective judgment of aesthetic value (1993, 138). Of course, this exclusion itself helps explain the success of autofiction as a strategy for legitimizing autobiographical writing, as the novelist Marie Darrieussecq ironically quips: "Since autobiography is questionable and conditional, and since all fiction is literary, let's bring autobiography into the field of fiction" (1996, 372–373). To put the point differently, this strategy mobilizes a postmodern, panfictionalist view of narrative ("all narrative is fictional") in order to claim a place within a literary regime that privileges fiction.

Some theorists, nevertheless, have successfully brought the fact/fiction distinctions of fiction theory into dialogue with approaches to autofiction. Arnaud Schmitt returns to Hamburger's (rather than Schaeffer's) conception of "feint" in order to define "self-narration" (*autonarration*), which he prefers as a term over "autofiction," as a "loosely referential literary genre" (2010, 129) that admits of degrees of proximity to reality (2007, 22), and draws on the formal resources of the novel to prioritize self-exploration and self-expression over precise factual accuracy. Self-narration amounts to a "more sophisticated" (2010, 133) mode of autobiography, specific to twentieth-century conceptions of the self. Frank Zipfel prefaces his reflection on autofiction with a definition of fiction as a rule-governed speech act, which produces a narrative with a "non-real" story that is to be received with an attitude of "make-believe" (2009, 289). He then distinguishes between three conceptions of autofiction: autofiction as a particular form of autobiography that (debatably) conflates fiction with narrative construction (Doubrovsky's definition) (290); autofiction as a particular kind of fictional telling (corresponding to Colonna's "autofabulation"), where a fictional figure has the name of the author (302–303); and finally, autofiction as a combination of fictional and autobiographical pacts (304).

The recent revival of "non-communicational" theories of fiction, such as Sylvie Patron's "optional-narrator" approach, which relates Hamburger's positions to those of Ann Banfield and S.-Y. Kuroda (Patron 2009), invites us to rethink the question of the speaker in both factual and fictional narratives. In this light, we may perhaps move beyond the simple binary of the identity/nonidentity of narrator and author that leaves no space for autofiction as a third term. In the domain of autofiction studies, Schmitt's return to Hamburger's conception of "feint" points to some intriguing possibilities, while reminding us of the ambiguous proximity of first-person fiction to autobiography. Without pursuing this last issue fully, I will focus on the question of the combined reading pact, following Schmitt's argument against the possibility of a "simultaneous approach" (2010, 128), as well as Zipfel's claim that readers in fact switch between modes of reading (2009, 306). In this volume, Martina Wagner-Egelhaaf (Chap. 2) and Alexandra Effe and Alison Gibbons (Chap. 4) also make the case for an oscillation in the reader's attitude to autofictional texts. Such oscillations, I would argue, require a fine-tuned attention to the shifting voice(s) of the work. Speaking of non-Francophone autofiction, Karen

Ferreira-Meyers points to a general consensus that readers remain "very much able to see and keep a line of demarcation between fact and fiction" (2018, 42). Françoise Lavocat (2016, 522) has argued for the broader necessity of just such a demarcation, noting that apprehending the modes of hybridization between the fictional and the factual need not entail erasing the contours of either sphere.

To apprehend these contours, it is helpful to turn to Richard Walsh's account of fictionality as "a distinctive rhetorical resource, functioning directly as part of the pragmatics of serious conversation" (2007, 1). Such "rhetorical" approaches, which distinguish between fiction as a genre and "fictionality as a quality or fictive discourse as a mode" (Nielsen, Phelan, and Walsh 2014, 62), allow for a distinction between "local" and "global" fictionality, such that nonfictional texts can contain "passages of fictionality" (67). In practice, as we shall see, the local and global are not entirely separable: for instance, particular formal devices that function as "signposts of fictionality" in a fictional context can produce different effects in a factual one. Still, when applied to autodiegetic narratives, the distinction between local and global fictionality allows us to theorize forms of hybridity that do not erase the border between fact and fiction or require the simultaneous adoption of contradictory modes of reading. Autofictional texts themselves help us draw out some of these distinctions and theorize kinds and degrees of fictionality. To demonstrate this point, I now turn to a few specific cases. Needless to say, these cases do not cover all configurations of the fact/fiction relationship or the great variety of autofictional practices. They do, however, serve to exemplify the operations and effects of fictionality and factuality at the level of narrative voice and readerly contracts, and moreover showcase a variety of autofictional texts across Anglophone, Francophone, and Scandinavian literatures.

I/Not I

The assertion, "It is I and it is not I," which constitutes for Genette the fundamental contradiction of autofiction (1993, 77), is in fact a common claim in both fictional and factual autodiegetic narratives. Generally speaking, it does not open a breach at the level of the text's pragmatic contract, but rather functions on the thematic level to expresses a non-unitary conception of the self. However, narrative voice and conceptions of selfhood are not always easily separable, especially when what is at stake is not only the relationship between a narrated and narrating *I* but also experimentation with new uses of the first person. The French writer Annie Ernaux, for instance, describes her use of the "transpersonal I" as an attempt to grasp social and familial reality: "The *I* that I use seems to me an impersonal form, barely gendered, sometimes more an utterance by the 'other' than by 'me': a transpersonal form, in short. It is not a means of constructing an identity through a text, of self-fictionalizing myself [*de m'autofictionner*]" (Ernaux 1993, 221; my translation).

Ernaux rejects the term *autofiction*, repeatedly insisting on her scrupulous adherence to the factual. Her works since *La Place* (1983; translated as *A Man's Place* [1996]) can certainly not be considered fiction in the sense of involving "shared ludic feint," in Schaeffer's terms. Still, the quotation above illustrates the enunciative gap that she opens up within the *I* itself. In the phrase, "The *I* that I use," are both instances of the pronoun transpersonal? Or does a personal *I* (that of the author) authorize and instrumentalize the transpersonal form (of the narrator)? This kind of metadiscursive commentary that introduces a split within the first person is also present in Ernaux's literary works. If there is any destabilizing of the referential ground of Ernaux's texts, it surely lies in the simultaneous impossibility and necessity of this "I-Origo" (to use Hamburger's term). Ernaux's experiments with the *I* invent an ambiguous space of projection, positioned between the individual and the collective. In *Les Années* (2008; translated as *The Years* [2017]), she extends the experiment to other pronouns: the impersonal *on* (one), the third-person *elle* (she), and the first-person plural *nous* (we):

> We [*on*] changed [*changeait*] plates for dessert, quite mortified [*mortifiée*] that our *fondue bourguignonne* had not been greeted with the expected congratulations, but with curiosity and comments that were disappointing at best, considering the trouble we'd gone to [*qu'on s'était donné*] with the sauces, and even a touch condescending. (Ernaux 2017, 91; French original: 2008, 97)

Globally, in its narrative framing and paratextual apparatus, *Les Années* remains a work of nonfiction. Still, the "I-Origo" that anchors the deixis in a given time and place is troubled by Ernaux's play with pronouns. In the passage above, for instance, the impersonal pronoun *on* is paired with the feminine singular gender agreement of *mortifiée*, while the imperfect tense suggests an iterative action somewhat incompatible with the specific scene of the failed *fondue bourguignonne*. What we are invited to participate in is not ludic pretense, but rather an interpretative operation that transforms a specific scene and personal feeling into a general scenario and a broader social symptom, while still maintaining a tension between the singular and the collective.

Many other writers also experiment with the first person without necessarily troubling the foundations of the autobiographical pact. Édouard Louis's *En finir avec Eddy Bellegueule* (2014; translated as *The End of Eddy* [2017]) stages in its title the desire for a violent break between the child Eddy Bellegueule (and his social milieu) and the narrating subject, the author Édouard Louis. This onomastic split, along with the designation "novel" (roman) on the book's cover, may help to account for the frequent characterization of this work (and Louis's other works) as autofiction, but in terms of global factuality, the autobiographical pact does not seem to be in question. Like Ernaux's works, those of Louis rule out overt fictionalization, as they rely on the referential force of self-exposure as the basis for the contagious sense of shame that confronts the reader with the violence of social and sexual norms.

We might contrast these cases with some globally fictional first-person narratives that are sometimes characterized as autofiction, and which share Ernaux's concern with intersubjectivity and the transpersonal. In Rachel Cusk's "Outline" trilogy (*Outline* [2014], *Transit* [2017], and *Kudos* [2018]), the narrator appears only in her interactions with others.[3] The basic principle of the work is articulated in the first volume, *Outline*, in a momentary *mise en abyme*—voiced not by the main narrator but by another character, Anne, who describes her conversation with a man sitting next to her on a plane:

> in everything he said about himself, she found in her own nature a corresponding negative. This anti-description, for want of a better way of putting it, had made something clear to her by a reverse kind of exposition: while he talked she began to see herself as a shape, an outline, with all the detail filled in around it while the shape itself remained blank. Yet this shape, even while its content remained unknown, gave her for the first time since the incident a sense of who she now was. (Cusk 2014, 239–240)

The narrator, a writer named Faye (although she is only named once in each book of the trilogy), records Anne's theory of fragile selfhood with the same passivity as she receives other characters' impressions and ideas. Although Faye clearly shares several characteristics with Cusk (biographical features that serve as "identification operators," as in the cases analyzed by Arnaud Schmitt in this volume), our desire to identify them stems above all from the attentive, receptive, and porous point of view that the narrative invites us to inhabit, by recording less Faye's own interiority than the voluble self-disclosures of those she encounters. The first-person subject at the center of the text is concerned less with direct self-narration than with a curious form of exteriorization, as those around the narrator offer reflections on everyday life, human relationships, and the human condition in extended monologues.

The trilogy produces what we might call an "autofictional effect," despite the lack of onomastic identity between author and character. The effect goes beyond the possibility of reading these texts as fictionalized autobiography (seeing Faye as a version of Cusk), although that is certainly one interpretative option. It has to do with the ambiguities and discomfort that Cusk produces by reversing the standard fictional strategies for representing consciousness. We may recall that Dorrit Cohn's "signposts of fictionality" involve, above all, techniques for the representation of consciousness. Cusk turns this novelistic interiority inside out, as the narrator simply receives the externalized thoughts of others. A metanarrative moment toward the end of the third volume, *Kudos*, acknowledges and exploits the artifice of this technique. Over dinner at a writers' conference, a woman named Sophia delivers an extended monologue on marriage, motherhood, divorce, her relationship to men, and her own sense of self, as her audience gradually becomes "visibly uncomfortable" with such self-exhibition (Cusk 2018, 162). Another novelist later remarks that "things had got pretty intense back there" (164). The scene foregrounds Cusk's own writing technique in the form of a fictional writer's inappropriate confession, raising the discomforting question of who is actually speaking in the novel's monologues. Throughout her trilogy, Cusk sustains the intensity of a multicentered subjectivity that is not performed as much as it is compulsively exuded. It emanates from individuals while also constituting an impersonal, diffracted, or projected version of the narrator's own consciousness.

We might compare this reading experience with another case where a displaced *I* governs an ambiguously fictional account. Olivia Laing's *Crudo* is presented as a novel in both its subtitle and the publisher's disclaimer at the beginning of the book: "*Crudo* is a work of fiction. Incidents, dialogue, and characters, with the exception of certain public and historical figures, are products of the author's imagination or are used fictitiously." The frequency of such disclaimers in contemporary literature is itself symptomatic, indicating the presence not just of fiction but of fictionalization. A person used fictitiously is not quite a fictional character, but a figure that draws us into the realm of the counterfactual (see Gallagher 2018; Prendergast 2019). The novel's opening establishes a very particular kind of novelistic frame:

> Kathy, by which I mean I, was getting married. Kathy, by which I mean I, had just got off a plane from New York. It was 19:45 on 13 May 2017. She'd been upgraded to business, she was feeling fancy, she bought two bottles of duty-free champagne in orange boxes, that was the kind of person she was going to be from now on. Kathy was met at the airport by the man she was living with, soon to become the man she was going to marry, soon, presumably, to become the man she had married and so on till death. (Laing 2018a, 1)

What displacement of meaning and self does the first sentence enact, exactly? Who does "I" refer to? Does Kathy stand in for Laing, the extradiegetic author? Does "she" refer to Kathy or Laing? Or does "she" stand in for "I," in an enunciative distancing of the intradiegetic narrator, complete with its own form of self-ironizing free indirect discourse ("that was the kind of person she was going to be from now on")?

The book's following pages complicate things further as we learn that Kathy's lover will break up with her because he does not think two writers should be together: "Kathy had written several books—*Great Expectations, Blood and Guts in High School*, I expect you've heard of them. The man with whom she was sleeping had not written any books. Kathy was angry. I mean I. I was angry" (1–2). Serving as a kind of referential "punctum" (Barthes 2002, 5:809) the book titles pierce through the fiction to link the character-narrator with Kathy Acker, the late author of *Great Expectations* (1982) and *Blood and Guts in High School* (1984). For the hesitant reader, the phrase, "I expect you've heard of them," serves as a signpost of factuality (to adapt Cohn's term). Or more precisely, it is a signpost of counterfactuality, which throws a possible version of Kathy Acker, still alive, into a post-Brexit Britain where she lives a life that in some way resembles that of Olivia Laing. None of this play with the authorial/narratorial persona or with referential elements entirely dissolves the novelistic frame: the *I* retains the identity of a fictional Kathy or counterfactual Kathy Acker. Still, it is not surprising that *Crudo* has been read as autofiction, despite Laing's own dislike of the term (Laing 2018b). This reception is conditioned by a number of factors, not least the opening's dramatic staging of the "deictic displacement" often associated with fiction (Hamburger 1973, 127–128). When foregrounded in this way, the signpost of fictionality becomes a signpost of *fictionalization*, only accentuating the referential uncertainty surrounding the first-person narrator and thereby encouraging an autofictional reading, regardless of the author's stated intention.

AUTOFICTION: A NOVEL

Cusk's and Laing's books both proclaim themselves to be novels, but so does Édouard Louis's primarily autobiographical narrative. The genre designation on its own—the paratextual indication "a novel" on the book's cover or title page, often appearing as a subtitle—has become an extremely fragile signpost of fictionality, even as it still functions as a marker of literary prestige. Detachment from direct *autobiographical* enunciation, in the cases of Cusk's trilogy and Laing's *Crudo*, still hinges on the proper name, whether it is discreet or insistent in its presence (Cusk's self-effacing "Faye" versus Laing's "Kathy"). In French-language literature, in particular, the indication *roman* very frequently coexists with a broadly referential pact and produces an ambivalent reception—including when these works cross into other languages, and especially into an Anglophone literary market characterized by a clearer-cut fiction/nonfiction distinction.

Another of these designated "novels," Christophe Boltanski's *La Cache* (2015; translated as *The Safe House* [2017]) is an autobiographical story of the Boltanski family, told via a description of spaces in the family home, including the "in-between"—the tiny storage room where the author's grandfather Étienne Boltanski hid out during the war (2017, 159). Boltanski's tale of his grandparents' home is organized around this secret place, the tiny safe house within the house. It is also a story about names: proper names that have been altered, rejected, or reinvented, and are no longer entirely "proper" (122) bear the problematic trace of an obscured origin, of the path that led the "Bolts" from Russia to France. We should note here that "Boltanski" is now a household name in French intellectual and artistic life: Christophe's uncle is the artist Christian Boltanski, his father the sociologist Luc Boltanski. But Boltanski (Christophe) explores what is hidden behind the public life of his eccentric family. In any case, this kind of investigation of names and identities (tied in this case to the condition of the Jewish diaspora in Europe) does not in itself undermine the autobiographical contract founded on the proper name.

Where, then, are the sites of fictionalization in Boltanski's account? The book's structure is non-linear, organized around spaces (rooms, but also the family car) treated as extensions of characters; it delves into family mythologies. This approach might be contrasted with the novels of the author's grandmother, who, publishing under the penname "Annie Lauran," "advocated a 'tape-recorder literature,' which depended on strictly cataloguing real life" (9). Boltanski, for his part, adopts a mode of writing that does not appear strictly documentary but adapts techniques sometimes associated with fiction. Consider the following use of "penetrative" narrative devices that Cohn (1999, 16) claims are "unavailable to narrators who aim for referential (nonfictional) presentation":

> She didn't so much want to rediscover her youth (Rediscover what? The abandonment she'd been a victim of? Her godmother? Polio? The war?) or thwart old age. She wanted to escape time altogether. No beginning, no end. No path sewn with obstacles to avoid. She wanted to be ageless. A state that was neither tender nor ungrateful nor green nor ripe. Not canonical, but undetermined or absent. She would have liked to float in a vague space. Eternally in between. (Boltanski 2017, 146)

The reader faced with this passage has different options. One is to read it as the site of a local fictionalization within a globally factual narrative, attributing the thoughts of the grandmother (Marie-Élise/Myriam/Annie Lauran) to the imaginative speculation of the author. Another option is to infer that the account is based on family archives, conversation, and oral tradition, but that this documentary-testimonial basis remains implicit in the text. The focalization remains ambiguous, between inner and outer. The presentation of the grandmother's mental states serves as an "immersion vector," to borrow Jean-Marie Schaeffer's term for "ludic feints, ludic beginnings, that the creators utilize to give birth to a fictional universe and that permit the receivers to reactivate this universe mimetically" (2010, 218). In this case, however, the "ludic feint of mental acts" (Schaeffer 2010, 219) does not serve as a gateway to a fictional universe; we do not read the book as fiction, exactly, but maintain a distinction between the *fictional* and the *fictionalized* that determines our reading of the formal indices. In any case, it is precisely the book's referential ground that makes visible the work of fictionalization—in this instance, Boltanski's transformation of a set of intensely private individuals and an eccentric family unit into characters whose lives we can follow.

What this example illustrates is also the difficulty of moving from local effects of fictionalization to a definition of autofiction as a genre. It may be more useful, as we have also seen with our other cases, to consider a range of strategies and textual features that can produce autofictional effects. The forms of hybridity and the relationship between global and local factuality and fictionality vary widely. Karl Ove Knausgaard's minute descriptions of attending a children's birthday party (2013, 21–59), eating cornflakes (56–57), or making a cup of tea (2014, 372), for instance, produce a different kind of fictional effect from Boltanski's use of free indirect discourse. Knausgaard's *Min kamp* (*My Struggle*) transports into self-narration the apparently superfluous details that Roland Barthes (2002, 3:25) associates with the "reality effect" in nineteenth-century literature. Used in a nonfictional, autobiographical context, however, they serve to capture the texture of daily experience and to cultivate a deliberate form of egalitarian, undifferentiated attention (see Lerner 2014). This hyperrealism appears as both acutely phenomenological and highly artificial, in that such minute recording evidently exceeds the capacities of memory. This is fictionalized reconstruction, deployed in the service of an overall autobiographical project.

Camille Laurens employs fictionalization to quite different effect in *Dans ces bras-là* (2000; translated as *In His Arms* [2004]), which integrates self-exploration into a fictional frame by staging a set of confessional dialogues with a psychoanalyst. The direct expression of the fictional pact takes the ambiguous form of a hypothetical account of a future book, narrated by someone who resembles the author but is not identical to her: "I wouldn't be the woman in the book" (2004, 7). Is it the author or the narrator who imagines the (this?) book? This paradoxical assertion perhaps brings us as close as we can come to an overtly autofictional pact. It also creates an enunciative distance that is in tension with the intimate thematic content of the book. Indeed, Laurens's strategies of fictionalization are in part a form of self-protection: Laurens herself describes them as attempts to bypass censorship in its various forms (from self-censorship to lawsuits for invasion of privacy[4]), as well as a means of allowing the reader a margin of manoeuver (2007, 224–225). Fictionalization appears here as a strategy of subterfuge, allowing Laurens to explore the limits of the sayable while evading some of the risks and commitments of truth-telling.

* * *

The above analyses can only scratch the surface of the range of practices and effects that shape the territory of the autofictional. Still, I hope to have shown where we can begin to locate the fictional in autobiographical writing, or, conversely, the factual in fictional first-person narratives. Literary theory, as Gasparini notes (2008, 246), has historically had difficulty tackling generic hybridity, but it can nevertheless supply us with tools for taking on this task. Theories of fiction and fictionality can help us avoid the pitfalls of a panfictionalist position that would ultimately deny any specificity to the autofictional (by identifying all narrative with fiction), and they give us tools for analyzing the textual strategies that produce particular autofictional effects. Autofictional texts, in turn, can shed light on key debates in the theory of fiction, for instance, in their complex play with forms of deictic displacement and other signposts of fictionality. By presenting us with a wide range of configurations of the fact/fiction relationship, these works make the nature and affordances of fictionality visible, and they illustrate the multiple forms that literary hybridity can take. In this sense, it is perhaps not possible to define a single kind of hybrid that would constitute the genre of autofiction. Broadly speaking, however, autofictional texts present us not with autonomous fictional worlds, but with sites of fictionalization where the referential ground of the *I* is maintained to a greater or lesser extent. As a corollary, different forms and degrees of fictionality are present at different moments or within particular aspects of the work, and produce specific effects. The autofictional is also a complex phenomenon of reception. Autofictional texts offer a salutary challenge to literary theory by highlighting the divide between ontological theories and pragmatic approaches, or between communicational and non-communicational theories of fictional discourse—reopening, for instance, the question of the distinction between fiction and feint. Finally, far from erasing all boundaries, these works bring new attention to the interactions of the factual and the fictional. While autofictional writing sometimes provokes epistemic anxiety and even moral condemnation in the so-called post-truth era, its contemporary forms can also be read as a response to this moment, revealing authors' heightened awareness of the stakes of both fiction and truth-telling.

Notes

1. "Fiction, d'événements et de faits strictement réels" (Doubrovsky 1977).
2. Hamburger applies a distinction between "fictive," to refer to the ontological status of invented events, characters, and entities, and "fictional," to refer to a mode of discourse. However, this distinction is not used in most of the English- and French-language criticism that I discuss, and I do not follow it in my own analysis, but instead use "fictional" throughout.
3. Aligning Cusk's *Outline* with Francophone autofiction, Jensen (2018, 65–66) associates autofiction with a process of self-erasure that de-centers the I, aiming to formulate "a new kind of human subject, one whose *intersubjectivity* (I, me, us) generates a kind of aesthetic intimacy" (69–70; original emphasis).
4. Gisèle Sapiro, considering among other examples the lawsuit (unsuccessfully) brought by Laurens's ex-husband against *L'Amour, roman* (Laurens 2003), notes that fictionalization does not always constitute a sufficient condition for bypassing French privacy laws, although it can serve as evidence for the defense (Sapiro 2013, 107).

Works Cited

Acker, Kathy. 1982. *Great Expectations*. New York: Grove Press.
———. 1984. *Blood and Guts in High School*. New York: Grove Press.
Barthes, Roland. 2002. *Œuvres complètes*. Edited by Éric Marty. 5 vols. Paris: Seuil.
Bersani, Jacques, Jacques Lecarme, and Bruno Vercier. 1982. *La Littérature en France depuis 1968*. Paris: Bordas.
Boltanski, Christophe. 2015. *La Cache*. Paris: Stock.
———. 2017. *The Safe House*. Translated by Laura Marris. Chicago: University of Chicago Press. Originally published in French as *La Cache* (Paris: Stock, 2015).
Caïra, Olivier. 2011. *Définir la fiction: Du roman au jeu d'échecs*. Paris: Éditions de l'EHESS.
Cohn, Dorrit. 1999. *The Distinction of Fiction*. Baltimore and London: Johns Hopkins University Press.
Colonna, Vincent. 2004. *Autofiction et autres mythomanies littéraires*. Paris: Tristram.
Cusk, Rachel. 2014. *Outline: A Novel*. London: Faber & Faber.
———. 2017. *Transit: A Novel*. London: Faber & Faber.
———. 2018. *Kudos: A Novel*. London: Faber & Faber.
Cusset, Catherine. 2012. *The Limits of Autofiction*. Conference presentation, 2012. http://www.catherinecusset.co.uk/wp-content/uploads/2013/02/THE-LIMITS-OF-AUTOFICTION.pdf. Accessed Mar 3, 2021.

Darrieussecq, Marie. 1996. L'Autofiction: un genre pas sérieux. *Poétique* 107: 369–380.
Doubrovsky, Serge. 1977. *Fils*. Paris: Galilée.
———. 2005. L'autofiction selon Doubrovsky. Interview by Philippe Vilain. In *Défense de Narcisse*, ed. Philippe Vilain, 169–235. Paris: Grasset.
Ernaux, Annie. 1983. *La Place*. Paris: Gallimard.
———. 1993. Vers un je transpersonnel. In *Autofictions & Cie*, ed. Serge Doubrovsky, Jacques Lecarme, and Philippe Lejeune. *Cahiers RITM*, no. 6, 219–21. Nanterre: Université Paris X.
———. 1996. *A Man's Place*. Translated by Tayla Leslie. New York, NY: Seven Stories Press. First published as *La Place* (Paris: Gallimard, 1983).
———. 2008. *Les Années*. Paris: Gallimard.
———. 2017. *The Years*. Translated by Alison L. Strayer. New York, NY: Seven Stories Press. First published as *Les Années* (Paris: Gallimard, 2008).
Ferreira-Myers, Karen. 2018. Does Autofiction Belong to French or Francophone Authors and Readers Only? In *Autofiction in English*, ed. Hywel Dix, 27–40. Cham: Palgrave Macmillan.
Frege, Gottlob. (1892) 1948. On Sense and Reference. Translated by Max Black. *The Philosophical Review* 57 (3): 209–230.
Gallagher, Catherine. 2018. *Telling It Like It Wasn't: The Counterfactual Imagination in History and Fiction*. Chicago: University of Chicago Press.
Gasparini, Philippe. 2008. *Autofiction: Une aventure du language*. *Poétique*. Paris: Seuil.
Genette, Gérard. 1993. *Fiction and Diction*. Translated by Catherine Porter. Ithaca, NY: Cornell University Press. First published in French as *Fiction et diction* (Paris: Seuil, 1991).
Hamburger, Käte. 1973. *The Logic of Literature*. Translated by Marilynn J. Rose. 2nd revised edition. Bloomington and Indianapolis: Indiana University Press. First published in German as *Die Logik der Dichtung* (Stuttgart: Ernst Klett Verlag, 1957).
Jeannelle, Jean-Louis. 2013. Le procès de l'autofiction. *Études: Revue de culture contemporaine* 419 (9): 221–230.
Jensen, Meg. 2018. How Art Constitutes the Human: Aesthetics, Empathy and the Interesting in Autofiction. In *Autofiction in English*, ed. Hywel Dix, 65–83. Cham: Palgrave Macmillan.
Knausgaard, Karl Ove. 2013. *My Struggle: Book 2: A Man in Love*. Translated by Don Bartlett. New York: Farrar, Straus and Giroux. First published in Norwegian as *Min kamp 2* (Oslo: Oktober, 2009).
———. 2014. *My Struggle: Book 3: Boyhood*. Translated by Don Bartlett. New York: Farrar, Straus and Giroux. First published in Norwegian as *Min kamp 3* (Oslo: Oktober, 2009).
Kripke, Saul A. 1972 (1980). *Naming and Necessity*. Oxford: Blackwell.

Laing, Olivia. 2018a. *Crudo: A Novel*. London: Picador.
———. 2018b. Becoming Kathy Acker: An Interview with Olivia Laing. Interview by Chris Kraus. *The Paris Review*, Sept. 11, 2018. https://www.theparisreview.org/blog/2018/09/11/becoming-kathy-acker-an-interview-with-olivia-laing/. Accessed Mar. 30, 2021.
Laurens, Camille. 2003. *L'Amour, roman*. Paris: P.O.L.
———. 2004. *In His Arms: A Novel*. Translated by Ian Monk. New York: Random House. First published in French as *Dans ces bras-là* (Paris: P.O.L, 2000).
———. 2007. (Se) dire et (s')interdire. In *Genèse et autofiction*, ed. Jean-Louis Jeannelle and Catherine Viollet, 221–228. Louvain-la-Neuve: Academia Bruylant.
Lavocat, Françoise. 2016. *Fait et fiction: Pour une frontière*. Poétique. Paris: Seuil.
Lejeune, Philippe. (1975) 1996. *Le Pacte autobiographique*. 2nd ed. Collection Points Essais. Paris: Seuil.
———. 1986. *Moi aussi*. Poétique. Paris: Seuil.
———. 2005. *Signes de vie: le pacte autobiographique 2*. Paris: Seuil.
———. 2007. Le Journal comme 'antifiction.'. *Poétique* 149: 3–14.
Lerner, Ben. 2014. "Each Cornflake." Review of My Struggle, vol. 3 by Karl Ove Knausgaard. *London Review of Books*, May 21, 2014. https://www.lrb.co.uk/the-paper/v36/n10/ben-lerner/each-cornflake. Accessed Mar 30 2021.
Lewis, David. 1978. Truth in Fiction. *American Philosophical Quarterly* 15 (1): 37–46.
Louis, Édouard. 2017. *The End of Eddy*. Translated by Michael Lucey. New York: Farrar, Straus and Giroux. Originally published in French as *En finir avec Eddy Bellegueule* (Paris: Seuil, 2014).
Nielsen, Henrik Skov, James Phelan, and Richard Walsh. 2014. Ten Theses about Fictionality. *Narrative* 23 (1): 61–73. https://doi.org/10.1353/nar.2015.0005.
Patron, Sylvie. 2009. *Le Narrateur: Introduction à la théorie narrative*. Paris: Armand Colin.
Pavel, Thomas G. 1986. *Fictional Worlds*. Cambridge, MA: Harvard University Press.
Petit, Marc. 1999. *Éloge de la fiction*. Paris: Fayard.
Prendergast, Christopher. 2019. *Counterfactuals: Paths of the Might Have Been*. London: Bloomsbury Academic.
Ryan, Marie-Laure. 1997. Postmodernism and the Doctrine of Panfictionality. *Narrative* 5 (2): 165–187.
Ryle, Gilbert. 1933. Imaginary Objects. *Proceedings of the Aristotelian Society* 12: 18–43.
Sapiro, Gisèle. 2013. Droits et devoirs de la fiction littéraire en régime démocratique: Du réalisme à l'autofiction. *Revue critique de fixxion française contemporaine* 6: 97–110.

Schaeffer, Jean-Marie. 2010. *Why Fiction?* Translated by Dorrit Cohn. Lincoln, NE: University of Nebraska Press. First published in French as *Pourquoi la fiction?* (Paris: Seuil, 1999).

Schmitt, Arnaud. 2007. La perspective de l'autonarration. *Poetique* 149: 15–29.

———. 2010. Making the Case for Self-Narration Against Autofiction. *A/b: Auto/Biography Studies* 25 (1): 122–137. https://doi.org/10.1080/08989575.2010.10815365.

Searle, John R. 1975. The Logical Status of Fictional Discourse. *New Literary History* 6 (2): 319–332. https://doi.org/10.2307/468422.

Vilain, Philippe. 2005. *Défense de Narcisse*. Paris: Grasset.

Walsh, Richard. 2007. *The Rhetoric of Fictionality: Narrative Theory and the Idea of Fiction*. Columbus, OH: Ohio State University Press.

Walton, Kendall L. 1990. *Mimesis as Make-Believe: On The Foundations of the Representational Arts*. Cambridge, MA and London: Harvard University Press.

Zipfel, Frank. 2009. Autofiktion: Zwischen den Grenzen von Faktualität, Fiktionalität und Literarität? In *Grenzen der Literatur: zu Begriff und Phänomen des Literarischen*, ed. Simone Winko, Fotis Jannidis, and Gerhard Lauer, 285–314. Berlin: De Gruyter.

Open Access This chapter is licensed under the terms of the Creative Commons Attribution 4.0 International License (http://creativecommons.org/licenses/by/4.0/), which permits use, sharing, adaptation, distribution and reproduction in any medium or format, as long as you give appropriate credit to the original author(s) and the source, provide a link to the Creative Commons licence and indicate if changes were made.

The images or other third party material in this chapter are included in the chapter's Creative Commons licence, unless indicated otherwise in a credit line to the material. If material is not included in the chapter's Creative Commons licence and your intended use is not permitted by statutory regulation or exceeds the permitted use, you will need to obtain permission directly from the copyright holder.

CHAPTER 4

A Cognitive Perspective on Autofictional Writing, Texts, and Reading

Alexandra Effe and Alison Gibbons

The early twenty-first century is witnessing a boom in autofiction, with the genre now a global publishing trend that enjoys cultural prestige and such a prosperous readership that the moniker has become its own marketing tool. Scholarly accounts have typically taken a literary critical perspective, positioning autofictions as contemporary cultural products. Marjorie Worthington argues that autofiction is "a symptom of the declining cultural capital of the traditional figure of the author" (2018, 6), while Hywel Dix suggests three impetuses for the autofiction boom: "a relative increase in the status of women's writing; the changing nature of the publishing industry, including the advent of self-publishing; and the saturation of the print and broadcast media with so-called 'reality' narratives" (2018, 10). What is missing from these perspectives is an account of autofiction not only as a cultural artifact in and of itself but also as part of a more holistic literary event, which includes writer and readers.

A. Effe (✉)
University of Oslo, Oslo, Norway
e-mail: alexandra.effe@ilos.uio.no

A. Gibbons
Sheffield Hallam University, Sheffield, UK

© The Author(s) 2022
A. Effe, H. Lawlor (eds.), *The Autofictional*, Palgrave Studies in Life Writing, https://doi.org/10.1007/978-3-030-78440-9_4

Studies of autofiction frequently make claims about readers and the reading experience: Worthington writes of "the constantly shifting reading strategies that autofiction requires" (2018, 5); Frank Zipfel names "the specificity of autofiction" in a narrow definition as "the unresolvable paradox of [...] contradictory reading instructions" (2005, 36); and Henrik Skov Nielsen describes autofictional texts as "overdetermined" because they present themselves, either at the same time or at different times, "as both fiction and nonfiction" (2011, 131). Consequently, many critics argue that reading autofiction involves an oscillation between, or a combination of, two attitudes of reception, what Lejeune (1989) saw as different contracts or pacts of reading: autobiographical and fictional. We agree with these critics' theoretical instincts. Nevertheless, to advance understanding of autofiction, and to evidence claims about the autofictional text and its reading experience, such assertions require further substantiation.

The role of the author as producer of autofiction is discussed less frequently, but is equally subject to critical conjecture. Siddharth Srikanth, for instance, defines autofiction as "a work in which the author is the protagonist, in which the author's biographical background and life experiences inform the nonfictionality of the work and in which the author combines fictionality and nonfictionality at length *for his or her purpose*" (2019, 353; our emphasis). These purposes, however, are unearthed through Srikanth's own critical interpretation, leading him to suggest that J. M. Coetzee "uses" *Summertime*—which revolves around the idea that a biographer interviews acquaintances of the recently deceased author— "to evaluate his own writing" (360). Another way in which autofictional writing is approached is through theories and studies of creative writing. Celia Hunt considers the personal gains of self-exploration through reflexive writing as work-in-progress and argues that autofictional writing "reveals itself to be a cognitive-emotional tool with, potentially, very powerful therapeutic benefits" (2018, 193). Her study does not, however, consider the intentions of published writers of autofiction. Similarly, Amelia Walker is interested in how autofictional texts can be used in teaching "personal reflective writing" (2018, 206).

In this chapter, we redress the balance between attention to autofictional texts, autofictional writing, and autofictional reading. We apply a cognitive and empirically grounded approach which offers a holistic account of the autofictional literary experience. The approach is holistic in that it not only explores the textual and narrative dynamics that signpost autofiction as at the same time autobiographical and fictional; it additionally, and significantly, considers both production and reception. We draw on three case studies: Philip Roth's *The Facts* (1988), Olivia Laing's *Crudo* (2018), and Ben Lerner's *10:04* (2014). These texts exhibit different degrees of fictionality and have different affordances and effects. Roth's *The Facts* reads like a primarily autobiographical narrative, signaling fictionality through the letters which frame it, one by a "Roth" author-character[1] and the other by a fictional character named Nathan Zuckerman who is often interpreted as Roth's alter ego. Laing's *Crudo* blends the narrative events of the author's real life in 2017 with the biographical details of the real, but by then long deceased, writer Kathy Acker. While Ben Lerner's *10:04* features a first-person narrator referred to once as "Ben" who shares much of the author's personal history, the narrative is predominantly fictional. Taken together, these works illustrate some of the variety of autofictional texts. Based on empirical studies concerning the processing of factual and fictional modes of discourse and accounts of the writing process by authors, we offer definitions of autofictional reading and writing. These definitions provide the basis for our discussion of the cognitive affordances and effects of autofictional modes in *The Facts*, *Crudo*, and *10:04*.

Autofictional Reading

Building on Alison Gibbons's argument that autofiction "is not only a literary genre, but also a reading strategy" (2019, 411), we suggest that there is a distinct mode of autofictional reading which responds to a text's invitations to be read as simultaneously fictional and factual. Readers draw on cognitive schemata to guide their expectations and responses in reading. Cognitive schemata are abstract representations of knowledge gained from experience about objects and situations; this knowledge helps to guide actions and expectations in the world (Stockwell 2019, 103–118). Schemata also help in managing reading expectations and behavior, with readers possessing schemata for genre, text-type, text-media such as digital fiction, and specific narratives/texts (e.g. Bell 2014; Cook 1994; Gibbons 2016; Mason 2019). Empirical studies indicate that readers also have cognitive schemata related to fiction and non-fiction. We therefore claim that readers approach an autofictional text with two kinds of acquired cognitive schemata: those for factual and those for fictional texts.

Evidence that genre expectations can influence how readers approach, process, and build mental representations can be found in cognitive, experimental, and developmental psychology (see Gibbons 2021b). Several studies have tested whether readers' perceptions of fictionality influence engagement, with participants informed in paratextual instructions that the same extract is either factual or fictional. Differences in reading times between the two conditions demonstrate that reading non-fiction involves prioritizing causal-situation information and disregarding contradictory or irrelevant details, while reading fiction entails building more detailed mental representations (Zwaan 1994), and that participants are more likely to scrutinize factual texts (Green et al. 2006). Deborah A. Prentice and Richard J. Gerrig (1999) took a different experimental approach by manipulating the details of a story to create two versions: one which primarily contained "contextual details," specific to the fictional storyworld; and another that primarily contained "context-free assertions," which generally hold and conform to real-world knowledge. Their results again indicate that readers process non-fiction more systematically than fiction.

Torsten Pettersson's (2016) study is relevant, in terms of this chapter's concerns, as he presented participants with an extract from the first volume of Karl Ove Knausgaard's *My Struggle* series, a now canonical example of contemporary autofiction. Pettersson manipulated paratextual framing to guide participants' expectations as to a text's factual or fictional status. The response data Pettersson collected was both quantitative and qualitative; the latter being particularly unusual as studies in experimental psychology generally collect the former. Based on the qualitative data, Pettersson concludes that "fiction stories are described as a source of knowledge, insight, or increased mental ability" (2016, n.p.). His qualitative analysis therefore adds further support for the influence of readers' schematic expectations about fictionality and factuality; in this case, the bearing that these expectations can have on the experience of reading autofiction.

One potential drawback of bringing such empirical data to bear on a discussion of autofiction is that, because experimental studies require easily controllable variables, they tend to take a binary view of factual and fictional genres. Such a view is ultimately insufficient for understanding autofiction, as well as autofictional modes of writing and reading. Text comprehension studies demonstrate that sentences that involve inconsistencies or clashes in fictionality conditions (e.g. when a fictional character is said to meet a real person) are easily detected (Yang and Xue 2014, 2015). On the one hand, this means that readers should be able to distinguish between textual beings that are known to them as representing real people and those that are known to be fictional inventions. The same logic thus applies to other aspects of the text, such as real versus fictional events, places, and so on. On the other hand, this does not resolve the ambiguity of autofiction, wherein the author-character can bear the real author's name but in every other respect be invented.

Indeed, empirical studies show that factors other than framing and real-world reference of entities or events also affect reader engagement. Two recent neuroimaging studies show, for example, that different neural patterns are activated when reading about real people and fictional characters (in the former case, emotional engagement is higher), but also that the decisive factor seems not to be fictionality but personal relevance (Abraham and von Cramon 2009; Abraham, von Cramon, and Schubotz 2008). Two earlier studies (Seilman and Larsen 1989; Larsen and Seilman 1988) find that literary/fictional as opposed to expository texts create more personal remindings (the technical term for spontaneous recollection of experiences) in which the reader has an active role rather than simply being an observer. Together, then, these experiments show that the cognitive operations involved in reading—whether fictional, factual, or hybrid texts—are too complex to be explained through framing alone.

Overall, the findings of empirical studies show that readers have cognitive schemata related to fiction and non-fiction and this affords credence to existing literary critical intuitions about reading autofiction (discussed in this chapter's introduction). As well as generating a combination of or oscillation in reading stances, however, autofictions often contain moments of ambiguity in which the reference to or departure of an element to or from the real world cannot be resolved. Consequently, we define autofictional reading as a mode in which readers approach the text with two overarching schemata, either in combination or in quick oscillation, and in which they often experience moments of tension or uncertainty about the communicative intention (fictionality/factuality) and/or ontological status (fictive or real) of entities and elements. The factual schema leads readers to approach a text for information about the real world, the real author, and to evaluate the relevance of this information for themselves and their own lives. The fictional schema encourages readers to approach the text for diversion and aesthetic pleasure, for indirect knowledge and general truths: it means paying attention to thematic meanings and refraining from applying standards of empirical verification or falsification. The effects of such tensions and uncertainties have not been tested, but we offer suppositions about potential effects in the subsequent discussion of our three case studies.

AUTOFICTIONAL WRITING

Just as we maintain that there is a specific autofictional mode of reading, we also argue that there is a mode of autofictional writing. Autofictional writing refers to the intentional production of a text both as autobiographical and as fictional, and the complementary intention that the text be recognized as such. The author aims to represent their self, or a dimension of their self, while also purposefully taking creative liberties in the act of self-narration. This is what we call an act of *autofictionalization*.[2] Autofictional writing is thus distinct from lying and misremembering—as Henrik Skov Nielsen, James Phelan, and Richard Walsh (2015) note for fictionality generally—and aims at something in addition to self-representation. Potential goals of the intentional act of autofictionalization include those associated with fictional modes in general (e.g. aesthetic pleasure, indirect learning, general or indirect truth), but there are also goals particular to the autofictional mode. These include creative, explorative thinking in the pursuit of self-understanding, self-performance and self-creation, and readerly positioning (with the aim, for example, of anticipating objections or of inviting reader engagement).

As yet, there is no empirical research into autofictional writing, though Hunt's observations on the therapeutic effects of fictionalizing strategies in creative life writing constitute a step in this direction. On the basis of students' self-reports and with recourse to comments by writers like Doubrovsky, Hunt argues that autofictional writing means "work[ing] in the autobiographical space with fictional/poetic techniques" (2018, 192), and creating a position of simultaneously being inside oneself and observing the self from the outside (2004, 156; 2018, 185). This is possible if writers suspend Lejeune's autobiographical pact in favor of a pact with themselves that entails "loosen[ing] control of the writing process so that space for the imagination opens within an autobiographical frame" (Hunt 2018, 190–191). The ways in which Philip Roth, Olivia Laing, and Ben Lerner describe their practice in interviews support Hunt's assertions.

Furthermore, the authors' commentaries on *The Facts*, *Crudo*, and *10:04* show their aims and strategies to be more diverse than those which interest Hunt, and allow conclusions to be drawn about the affordances of autofictional writing. While autofictional texts in particular make it difficult to draw a purposeful boundary between statements within the text, for example, by authorial alter egos, and statements outside the partially fictional universe, we focus on the latter in this section and consider the former in the next.

Throughout his oeuvre, Philip Roth has not only created fictionalized self-representations of different degrees but also written autobiographically without markers of fictionality. *The Facts* (1988) is more strongly and more explicitly autobiographical: in interviews, Roth repeatedly attests to the "facts" in this particular text but also stresses that he could not have presented them without fictional qualifiers and challenges. The fictive character Zuckerman speaks in a fictional letter at the end of the book, voicing, and thus anticipating, objections to Roth's autobiographical narrative. In interview, Roth speaks of this as "covering [all the] bases" (Roth 1988a, 223) but also says that he intended for Zuckerman's countervoice to give readers interpretative possibilities and alternative perspectives in order to "enlarge [their] perception of the book" (224). Roth's comments reveal both other- and self-directed intentions. For the writer, according to Roth, Zuckerman as autofictional countervoice constitutes "a genuine challenge to the book" that comes from Roth himself (223). Roth began writing the facts, he explains, after what he describes in the book as "minor surgery" that "turned into a prolonged physical ordeal that led to a depression" and carried him "to the edge of emotional and mental dissolution" (Roth 1988b, 5). His aim, as he characterizes it in his book,, was to "retrieve [his] vitality, to transform [himself into himself]" by way of "rendering experience untransformed." Zuckerman's voice challenges the endeavor of retrieving bare facts and an untransformed self. *The Facts* appears to constitute Roth's own attempt at figuring out where he stands between the conflicting positions of his two alter egos—the one equating fictionalization with lying and disguise, and longing to find a self that is untransformed, and the other acknowledging the impossibility of such an attempt as he conceives of acts of fictionalization as self-creation and, in consequence, of autofictional writing as a means of insight into himself and as a more truthful kind of autobiography.

Crudo is the result of Olivia Laing's decision "to take [her] own life and times and transpose them into the Kathy Acker person," motivated by the wish to "see what would happen if [she] recorded everything that was going on around [her], from [her] own wedding to Trump's tweets threatening nuclear war, from the perspective of this cartoonish, hyper-anxious, paranoid figure" (Laing 2018c). Her writerly process purportedly involved writing every day, combining reflections on her own daily personal life, the representation of world news in the media (including on social media), and entwining this with the late Kathy Acker by randomly flipping through Acker's novels until she found something that spoke to the day's news (Laing 2018b). Laing combines her own identity, voice, perspective, and experience with those of someone else. She expresses reservations about the term "autofiction,"[3] but what she describes can nonetheless be understood as a strategy with cognitive affordances characteristic of autofictional writing. She characterizes these in terms of liberation and self-transformation, and as effecting a distancing and displacement that comes with new perspectives on self and world. The ploy of writing as or through Kathy, Laing says, allowed her to get away "from both direct reportage and labored, self-absorbed confessional writing," by adopting the perspective of "a character that could observe the turbulence [of the summer of 2017] in an exaggerated, frenetic, paranoid way," "a made-up perspective from which to view a real moment" (Laing 2018b). Laing, moreover, describes autofictional writing as enabling her to speak and think more freely, and even to transform herself, at least for the duration of writing. "Writing as Kathy," Laing says, "as this hybrid Frankenstein composite of me and Acker," "to invent the character and to help [her]self to the ravishing grab bag of Acker's own work," was "immediately liberating," allowing her to "say anything," to "zigzag between topics," and to "talk about both the political and the personal without getting bogged down" (Laing 2018b). The autofictional mode, in sum, allows Laing to develop new perspectives on herself and the world, and to, momentarily at least, transform her (experience of) self.

Ben Lerner explains in interviews that his interest lies not in the distinction between reality and fiction but in what stories do (David 2016). He is concerned with "how we live fictions, how fictions have real effects, become facts in that sense, and how our experience of the world changes depending on its arrangement into one narrative or another" (Lerner 2014b). Lerner, therefore, explains autofictional self-referentiality as an attempt to be sincere rather than ironic, which for him entails exploring "how fiction functions in our real lives—for good and for ill" rather than "mocking fiction's ability to make contact with anything outside of itself" (Lerner 2014b). Autofictional writing can constitute such a sincere exploration of the effects of stories, including fictional stories, in the author's life, and in that of the reader. These real-world effects of storytelling are what Lerner's autofictional practice arguably not only depicts but also aims to generate. The narrator of Lerner's book refers to "the utopian glimmer of fiction" (2014a, 54), and Lerner's reflections on the potential of (fictional) storytelling invite an explanation of this utopian potential in terms of the cognitive affordances and effects of an autofictional mode.

Ultimately, Roth, Laing, and Lerner each talk about their intentions and writing strategies in terms that reveal the impulse of autofictional writing. In the next section, we examine how their books activate factual and fictional schemata, and in consequence create specifically autofictional effects.

AUTOFICTIONAL TEXTS

The Facts, *Crudo*, and *10:04* all invite modes of autofictional reading. Because works of autofiction are by definition self-reflexive, albeit to different degrees, they often reveal how writers of autofiction conceptualize their craft: what they think about autobiographical writing, how they conceive of their act of fictionalization, and especially the act of autofictionalization. In this section, we link the formal makeup of these three autofictional texts to intimations of intentions in autofictional writing and the cognitive experience of autofictional reading.

Philip Roth

The title of Philip Roth's *The Facts* foregrounds the work's global factuality, while its autofictionality is made apparent by its subtitle "*A Novelist's Autobiography.*" While its primary generic coding is "autobiography," the pre-modification carries a double meaning: on the one hand, it signals possession—the self-narration and the life being storied belong to the novelist Philip Roth; on the other hand, it intimates that techniques of fictionalization and literary craftsmanship have been used in the telling of Roth's life story. Roth also presents readers with an epigraph attributed to "Nathan Zuckerman, in *The Counterlife*," one of several earlier novels by Roth in which Zuckerman appears as a fictional alter ego.[4] In the epigraph,

Zuckerman—or Roth—comments on the cross-influence of life and text: "And as he spoke, I was thinking, *the kind of stories that people turn life into, the kind of lives that people turn stories into*" (original emphasis). By quoting his fictional character in an epigraph—a type of discourse commonly reserved for the words of real people—Roth puts the distinction between fictional characters and historical people under threat. At the same time, Roth signals through the epigraph that he uses Zuckerman as mouthpiece. The effect is an ontological ambiguity between the author and the character, the factual and the fictional, which gestures toward the need to engage with *The Facts* through an autofictional mode of reading.

Framing the central narrative of *The Facts* are two letters: the first, from "Roth" to Zuckerman; the second, Zuckerman's reply. In their letters, the pair discuss the truth value of this ostensible manuscript in relation to Roth's historical creation of explicitly fictionalized author surrogates. The discussion is apt, since, as Berryman puts it, "Roth has long used this figure [Zuckerman] to hold a dialogue with himself" (1990, 177). The framing letters constitute invitations for autofictional reading as they highlight the difference between Roth, as real author, and these two textual impersonations. This invitation is intensified through the letters' content: "Roth" and Zuckerman debate the role of acts of imagination in memory, the relation of these acts to truth, and the power of fiction to (trans)form the self.

In the opening letter, "Roth" recognizes that what defines a fact is contentious, especially in autobiographical narration, as "the facts are never just coming at you but are incorporated by an imagination that is formed by your previous experience," and that "[m]emories of the past are not memories of facts but memories of your imagining of the facts" (1988b, 8). In contrast, in his previous use of Zuckerman as a character in his fiction—in acts of autofictionalization, to use our terms—Roth, by his surrogate's account, set himself the following rules: "imagin[ing] things not quite as they had happened to me or things that never happened to me or things that couldn't possibly have happened to me happening to an agent, a projection of mine, to a kind of me" (6).

The "Roth" and Zuckerman surrogates present differing opinions on the affordances and effects of acts of autofictionalization. For "Roth," they constitute "masks, disguises, distortions, and lies" (6), from which he claims to want to move away. Zuckerman, on the other hand, expresses doubt in his reply about whether such undisguised autobiography is possible, all the more so for a writer like Roth who has been formed or transformed by writing in autofictional modes: "My guess is that you've written metamorphoses of yourself so many times, you no longer have any idea what *you* are or ever were. By now what you are is a walking text" (162; original emphasis). Zuckerman highlights the affordances of autofictional writing for self-insight and a more honest form of self-representation. He is of the opinion that "in the fiction you can be so much more truthful" (162), that "there is mystery upon mystery to be uncovered once you abandon the disguises of autobiography and hand the facts over for imagination to work on" (185), and that it is "through *dis*simulation that you find your freedom from the falsifying requisites of 'candor'" (185; original emphasis). The dispute between the two alter egos warns readers against naively mining Roth's oeuvre for biographical details or criticizing it for omissions or misrepresentations.[5]

While the letters comment on acts of autofictionalization, they also constitute such an act. The ploy functions to counsel readers against reading *The Facts* as straightforwardly autobiographical (or, indeed, as straightforwardly fictional). *The Facts* does contain verifiable details: biographical events, such as the death of Roth's first wife in a car accident; references to Roth's own work on his journey to becoming a successful writer; mentions of published journalism about and critical responses to his life and work. Nevertheless, "Roth" is at pains to emphasize the fallibility of his memories. Recounting his interview for a place at Bucknell University in 1951, "Roth" writes that his interviewer was "a courteous middle-aged woman whose name I've by now forgotten" (43). To cover the gap in memory, "Roth" openly resorts to invention: "Miss Blake, let's call her" (43). Later, he claims to have completely forgotten a disciplinary hearing in front of the student–faculty Board of Publications: "I don't remember it at all and was only recently reminded that it took place by my former teacher, Mildred Martin" (67). To piece the episode together, he requested that "Mildred—who is now eighty three—sen[d] me entries from her 1953–1954 journals" (67), some material from which has purportedly been included in *The Facts* (69). While some elements of *The Facts* necessarily engender a factual schema for reading, this is undercut somewhat by such blatant memory blanks. Even in the closing letter, Zuckerman casts doubt on the wholesale veracity of *The Facts*, advising the author "I think you must give Josie her real name" (178); "Josie" being the character-pseudonym given to the first wife of "Roth" in the book.

Acts of fictionalization and autofictionalization throughout *The Facts* continually disrupt reading the book through an uncomplicatedly factual schema. Rather, the book openly debates and problematizes the distinction between factual and fictional schemata, asking instead to be read in an autofictional mode. The countervoices provided by "Roth" and Zuckerman serve to destabilize Roth's self-presentation, allowing him to challenge his own memory and self-construction, and inviting readers to explore a range of interpretative possibilities.

Olivia Laing

Crudo is Olivia Laing's debut novel and a departure from her established profile as a writer of non-fiction. The work bears no subtitle providing its generic description but is marketed, on online bookselling sites and in published reviews, as a novel. Its bizarre epigraph—"*The cheap 12 inch sq. marble tiles behind the speaker at UN always bothered me. I will replace with beautiful marble slabs if they ask me*" (original emphasis)—is unattributed on the page itself but is later identified, in the book's appended list of sources (2018a, 135), as words tweeted by Donald Trump (3 October 2012). The epigraph therefore sets up a tension in terms of the book's overarching fictional schema. Trump's tweet is a context-free assertion of sorts; here, its extratextual reality appears to enter into the fictional university of *Crudo*.

The novel's opening is composed as a curious combination of both first and third person: "Kathy, by which I mean I, was getting married. Kathy, by which I mean I, had just got off a plane from New York. It was 19:45 on 14 May 2017" (1). As the narrative continues, readers learn that "Kathy had written several books—*Great Expectations, Blood and Guts in High School*, I expect you've heard of them" (1). The named texts, particularly the latter, are easily identifiable to informed readers as Kathy Acker's published works. However, as the real Kathy Acker died in 1997, the 2017 airport arrival described at the start of *Crudo* is a logical impossibility, at least according to a factual, biographical schema. In consequence, the narrator and "Kathy," at the start of the novel and at various points thereafter, come together and fracture apart in fluctuating subjective transpositions. As such, the opening signals, at least to one reviewer, that "the novel is several things at once: a work of autofiction detailing key events in Laing's life, a counterfactual fiction in which Kathy Acker is alive and getting married and a rigorous piece of fictional appropriation" (Kitamura 2018, 10). The play of subjectivities so central to *Crudo* is at the heart of its autofictional ambiguity. While Kathy Acker was a real person, the persona in *Crudo* is fabricated by, and merged with, Laing; the "Kathy"/I persona, therefore, represents freedom to depart from traditional autobiographical representation, including aims at factual accuracy. *Crudo* thus demands an autofictional mode of reading: readers must oscillate between imagining "Kathy" as a fictionalized counterpart of Kathy Acker reacting to the real events of 2017 and simultaneously attributing these reactions, as belonging, and happening, to Laing herself.

As mentioned, in interviews Laing has openly discussed her compositional method for *Crudo*. In the early pages of the novel, her writing process is transposed into the routine of "Kathy": "Kathy was writing everything down in her notebook, and had become abruptly anxious that she might exhaust the present and find herself out at the front, alone on the crest of time" (8). In *Crudo*, engagement with "the present" takes place largely through digital media, from which Laing quotes freely and in so doing weaves real events and, more importantly, the voices of real people, into the fabric of her book. Worried about the increasingly tense relationship between the United States and North Korea, for example, "Kathy" decides to consult Trump's Twitter account:

> It was worse than she'd expected. He was retweeting Fox News about jets in Guam that could fight tonight, but he was also taking time out to trashtalk the FailingNewYorkTimes. My first order as President was to renovate and modernize our nuclear arsenal. It is now far stronger and more powerful than ever before …… Hopefully we will never have to use this power, but there will never be a time that we are not the most powerful nation in the world! (42–43)

The first-person voice here once again belongs to Donald Trump via Twitter (9 August 2017). The list, "Something Borrowed," at the end of *Crudo* (135–141) discloses appropriated material from real-world textual sources included in the book. A significant number are from Kathy Acker's work; others are taken from Twitter as well as news and magazine sources. Although Acker fans might notice the inclusion of the dead writer's material, it seems unlikely that readers will be familiar with all of Laing's appropriated sources. Factual and fictional materials thus repeatedly intrude into *Crudo*, at times imperceptibly. The appended source list does acknowledge them, however, and, in so doing, makes readers aware of how Laing merges modes of discourse (news, social media, autobiography, and novel) and voices (Acker's, Laing's, and those of fictional characters as well as other real-world people).

In *Crudo*, "Kathy" thinks, "[t]his was the problem with history, it was too easy to provide the furnishings but forget the attitudes, the way you became a different person according to what knowledge was available, what experiences were fresh and what had not yet arisen in a personal and global frame" (82). Capturing the attitudes of other people is, according to "Kathy"/Laing, "the province of the novel, that hopeless apparatus of guesswork and supposition, with which Kathy liked to have as little traffic as possible. She wrote fiction, sure, but she populated it with the already extant, the pre-packaged and ready-made"; "it was economic also stylish to help yourself to the grab bag of the actual" (84). Appropriated intertextual material and context-free assertions about 2017 intermingle with "Kathy"'s experiences of Laing's autobiographical life (such as her wedding). *Crudo* is driven consequently not only by acts of autofictionalization but a form of collective socio-historical commentary which, by placing Laing and "Kathy" in the wider context, seems to be an attempt to capture not only the events of 2017 but the spirit of the times.

Within *Crudo*, "Kathy"/Laing admits to longing for some sort of interpersonal liberation: "She was bored, [...] wanted novelty and heat, [...] wanted to unhook herself" (72). Writing, especially autofictional writing, seems to make this possible. Toward the end of *Crudo*, "Kathy"/Laing repeatedly stresses that "she c[an't] settle" (113), switches furniture, flats, cities, "want[s] a new coat, a new figure, a new lease of life," "want[s] someone else's life" (113). She realizes that this is possible in writing: "Writing, she can be anyone. On the page the I dissolves, becomes amorphous, proliferates wildly. Kathy takes on increasingly preposterous guises, slips the knot of her own contemptible identity" (125). Just as Zuckerman advises "Roth" in *The Facts* that freedom can be found only if the pursuit of autobiographical accuracy is abandoned, "Kathy"/Laing finds release by borrowing from the lives of others, both real and imagined.

Ultimately, *Crudo*'s composition not only problematizes any reading that seeks to pigeonhole the work through a wholly fictional or factual schema; it also encodes the experience of living in a social media–saturated culture, in which reality and textual mediation are sometimes difficult to separate. The result is a disorientating literary experience—in other words, an autofictional effect.

Ben Lerner

Ben Lerner's *10:04* is subtitled "*A Novel.*" The three-part narrative features two author figures, presented as fictionalized versions of Lerner. "Ben," the first-person narrator of the first and third parts, is a writer who lives in Brooklyn (as does Ben Lerner), writes one of Lerner's poems ("The Dark Threw Patches Down Upon Me"), and is working on a book that turns out to be *10:04* itself. Part two consists of one of Lerner's previously published short stories, featuring the second author-character, this time referred to in the third person as "the author," who has made a debut with a novel identifiable to readers familiar with Lerner's previous work as *Leaving the Atocha Station*—Lerner's first novel, published in 2011. Thus, while *10:04*'s subtitle immediately activates a fictional schema for readers, an autobiographical reading is simultaneously invited through the onomastic and biographical correspondences between author and protagonist and the references to actual publications that the author and character share. *10:04*, in sum, signals an autofictional text and produces a corresponding reading mode.

There are, moreover, several instances within *10:04* in which the (real) effects of (fictional) stories are thematized. "Ben" is, for example, advised by a friend against writing "about medical stuff," since, the friend claims, "you believe, even though you'll deny it, that writing has some kind of magical power" and are "crazy enough to make your fiction come true somehow" (Lerner 2014a, 137–138). The narrator validates this allegation by first denying it and then confessing the dishonesty of his denial in the narration. In another instance, "the author" takes a stance against autobiographical readings of his/Lerner's first novel, but follows suit with the acknowledgment that, as the narrator of this book "was characterized above all by his anxiety regarding the disconnect between his internal experience and his social self-presentation, the more intensely the author worried about distinguishing himself from the narrator, the more he felt he had become him" (66). The act of (auto-)fictional distancing, these comments suggest, creates distance between author and narrator or character, but in turn transform the author. Through these instances of metanarrative commentary, *10:04* thus invites the kind of autobiographical, or rather autofictional reading, that the author-characters reject.

In the first pages of *10:04*, Lerner sets up the premise that the book that "Ben" has been commissioned to write is *10:04* itself. At the end of *10:04*'s opening scene, a celebratory meal in a Manhattan seafood restaurant,

"Ben" promises "a novel" to his fellow diner and publisher in which their own act of "eating cephalopods" will "become the opening scene" (4). The genre designator "novel" together with the word "scene" clashes with the metatextual information about the author's own process of writing. As the author-character is writing the very artifact we are reading, *10:04* must be seen as both an autobiographical narrativization of the writing process *and* a fictional representation of a writer-character. The clash demands combining or oscillating between the fictional and the autobiographical mode—a demand that is reiterated at intervals throughout the book. It is most apparent in other instances of indexicality; for example, when the narrator suggests, "say that it was standing there that I decided to replace the book I'd proposed with the book you're reading now, a work that, like a poem, is neither fiction nor nonfiction, but a flickering between them" (194). Lerner makes the movement from fictional story to real world materiality palpable even when the narrator puts before us the following image: "a bright glow to the east among the dark towers of the Financial District, like the eyeshine of some animal" (237). The light, we are told, comes from the Goldman Sachs building, and the narrator refers us to "photographs in which one of the few illuminated buildings in the skyline was the investment banking firm, an image," he notes in passing, "I'd use for the cover of my book" (237). Through this reference to the photograph, the book that "Ben" has been writing materializes in the reader's hands, at least if they have the US edition of *10:04*, which features this very image on its cover. *10:04* is, in other words, a book "on the very edge of fiction" (237)—a book oscillating between the fictional and the autobiographical.

Elsewhere, we have both argued that *10:04* has the potential to affect how readers think, feel, and possibly act in the real-world context of climate change and globalization. Gibbons (2021a) stresses that *10:04* creates an "affective effect" (144) of the anticipated future for readers and that *10:04* "positions Ben's anxieties as already part of a reader's past and present" making the potential future apocalypse "feel more meaningful to readers" (142). Alexandra Effe (2021) argues that *10:04* "works toward change by calling on the reader to take action in reality" and that Lerner's text has high potential for inciting readers to do so as the autofictional dimension creates a feeling of direct relevance for readers in combination with the sense of possibility for transformation (739). Lee Konstantinou categorizes Lerner more generally in a group of "affective neorealists" (2018, 111), who aim to "facilitate new powers for fiction" (120).

Empirical data on factual and fictional reading modes and Lerner's own reflections on autofictionalization offer a possible explanation for the potential cognitive-affective effects of his book.

* * *

In this chapter, we have argued that autofictional texts should not be considered in isolation but rather as part of a literary event that includes the intentional production of an autofictional mode of writing and a corresponding autofictional mode of reading. Empirical data—in the form of writers' self-reports in interviews and evidence from psychology concerning the cognitive-affective dimensions of fictional and factual reading modes—has enabled us to substantiate our claims and form theoretically and empirically grounded hypotheses about autofictional writing and reading. Writers' own reflections, both in interviews and within their works, provide insight into the motivations for and cognitive affordances of their acts of autofictionalization, from interrogating memories to coming to terms with living in a contemporary society in which social media fuels a post-truth culture and climate change creates an uncertain future. Furthermore, readers of *The Facts*, *Crudo*, and *10:04* are likely to recognize and feel the rootedness of these works in their real-world contexts, be that a single author coming to terms with their life and the reception of their work, the disorientation of our media-saturated contemporary culture, or the reality of climate change. This rootedness in reality is likely to create personal relevance which, empirical studies suggest, is linked to higher emotional involvement—that is, to an affective effect. The fictional dimension of autofiction, in turn, is likely to lead readers to create detailed mental representations and contemplate contradictory elements, such as different author avatars and different depicted realities. Such contemplation will also mean more critical, perhaps also more creative, engagements with the text, including the ways in which readers relate to autofictions and what changes they themselves might put into action in their lives. The cognitive and holistic perspective adopted in this chapter, combined with attention to the textual and paratextual apparatus of a work, has allowed us to draw out and to better understand such effects and affects. Especially in the light of the personal and psychological dimension of much autofictional literature, we believe that this perspective is ultimately best placed to account for the affordances and affective resonances of autofiction as a holistic literary experience.

Notes

1. When names are placed in inverted commas, we are referring to characters and author-avatars as textual beings in our case studies.
2. To our knowledge, our use of the term is novel, although Walker (2018) speaks of "autofictionalizing reflective writing strategies" (in the title of her chapter).
3. Laing feels that the term "autofiction" diminishes her understanding of novels as "an intimate communication between writer and reader with personal stakes" (Laing 2018b).
4. Berryman (1990) discusses Zuckerman as Roth's self-portrait throughout the author's work.
5. *The Facts* can thus be seen as a reply to select Jewish-American readers, reading what Roth intended as satires as autobiographical, criticizing him for betraying a Jewish community, and accusing him of self-hatred. *The Facts* seems to put the record straight, but the autofictional dimension also qualifies "the facts" that *The Facts* provides. For an account of *The Facts* as an ambiguous act of righting the record, see also Wirth-Nesher (2007, 158–64).

Works Cited

Abraham, Anna, and D. Yves von Cramon. 2009. Reality = Relevance? Insights from Spontaneous Modulations of the Brain's Default Network when Telling Apart Reality from Fiction. *PLoS One* 4 (3): 1–9.

Abraham, Anna, D. Yves von Cramon, and Ricarda I. Schubotz. 2008. Meeting George Bush versus Meeting Cinderella: The Neural Response When Telling Apart What is Real from What is Fictional in the Context of Our Reality. *Journal of Cognitive Neuroscience* 20 (6): 965–976.

Bell, Alice. 2014. Schema Theory, Hypertext Fiction and Links. *Style* 48 (2): 140–161.

Berryman, Charles. 1990. Philip Roth and Nathan Zuckerman: A Portrait of the Artist as a Young Prometheus. *Contemporary Literature* 31 (2): 177–190.

Cook, Guy. 1994. *Discourse and Literature*. Oxford: Oxford University Press.

David, Thomas. 2016. Ben Lerners Roman *22:04*: Hat es dieses Brooklyn je gegeben? http://www.faz.net/aktuell/feuilleton/buecher/autoren/ben-lerner-ueber-seinen-roman-22-04-14028724.html. Accessed Mar 30, 2021.

Dix, Hywel. 2018. Introduction: Autofiction in English: The Story so Far. In *Autofiction in English*, ed. Hywel Dix, 1–23. Cham: Palgrave Macmillan.

Effe, Alexandra. 2021. Ben Lerner's *10:04* and the "Utopian Glimmer of [Auto]fiction." *Modern Fiction Studies* 67 (4): 739–757.

Gibbons, Alison. 2016. Multimodality, Cognitive Poetics, and Genre: Reading Grady Hendrix's Novel *Horrorstör*. *Multimodal Communication* 5 (1): 15–29.

———. 2019. The 'Dissolving Margins' of Elena Ferrante and the Neapolitan Novels: A Cognitive Approach to Fictionality, Authorial Intentionality, and Autofictional Reading Strategies. *Narrative Inquiry* 29 (2): 389–415.

———. 2021a. Metamodernism, the Anthropocene, and the Resurgence of Historicity: Ben Lerner's *10:04* and 'the utopian glimmer of fiction.'. *Critique: Studies in Contemporary Fiction* 62 (2): 137–151. https://doi.org/10.108 0/00111619.2020.1784828.

———. 2021b. 'Why do you insist Alana is not real?': Visitors' Perceptions of the Fictionality of Andi and Lance Olsen's 'There's No Place Like Time' Exhibition. In *Style and Reader Response: Minds, Media, Methods*, ed. Alice Bell, Sam Browse, Alison Gibbons, and David Peplow, 101–121. Amsterdam: John Benjamins.

Green, Melanie C., Jennifer Garst, Timothy C. Brock, and Sungeun Chung. 2006. Fact Versus Fiction Labeling: Persuasion Parity Despite Heightened Scrutiny of Fact. *Media Psychology* 8: 267–285.

Hunt, Celia. 2004. Writing and Reflexivity: Training to Facilitate Writing for Personal Development. In *Creative Writing in Health and Social Care*, ed. Fiona Sampson, 154-169. London: Jessica Kingsley.

———. 2018. Autofiction as a Reflexive Mode of Thought: Implications for Personal Development. In *Autofiction in English*, ed. Hywel Dix, 179–196. Cham: Palgrave Macmillan.

Kitamura, Katie. 2018. Anxieties of Influence. *The New York Times Book Review*, October 7.

Konstantinou, Lee. 2018. Neorealist Fiction. In *American Literature in Transition: 2000–2010*, ed. Rachel Greenwald Smith, 109–124. Cambridge: Cambridge University Press.

Laing, Olivia. 2018a. *Crudo*. London: Picador.

———. 2018b. Becoming Kathy Acker: An Interview with Olivia Laing. Interview by Chris Kraus, *The Paris Review*, September 11, 2018. https://www.theparisreview.org/blog/2018/09/11/becoming-kathy-acker-an-interview-with-olivia-laing/. Accessed Apr 1, 2021.

———. 2018c. Olivia Laing: 'I Stopped Being Able to Distinguish News from Rumour, Paranoia and Supposition.' Interview by Anna Leszkiewicz, *New Statesman*, November 2, 2018. https://www.newstatesman.com/culture/books/2018/11/olivia-laing-i-stopped-being-able-distinguish-news-rumour-paranoia-and. Accessed Mar 30, 2021.

Larsen, Steen F., and Uffe Seilman. 1988. Personal Remindings While Reading Literature. *Text* 8 (4): 411–430.

Lejeune, Philippe. 1989. The Autobiographical Pact. In *On Autobiography*, translated by Katherine Leary, 3–30. Minneapolis: University of Minnesota Press.
Lerner, Ben. 2014a. *10:04*. London: Granta.
———. 2014b. Ben Lerner. Interview by Tao Lin, *The Believer*, September 4, 2014. https://believermag.com/an-interview-with-ben-lerner/. Accessed Apr 1, 2021.
Mason, Jessica. 2019. *Intertextuality in Practice*. Amsterdam; Philadelphia, PA: John Benjamins.
Nielsen, Henrik Skov. 2011. What's in a Name? Double Exposures in *Lunar Park*. In *Bret Easton Ellis: American Psycho/Glamorama/Lunar Park*, ed. Naomi Mandel, 129–142. London: Continuum.
Nielsen, Henrik Skov, James Phelan, and Richard Walsh. 2015. Ten Theses about Fictionality. *Narrative* 23 (1): 74–100.
Pettersson, Torsten. 2016. Fictionality and the Empirical Study of Literature. *CLCWeb: Comparative Literature and Culture* 18 (2). https://docs.lib.purdue.edu/clcweb/vol18/iss2/3/. Accessed Mar 30, 2021.
Prentice, Deborah A., and Richard J. Gerrig. 1999. Exploring the Boundary between Fiction and Reality. In *Dual-Process Theories in Social Psychology*, ed. Shelley Chaiken and Yaacov Trope, 529–546. New York: Guilford Press.
Roth, Philip. 1988a. PW Interviews: Philip Roth. Interview by Katharine Weber. In *Conversations with Philip Roth*, edited by George J. Searles, 220–225. Jackson: University Press of Mississippi, 1992. Reprinted from the August 26, 1988 issue of *Publishers Weekly*.
———. 1988b. *The Facts: A Novelist's Autobiography*. London: Penguin Random House.
Seilman, Uffe, and Steen F. Larsen. 1989. Personal Resonance to Literature: A Study of Remindings While Reading. *Poetics* 18 (1): 165–177.
Srikanth, Siddharth. 2019. Fictionality and Autofiction. *Style* 63 (3): 344–363.
Stockwell, Peter. 2019. *Cognitive Poetics: An Introduction*. 2nd ed. London; New York: Routledge.
Walker, Amelia. 2018. Autofictionalizing Reflective Writing Pedagogies: Risks and Possibilities. In *Autofiction in English*, ed. Hywel Dix, 198–215. Cham: Palgrave Macmillan.
Wirth-Nesher, Hana. 2007. Roth's Autobiographical Writings. In *The Cambridge Companion to Philip Roth*, ed. Timothy Parrish, 158–172. Cambridge: Cambridge University Press.
Worthington, Marjorie. 2018. *The Story of "Me": Contemporary American Autofiction*. Lincoln, NE: University of Nebraska Press.
Yang, Jie, and Jin Xue. 2014. Distinguishing Different Fictional Worlds during Sentence Comprehension: ERP Evidence. *Psychophysiology* 51: 42–51.

———. 2015. Reality/Fiction Distinction and Fiction/Fiction Distinction during Sentence Comprehension. *Universal Journal of Psychology* 3 (6): 165–175.

Zipfel, Frank. 2005. Autofiction. In *Routledge Encyclopedia of Narrative Theory*, ed. David Herman, Manfred Jahn, and Marie-Laure Ryan, 36–37. London: Routledge.

Zwaan, Rolf A. 1994. Effect of Genre Expectations on Text Comprehension. *Journal of Experimental Psychology: Learning, Memory and Cognition* 20: 920–933.

Open Access This chapter is licensed under the terms of the Creative Commons Attribution 4.0 International License (http://creativecommons.org/licenses/by/4.0/), which permits use, sharing, adaptation, distribution and reproduction in any medium or format, as long as you give appropriate credit to the original author(s) and the source, provide a link to the Creative Commons licence and indicate if changes were made.

The images or other third party material in this chapter are included in the chapter's Creative Commons licence, unless indicated otherwise in a credit line to the material. If material is not included in the chapter's Creative Commons licence and your intended use is not permitted by statutory regulation or exceeds the permitted use, you will need to obtain permission directly from the copyright holder.

CHAPTER 5

"The Pragmatics of Autofiction"

Arnaud Schmitt

Any research project focusing in one way or another on autofiction should state what is meant by the term in that particular context. Indeed, Karen Ferreira-Meyers rightfully points out that "[t]here are numerous examples of academic writers including the terms 'autofiction' or 'autofictional' in their analyses without providing further details" (2018, 33–34). Furthermore, authors would also be well advised to keep in mind that, as Marjorie Worthington notes about her own approach, the definition with which one is working "is only one of many in circulation" (2018, 6). Consequently, let me start by reiterating in a concise way my own understanding of autofiction (as Martina Wagner-Egelhaaf also urges us to do in her contribution to this volume [see Chap. 2]). Autofiction, in my understanding of the term, is neither a new autobiographical form nor a hybrid genre, but should instead be regarded as "a hyperbolic form of autobiographical novel," even "a baroque version" of it. It operatively rests on "paroxysmal associations" and "an extravagant presence of the author within her/his own fiction, a presence that follows the tradition of the

A. Schmitt (✉)
University of Bordeaux, Bordeaux, France
e-mail: arnaud.schmitt@u-bordeaux.fr

© The Author(s) 2022
A. Effe, H. Lawlor (eds.), *The Autofictional*, Palgrave Studies in Life Writing, https://doi.org/10.1007/978-3-030-78440-9_5

autobiographical novel but also upends it" (Schmitt 2020, 9), a *presence* that can be quite simply defined as an avatar of the author within her own fiction. Thus, autofiction, as I use the term, is to be understood primarily as a fictional genre.

However, my purpose in this chapter is not to develop this, ultimately simple enough, definition any further, but to illustrate how the aforementioned "associations" actually function. For a relatively new literary concept, autofiction has been extensively defined, even over-defined for some (for instance, on the "theoretical soap opera" surrounding autofiction in France, see Worthington 2018, 3). Although I draw on select theoretical contributions (for instance, by Worthington and Hywel Dix), I adopt a more practical approach by studying what I have dubbed "the pragmatics of autofiction," in keeping with the methodology that Gasparini partially adopted in *Est-il Je?* 16 years ago, concretely identifying stylistic, rhetorical, or paratextual elements in texts clearly identified as autofictions, or at least as ambiguous autobiographical novels, or in line with what Worthington accomplished in some chapters of *The Story of "Me": Contemporary American Autofiction*, which consists in studying the actual textual signals and tropes that suddenly or progressively turn an autobiographical novel into autofiction.

In his introduction to *Autofiction in English*, Dix writes that "one of the key questions to be explored throughout this volume is whether the definition, components, characteristics and theories of autofiction remain the same when transplanted from French into English, or whether the components themselves undergo modification when the context changes" (2018, 5). It is my belief that, even though theoretical approaches may differ,[1] the practice of autofiction as a particular form of autobiographical fiction is common to many countries' literary traditions. Apart from the usual cultural and historical discrepancies, the operative forms of US and French autofictions do not fundamentally differ, which is why the late arrival of the term autofiction in the theoretical lexicon of Anglophone academia remains surprising, as "[t]here was nothing, absolutely nothing, in the first steps toward coining, defining and deepening the concept of autofiction that barred it from being accepted worldwide" (Ferreira-Meyers 2018, 27). Indeed, "novels that feature a character who shares his/her name with the author," one of the most salient features of autofiction, can be regarded as "a phenomenon of contemporary American fiction that took shape in the late 1960s and early 1970s and continues in earnest today [...] when it has become a postmodern trope" (Worthington

2018, 1). Ferreira-Meyers differentiates between these so-called postmodern tropes and the rise of a new kind of autofictional writing, which Jonathan Sturgeon describes as "autofictions that vigorously reasserted the self" through "the induction of a new class of memoiristic, autobiographical, and metafictional novels—we can call them autofictions—that jettison the logic of postmodernism in favor of a new position" (2018, 33). Worthington certainly underlines this new fad in American letters as, according to her, "[t]he autofictional trope has become so common in American fiction that it almost seems a requirement for contemporary authors to engage in it," although again she finds it odd that "there has been little critical discussion of this trend" (2018, 1). But even though "autofictions themselves have proliferated in recent American literature" (10), she is also careful to insist that this recent proliferation stems from "a fictional tradition sixty years in the making" (4).

I have differentiated between theoretical and literary traditions when it comes to autofiction and, by referencing Worthington and Dix's research, claimed that despite the lack of "critical discussion of this trend," the practice of autofictional writing is very lively, maybe paradoxically even more so in the US than in France nowadays. I would now like to turn to my two case studies, Ben Lerner's *10:04* (2014) and Siri Hustvedt's *Memories of the Future* (2019), and justify my choice of primary texts. Published 5 years apart and written by authors of different genders and belonging to different generations (Lerner is 41 and Hustvedt 65), neither of these books is explicitly advertised as autofiction. Nonetheless, critics have not missed the opportunity to point out the highly autofictional logic of these authors' narrative strategies,[2] and rightfully so, for, as we will see, both display archetypal features of autofiction. But in the domain of autofiction, it is now widely known that authors should not be trusted, and nor should the generic designation indicated on a book's cover. It is part of the autofictional game to muddy the waters as early as possible in the reader's experience of the text, epitextually and peritextually. As regards these two works, they were either, depending on the edition, labeled "a novel" or no reference was made to the genre of the text. Nevertheless, both authors drop recurring references to their own biographical data. Ben Lerner's first novel *Leaving the Atocha Station* is more or less remotely based on the author's own experience in Madrid ("no one will be surprised to hear that he has indeed spent a year doing some sort of research in Madrid" [Turner 2012]) and the narrator Adam Gordon is, like Lerner, a young American poet and shares other biographical traits with him. As for Siri Hustvedt, whether in fictional (*The Sorrows of an American*) or nonfictional (*The Shaking Woman or A History of My Nerves*) form, she is known for inserting more or less explicit references to her own life into her work. Does this mean that readers were primed to read *10:04* and *Memories of the Future* as autofictional? Such a reading was certainly invited, although some readers may still have read the books as ordinary novels. As different as their authors' backgrounds might be, these two texts, published in the current proliferation of US autofiction and thus symptomatic of a literary trend, share many defining features that can help us better understand how autofiction actually works. We will see that these features can be divided between primary, or essential ones without which a text cannot be identified as autofictional, and secondary ones, or what I will call "enhancers," elements that enhance the reader's perception of a text as autofictional but do not initiate such a perception.

What's in a Name?

Much has been written about autofiction's onomastic criterion, as many theorists regard it as a defining one, even *the* defining one in some cases (as is the case for Colonna 2004). Conferring your name on your narrator is a way for writers, especially writers whose biographical contours remain mostly unknown by their putative readers (which was certainly the case when Lerner published *10:04*, only his second novel), to bring to their readers' attention a closeness, or a similarity, between themselves and their narrators that might not be apparent otherwise. In other words, it is a way of starting the autofictional game by projecting a narrator very similar to you, named after you, into a world that may otherwise be fictional. Gasparini relevantly pointed out that autofictional texts are "saturated by conjunctional and disjunctional signs between the two instances [facts and fiction]"[3] (2004, 13; my translation), stating that "right from its very beginning, the double movement of confession and denial has been constitutive of the autobiographical novel"[4] (32; my translation), and the same can be said about autofiction. Inserting your name into your text is an easy way for the author to fulfill the confessional and the conjunctional function, and both Lerner and Hustvedt resort to it, although in different ways. Lerner's narrator is referred to as "Ben." Hustvedt's narrator refers several times to her younger self as "S.H." Refraining from using your full name while using your first name or your initials is obviously nothing new and is a way of suggesting proximity while maintaining a form of distance, which is characteristic of autofiction. Worthington sees an identical strategy in Bret Easton Ellis's *Lunar Park* and reaches a similar conclusion: "*Lunar Park* toys with readers' sense of reality by depicting a 'Bret' whose biography is simultaneously similar to yet often distinct from that of the extratextual Ellis. The two become divergent yet metaleptically interconnected identities: this is the defining characteristic of autofiction" (2018, 2). Without referring to Gasparini, she nevertheless puts forward very similar analyses to the ones quoted above: "The primary defining trait of autofiction as I define it is the inclusion of a characterized version of the author, usually as the protagonist. […] although they share a name, the protagonists and the authors are not identical to one another" (2018, 2). In my two case studies, they do not exactly "share a name" (merely a first name or initials), but the effect can be seen as similar.

To answer the Shakespearian question of this section's title, a reader can find in a name, even in a first name or initials, a strong hint of an autofictional intent. This onomastic nod to the author can be, and often is, supplemented with the insertion of autobiographical data. As expounded above, I equate autofiction with self-fictionalization, projecting one's self into a fictional world. This echoes Genette's definition,[5] but acknowledges that the projection may involve a form of ontological introspection on the part of the author who has an opportunity to contemplate himself or herself in a life that is sometimes not so drastically different from their real life. *10:04*'s almost programmatic epigraph reads:

> The Hassidim tell a story about the world to come that says everything there will be just as it is here. Just as our room is now, so it will be in the world to come; where our baby sleeps now, there too it will sleep in the other world. And the clothes we wear in this world, those too we will wear there. Everything will be as it is now, just a little different. (Lerner 2014, 1)

This last sentence is repeated throughout the book in various forms, as if the author were particularly keen on the reader not losing sight of this prism through which to read the book. Lerner implements a differentiation that keeps his real self at bay but always within sight. In a way, Lerner's "now"—his real-life present—is not substantially different from the fictional world of *10:04*, but it is in the distance, the more or less perceptible gap, between life and art that autofiction exists. In fact, another reference to an autofictional blueprint can be found later in the text: "The poem, like most of my poems, and like the story I'd promised to expand, conflated fact and fiction [...] part of what I loved about poetry was how the distinction between fiction and nonfiction didn't obtain, how the correspondence between text and world was less important than the intensities of the poem itself [...]" (2014, 170–171). Through "Ben," Lerner keeps "conflating fact and fiction," toying with the reader's horizon of expectation.

Trying to go beyond the onomastic criterion, Gasparini asked this seminal question: "Why not admit that, besides a family name and a first name, a whole series of hero/author identification operators exist: their age, their socio-cultural background, their profession, their aspirations, etc.?"[6] (2004, 25; my translation). Indeed, a stronger case can be made for labeling a text as autofiction when there is a certain resemblance between narrator and author based on similar biographical features than when the only conjunction is the name. Without these "identification operators," the name remains empty (to carry the Shakespearian metaphor further). Worthington notes that in the case of *Lunar Park*, the "onomastic connection between 'Bret' and Ellis makes that point more vividly than a purely fictional character could, for it lends a patina of 'reality' to an otherwise patently fictional situation" (2018, 3). But one could counterargue that a "patina" is not enough to uphold an autofictional reading and, what is more, there are more connections between "Bret" and the author than a simple first name, especially in the first chapter which generously taps into Ellis's biographical background, which has been epitextually documented.

As far as *10:04* is concerned, identification operators are plentiful. The narrator and protagonist is a poet and a writer who published a short story entitled "The Golden Vanity" in *The New Yorker*—Ben Lerner published this short story, exactly the same as the one found in the book's second chapter, 2 years prior to the publication of *10:04*—to which constant references are made throughout the book (for instance: "'But you need to keep the New Yorker story in there, I think'" [Lerner 2014, 157]); exactly like Lerner, the narrator was born in 1979 ("1985, when I was six" [6]) and grew up in Topeka ("my entire childhood in Topeka" [14]) and after several collections of poems published a first novel in which "the protagonist tells people his mother is dead" (138), as Lerner's narrator Adam does in *Leaving the Atocha Station* (2011). This last element obviously requires knowledge of Lerner's first novel. Indeed, all his prose works are connected by means of intertextual references like this one. Many others can be found in his latest novel *The Topeka School* (2019), which centers on the protagonist's youth in Topeka and his family life (unsurprisingly evoking what we know about the author's). Not all, but enough, parallels can be detected simply through the respective peritexts, and the first elements are quite easy to encounter epitextually in interviews or book reviews. Parallels are thus apparent even for someone who is not particularly interested in making detailed connections, but, of course, autofiction only makes sense, only exists, if there are readers who find such connections fruitful.

Siri Hustvedt employs similar techniques. We find, in *Memories of the Future*, typical autofictional tropes about the equivocality of the narrative voice and overall project. The narrator speaks of "a voice that is at once mine and not quite mine anymore" (2019, 11) and reflects on pronoun use: "And I, or she (easier to say she)" (37). The narrator's background also matches Hustvedt's: a woman in her 60s who grew up in Minnesota and moved to New York to study at Columbia and become a writer. However, there are also discrepancies. Siri Hustvedt is married to fellow writer Paul Auster whereas in the novel, S.H.'s husband's name is Walter and he is a mathematician. Moreover, although the author's and the narrator's daughters are both musicians, again names differ (Sophie in real life, Freya in the book). *Memories of the Future* is composed of three interweaving texts, or narrative layers: the journal that S.H.'s younger self kept, long excerpts from what seems to be her first novel—which echoes Hustvedt's own first novel, *The Blindfold*, which focuses on a young woman also of Norwegian descent from Minnesota, who has just moved to Manhattan's Upper West Side to study at Columbia in the 1970s—and finally comments from S.H. in the narrative's present. Thus, Hustvedt sets up the typical (for autofiction) conjunctions and disjunctions, similarities and dissimilarities with her biographical background. Similar to *10:04*, the author's and the narrator's personas are very much alike in many aspects, enough for the reader willing to adopt an autofictional mind-frame. Resorting to autobiographical data is a necessary step to implement the necessary process of recognition. Indeed, if autofiction is the same (an autobiographical narrator or protagonist) but different (transposed into an overall fictional narrative), then to read these differences, one must first set up similarities.

"Enhancers"

To create a sense of autofiction, that is to say, to make the reader aware of a form of saturation of autobiographical references in a novel, the author can rely on two types of elements: primary criteria and secondary ones. The former are to some extent compulsory; without them autofiction cannot work. The latter enhance the sense of the autofictional without creating it in the first place. There are only two kinds of primary criteria: onomastic correspondence and similarities in biographical background between author and narrator. I claim that it is inconceivable to consider a work as autofictional if there is not at least one of these elements in place, as they constitute the necessary signal. Secondary elements, which I call "enhancers," contribute to the reader's awareness of the necessary ambiguousness of the generic status of the text, but do not create it.

Metafiction

The first kind of enhancer that I would like to explore, used by both Hustvedt and Lerner, is metafiction. This typically postmodern device has been associated on many occasions with autofiction, Worthington recently going as far as stating that "autofiction is a highly metafictional genre" (2018, 3) or, as we saw above, Sturgeon equating autofictions with "memoiristic, autobiographical, and metafictional novels." However, it is my contention that autofictional and metafictional texts are dissimilar in many ways, but thrive on the same narrative environment: unstable narrative centers and authorial intrusions. The fact that some texts are both metafictional and autofictional does not mean that they are similar, simply that metafictional and autofictional elements can work together. Many autofictions do not include metafictional elements. *Lunar Park* is yet again a good example. Ellis's references to Patrick Bateman, the notorious character from *American Psycho*, are not metafictional, but intertextual.

Some theorists who resort to these analogies between autofiction and metafiction even omit to differentiate between metatextuality and metafiction. In *La Figure de l'auteur*, Maurice Couturier makes a useful distinction between the two practices, reminding us that, according to Patricia Waugh, metafictional writers "explore a theory of fiction through the practice of writing fiction" (Waugh 1984, 2), whereas metatextuality consists in embedding texts whose origin is problematic because they are originally non-literary, even if the distinction between both terms can occasionally be "thin" (Couturier 1995, 77; my translation). He goes on to compare John Barth's *LETTERS*, a metafictional text according to him as it is built on other fictions (the novels previously published by the author), to Richardson's *Pamela*, which is metatextual as the letters embedded in it did not have a literary status prior to their inclusion in the novel (77). Thus, *Memories of the Future* may be seen as both metafictional (the main narrative embeds S.H.'s first novel) and metatextual (it also embeds the journal of the younger S.H.). Similarly, *10:04* comprises Lerner's short story "The Golden Vanity," which first appeared in *The New Yorker*, but also "To the Future," a short piece about the apatosaurus written, the reader is told, by the narrator in collaboration with the young Roberto Cortiz (a non-literary text that turns out not to be as fictional as we might imagine at first, as we learn in the acknowledgments that "[t]he narrator's collaboration with 'Roberto' is based on a self-published book [he] cowrote with Elias Garcia, but 'Roberto' is otherwise a work of fiction"). Multiple layers of narrative make texts either metatextual, metafictional, or both, but as far as autofiction is concerned, they enhance the impression of confusion regarding the source of the narrative. By virtue of the increased hermeneutical effort required to make sense of the text, the reader's attention is drawn to the noncongruent origins of the narrative's components. By mixing fictional and non-literary texts, the book also echoes autofiction's mix of facts and fiction.

Memories of the Future and *10:04* are also metafictional in that, on several occasions, the respective texts refer to their own status as artifacts. For instance, in Hustvedt's book, S.H.'s mother asks her about the book she is writing, the frame narrative in other words: "She asks me about this book, and I tell her I am in the middle of it. 'You are writing about your life, your *own* life?' Only one year of it, I explain" (2019, 158). Lerner's narrator and other characters also make multiple references to the narrator's own work as a writer, for instance: "How exactly will you expand the story" (2014, 4) and "[...] over the next week, I began to work on a story, outlining much of it in my notebook while sitting in the theater. The story would involve a series of transpositions [...]" (54). The narrator then describes what will eventually become "The Golden Vanity," Lerner's real embedded short story. As in *Memories of the Future*, according to a metafictional logic, some characters in *10:04* display an awareness of the narrator's status as a writer: "I don't want what we're doing to just end up as notes for a novel" (137). Passages like these not only emphasize the splitting of the narrative voice—that of the narrator and her younger self, in

Memories of the Future, or that of the narrator and his imagined self, in *10:04*—they also inevitably evoke the very nature of autofiction: one real self and one invented self projected into a novel by a real self, a novel that is also, in the cases discussed here at least, strongly inspired by, even based on the author's life. We will see below that the switch between tenses in both texts further reinforces this perception of narrative complexity and generates an isotopy of division, of estrangement.

Time, Tenses, and the Fallibility of Memory

Mimicking the chronological progression of traditional autobiographical form, autofiction is normally retrospective, an older self remembering or revisiting their past life. For Lejeune, this forms part of his definition of autobiography: "we call 'autobiography' the retrospective prose narrative of someone's own existence" (1971, 14; my translation).[7] In autofiction, it is more precise to speak of an older self projecting himself or herself into an imaginary past. While Hustvedt complies with this narrative rule, Lerner offers a different, prospective version. Indeed, modeling his novel on autofiction's principle of projection, he builds his narrative not only on the concept of everything being, in the future, "as it is now, just a little different," but also on the idea of "projecting [himself] into the future" (2014, 109), a phrase which, similar to the Hassidic story, is repeated throughout the novel—for instance: "I'll project myself into several futures simultaneously" (4)—and represents the narrative trigger of many passages such as the following one: "I imagined trying to explain all of this to a future child [...]" (91). However, despite this distinction between Hustvedt's traditionally retrospective narrative (the title of which paradoxically seems to imply the opposite) and Lerner's prospective one, nothing fundamentally changes: indeed, both are narrated *after the fact*, in a timeframe when the past can be reimagined as autofiction. Lerner projects himself into a future which he has already imagined when he starts narrating it. The narrative can be prospective, but the narrating act is always retrospective (it narrates what has happened, or what the author has imagined). In a fashion typical of any life narrative (even those that encompass only a particular period), *Memories of the Future* and *10:04* hinge on two periods, the past and the present, classically embodied by the *narrated* I and the *narrating* I. This is a narrative configuration that autofiction has widely embraced in its attempt to resemble autobiography, sometimes as closely as possible. Our two case studies do not depart from this rule, enhancing this ontological duality by implementing recurring tense shifts, mostly from past to present tense and vice versa. Below are just a few examples:

10:04: "We sat and watched the traffic and I am kidding and I am not kidding when I say that I intuited an alien intelligence [...]" (Lerner 2014, 3); "I want to say I felt stoned, did say to Alex [...]" (19); "When the workers had moved on to Creeley's house and I could read—I can only read if it's quiet, but I can write against noise [...]" (173); "They looked two-dimensional, like cardboard cutouts in a stagecraft foreground. Lower Manhattan was black behind us, its densities intuitive. The fireworks celebrating the completion of the bridge exploded above us in 1883, spidering out across the page. The moon is high in the sky and you can see its light on the water." (239)

Memories of the Future: "I remember the eerie illumination that came through the broken blinds the first night I slept in apartment 2B on August 25" (Hustvedt 2019, 4); "I am still in New York, but the city I lived in then is not the city I inhabit now" (10); "Were you disappointed, Fanny? Maybe you didn't care? It seems I like girls more in my fantasies than in real life" (155–156); "They cross the street in our past but in their present and, as they walk, I adopt the present tense because you and I are with them now. It is May 17, 1979 [...]." (211)

These tense shifts emphasize the chronological and ontological separation of events and narration, thus undermining the credibility of these facts as they put the stress on distance rather than accuracy. Even if many authors of memoirs proceed in a similar fashion, questioning their ability to remember properly by drawing the reader's attention as much to the present of narration as to the past narrative, in memoirs such challenges to the narrative itself nevertheless take place within the framework of a reading contract that claims commitment to sincerity, if not accuracy. Autofiction undercuts this commitment, at times even ridiculing it. For doing so, it uses the same rhetorical strategy as autobiography, namely, focusing on the doubling of the authorial presence in the text, but in an autofictional context this distance has a stronger impact and resonance, as autofiction thrives on the kind of ambiguity that can emerge from the distance between narrated and narrating self. The same can be said regarding the fallibility of memory.

Memories of the Future resorts to the modern autobiographical trope of confessing to the flaws of one's memory more than *10:04*. As we see in texts such as *The Shaking Woman or A History of My Nerves* and many recent interviews,[8] Siri Hustvedt is well aware of recent cognitive research on memory. There are countless studies on the limits of mnemonic capacity, from landmark texts such as Christopher Chabris and Daniel Simons's *The Invisible Gorilla* (2011) to more recent research such as Mark Rowlands's *Memory and the Self*. Rowlands sums up the irony of memory's limitations: "But by the time you need memory the most, it is beginning to become clear just how unreliable this faculty is. And it isn't going to get any better—quite the contrary, in fact. As a general rule of thumb: the more important memory becomes in your life, the less you can or should rely on it" (2017, 6). Hustvedt integrates this knowledge into her autofiction by making her older narrating "I" constantly lament her limited ability to remember:

> If you are one of those readers who relishes memoirs filled with impossibly specific memories, I have this to say: those authors who claim perfect recall of their hash browns decades later are not to be trusted. (3)
> The past is fragile, as fragile as bones grown brittle with age [...]. (13)
> I have no memory of Wanda [a person mentioned in her journal]. (17)
> I have pictures in my mind that have lasted, but their accuracy is something I can't vouch for. (77)
> I can't recover the now of it. It is a withered now. (91)
> But what do I actually remember? [...] I find bits and pieces of recollections in various modes that have no particular order [...]. (93)

I have argued elsewhere (Schmitt 2011) that "coming clean" about the limitations of our mnemonic efforts and still attempting to build a self-narrative is not a contradiction, and that this is more or less what we have to do every day. However, the complexities of the process of remembering and its flawed results remain an oft-cited *raison d'être* of autofiction. Gasparini emphasized this aspect when he stated that disrupting "the representation of the time of memory in fiction and autobiography" by "constantly confronting one's personal history with mnemonic capacities" (2004, 229; my translation)[9] is part of autofiction's own history. Autofictionists are often suspicious of autobiography on account of the latter's perceived overreliance on memory's ability to conjure up accurate memories. This suspicion is part and parcel of autofiction's ethos and Hustvedt repeatedly taps into it to undermine her narrator's authority.

Apostrophe

As mentioned earlier, the common denominator between metafiction and autofiction is the will to navigate in the same text through several narrative layers. This hermeneutical navigation can be *descending*, that is to say, shifting from the frame narrative to the first embedded narrative, then to the next one and so on. In cases of *ascending* frames, characters might meet their author in a metaleptic upward move (although in this case, it can also be said that the author is descending into her fiction). This ascending movement normally allows readers to zoom out and embrace all the ins and outs of the text they are reading, its narrative hierarchy, in other words. One ancient way of zooming out is the apostrophe, an actor or coryphaeus directly addressing the audience, putting an end to or temporarily suspending their immersion. A modern version of the apostrophe is when the narrator of a work of fiction directly addresses readers, a device which is quite common (one can find many examples in Sterne's *Tristram Shandy*, for instance). The effect is slightly different, however, in an autofictional text. In this case, the apostrophe is a way of refocusing the reader's attention on the matter of different narrative times and on the identity of an addressee who may or may not be the author, in other words, on the context and intent of narration and its ambiguities.

Apostrophes are abundant in both texts:

Memories of the Future: "At least a year after the book you are reading now ends […]" (Hustvedt 2019, 118); "Tell me why I need you with me as my fellow traveler, my variously dear and crotchety other, my spouse for the book's duration. Why is it that I can feel your stride beside me as I write?" (128); "I need you as my intimate witness because without you, none of my stories will be real" (129); "Do not be misled. These stories are not extraneous to the question at hand" (181); "We all suffer and we all die, but you, the person who is reading this book right now, you are not dead yet. I may be dead, but you are not" (294); "I am going to tell you a secret now: There is a doctor in this story, but she arrives much later, well after the millennium has ended." (301)

10:04: "You might have seen us walking on Atlantic, tears streaming down her face, my arm around her shoulder […]" (Lerner 2014, 8); "Do you know what I mean if I say that when I reached the second floor […]" (14); "You might have seen me sitting there on the bench that midnight […]" (109); "Reader, we walked on" (234); "[…] maybe you saw me" (235); "[…] my book—not the one I was contracted to write about fraudulence, but the one I've written in its place for you, to you, on the very edge of fiction." (237)

Apostrophe is not a primary feature of autofiction, but drawing attention to the intersubjective nature of literary communication, emphasizing how meaning is built jointly by both narrator and addressee, fittingly serves autofiction's purpose to position a text "on the very edge of fiction," as Lerner's narrator claims is true for his writing, or at least on *a* narrative edge where authors can suddenly surface, confess to or lie about the nature of their text, and thereby sow the necessary seeds of doubt within the minds of their readers. Edges, limits, and boundaries are constituent parts of the topology of autofiction: "Unlike memoir or autobiography, autofiction often depicts its author-characters in clearly fictional situations, thus blurring the already hazy *boundaries* between fiction and nonfiction" (Worthington 2018, 2–3; my emphasis). For some theorists, like Lejeune, for instance, these boundaries are not "hazy" at all, but autofiction's very existence depends on creating an ambivalence. To exist as autofictions, to be seen as autofictional, these novels cannot content themselves with being only "primarily novels." They must also exist as *something else*, as potentially autobiographical, to be specific. Referring to controversial French autofictions such as Guibert's, Angot's, or Millet's, and their "outpouring of resentment and orgasms that can only create a neurotic atmosphere,"[10] Claire Debru went as far as claiming that "autofiction is born of neurosis" (2007, 54; my translation).[11] Being constantly on the edge in order to exist does also create, to some extent, a form of neurosis.

* * *

It has been the purpose of this chapter to show how these two autofictional texts "straddle the line," both rhetorically and stylistically, from a practical point of view. Indeed, if a "consensus definition of autofiction has become virtually impossible" (Mortimer 2009, 22), we should now focus less on deciding what autofiction is and more on what it means concretely, textually, for an author to project himself or herself into a text without an autobiographical pact. I have argued that there are some primary features without which autofiction does not exist and that it relies moreover on a series of tropes—enhancers, as I have called them. How these contribute to the interpretation of an ambiguous text by readers as autofiction might be the most important aspect of autofictional studies right now.

Autofiction has always been energized by an unresolved authenticity/sincerity dialectic. This dialectic is based on Lionel Trilling's (1972) *Sincerity and Authenticity* and especially on how Trilling conceives of authenticity, namely, "as something inward, personal, and hidden, the goal primarily of self-expression rather than other-directed communication" (Kelly 2010, 132) and tries to reassess the value of sincerity, especially in an autobiographical context. Autofiction, definitely leaning toward sincerity, albeit a sincerity that is in no way connected to accuracy, aims to produce an autobiographical *intent* without clearly identifying the autobiographical *content*, and the stylistic and rhetorical skills employed in the effort are worthy of scholarly investigation. Autofiction is not a case of split personality, but clearly one of split narration: the pronoun used by the author to refer to himself or herself, whether it is the first-person singular or the third, points in two directions that are hard to reconcile. It conjures up Dorrit Cohn's "disjunctive model" (1999, 126), the fundamental difference between narrator and author, which, for autofiction to make any sense, must somehow be or appear to be "rejoined." I have tried to demonstrate how two different authors have resorted to similar conjunctional means to bridge this gap—but not fully—and to bring to light their use of specific rhetorical tools, some essential, others secondary (enhancers), to create what I have called a sense of the autofictional.

Notes

1. "While in French and other Francophone literatures, the main focus remains on the endless discussion regarding truth, fact and fiction, the real and the 'made up,' other world literature stakeholders turn away from this debate and instead look for an answer on how to live and how to create, not on how to truthfully write how one lives" (Ferreira-Meyers 2018, 33).
2. See, for instance, Judith Shulevitz's review of *Memories of the Future* in *The New York Times* or Stephanie Bishop's (2015) piece on *10:04* in *The Sydney Review of Books*.
3. "[l]e texte est ainsi saturé par des signes de conjonction et de disjonction des deux instances."
4. "Dès ses origines, le double mouvement d'aveu et de déni est constitutif du roman autobiographique."
5. "I, the author, am going to tell you a story in which I am the hero, but which never happened to me" ("Moi, auteur, je vais vous raconter une histoire dont je suis le héros, mais qui ne m'est jamais arrivée"; Genette 1991, 86).

6. "Pourquoi ne pas admettre qu'il existe, outre les nom et prénom, toute une série d'opérateurs d'identification du héros avec l'auteur: leur âge, leur milieu socioculturel, leur profession, leurs aspirations, etc.?"
7. "Définition: nous appelons 'autobiographie' le récit rétrospectif en prose que quelqu'un fait de sa propre existence."
8. See, for instance, https://www.youtube.com/watch?v=MsbxlNyb7hE or https://www.youtube.com/watch?v=pzeMsrwOtJg
9. "la représentation du temps mémoriel dans le roman et dans l'autobiographie"; "en confrontant constamment l'histoire personnelle aux capacités de la mémoire."
10. "[…] le grand déballage de rancœurs et d'orgasmes ne peut qu'exhaler un climat névrotique […]."
11. "C'est bien dans la névrose que naît l'autofiction."

Works Cited

Bishop, Stephanie. 2015. The Same But Different: *10:04* by Ben Lerner. *The Sydney Review of Books*, February 6, 2015.
Chabris, Christopher, and Daniel Simons. 2011. *The Invisible Gorilla, and Other Ways our Intuition Deceives Us*. London: HarperCollins.
Cohn, Dorrit. 1999. *The Distinction of Fiction*. Baltimore: Johns Hopkins University Press.
Colonna, Vincent. 2004. *Autofiction et autres mythomanies littéraires*. Paris: Tristram.
Couturier, Maurice. 1995. *La Figure de l'auteur*. Paris: Éditions du Seuil.
Debru, Claire. 2007. Névrose de l'autofiction. *Revue des deux mondes* 2 (February): 43–64.
Dix, Hywel, ed. 2018. Introduction: Autofiction in English: The Story so Far. In *Autofiction in English*, ed. Hywel Dix, 1–23. Cham: Palgrave Macmillan.
Ferreira-Meyers, Karen. 2018. Does Autofiction Belong to French or Francophone Authors and Readers Only? In *Autofiction in English*, ed. Hywel Dix, 27–48. Cham: Palgrave Macmillan.
Gasparini, Philippe. 2004. *Est-il je?* In *Paris: Éditions du Seuil*.
Genette, Gérard. 1991. *Fiction et diction*. Paris: Éditions du Seuil.
Hustvedt, Siri. 2008. *The Sorrows of an American*. London: Sceptre.
———. 2009. *The Shaking Woman or a History of My Nerves*. New York: Henry Holt and Company.
———. 2019. *Memories of the Future*. London: Sceptre.
Kelly, Adam. 2010. David Foster Wallace and the New Sincerity in American Fiction. In *Consider David Foster Wallace: Critical Essays*, ed. David Hering, 131–146. Austin, TX: SSMG Press.
Lejeune, Philippe. 1971. *L'Autobiographie en France*. Paris: Armand Colin.

Lerner, Ben. 2011. *Leaving the Atocha Station*. London: Granta.
———. 2014. *10:04*. London: Granta.
———. 2019. *The Topeka School*. London: Granta.
Mortimer, Armine Kotin. 2009. Autofiction as Allofiction: Doubrovsky's 'L'Après-vivre'. *L'Esprit Créateur* 49 (3): 22–35.
Rowlands, Mark. 2017. *Memory and the Self: Phenomenology, Science and Autobiography*. Oxford: Oxford University Press.
Schmitt, Arnaud. 2011. Making the Case for Self-Narration against Autofiction. *a/b: Auto/Biography Studies* 25 (2): 122–137.
———. 2020. Avatars as the Raison d'Être of Autofiction. *Life Writing*, published online April 27, 2020. https://doi.org/10.1080/14484528.2020.1753486.
Shulevitz, Judith. 2019. Was That Really Me? A Novelist Discovers Her Younger Self. *The New York Times*, March 26, 2019.
Trilling, Lionel. 1972. *Sincerity and Authenticity*. Cambridge: Harvard University Press.
Turner, Jenny. 2012. *Leaving the Atocha Station* by Ben Lerner—Review. *The Guardian*, July 12, 2012.
Waugh, Patricia. 1984. *Metafiction, The Theory and Practice of Self-Conscious Fiction*. London, Routledge.
Worthington, Marjorie. 2018. *The Story of "Me": Contemporary American Autofiction*. Lincoln, NE: University of Nebraska Press.

Open Access This chapter is licensed under the terms of the Creative Commons Attribution 4.0 International License (http://creativecommons.org/licenses/by/4.0/), which permits use, sharing, adaptation, distribution and reproduction in any medium or format, as long as you give appropriate credit to the original author(s) and the source, provide a link to the Creative Commons licence and indicate if changes were made.

The images or other third party material in this chapter are included in the chapter's Creative Commons licence, unless indicated otherwise in a credit line to the material. If material is not included in the chapter's Creative Commons licence and your intended use is not permitted by statutory regulation or exceeds the permitted use, you will need to obtain permission directly from the copyright holder.

CHAPTER 6

The Autofictional in Serial, Literary Works

Ricarda Menn and Melissa Schuh

> *Other thoughts were coming up, the thoughts and calculations she had not meant to make, but they rushed forward, and there was something extraordinary behind them, something that was part of the sky, of her own particular sky as she knew it.*
> —(Richardson 1921, 13–14)

Reflecting on her mental processes, Miriam, the autobiographical protagonist of Dorothy Richardson's *PILGRIMAGE*[1] (first published between 1915 and 1935), recognizes something unique in her thoughts and likens it to "her own particular sky" (1921, 14). This description continues to present her perceptions as shifting till the sky "was just the flat sky of everyday, part of London; with nothing particular to say" (14), suggesting

---

R. Menn (✉)
Institute for Advanced Study in the Humanities (KWI), Essen, Germany
e-mail: ricarda.menn@kwi-nrw.de

M. Schuh
Christian-Albrechts-University Kiel, Kiel, Germany
e-mail: schuh@anglistik.uni-kiel.de

© The Author(s) 2022
A. Effe, H. Lawlor (eds.), *The Autofictional*, Palgrave Studies in Life Writing, https://doi.org/10.1007/978-3-030-78440-9_6

an introspective focus on individual subjectivity that is aligned with the purpose of representing a complex sense of self. Autobiographical and autofictional texts may both aim to do so, but Serge Doubrovsky, who coined the term *autofiction* in the 1970s, emphasizes complexity in the sense of lack of unity as specific to autofiction:

> Unlike autobiography, which explains and unifies, which wants to get hold of and unravel the threads of someone's destiny, autofiction doesn't perceive someone's life to be a whole. It is only concerned with separate fragments, with broken up chunks of existence, and a divided subject who doesn't coincide with him or herself. (Doubrovsky 1999, back cover, translated by and quoted in Jones 2010, 176)

Doubrovsky's emphasis on a fragmented self that requires fictionalization is significant. As E.H. Jones notes in her article on the history of autofiction as a neologism, Doubrovsky proposes "a work in which author, protagonist and narrator all bore the same name, but which did not make the simple truth claims of conventional autobiography" (2010, 176). Doubrovsky's process of fictionalization emphasizes a distinction between content and form as, respectively, factual and fictional. In a slightly different manner, Gérard Genette describes the contradiction inherent in autofictional writing as "It is I and it is not I" (1993, 77), a paradox which attests to the play with homology and alterity at work in autofictional narratives. In disentangling these diverse approaches to autofiction, Jones stresses that "[a]utofiction, as opposed to autobiography, then, is highly attuned with an age in which the subject is no longer accepted to be a unified, simple whole" (2010, 177). In response to conventions of autobiographical unity, autofiction fictionalizes the narrated self and thus promotes a sense of unstable subjectivity. Crucially, this non-linear conception of the self, which constitutes what we call an autofictional sense of self, structures serially published life narratives. In this context, seriality is a largely understudied phenomenon: Nicole Stamant (2014) has investigated twentieth-century serial memoirs by American authors as enabling a textual space for self-archivization, and Ricarda Menn (2018) considers seriality in John Burnside's autofictions. Usually consisting of more than two installments, serial works disrupt demands on autobiographical singularity and textual closure. A sense of deliberate multiplicity in representing the self tends to emerge from more than two texts. Multi-volume self-narratives oppose a view of autobiography as "a genre of last words" (Gilmore 2001, 96) and instead present the narrated self as potentially open-ended, subject to reinterpretation and contradictions. Autofictional and serial life narratives thus both transgress and experiment with autobiography's generic conventions.

Western autobiography has traditionally been the domain of "great men," telling their stories with claims to the significance of exemplary lives, invoking truth, confession, and the totality of the entire life (from childhood to old age). St. Augustine's *Confessions* (published between 397 and 401) is often regarded as a precursor of modern autobiography, but the term was coined only in the late eighteenth century (*OED Online*, n.d.). Individual spiritual accounts, such as conversion narratives, indicate autobiography's Christian roots in the practice of confession. Owing to the history of the autobiographical canon as adhering to formal conventions of non-fiction while representing the lives of prominent men, traditional autobiography has also had a privileged standing within life writing discourse and criticism. James Olney observes that "in the works of three authors one can trace the central line of life writing in the Western world. St. Augustine, Jean-Jacques Rousseau and Samuel Beckett: each of them is crucial; no others are necessary" (Olney 1997, 554). This statement illustrates the canonical weight ascribed to dominant examples of white male autobiographical writing in the study of life writing. Many critics have asserted that the established canon of autobiography reflects hierarchies of power which neglect the voices of minorities, whose experiences differ from this pattern of telling a prominent man's exemplary life. As a form of representation that counters autobiographical norms and departs from autobiography's supposed unity and literary prestige, autofictional texts undermine established conceptions of autobiography. The same holds for serial forms of life writing. Autofictional, serial forms offer a discontinuous rather than unified sense of the self through the foregrounding of fictionality and by deferring textual closure with a serial exploration of the self.

We conceive of serial, literary autofictions as an experimental form of life narrative. In this context, the autofictional mode juxtaposes imagined and referential dimensions contributing to self-representation. Strategies of fictionalization and creative self-invention characterize different manifestations of the autofictional. As it is predominantly literary, professional authors who write and publish such texts, we argue that an insistence on the literary and aesthetic capacities for self-narrativization is integral to this mode of self-presentation. The use of multi-volume publication for doing so entails a sense of self that is unfinished, contingent, and subject to revision.

As serial autofiction already encompasses a degree of experimentation in its serial representation of life and self as well as its crossing of autobiographical and fictional frames of reference, the additional qualification of literary serial autofiction might appear superfluous at best, and unnecessarily exclusionary at worst. Literariness, or the literary, invites similar criticism to autobiography in terms of its evaluative and possibly normative sense of innovation and value. This is not to say that all autofiction has to be literary or that non-professional authors who are less established or earn their living primarily from other ventures—such as celebrities including politicians, athletes, and actors—may not engage in aesthetically challenging forms of self-presentation. However, the combination of the serial, the literary, and the autofictional occurs dominantly with established authors. Melissa Schuh (2020) discusses the literary in autobiography along similar lines, considering expectations of innovation and late style in the works of established novelists. Autofictions are often written by established authors, which implies the literary in two dimensions. The first relates to the image and authorial performance of writers, who tend to fashion themselves and/or be styled by others as a professional author, thus evoking expectations of literary skill and value. The second dimension encompasses the degree and kind of experimentation that an autofictional text displays in order to communicate a particular autobiographical act. Seriality underpins both dimensions of literary life writing. Professional writers may use techniques of serialization to present narratively complex self-representations. This can include novels that contain only some autobiographical references or distinctly self-reflexive works that more explicitly evoke an autobiographical context and showcase their fictionality. The autofictional describes such literary endeavors of experimenting with the self and is enhanced by the serial publication of several installments.

The discourse surrounding serially expansive works of autofiction is dominated by male authors—exemplified by Karl Ove Knausgaard's *MY STRUGGLE* (first published between 2009 and 2011) serial spanning over 4000 pages—although women writers too (e.g. Rachel Cusk, Olivia Laing, or Sheila Heti) engage in both extensive and serial self-representation. To balance a discussion that tends to be weighted heavily toward male authors, we showcase serial, literary autofiction by women, specifically Dorothy Richardson, Doris Lessing, and Rachel Cusk. While Marcel Proust's canonical, semi-autobiographical novel *À LA*

RECHERCHE DU TEMPS PERDU (first published between 1913 and 1927) continues to be named as a prominent example of autofiction, Richardson's *PILGRIMAGE* remains an under-discussed multi-volume modernist example of autobiographical writing. Nevertheless, recent scholarly attention has resulted in the publication of an *Oxford Edition of the Works of Dorothy Richardson* (2020), which foregrounds aesthetic inconsistencies within and across *PILGRIMAGE*'s volumes as part of Richardson's experimental style. This edition highlights *PILGRIMAGE* as an unfinished series of developing experiments but is not primarily concerned with its generic hybridity and seriality. Our consideration of *PILGRIMAGE* as a modern precursor to serial, literary autofictions will show how modernist techniques, such as stream-of-consciousness narration, can contribute to an autofictional sense of the self, namely, of the self as fictionalized, contingent, and complex. Although Lessing's fiction has garnered significant attention, most notably *The Golden Notebook* (1962) as a feminist and postmodern novel, her experiment with diverse serializing strategies in her autobiographically informed texts, which we will discuss as autofictional, has so far received less critical attention than the work of prominent male contemporaries also engaging in serialized and fictionalized self-writing, such as Philip Roth and J.M. Coetzee. While not completely on par with the fame of Knausgaard's *MY STRUGGLE* series, Cusk's *OUTLINE* serial has attracted ample attention as autofiction, but her experiments with subjectivity through externalization and her use of serialization have not yet been explored.

We illustrate generic and narrative specificities of literary, serial autofiction, and discuss diachronic precursors. By considering how serial publication enhances autofictional experimentation, we also show its unique narrative and aesthetic affordances. Specifically, we showcase the interconnection of serial publication and serializing narrative techniques. In doing so, we argue that serial, literary autofictions denominate a fruitfully distinct sub-category within the wider field of autofiction. Reading related works as serially connected rather than as individual, stand-alone texts has new ramifications for the study of such texts. It highlights overarching developments, including cross-connections and different degrees in shaping self-representation and fictionalization. Similarly, conceiving of the autofictional as a mode rather than a generic absolute enables a view on different constellations across an oeuvre, such as autofictional themes, autobiographical alter egos, strategies of experimenting with subjectivity, and changing perceptions of the self and its experiences. A focus on serial and literary techniques and affordances offers a new approach to autofictional writing that acknowledges a writer's oeuvre as a dynamic site of self-expression rather than a unified and closed whole.

SERIAL CHAPTERS: DOROTHY RICHARDSON

Richardson's *PILGRIMAGE* comprises a sequence of 12 novels published during her lifetime: *Pointed Roofs* (1915), *Backwater* (1916), *Honeycomb* (1917), *The Tunnel* (1919), *Interim* (1920), *Deadlock* (1921), *Revolving Lights* (1922), *The Trap* (1925), *Oberland* (1928), *Dawn's Left Hand* (1931), *Clear Horizon* (1935), and *Dimple Hill* (1938). A 13th, unfinished volume titled *March Moonlight* was published posthumously in 1967. *PILGRIMAGE* is interpreted as incomplete; Adam Guy and Scott McCracken have described it as "consciously a work in progress" (2020, 112). The author herself considered *PILGRIMAGE*'s volumes as chapters of a whole rather than conventional installments in a series (as noted in Hanscombe 1979, 1 and Guy and McCracken 2020, 112). *PILGRIMAGE* recounts the experiences of Miriam Hendersen, who functions as an alter ego for Richardson. While Richardson herself resisted autobiographical interpretations of Miriam as an explicit alter ego by concealing personal biographical information about herself during her lifetime (Winning 1998, 215) and stating "I am not Miriam" to the editor Edward Garnett (Garnett 1924, 12, as quoted in Guy and McCracken 2020, 117), *PILGRIMAGE* has been read both as a novel and as a form of autobiographical writing. We propose that the blurring of recognizable autobiographical experience with fictional elements makes the novel sequence autofictional. Although the use of a differently named protagonist underlines the conceptualization of the text first and foremost as a novel, Miriam's life bears such an undeniable resemblance to Richardson's that critics have remarked on the importance of reading Richardson's life in combination with *PILGRIMAGE*. Gloria Fromm notes in her biography of Richardson: "it would seem that in Dorothy Richardson's case at least, the critic and the biographer must truly join forces" (1994, xvii). Joanne Winning posits that "the text of *PILGRIMAGE* is founded upon a fundamental slippage between autobiography and fiction" (1998, 213).

Reading *PILGRIMAGE* as an early example of autofictional experimentation entails an acknowledgment of how life and art are entangled in an ongoing process of writing and rewriting. Therefore, to see it as an experimental and incomplete work in progress is essential to its interpretation. *PILGRIMAGE* has been perceived as experimental in terms of formal innovation from the time of its publication, and critics have remarked on the serial dimension of its formal experiments. As Guy and McCracken argue, *PILGRIMAGE* shows "the particularity of individual experiments rather than a vague essence of 'experimentalism'" (2020, 111; original emphasis). Rather than being experimental for engaging in "modernist aesthetics in general," *PILGRIMAGE* offers a series of different experiments in narrating Miriam's experiences and self (111). Guy and McCracken's emphasis on the plural and serial dimension of Richardson's experiment with *PILGRIMAGE* supports a consideration of its serial strategies.

Autofiction is associated with a sense of innovation with regard to the representation of self, life, and authorship. In this context, it is significant that, as the first published English example of an exclusive stream-of-consciousness style of narration, *Pointed Roofs* (the first volume of *PILGRIMAGE*) renders Miriam's experiences with an unprecedented commitment to the protagonist's perspective. *PILGRIMAGE* as a whole reflects her views, thoughts, and perceptions, without the obvious intervention of an external narrator or other focalizers. The narrative adopts Miriam's perspective through heterodiegetic third-person narration and internal focalization, and some sections exclusively narrate her thoughts:

> It was a fool's errand. ... To undertake to go to the German school and teach ... to be going there ... with nothing to give. The moment would come when there would be a class sitting round a table waiting for her to speak. She imagined one of the rooms at the old school, full of scornful girls. ... How was English taught? How did you begin? English grammar ... in German? Her heart beat in her throat. She had never thought of that ... the rules of English grammar? (Richardson 2002, 28)

On the train journey to starting work as a teacher at a German school in Hanover, Miriam is confronted by doubts about her undertaking. She imagines herself exposed to her students' "scornful" ridicule in a classroom like those at her old school and voices insecurity about teaching English, particularly English grammar. Richardson's use of incomplete sentences and punctuation to reflect ellipses in Miriam's thoughts highlights the fragmented form of the protagonist's train of thought typographically. The stream-of-consciousness narration privileges and individualizes Miriam's perspective, and challenges the reader to follow and make sense of Miriam's views without the guidance of a narrator's metaperspective.

Guy and McCracken suggest that "Richardson's aim was for an open design marked by gaps and silences that grant the reader a collaborative role in the creation of the narrative" (2020, 113). Similarly, Annika J. Lindskog argues that Richardson elicits "the reader's cooperation" in the creation of the literary work, so "that the ellipses and commas function as visual components of the literary work, representing and illustrating thought-processes and states of mind that are essentially non-verbal" (2014, 7). *PILGRIMAGE*'s experimental style encourages readerly engagement with the representation of a mind—and, by extension, a life—and showcases the narrative construction of lived experience as a difficult and ongoing process. As exemplified in Richardson's use of ellipses, Miriam's experience is complex and challenging to follow. Her perspective is represented through a fragmented, associative narrative structure, suggesting that a life should be perceived in its fleeting and jarring facets, thus differing from traditional autobiographical tropes of unity and coherence. Furthermore, the displacement of this perspective onto an alter ego and the fictionalized representation of impressions and thought processes contribute to the autofictional dimension of the novel sequence. This combination of experimental renderings of individual perspective and fictionalization of autobiographical experience constitutes an autofictional approach to self-presentation.

This autofictional strategy of experimentation and fictionalization is furthered by *PILGRIMAGE*'s conception as a series of chapters. John Mepham has remarked on how Richardson's style in *PILGRIMAGE* was perceived as "unreadable" by contemporaries owing to its experimentation, suggesting that her formal experiments might have been received more in line with other modernist classics, such as James Joyce's *Ulysses* (1920) and Virginia Woolf's *Mrs Dalloway* (1925), had the first three volumes been published as "a separate work" (2000, 451). In comparison to Joyce's and Woolf's more generally experimentalist writing, Richardson undertakes an explicitly autofictional series of experiments with *PILGRIMAGE*. The shifts in style between volumes reflect how the perspective on a life may change, depending on the writing moment, creating in these serial parts an autofictional sense of the self as contingent, changing, and multi-faceted. This autofictional sense of the self relies on the creative use of fictionality to enable an ongoing invention and re-invention of the self. Rather than simply reflecting the broader experience and perception of modern life, *PILGRIMAGE* renders an autofictional self through fictionalization and serial, ongoing, and incomplete experimentation.

PILGRIMAGE contains self-conscious reflections on truth and the process of writing, which is a common characteristic of much autofiction, and especially prominent in literary autofiction. In *Deadlock*, Miriam observes gender-based differences in thinking, speaking, and writing:

> These afterthoughts always came, answering the man's phrase; but they had not prevented his description from coming up always now together with any thoughts about the house. There was a truth in it, but not anything of the whole truth. It was like a photograph … it made you see the slatternly servant and the house and the dreadful looking people going in and out. Clever phrases that make you see things by a deliberate arrangement, leave an impression that is false to life. But men do see life in this way, disposing of things and rushing on with their talk; they think like that, all their thoughts false to life; everything neatly described in single phrases that are not true. Starting with a false statement they go on piling up their books. That man never saw how extraordinary it was that there should be anybody, waiting for anything. But why did their clever phrases keep on coming up in one's mind? (Richardson 1921, 5)

Miriam judges men's "clever phrases" as deliberately arranged and "false to life." She compares a man's description to a carefully composed photograph, suggesting that the resulting impression contains some truth "but not anything of the whole truth." *PILGRIMAGE*'s representation of Miriam's mind and experiences provides a countervoice to the male discourse that Miriam criticizes here. Instead of offering "everything neatly described in single phrases," Miriam's thoughts are represented in a seemingly unedited stream, shifting back and forth between impressions, associations, and topics:

> Some clue had been missed. There was something incomplete in the thought that had come just now and seemed so convincing. She turned back and faced the self that had said one ought to meet everything in life with one's eyes on the sky. It had flashed in and out, between her thoughts. Now it seemed alien. (Richardson 1921, 13)

Although Richardson arranges Miriam's perspective just as deliberately as the male discourse described in this passage, the emphasis of this construction is on fragmentation rather than unity. Miriam describes gaps in her thoughts, recognizing "something incomplete." She perceives herself moreover in this moment as different from "the self that had said one ought to meet everything in life with one's eyes on the sky," thus conceptualizing this earlier self as changing and dependent on the present time of recollection. She also claims ownership of her impressions a few lines further by proposing the idea of "her own particular sky as she knew it" (1921, 13), rejecting a universalizing representation of individual experience. While the techniques Richardson uses to describe Miriam's life—such as stream-of-consciousness narration and excessive punctuation—are undoubtedly modernist in their rendering of perception, impression, and the mind, these strategies also serve to represent self and life as fluid and complex, which is a characteristic aim of many autofictional texts. *PILGRIMAGE*'s serial and unfinished form foregrounds life as a work in process and a series of narrative experiments, while its self-reflexive ideas about writing and truth constitute a metatextual focus on the writing life, thus providing a modernist example of both serial and literary autofiction.

A Serial Oeuvre: Doris Lessing

Doris Lessing, winner of the Nobel Prize for Literature (2007) and arguably best known for her 1962 novel *The Golden Notebook*, is an author who has written many autobiographically informed books and has experimented with different forms of multi-volume, serial publication throughout her career. She has released five explicitly autobiographical works. Two are presented as volumes of her autobiography—*Under My Skin: Volume One of My Autobiography, 1919–1949* (1994) and *Walking in the Shade: Volume Two of My Autobiography, 1949–1962* (1997)—and three without such generic designation, but with names that could apply equally well to memoirs or fictional texts: *Going Home* (1957), *African Laughter: Four Visits to Zimbabwe* (1992), and *Alfred & Emily* (2008). While the two volumes of her autobiography trace developments of her life in a linear and chronological manner, her memoirs provide more episodic insights into her relations to Africa and her family life. Alongside these, Lessing has also published a serial of five autobiographically informed novels, the *CHILDREN OF VIOLENCE* serial (first published between 1952 and 1969) centering on her authorial alter ego Martha Quest. Ángeles de la Concha observes that through these texts Lessing rewrites parts of her youth from the "vantage point of her own old age" (2016, 171). Lessing herself, in her autobiography *Walking in the Shade*, describes "Martha Quest, [her] third book," as "more or less autobiographical" (1997, 16). Lessing's writings—both her overtly autobiographical works and her novels—are characterized by recurrent narrative motifs such as the author's self-understanding as determined by her early years in Africa and reflections on crafting both her fictional and autobiographical texts.

For instance, *Walking in the Shade* presents a linear first-person account of the years 1949–1962 and includes reflections on literary authorship and the crafting of an autobiographical text:

> I have far too much material for this second volume. Nothing can be more tedious than a book of memoirs millions of words long. A little book called *In Pursuit of English*, written when I was still close to that time, will add depth and detail to those first months in London. At once, problems—literary problems. What I say in it is true enough. [...] But there is no doubt that while "true," the book is not as true as what I would write now. It is a question of tone, and that is no simple matter. That little book is more like a novel; it has the shape and pace of one. It is too well shaped for life. (Lessing 1997, 4)

In this passage we can see how Lessing's profession as a novelist determines the story of her life: she does not only refer to the experience of her arrival in London as "material" for a narrative but also stresses that one of her novels represents this period of her life. However, in this context, she also differentiates between the truth of a novel and the truth of an autobiographical account. For her, these two forms of truth are endowed with different purposes: where a novel subscribes to certain aesthetic criteria (to be "well shaped"), a life narrative seems less polished. As she mentions the abundance of material available, readers are made aware that her autobiographical writing, like her fictional style, too, is invested in shaping and arranging. Much like Richardson's commentary on men's self-fashioning style of writing, Lessing's writing also reveals its own constructedness. *Walking in the Shade* establishes intertextual connections between *In Pursuit of English* (1960) and Lessing's autobiographical volumes as well as other novels by her, such as the first installment of her Martha Quest serial. In this sense, reflections on her own literary authorship characterize her life stories and at the same time complicate clear-cut distinctions, as—despite distinct generic markers—her fictional and autobiographical accounts potentially overlap.

To a different degree, Lessing's profession as a novelist also resonates in her memoir *Alfred & Emily*. Divided into two parts, the second half of this text is more conventionally (auto)biographical in narrating the life of her parents, but the first part shows Lessing imagining an alternative life for them—one in which the First World War did not take place. Dorothee Birke reads this scenario as "counterfactual," given that Lessing sketches and fictionalizes an alternative reality (2015, 141). This deliberate fictionalizing can be seen as emblematic of an ongoing probing of different forms of representation which characterizes Lessing's autobiographical oeuvre. Ranging from travel memoir (*Going Home* and *African Laughter*) to fictionalizing her parent's biography or inserting herself as an authorial alter ego in the Martha Quest novels, Lessing's experimentation with different forms of autobiography chimes with the skepticism and ambivalence toward autobiographical unity that is characteristic of much autofictional writing. This disavowal of autobiographical unity is reflected moreover in her use of serial forms, which similarly undermines a sense of a stable, textually unified self.

In his consideration of the economic interconnections of seriality and mass media, Roger Hagedorn points out how "the serial proper" centers on "the narrative developed in one episode [which] interlocks with previous and subsequent episodes, on the basis of a play of unresolved narrative questions" (1988, 7). This interlocking does not only imply several installments but also that the "break" (7) between distinct episodes is a moment of suspense and a commercial factor ensuring the consumption of the ongoing serial. What is crucial in Hagedorn's account is that, even though he focuses primarily on the serial proper and its medial affordances for economic purposes, he offers two variants of it: "serialized publication of lengthy narratives in relatively self-sufficient episodes or chapters [...] [in which] the narrative structure is unaffected by its mode of presentation" (8), and, in contrast, "series of independent, complete episodes which interrelate through the use of recurring characters and a basic diegetic situation, but not in terms of any overall narrative structure" (8). However, Lessing's two-volume autobiography—*Under My Skin: Volume One of My Autobiography, 1919–1949* and *Walking in the Shade: Volume Two of My Autobiography, 1949–1962*—complicates such clear distinctions. She refers to both of these texts as "My Autobiography" in the singular, which, alongside the reference to "volumes," would initially suggest the serialization of one text. This is underscored by chronological linearity—the years up to 1949 are covered in volume one and the years 1949–1962 in the second part. Yet, in contrast to the serialization of an already finished story, Lessing's two volumes illustrate a supplementary continuation, staging her autobiographical endeavor as ongoing rather than closed-off. As each volume functions as a stand-alone text, they do not constitute a serialization akin to serialized novels but rather rely on a serial connection. Lessing, in sum, not only experiments with diverse subgenres of life writing but also employs different serializing strategies. Whereas *CHILDREN OF VIOLENCE* constitutes a serial of interconnected novels, a sense of serial supplementation structures her two autobiographical volumes. Conversely, her three memoirs, offering more episodic insights into her life, appear as a temporally dispersed series. This diversity of self-referential practices constitutes an autofictional way of experimenting with conventions of autobiographical and textual unity.

Serial Episodes: Rachel Cusk

Following three memoirs—*A Life's Work* (2001), *The Last Supper* (2009), and *Aftermath* (2012)—Canadian-born, Britain-based novelist Rachel Cusk published an autofictional trilogy between 2014 and 2018. *Outline* (2014), *Transit* (2016), and *Kudos* (2018) are referred to as the *OUTLINE* trilogy by Cusk's US publisher Macmillan and paratextually labeled by a unifying cover design. The trilogy engages in a serial form of dispersing subjectivity across several parts. All three volumes follow Faye—whose name is mentioned only once in each text—as she recounts a series of conversations with people she meets on her travels, at literary festivals, or at writing workshops. The set-up of smaller, serialized segments rather than a linearly unfolding storyline thus mirrors the trilogy's form by serializing both form and content. This translates into the respective novels' chapter structures: the first volume is split into ten distinct chapters labeled with roman numerals. *Transit* and *Kudos* offer a variation: instead of numerical sub-parts, they mark the beginning of a new episode or chapter with a gap instead of a chapter heading. These two texts enhance the impression of non-connectedness between narrated episodes by only giving a minimal sub-structure to the narratives. The listing of distinct chapters and episodes across all three parts establishes neither a chronological nor a thematic connection. Despite these slight variations in chapter structures, the entire trilogy is built around serially ordered but not causally linked parts, contributing to an overall effect of narrative fragmentation.

OUTLINE has been compared to Knausgaard and his expansive *MY STRUGGLE* serial, although the serials differ considerably from one another in terms of their respective scopes and styles. Knausgaard's six volumes span over 4000 pages, Cusk's three volumes amount to fewer than 700. In a related manner, the author-narrator of Knausgaard's serial recounts his life unambiguously and in great detail, whereas Cusk's trilogy uses a more elusive, externalized, and distanced narrative perspective. Instead of directly recounting personal experiences, the first-person narrator Faye relays stories she is told by others and continually, albeit indirectly, inserts her own perspective into the account of others. In contrast to Cusk's straightforwardly autobiographical first-person account in her memoirs—each centering on an episode of the author's life, such as childbirth or divorce—the narrative style of *OUTLINE* externalizes subjectivity. Even though Faye selects and arranges the stories she receives from others, she remains elusive, or as Alison James notes in her contribution to this volume, "an impersonal, diffracted, or projected version of the narrator's own consciousness" (p. 51).

The structural make-up of *OUTLINE* illustrates what Genette considers essential to autofiction, namely, the paradoxical statement "It is I and it is not I" (1993, 77): both Cusk and Faye are middle-aged novelists, mothers of two children, and divorced. Besides the difference in their names, Cusk has two daughters whereas Faye is mother to two sons. Through the parallel structure of evoking yet undermining autobiographical reference, Faye thus appears as an autofictional alter ego of Cusk. In a passage toward the end of Outline, the externalization of events by Faye becomes further removed as Faye recounts an incident she learns about from a novelist, Anne, by subsuming Anne's perspective:

> The longer she listened to his answer, the more she felt that something fundamental was being delineated, something not about him but about her. He was describing, she realized, a distinction that seemed to grow clearer and clearer the more he talked, a distinction he stood on one side of while she, it became increasingly apparent, stood on the other. He was describing, in other words, what she herself was not: in everything he said about himself, she found in her own nature a corresponding negative. This anti-description, for want of a better way of putting it, had made something clear to her by a

reverse kind of exposition: while he talked she began to see herself as a shape, an outline, with all the detail filled in around it while the shape itself remained blank. Yet this shape, even while its content remained unknown, gave her for the first time since the incident a sense of who she now was. (Cusk 2014, 240)

Through summarizing and relaying an event she did not experience herself but only learns about from Anne, an even more indirect and remote mode of storytelling is evoked. Syntactically, this is underlined by the use of indirect speech and a complete absence of the first-person pronoun. Obvious parallels between Faye and Anne—both are divorced, novelists, teach writing in Athens, and recount conversations during their respective flights to Greece—invite a reading in which Anne functions as a textual stand-in for Faye or even a metatextual stand-in for the author Cusk. At the same time, Faye's and Anne's perspectives emerge only as a foil to the male conversation partner, which furthers the externalization of subjectivity as *OUTLINE*'s central autofictional technique. What is more, this technique here carries a distinct gender dynamic. Initially, the emergence of a female character only as the counterpart of her male pendant poses an implicit critique to a dominant conversation partner. Filtering Anne's account through Faye's voice—James describes this as a *"mise en abyme"* (this volume, p. 50)—the anti-description poses a challenge to reliability and thus questions the authority the conversation initially indicated. In this sense, the entire serial is structured around the aesthetic principle of providing only outlines of events and persons. Alongside the fragmentary chapter structure, Cusk's trilogy showcases an autofictional style that disavows textual unity by refusing linear structure and direct self-presentation. Instead, the externalization of self-description and the serializing of episodes are embraced as central techniques for autofictional self-presentation.

* * *

Serial, literary autofiction, as a specific sub-category of autofiction, displays particular narrative characteristics that promote a sense of self, life, and identity as unstable, multi-faceted, and contingent. Often written by professional authors, these texts show their formal experimentation and literary form in distinct ways, thereby illustrating how life narrative is not solely about accurate remembering but is just as dependent on fictionalization, self-imagination, and creative self-invention. Our case studies have allowed us to distinguish different kinds of serialized autofictional practice: the serialization of a life story into discrete parts (as we saw in Richardson's *PILGRIMAGE*), serials consisting of thematically and conceptually interwoven works (in Cusk's *OUTLINE*) but also series of only tangentially related works which loosely build on similar strategies and motifs (as in Lessing's narratives). In all cases, seriality destabilizes notions of self and life as unified and emphasizes life as ongoing, disjointed, and potentially subject to revision. Serial structures and forms of publication thus enhance autofictional experimentation in their foregrounding of the unstable and open-ended nature of a self and self-writing.

As our case studies from across the twentieth and twenty-first centuries show, autofictional elements may appear in various forms: for instance, in the form of texts featuring an authorial alter ego, playing with tensions of similarity and difference between autobiographical parallels and fictionalized elements, or in experimental shifts of style and aesthetic across different serial installments of self-representation. Rather than perceiving autofiction's conceptual openness as a weakness, we embrace its terminological flexibility to describe texts that voice dissatisfactions with claims of autobiographical unity. By using the adjective (autofictional) rather than the noun, we can extend the scope of the study of autofiction and consider a range of strategies and constellations that constitute experimental and literary means of self-representation. Considering several—possibly unconnected or only marginally connected—texts as part of an autofictional serial enables an extended view on textual and aesthetic continuities, developments, and literary experimentation. Serial structures in autofictional works reveal different constellations of contingency, creative revision, and the instabilities of a work in progress. In this sense, such an approach challenges the self-containment of an individual work, just as autofictional modes of self-narrativization challenge linear, unifying understandings of subjectivity.

Note

1. We use capitals to distinguish the titles of series and serials from individual texts.

Works Cited

"autobiography", n.d. The *OED Online*. March 2021. Oxford University Press. https://www.oed.com/view/Entry/13379?redirectedfrom=autobiography. Accessed Mar 30, 2021.

Birke, Dorothee. 2015. Doris Lessing's 'Alfred and Emily' and the Ethics of Narrated Memory. In *Narrated Communities, Narrated Realities: Narration as Cognitive Processing and Cultural Practice*, ed. Herrmann Blume, Christoph Leitgelb, and Michael Rössner, 141–151. Leiden: Brill Rodopi.

Cusk, Rachel. 2014. *Outline*. London: Faber & Faber.

De La Concha, Ángeles. 2016. Rewriting the Story, Restorying the Self: Doris Lessing's Experiments in Life Writing. In *Traces of Aging: Old Age and Memory in Contemporary Narrative*, ed. Marta Cerezo Moreno and Nieves Pascual Soler, 169–188. Bielefeld: Transcript.

Doubrovsky, Serge. 1999. *Laissé pour conte*. Paris: Grasset.

Fromm, Gloria. 1994. *Dorothy Richardson: A Biography*. Athens, GA: University of Georgia Press.

Garnett, Edward. 1924. Women of the Day: Miss Dorothy Richardson. *Yorkshire Post*, March 3, 1924.

Genette, Gérard. 1993. *Fiction and Diction*. Translated by Catherine Porter. Ithaca, NY: Cornell University Press. First published in French as *Fiction et diction* (Paris: Seuil, 1991).

Gilmore, Leigh. 2001. *The Limits of Autobiography: Trauma and Testimony*. Ithaca, NY: Cornell University Press.

Guy, Adam, and Scott McCracken. 2020. Editing Experiment: The New Modernist Editing and Dorothy Richardson's *Pilgrimage*. *Modernist Cultures* 15 (1): 110–131.

Hagedorn, Roger. 1988. Technology and Economic Exploitation: The Serial as a Form of Narrative Presentation. *Wide Angle* 1 (4): 4–12.

Hanscombe, Gillian E. 1979. Introduction. In *Pilgrimage 1*, ed. Dorothy Richardson, 1–7. London: Virago.

Jones, E.H. 2010. Autofiction: A Brief History of a Neologism. In *Life Writing: Essays on Autobiography, Biography and Literature*, ed. Richard Bradford, 174–184. Basingstoke: Palgrave Macmillan.

Lessing, Doris. 1997. *Walking in the Shade: Volume Two of My Autobiography, 1949–1962*. New York: Harper Collins.

Lindskog, Annika J. 2014. Dorothy Richardson and the Grammar of the Mind. *Pilgrimages: A Journal of Dorothy Richardson Studies* 6: 6–24.

Menn, Ricarda. 2018. Unpicked and Remade: Creative Imperatives in John Burnside's Autofictions. In *Autofiction in English*, ed. Hywel Dix, 163–178. Cham: Palgrave Macmillan.

Mepham, John. 2000. Dorothy Richardson's 'Unreadability': Graphic Style and Narrative Strategy in a Modernist Novel. *English Literature in Transition, 1880–1920* 43 (4): 449–464.

Olney, James. 1997. Transmogrifications of Life Writing. *The Southern Review* 33 (3): 554–604.

Richardson, Dorothy. 2002. *Pilgrimage I, Pointed Roofs*. London: Virago.

———. 2020. *The Oxford Edition of the Works of Dorothy Richardson, Volume IV: Pilgrimage 1 & 2, Pointed Roofs, Backwater*. Edited by Scott McCracken. Oxford: Oxford University Press.

———. 1921. *Deadlock*. New York: Alfred A. Knopf.

Schuh, Melissa. 2020. 'Which I presume is permitted, since we are talking about a writer': Lateness, Memory, and Imagination in Literary Autobiography. *The European Journal of Life Writing* 9: 111–130.

Stamant, Nicole. 2014. *Serial Memoir: Archiving American Lives*. Basingstoke: Palgrave Macmillan.

Winning, Joanne. 1998. '"The Past" is with me, seen anew': Biography's End in Dorothy Richardson's *Pilgrimage*. In *Writing the Lives of Writers*, ed. Warwick Gould and Thomas F. Staley, 212–223. Basingstoke: Palgrave Macmillan.

Open Access This chapter is licensed under the terms of the Creative Commons Attribution 4.0 International License (http://creativecommons.org/licenses/by/4.0/), which permits use, sharing, adaptation, distribution and reproduction in any medium or format, as long as you give appropriate credit to the original author(s) and the source, provide a link to the Creative Commons licence and indicate if changes were made.

The images or other third party material in this chapter are included in the chapter's Creative Commons licence, unless indicated otherwise in a credit line to the material. If material is not included in the chapter's Creative Commons licence and your intended use is not permitted by statutory regulation or exceeds the permitted use, you will need to obtain permission directly from the copyright holder.

PART II

Affordances

CHAPTER 7

Metanarrative Autofiction: Critical Engagement with Cultural Narrative Models

Hanna Meretoja

While the view that narrative is integral to humans' mode of making sense of the world has shaped the "narrative turn" in the humanities and social sciences since the 1980s (Ricœur 1983; Hyvärinen 2008; Meretoja 2014), in the twenty-first century society more broadly has become obsessed with narratives (see Polletta 2006; Salmon 2010; Fernandes 2017; Mäkelä & Meretoja 2022). The notion of finding one's own narrative has pervaded culture at large, and it has been put to extensive commercial use. Contemporary fiction is increasingly responding to this trend by critically reflecting on how cultural narrative models shape our lives. While metafiction (Hutcheon 1980; Waugh 1984; Currie 2014) was a key characteristic of postmodernist literature and art, an important form of self-reflexivity in contemporary literary fiction is "metanarrativity"—self-aware reflection not only on the narratives' own narrativity but also on cultural processes of narrative sense-making and on the roles that narrative practices play in our lives. This is particularly salient in autofictional writing, which centers

H. Meretoja (✉)
University of Turku, Turku, Finland
e-mail: hailme@utu.fi

on the relationship between the real and the imaginary, life and its narrativization.[1]

To date, metanarratives have been studied from two different perspectives. First, the term "metanarrative" is used in critical theory, particularly in connection to postmodernism, predominantly with reference to what Jean-François Lyotard (1979) called "grand narratives" (*grands récits*)— master narratives that seek to offer legitimation through the anticipated completion of a master idea (such as narratives of Marxism and the Enlightenment). It is misleading, however, to call Lyotardian master narratives "metanarratives" because the prefix "meta-" suggests that they are narratives *about* narratives. Master narratives, in contrast, mask their own narrativity. Second, metanarrativity (or metanarrative commentary) is a narratological term for self-reflexive narration in which the narrators reflect on their own process of narration (see, e.g., Fludernik 1996, 2003; Neumann and Nünning 2014; Macrae 2019).

These approaches leave out two central dimensions of self-reflexive storytelling: metanarrative fiction is characterized by critical reflection on, first, the *significance of cultural narratives* for individuals and communities and, second, the *functions of narratives* in our lives. In this chapter, I explore how what I call "metanarrative autofiction" makes narrative its theme through critical engagement with cultural narrative models of sense-making. While *metafictional* autofiction focuses on issues of fictionality in narrating lives, *metanarrative* autofiction, as I define it, reflects on the role of narratives (both fictional and nonfictional) in the processes in which we make sense of our lives. My notion is thus also different from what one might call metanarrative autobiography—a term that Bianca Theisen uses for autobiographical texts that highlight the "codes that have governed the writing of autobiographies" (2003, 11), and which could logically also be used to designate autobiographical texts reflecting on the act of narration in general, as well as those reflecting on cultural narrative templates. Metanarrative autofiction, in distinction from metanarrative autobiography, focuses in addition on the relation between the real and the imaginary, as is characteristic of autofiction in general, and often employs experimental narrative strategies in the process. In particular, I analyze the affordances of metanarrative autofiction by focusing on how it deals with the nature and conditions of narrative agency.

The notion of *narrative agency* has been used to foreground the role of narrative self-interpretation in bringing about the "integration of the self over time"—a process that is "dynamic, provisional and open to change and revision" (Mackenzie 2008, 11–12). However, I have argued (Meretoja 2018, 11–12) that the narrative dimension of agency is not merely at play in processes of self-interpretation, but forms, more broadly, a constitutive aspect of our agency as we participate, through our actions and inactions, in narrative practices that perpetuate and challenge social structures. The concept of narrative agency signals that culturally mediated narrative interpretations play an important role in constituting us as subjects capable of action, while simultaneously alerting us to how narrative agency is socially conditioned. Our narrative agency means our ability to navigate our narrative environments: use and engage with narratives that are culturally available to us, to analyze and challenge them, and to practice agential choice over which narratives we use and how we narratively interpret our lives and the world around us. Narrative agency can be amplified or diminished, and agentic power is unevenly distributed both within societies and across the globe. Amplified narrative agency can manifest itself, for example, as enhanced awareness of one's possibilities of action, affect, and thought in relation to one's narrative environments and as the ability to imagine different modes of living a fulfilling life.

I take narrative agency to include three central dimensions. First, it involves *narrative awareness*: awareness of different narrative perspectives and of the cultural repertoire of narratives that circulate in our cultural environments and provide us with models of sense-making. Second, it includes *narrative imagination*: the capacity to imagine beyond what appears to be self-evident in the present (see Andrews 2014; Brockmeier 2015) and to engage with the culturally available repertoire of narratives critically and creatively in ways that expand one's "sense of the possible" (Meretoja 2018, 20, 90–97). Its third aspect is *narrative dialogicality*: the capacity to enter into relationships and be part of communities that have their own shared "narrative in-betweens" (Meretoja 2018, 117–125), that is, intersubjective mythologies and narrative sense-making systems, and to participate in their renewal, challenging, and transformation.

An important strand of contemporary autofiction problematizes the pressure to create a single, coherent life story, articulating how the self is constituted in relation to narratives that are only partly our own, unearthing the normative aspects of the cultural narrative models that are imposed on us, and exploring alternatives to dominant models of how to live and narrate a fulfilling life. In this chapter, I will analyze three examples of such contemporary metanarrative autofiction, showing how the respective texts display and work through the three dimensions of narrative agency. I propose that in so doing they contribute to shaping narrative agency in our culture at large.

Narrative, Memory, and Imagination in Ernaux's *Les Années*

The form of Annie Ernaux's *Les Années* is highly experimental. It avoids the first-person singular pronoun and, instead, oscillates between the third-person singular (*elle*/she) and the first-person plural (*nous*/we). "Ernaux" the narrator refers to herself/the protagonist as "she" (*elle*) and to her generation or peer-group as "we" (*nous*).[2] This impersonal autobiography charts the change of times through the itinerary of her own life, linking the unfolding of an individual life to historical events and change of fashions and mentalities. It compellingly entwines the personal and the collective by showing how the most personal experience takes place in a space shaped by collective forces and how major historical events are experienced differently by each individual. I will focus here on how *Les Années* thematizes the narrative aspect of memory and imagination.

Ernaux's autobiographical impulse seems to arise from a sense of the past disappearing. Aging and serious illness (breast cancer) prompt her to narrate her life and seek a fitting form for such an endeavor.[3] The narrator feels that there is "something too permanent about 'I,' something shrunken and stifling, whereas 'she' is too exterior and remote" (2017, 169–170/2008, 187–188).[4] Illness and aging produce a sense of transience and a felt need to leave a trace. Writing is about constructing and preserving a past in order to have a sense of the multitude of who one has been and who one is now and to see that process in relation to other people:

> She doesn't know what she wants from these inventories, except maybe through the accumulation of memories of objects, to again become the person she was at such and such a time. She would like to assemble these multiple images of herself, separate and discordant, thread them together with the story of her existence, starting with her birth during World War II up until the present day. Therefore, an existence that is singular but also merged with the movements of a generation. (169/187)

"Ernaux" wants to remember, to take stock of her life, but with a keen awareness of how her personal memory is entwined with collective imagination. Even highly subjective bodily experience is mediated by cultural narrative models of sense-making:

> She has mined her intuition of what her book's form will be from another sensation, the one that engulfs her when, starting with a frozen memory-image of herself with other kids on a hospital bed after tonsil surgery, after the war, or crossing Paris on a bus in July of 1968, she seems to melt into an indistinct whole whose parts she manages to pull free, one at a time, through an effort of critical consciousness: elements of herself, customs, gestures, words, etc. […] Then, in a state of profound, almost dazzling satisfaction, she finds something that the image from personal memory doesn't give her on its own: a kind of vast collective sensation that takes her consciousness, her entire being, into itself. (223–224/250)

Falling ill is an intensely personal experience, but Ernaux shows that it also has a collective dimension and is affected by cultural narratives of illness. How we think about cancer as disease, for example, is shaped by narratives of restitution and recovery that dominate the media. "Ernaux" mentions the illness almost in passing as a trivial thing that seems to affect all women of her generation:

> a tumour of the kind that seems to burgeon in the breasts of all women her age, and appeared to her a normal occurrence, almost, because the things we most fear happen. At the same time she received the news that a baby was growing in the womb of her eldest son's partner—the ultrasound revealed a girl, and meanwhile she'd lost all her hair as a result of chemotherapy. This replacement of herself in the world, without delay, profoundly disturbed her. (220/246)

First, in terms of the three aspects of narrative agency, *Les Années* is permeated with narrative awareness. Each memory is recounted so that the personal and the collective intersect. Personal experiences are shown to take shape in a cultural context that functions as a "space of experience" (Koselleck 2004) that allows certain experiences and disallows others. Ernaux uses this Koselleckian concept when she speaks of "[t]he space of experience" that "lost its familiar contours" (2017, 170/2008, 188). The narrator acknowledges that we not only share experience of great historical events ("our landmarks, 1968 and 1981" [170/188]) but "a great deal of shared experience that left no conscious trace" (180/200) and is linked to shared habits and assumptions. By articulating cultural narratives underlying such shared assumptions, *Les Années* brings elements of the narrative unconscious to the level of narrative awareness (see also Meretoja 2018, 18–21; Freeman 2010, 105, 120).

Narrative awareness also involves awareness of how people search for "models of existence in space and time" (108/118). *Les Années* depicts how people create their "personal Pantheon" (119/130), their personal mythology of figures they adore and from whom they seek guidance and inspiration. Literature and other arts as well as advertising provide narrative "models for how to live, behave, and furnish the home. It was society's cultural educator" (111/122). Ernaux disenchants the Pantheon of narrative models by showing how not only intellectual heroes but also mundane advertising plays a crucial role in providing us with models to live by. The text emphasizes how the most personal mythology often turns out to be anything but personal: it is entangled with the story economy of the times and its commercial interests.

Second, an equally important aspect of Ernaux's metanarrative autofictional mode of writing is the way it charts changes in collective narrative imagination. The narrator repeatedly refers explicitly to imagination (to "teenage imagination" [146/161], for example, or to the way in which "[t]he *banlieues* loomed large in the popular imagination" [141/155]). In a sense, her text is a cultural history of the transformations of public imagination. It also acknowledges that collective imagination is heterogeneous and plural. The immigrants, for example, have their own "imagination, which annoyed us insofar as it was focused elsewhere, on Algeria and Palestine" (173/192).

The narrative is permeated by reflection on how personal and collective narrative imagination constantly intersect and how individual memory is conditioned by cultural memory embedded in a specific social context. It is an organizing principle of Ernaux's autofictional writing that her life is told with an emphasis on what she remembered and what she imagined at the time. Who "Ernaux" is at a given point in her life is defined by what she remembers and dreams of at that time. At one point, she tells us, "[s]he has started to imagine herself outside of conjugal and family life" (115/126), for instance, and at another "[s]he no longer imagines herself lying on the beach or as a writer publishing her first book" (96/104). The narrator also acknowledges that she has to imagine the book, the impersonal autobiography, before she can write it. Then, however, this project is presented as only one aspect of her everyday life and of her narrative imagination that orients her to her future: "Even more than this book the future is the next man who will make her dream, buy new clothes, and wait: for a letter, a phone call, a message on the answering machine" (170/188). Ernaux emphasizes that our dreams and memories (perceived as highly personal and unique) are ultimately dominated by quite banal everyday fantasies and anxieties that are largely shaped by cultural narrative models.

Third, Ernaux's autofictional writing is fundamentally relational. It acknowledges how individual life takes place within a social world in which it is part of the life of a whole generation. Much of her writing explores relationships, such as her intense love affair with a younger man while she undergoes breast cancer treatments. Ernaux's *L'Usage de la photo* (2005) documents this love affair through photos taken of their discarded clothes after they have had sex. In *Les Années*, the man "attracted her with his gentleness and his penchant for everything that makes one dream, books, music, films. This miraculous coincidence gave her a chance to triumph over death through love and eroticism" (220–221/246). Ernaux thematizes the narratively shaped intersubjective space between people, the narrative in-between that allows us to talk about certain experiences but not others. The narrator repeatedly reflects on what can be said and thought in a particular social and cultural world, experiencing as tormenting the inability to express one's thoughts and feelings:

> At every moment in time, next to the things it seems natural to do and say, and next to the ones we're told to think—no less by books or ads in the Métro than by funny stories—are other things that society hushes up without knowing it is doing so. Thus it condemns to lonely suffering all the people who feel but cannot name these things. Then the silence breaks […] and words burst forth, recognized at last, while underneath other silences start to form. (97/105)

In *Les Années*, illness, death, and aging are surrounded by silence. Through writing, Ernaux creates an intersubjective space of memory and imagination that makes it possible to fill in one of these silences through the anticipation of one's own death: "The future is replaced by a sense of urgency that torments her. She is afraid that as she ages her memory will become cloudy and silent, as it was in her first years of life, which she won't remember anymore. […] Now's the time to give form to her future absence through writing" (222/248–249). In connection to this intertwinement of presence and absence, she writes about "palimpsest time"

(223/249).[5] This is a layered time in which the past is overwritten by the present and future: "What matters to her, on the contrary, is to seize this time that comprises her life on Earth at a given period, the time that has coursed through her, the world she has recorded merely by living" (223/250). Such an acute sense of temporality and finitude marks her whole process of life writing.

Overall, a key affordance of Ernaux's experimental metanarrative autofictional writing is that it allows her to acknowledge how much of our existence is not a matter of action but of being acted upon. We are as much a product of what happens to us as we are centers of action and meaning that give sense and direction to our own lives. *Les Années* highlights the continuous dialogue between these two sides of our existence. We are socially conditioned, but we learn to become narrators of our lives who act as if we could simply choose a certain direction for our own lives and life-narrations. Yet, *Les Années* shows how deeply entrenched this narrative agency is in narratively constituted webs of relationships that shape what the individual, as a member of a generation, remembers and imagines.

Knausgaard's Essayistic Storytelling: The Search for Authenticity

An important theme in Karl Ove Knausgaard's (2009–2011) six-volume autofictional series *Min kamp* is the search for an authentic mode of being through a process of writing one's life. Integral to this is a search for authentic storytelling, which involves a struggle with culturally dominant narrative models he finds limiting. Telling the story of one's own life, an act of practicing narrative agency, opens up the possibility to turn from being a victim to an agent. At the same time, Knausgaard's autofictional series is shot through with a critical attitude toward narrativizing life. On the one hand, life is for him a flow of experiences, and narrative is deeply problematic insofar as it tries to stop the flow and appropriate life into a closed form. On the other hand, narrative is shown to be indispensable to being human. I argue that Knausgaard strives to find a form of fragmentary, essayistic, open-ended storytelling that deliberately avoids appropriation and closure.

The two primary ways in which Knausgaard's autofictional series contributes to narrative awareness are, first, by reflecting on the tension between life and narrative, and second, by drawing attention to, and critically reflecting on, cultural narratives that steer our lives, as the narrator observes in the sixth volume of the series: "We need to be alert whenever events shape themselves into narratives, for narratives belong to literature and not to life, and occurrences of the past seep into and absorb expectations of the future" (2018, 534/517). Occurrences pass quickly, but newspapers tell stories that give them a fixedness:

> The event is lifted out of its physical environment and its particular moment and goes from being without continuity to becoming a part of an ongoing, so-called news. Anything that cannot be explained, any unexpected accident or catastrophe, any instance of sudden death or incomprehensible malice is gathered here in the form of small narratives, and the mere fact of their being told is sufficient to put us at ease, to assure us that order exists. (2018, 651/627)

Min kamp suggests that narratives provide reassurance and a sense of control, but we should be aware of the flux of events that lies underneath the neat narratives that create a false illusion of order. An important way in which reality is ordered is through cultural narrative models.

Min kamp particularly reflects on cultural narrative models of masculinity, including models of being a father, husband, and artist. "Knausgaard" struggles with these models in trying to find his own path, which entails both a style of existence and a style of writing that he can consider authentic. He asks how he might turn his "almost inexhaustible" recollections "into a coherent narrative? And how to do so in such a way as to remain faithful to what was mine about them?" (2018, 66/68). He is largely aware of his debt to the tradition of Romanticism, which emphasizes that which is unique to each individual, but he also critically engages with this tradition by foregrounding our fundamental connectedness to other people.[6] He does not want to repeat the mistakes of his father; instead, he wants to be a committed, loving parent, whose children "shouldn't be afraid of their own father" (2014c, 248/246). I agree with Christian Refsum that, despite being criticized for individualism and egoism, "Knausgaard" strives "to find and maintain attachment, belonging, and love" (2020, 370). A deep commitment to his nuclear family is crucial to his sense of self; both love and writing are for him modes of renewal through which he searches for self-fulfillment and self-transformation. When caught between trying to be a good father/husband and a good writer, however, he ultimately privileges his ambitions as a writer in his struggle for authenticity.

It is first and foremost the conventionality of everyday routines and habits that oppresses him:

> perhaps it was the prefabricated nature of the days in this world I was reacting to, the rails of routine we followed, which made everything so predictable that we had to invest in entertainment to feel any hint of intensity? Every time I went out of the door I knew what was going to happen, what I was going to do. This was how it was on the micro level, I go to the supermarket and do the shopping, I go and sit down at a café with a newspaper, I fetch my children from the nursery, and this is how it was on the macro level, from the initial entry into society, the nursery, to the final exit, the old folks' home. (2014b, 75–76/67–68)

Crucial to Knausgaard's ethos—to the overall guiding beliefs and ideals that shape the narrative—is a search for authenticity characterized by the struggle of each individual to become who they are, against such obstacles as conventions, norms, and dominant narrative models. In particular, the narrator repeatedly places the singularity of what is happening to him against the generality of narrative models: "For a moment, it was as if I was entering a larger story than my own. The sons leaving home to bury their father, this was the story I suddenly found myself in" (2014a, 296/265). After a while, however, the "sensation of the great story had gone. We were not two sons, we were Yngve and Karl Ove; we were not going home but to Kristiansand; this was not a father we were burying, it was dad" (2014a, 297/266). He feels that taking up the Scandinavian model of a father who stays at home with the children takes something away from him: "When I pushed the buggy all over town and spent my days taking care of my child it was not the case that I was adding something to my life, that it became richer as a result; on the contrary, something was removed from it, part of myself, the bit relating to masculinity. […] I squeezed myself into a mould that was so small and so constricted that I could no longer move" (2014b, 99/87). Ultimately, "Knausgaard" resists one model—a distant, authoritative father-figure like his own—only to find himself diminished by the alternative model—the modern Scandinavian father-figure, which may be conceived as more in line with a traditionally female model. Awareness of these models allows him to gain critical distance from them, but being caught between them remains a struggle.

Knausgaard's contribution to narrative imagination is linked to his explicit interest in exploring "what is possible and what is not possible to say and do in a given day and age" (2018, 762/732). The sixth volume, for example, discusses the historical context that allowed Hitler to gain power and draws a parallel to the Utøya massacre in contemporary Norway.[7] In 1910, it would not have been possible for Hitler to become a political leader, the narrator muses (2018, 765/734), but in the 1930s a world emerged in which ordinary people, "we," became supporters of the Nazi regime. He analyzes how this launched a tradition that has enabled the rise of far-right extremism across contemporary Europe. He suggests that we cannot understand the rise of Nazism unless we acknowledge what he calls the "power of the we" (828/792), which implies that we ourselves could have been Nazis had we been born in a different time and place (see also Meretoja 2018, 217–254).

In *Min kamp*, narrative imagination also concerns the question of how to expand one's sense of the possible. What liberates "Knausgaard" and expands his sense of the possible is primarily art. He is trying to get hold of the singularity of who he is, under the pressure of narrative models, norms, and life trajectories forced on individuals. Linear narrative form represents conventionality for Knausgaard, which is why he struggles to give expression to what evades narrativization, and in this effort he turns to the fragmentary, essayistic form that he develops throughout his series. His search for authenticity combines an aesthetic of transiency and unfinishedness with an ethics and aesthetics of brutal honesty. Knausgaard attempts to create a narrative style that is as true to reality as possible. Tired of fiction, he wants to develop an aesthetics of truth that is animated by a hunger for reality: "The idea was to get as close as possible to my life" (2014b, 654/554).[8] For him, the search for authenticity is inextricably linked to the project of writing in which he displays the secrets of his soul as scrupulously and completely as possible. He seems to think that a brutally honest narrative that reveals his life in all its contradictory, messy complexity is key to integrity and authenticity.

Knausgaard contributes to narrative imagination by developing an aesthetics of brutal honesty that lays bare the destructiveness of the grind of everyday routines and narratives with which we structure them—an aesthetic he calls the "banality of the everyday" (2012). In a way, this is for Knausgaard not only an aesthetic but also an *ethos* used to justify placing art above the ethical commitments of family life and community life. Ultimately, only art is sacred for him. He pushes the limits of what can be said and done in literature in order to turn the tedious everyday life into something meaningful that makes life worth living: "Everyday life, with its duties and routines, was something I endured, not a thing I enjoyed, nor something that was meaningful or made me happy. […] I always longed to be away from it, and always had done. So the life I led was not my own. I tried to make it mine, this was my struggle, because of course I wanted it, but I failed, the longing for something else undermined all my efforts" (2014b, 75/67). Out of this failure grows the Knausgaardian narrative imaginary characterized by an oscillation between commitments to others and a search for authenticity.

In terms of dialogicality, *Min kamp* presents narrative as not only a matter of conventional cultural models that convey norms and stereotypical roles but also as a possibility of establishing connections with others. Narrative is for the narrator "a matter of communication, establishing community out of what was one's own" (2018, 65/67). Narrative is a process of giving meaning to the world, which is for him "not only our responsibility but also our obligation" (2018, 373/366), but this process only makes sense if we understand that language is the medium through which we enter into a dialogical relationship with others: "In the language I exist, but only if there is also a you to which the I of the speech act can relate, because if not how then should the I separate itself and find form?" (2018, 465/454). Hence, despite Knausgaard's attachment to the idea of a romantic genius searching for authenticity, he also recognizes that he is fundamentally dependent on and connected to others. One of the crucial tasks his narrator sets for himself is to explore these connections: "meaning arises out of cohesion, in the way we are connected to one another and our surroundings. This is the reason I write, trying to explore the connections of which I am a part" (630/606). At the same time, however, he says he wrote the series in an effort to free himself "from everything that ties" (2018, 982/942). Throughout the series, Knausgaard explores this fraught relationship with our fundamental relationality. Although relationality is often seen to be characteristic of women's autobiographical writing, Knausgaard shows that it can be a key issue for male writers too.

Narrative dialogicality involves awareness of how each narrative can be told from multiple perspectives and how our individual narratives enter into dialogue with those of others. Despite Knausgaard's commitment to truth, it is evident that his narrative is an interpretation, a selection: some things are left out, others told with excruciating detail. In making such choices, he practices his power of narrative agency. Narratives always represent a certain perspective, and the narrator of *Min kamp* makes clear that the series is primarily about his perspective, his truth, his shame, and anguish. It is a largely monological project, which can be considered ethically problematic, but "Knausgaard" also metanarratively foregrounds his own status as a narrator who selects what to tell and how to tell it. In fact, the self-reflexive dimension of the series entails that Knausgaard never pretends to tell the whole truth or the only truth. He aspires to tell *his* truth and to acknowledge how it necessarily takes shape in dialogical relationships, and often in tension with the truths of other people.

Nevertheless, as his life is entangled with those of others, he also has to consider the cost. Brutal honesty comes at the expense of those close to him, whom he turns into material for his art.[9] Hence, the series is ultimately permeated with a tension between an individualist search for authenticity and a relational sense of connectedness. Its narrative dialogicality contributes to a narrative in-between that makes it possible to verbalize shame, insecurity, and selfishness, a space that enables Knausgaard to become visible as an incomplete and imperfect person and writer in search of his own truth. He does this through essayistic, fragmentary storytelling that deliberately eschews narrative mastery and definitive answers to fundamental existential and ethical questions. His metanarrative reflections are grounded in a poetics of essayistic, explorative, fluid, and open-ended autofiction.

Swan's Autofictional Cancer (Counter-)Narrative

Astrid Swan's *Viimeinen kirjani* (*My Last Book*) is a genre-defying book about the author's journey to become a singer-songwriter, mother, and writer, while learning that she has incurable metastatic breast cancer. Swan's experimental narrative challenges linear narrativity and plays with the permeable border between fictionality and nonfictionality. It starts off like a fairytale: "Once upon a time there was a woman, who breast-fed her almost two-year-old, speaking child" (2019, 9).[10] Swan's way of dealing explicitly with her own experience of illness makes her book a memoir. While memoir, however, is traditionally seen as a nonfiction genre, Swan employs aesthetic strategies that draw attention to the process of experimental writing and give the text a quality of literariness. For example, the chapters are numbered in an irregular fashion—5, 30, 7, 24, 5, indicating her age at the time of the narrated events—which emphasizes the way she writes from the middle of events that refuse to settle into a linear, coherent narrative. Diary excerpts are interspersed with interior monologue, reflections on the past, snapshots of the present, and anticipation of the future into a collage-like assemblage. Throughout her book, "Swan" comments on her own process of narration and on cultural models for illness narratives. As she struggles with culturally dominant narratives of fighting breast cancer, she reflects on how lives are entangled with one another through shared narrative imagination and processes of co-telling in which lives are narrated collaboratively.

In terms of the three dimensions of narrative agency, Swan's book contributes to narrative awareness particularly through its critical engagement with cultural narrative models linked to narrating illness. She looks for stories in which she would recognize herself, but finds that the available repertoire of cancer narratives is limited: "It has been difficult to find narratives that reflect me back to myself" (138). The dominant cancer narratives emphasize battle and recovery. The metaphor of war, which portrays cancer patients as fighters, has been criticized since Susan Sontag's *Illness as Metaphor* (1978) but continues to dominate the culturally mediated narrative imagination concerning cancer (see also Ehrenreich 2001; Bleakley 2017). The battle narrative is problematic because it turns cancer patients into either winners or losers, the implication being that those who die did not fight hard enough (see Meretoja 2021, 38).

It is significant that Swan's narrator has problems not only with the dominant narrative of fighting cancer but also with such a counter-narrative as the feminist activist Audre Lorde's *The Cancer Journals* (1980), which is meant to be an empowering narrative that encourages breast cancer survivors to be proudly one-breasted: "I am not, after all, a valiant one-breasted warrior who carries her scars without shame. I want to camouflage" (Swan 2019, 243). She also finds problematic the normative pressure to be positive that is integral to culturally dominant narratives of illness: "Those who suggest I should look at everything a little more positively cannot fathom the form my life has taken" (254). Swan draws attention to the strong normative element of obligatory optimism. As Emilia Nielsen (2019) observes, in the culturally preferred cancer narrative one wages war on cancer with courage and optimism, as if recovery depended simply on the right attitude and enough willpower. Nielsen analyzes alternative stories, counter-narratives, that she calls disruptive breast cancer stories, and shows how they make room for a wider range of emotions in the experience of cancer. However, people rarely want to hear stories of anger or grief. Swan contributes to such disruptive counter-narratives by exploring complex, dark affects linked to the experience of facing terminal illness and the inevitably approaching death.

Swan's autofictional writing compellingly verbalizes aspects of both personal and collective narrative imagination. She frequently speculates on what could have been—on life trajectories that did not actualize. For example, as an exchange student in the US, she "receives a whole fast-forward of what-if-life": "What if I had been born elsewhere? What if my parents had been entirely different people? What if everything that happened had happened but in a different setting?" (2019, 81). Narratives are a vehicle of imagination, of imagining an elsewhere, which can be either a past elsewhere or a not-yet that could unfold one day. "Swan" tries to imagine her forebears, including her lost grandfather, an Ashkenazi Jew who had a nomadic lifestyle, but she also reflects on how weaving her family history into an imaginative narrative may grow into "a dangerous story inside of me" (52). Narratives are also a mode of reaching to the future, even beyond death. She refers to her "insatiable hunger of stories" (142), which is linked to a "fear of disappearing" (47), and suggests that stories are for her a mode of survival: "I live by stories" (46). This connects her to a literary tradition going all the way back to *One Thousand and One Nights* (see Meretoja 2018, 168). Survival through storytelling is connected to the need to imagine both where she comes from and where she is going.

My Last Book shows how we live at the intersection of a multitude of narratives and must deal with their tensions and contradictions: "for me both narratives are necessary and true" (68). Narrative imagination involves the ability to imagine the messiness of the narrative webs in which we are entangled. Although it is in the power of narrators to decide which versions of particular stories to tell and "what they emphasize" (60), she also acknowledges that life stories ultimately take shape through shared narrative imagination and processes of co-telling. This brings us to narrative dialogicality, which is a key aspect of *My Last Book*. The way Swan tells her life story emphasizes the profound relationality of our existence and the inextricable entanglement of our stories with the stories of others: "We are a million different shards in other people's stories." (147) No individual is separate from the lives of others and this entanglement of lives makes them messy and layered: "It is not a tidy operation. It's a messy chaos. My life does not dislodge from the lives of others. Neither do experiences. Everything is sedimented. We share habits, memories, trauma, genes, recipes, plans, daydreams, fears…" (30). "Swan" repeatedly foregrounds the connections between her stories and those of others: "Invisible filaments connect me to others, their stories and cultures" (53).

As she prepares for her own death, "Swan" works through the idea of letting go of being the protagonist of her own story and becoming, instead, a character in other people's, when she no longer exists, but lives on in the stories of those who knew her or listen to her music: "I become story. A metaphor and an evaporation. I become a character inhabiting the memories, material items and behaviors of these people, even in surprising situations. Strange entanglements—moments of presence after all" (284). Coming to terms with her own death is in many ways a process of letting go—first and foremost of control because we cannot govern our death and what happens to our loved ones afterward. This involves letting go of narrative mastery, which opens up the ability to enjoy the moment and its transience: "I take pleasure in the presence of the unknown. I deliberately enjoy that which is not in my control, of which I am not aware and cannot anticipate. This is my reason for loving the moment of waking up in the morning" (285). The process of creating a narrative in-between in which the end of her life is given meaning emerges as a process of collaborative storytelling in which she participates and which those close to her will uphold, reinterpret, and transform when she is gone.

Swan's book contributes to a narrative in-between in which it is possible to share experiences of fundamental vulnerability without being paralyzed by shame and feelings of inadequacy. It questions the dichotomy between health and illness, showing how much wellbeing and agency there can be in times of serious illness. Her metanarrative autofictional writing is thereby a contribution to the discussion on "health within illness" (Carel 2008). The concept of narrative agency provides an important new perspective in this discussion. While illness is commonly seen in terms of a radical impairment of agency, acknowledging how agency is mediated through cultural narratives allows us to appreciate both our limitations at times of good health and the agency that persists in times of illness. This approach invites us to explore how agency can be strengthened through narrative practices that cultivate narrative awareness, imagination, and dialogical relationality.

*　*　*

This chapter has delineated the emerging phenomenon of metanarrative autofiction that self-reflexively draws our attention to the complexities of having to navigate contemporary narrative environments, including critical engagement with the current storytelling boom. Through the examples linked to memory and imagination, authenticity, and illness, I have unearthed key affordances of metanarrative autofiction—particularly ways in which it reflects on culturally dominant narrative models and enriches the culturally available repertoire of narratives that can help us verbalize our experiences and imagine different life trajectories. Such autofiction explores entanglements between one's own narrative agency and narratives culturally imposed on us, and it provides critical perspectives on the ways in which cultural narrative models affect the space of possibility in which we narrate our lives and become who we are. Metanarrative autofiction is an important strand of contemporary literature globally, and it remains for future research to analyze this phenomenon through a wider selection of texts from various cultural contexts. The case studies analyzed in this chapter have shown that a focus on metanarrative autofiction as a distinct form of autofiction with specific affordances provides a new perspective on both agency and its narrative mediation. This approach has allowed us to see how contemporary metanarrative autofiction articulates the complex ways in which the cultural and social forces around us affect the narrative models through which we make sense of our own experiences and those of others, and how it can expand our sense of the possible.[11]

Notes

1. Metanarrative autofiction can be seen as a subcategory of autofiction, but I also see it as a subcategory of metanarrative fiction more broadly (fiction characterized by metanarrativity). I embrace the view outlined in the Introduction of this volume according to which the autofictional is not only a genre-descriptor but also "a mode, moment, and strategy." In this chapter, I focus on some of the key affordances of metanarrative autofictional modes of writing.
2. I will refer to the narrator-protagonist of her autofictional writing as "Ernaux" (the version of Ernaux that emerges from the text) and will similarly use "Knausgaard" and "Swan."
3. Aging engenders, in *Les Années*, a voice "marked by authority, but also by a new fragility, anxiety and fear" (Jordan 2011, 138).
4. Quotations are from the English translation (Ernaux 2017). In-text citations include references to both the translation and the original (separated by a slash). The same principle is applied in Knausgaard's case.
5. On palimpsest memory, see Silverman 2013.

6. On the Romantic roots of the idea of authenticity, see Taylor 1991.
7. The Utøya massacre refers to the July 22, 2011, attack in which Anders Breivik, a 32-year-old Norwegian right-wing extremist, shot dead 69 people attending the summer camp of the Workers Youth League on Utøya Island.
8. *My Struggle* can be seen as part of the phenomenon that Shields (2010) dubbed "reality hunger."
9. In an interview (2012), Knausgaard says that in this project he "gave away" his soul and he feels "a measure of guilt" for the hurt he has caused.
10. The translations are Swan's own, based on an unfinished English translation. I am grateful to Swan for providing me with these translations.
11. Work on this chapter has been funded by the Academy of Finland project Instrumental Narratives: The Limits of Storytelling and New Story-Critical Narrative Theory (project number 314769).

Works Cited

Andrews, Molly. 2014. *Narrative Imagination and Everyday Life*. Oxford: Oxford University Press.
Bleakley, Alan. 2017. *Thinking with Metaphors in Medicine: The State of the Art*. London: Routledge.
Brockmeier, Jens. 2015. *Beyond the Archive: Memory, Narrative, and the Autobiographical Process*. New York: Oxford University Press.
Carel, Havi. 2008. *Illness*. London: Routledge.
Currie, Mark. 2014. *Metafiction*. London: Routledge.
Ehrenreich, Barbara. 2001. Welcome to Cancerland. *Harper's Magazine*, November, 43–53.
Ernaux, Annie. 2005. *L'Usage de la photo*. Paris: Gallimard.
———. 2008. *Les Années*. Paris: Gallimard.
———. 2017. *The Years*. Translated by Alison L. Strayer. London: Fitzcarraldo.
Fernandes, Sujatha. 2017. *Curated Stories: The Uses and Misuses of Storytelling*. Oxford: Oxford University Press.
Fludernik, Monika. 1996. *Towards a "Natural" Narratology*. London: Routledge.
———. 2003. Metanarrative and Metafictional Commentary: From Metadiscursivity to Metanarration and Metafiction. *Poetica* 35: 1–39.
Freeman, Mark. 2010. *Hindsight: The Promise and Peril of Looking Backward*. New York: Oxford University Press.
Hutcheon, Linda. 1980. *Narcissistic Narrative: The Metafictional Paradox*. Waterloo: Wilfrid Laurier University Press.
Hyvärinen, Matti. 2008. Revisiting the Narrative Turns. *Life Writing* 7 (1): 69–82.
Jordan, Shirley. 2011. Writing Age: Annie Ernaux's *Les Années*. *Forum for Modern Language Studies* 47 (2): 138–149. https://doi.org/10.1093/fmls/cqq080.

Knausgaard, Karl Ove. 2009–2011. *Min kamp 1–6*. Oslo: Oktober.
———. 2012. "I Have Given Away My Soul." Interview by Jon Henley. *The Guardian*, March 9, 2012. https://www.theguardian.com/lifeandstyle/2012/mar/09/karl-ove-knausgaard-memoir-family. Accessed Apr 6, 2021.
———. 2014a. *A Death in the Family: My Struggle 1*. London: Vintage Books.
———. 2014b. *A Man in Love: My Struggle 2*. London: Vintage Books.
———. 2014c. *Boyhood Island: My Struggle 3*. London: Vintage Books.
———. 2018. *The End: My Struggle 6*. London: Harvill Secker.
Koselleck, Reinhart. 2004. *Futures Past: On the Semantics of Historical Time*. Translated by Keith Tribe. New York: Columbia University Press.
Lorde, Audre. 1980. *The Cancer Journals*. Argyle: Spinsters Ink.
Lyotard, Jean-François. 1979. *La Condition postmoderne: Rapport sur la savoir*. Paris: Minuit.
Mackenzie, Catriona. 2008. Introduction: Practical Identity and Narrative Agency. In *Practical Identity and Narrative Agency*, ed. Kim Atkins and Catriona Mackenzie, 1–28. London: Routledge.
Macrae, Andrea. 2019. *Discourse Deixis in Metafiction: The Language of Metanarration, Metalepsis and Disnarration*. New York: Routledge.
Mäkelä, Maria, and Hanna Meretoja. 2022. Critical Approaches to the Storytelling Boom. *Poetics Today* 43 (2) Do you want to remove "forthcoming"? The issue comes out in June 2022 and the issue number is 43 (2), so at this moment it is forthcoming, but if you prefer just 43 (2), that's also fine by me.
Meretoja, Hanna. 2014. *The Narrative Turn in Fiction and Theory: The Crisis and Return of Storytelling from Robbe-Grillet to Tournier*. Basingstoke: Palgrave Macmillan.
———. 2018. *The Ethics of Storytelling: Narrative Hermeneutics, History, and the Possible*. Oxford: Oxford University Press.
———. 2021. A Dialogics of Counter-Narratives. In *The Routledge Handbook of Counter-Narratives*, ed. Klarissa Lueg and Marianne Wolff Lundholt, 30–42. London: Routledge.
Neumann, Birgit, and Ansgar Nünning. 2014. Metanarration and Metafiction. In *The Living Handbook of Narratology*, ed. Peter Hühn, Jan Christoph Meister, John Pier, and Wolf Schmid. Hamburg: Hamburg University Press. https://www.lhn.uni-hamburg.de/node/50.html. Accessed Apr 6, 2021.
Nielsen, Emilia. 2019. *Disrupting Breast Cancer Narratives: Stories of Rage and Repair*. Toronto: University of Toronto Press.
Polletta, Francesca. 2006. *It Was Like a Fever: Storytelling in Protest and Politics*. London: University of Chicago Press.
Refsum, Christian. 2020. 'A Love Relationship Is Not a Place for Refuge, It Is The Place To Be': The Theme of Love in Karl Ove Knausgaard's *Min kamp*. *Scandinavian Studies* 92 (3): 369–389.
Ricœur, Paul. 1983. *Temps et récit 1*. Paris: Seuil.

Salmon, Christian. 2010. *Storytelling: Bewitching the Modern Mind*. London: Verso.
Shields, David. 2010. *Reality Hunger: A Manifesto*. New York: Vintage.
Silverman, Max. 2013. *Palimpsest Memory: The Holocaust and Colonialism in French and Francophone Fiction and Film*. New York & Oxford: Berghahn.
Sontag, Susan. 1978. *Illness as Metaphor*. New York: Farrar, Straus & Giroux.
Swan, Astrid. 2019. *Viimeinen kirjani*. Helsinki: Nemo.
Taylor, Charles. 1991. *The Ethics of Authenticity*. Cambridge, MA: Harvard University Press.
Theisen, Bianca. 2003. *Silenced Facts: Media Montages in Contemporary Austrian Literature*. Amsterdam: Rodopi.
Waugh, Patricia. 1984. *Metafiction: The Theory and Practice of Self-Conscious Fiction*. London: Methuen.

Open Access This chapter is licensed under the terms of the Creative Commons Attribution 4.0 International License (http://creativecommons.org/licenses/by/4.0/), which permits use, sharing, adaptation, distribution and reproduction in any medium or format, as long as you give appropriate credit to the original author(s) and the source, provide a link to the Creative Commons licence and indicate if changes were made.

The images or other third party material in this chapter are included in the chapter's Creative Commons licence, unless indicated otherwise in a credit line to the material. If material is not included in the chapter's Creative Commons licence and your intended use is not permitted by statutory regulation or exceeds the permitted use, you will need to obtain permission directly from the copyright holder.

CHAPTER 8

Multilingual Autofiction: Mobilizing Language(s)?

Helle Egendal

This chapter argues that multilingualism is a key autofictional strategy in transcultural autobiographical literature. My research on recent transcultural literature points to the increasing importance of multilingualism, which I interpret in relation to Mikhail Bakhtin's concept of polyglossia: the playful mixture of a multitude of national languages within the same text (Bakhtin 1981, 65). This multilingualism could—potentially—be seen as an expression of polyphony, a concept coined by Bakhtin to describe how life and literature are fundamentally structured by a diversity of voices and points of view (Bakhtin 1981). Multilingualism, used in this particular sense of the word, has the potential to become a powerful aesthetic strategy in multicultural literature. In this chapter, I will argue that in postmigrant literature published between 1990 and 2020, a new mode of multilingual autofiction can be identified.

The autofictional multilingual mode thrives across borders and cultures and seems to be independent of the geographical places of publication. In

H. Egendal (✉)
Freiburg, Germany
e-mail: helle.egendal@skandinavistik.uni-freiburg.de

this chapter, I will explore the works of three authors from Germany, Sweden, and Denmark: *Kanak Sprak: 24 Misstöne vom Rande der Gesellschaft* (*Kanak Sprak: 24 Discordant Notes from the Margin of Society*) (1995) by the German-Turkish author Feridun Zaimoğlu, *Ett öga rött* (*One Eye Red*) (2003) by the Swedish-Tunisian author Jonas Hassen Khemiri, and *Yahya Hassan* (2013) by the Danish-Palestinian author Yahya Hassan. What I refer to as multilingual autofiction emerges in each of these works in different guises, but to similarly powerful effect.[1] Their subtle play with the multi-layered and hybrid character of languages has a subversive impact on their respective political and historical contexts, giving each of the authors a penetrating voice in polemical contemporary debates. This chapter explores both the aesthetic scope and the political potential that these authors' multilingual autofictional strategies afford.

The elements of multilingualism and polyglossia have received little attention so far in research on autofiction.[2] Although several critics have considered the relationship between autobiography, autofiction, and multilingualism, including Martina Wagner-Egelhaaf (2006), Mirjam Gebauer (2009), Michaela Holdenried (2012), Wolfgang Behschnitt and An Willems (2012), and Marion Acker and Anne Fleig (2018), it is striking that the question and importance of multilingual autofictional literature is not mentioned in the recent overviews of autofiction provided by Iversen (2020) and Gronemann (2019). Owing to a combination of globalization, war, poverty, and natural disasters, the past thirty years have seen a significant increase in migration and thus in the prevalence of transcultural backgrounds.[3] Transcultural autofictional writing, as a result, is a rapidly expanding field.

Transcultural Authors and the Appeal of the Autofictional

Since Serge Doubrovsky coined the term "autofiction" in 1977, there has been a notable affinity between transcultural writers and autofictional modes. Acker and Fleig (2018) argue that one reason for this affinity is that, temporally, the growth of migrant literature and of autofiction coincided. Additionally, they state that:

> [a]part from this temporal coincidence, autofiction seems to appeal to many multilingual authors "in between," because of its constitutional ambiguity and its transgressing character of noticeable self-positioning. The

ambivalences and fractions of multilingual, transcultural affiliation meet an adequate expression in the ambivalence and inconsistency of autofictional texts between theory and practice, novel and autobiography, fact and fiction. (Acker and Fleig 2018, 22)[4]

As Acker and Fleig suggest, the oscillating structure of this postmodernist genre offers a space for negotiations of multicultural identity. A key component of a multicultural identity is the experience of living with more than one language. Mirjam Gebauer (2009, 114), Yildiz (2012, 10–13), and Acker and Fleig (2018, 20) describe such multilingual writers as experiencing a "double exclusion from the literary tradition." As early as the nineteenth century, German philosophers Johann Gottfried von Herder and Friedrich Schleiermacher were among those who advocated the idea that only "mother tongue" literature would be capable of creating masterpieces. Consequently, writings by transcultural authors would be excluded from the Parnassus of recognized literature, and, according to Gebauer, a tendency can be observed to consider these writings as "autobiographical" in the traditional, non-fictional sense of the word, and more specifically as "documents on cultural alterity." However, as classic autobiography is attached to the fundamental idea that expressions of "undisguised subjectivity" could only be expressed with authenticity by the mother tongue, these multilingual writers face an "autobiographical paradox," which also banishes them from the classic autobiographical genre (Gebauer 2009, 14). It is in the face of this generic no man's land that transcultural writers turn to autofiction. Whereas traditional autobiography is bound to the "exclusive intimacy of the mother tongue," autofiction operates with "the option of the playful rejection of cultural identification" and an open mind toward plural cultural and lingual relations (Acker and Fleig 2018, 23). The flexibility and variety of this autofictional play affords authors multiple ways in which to express and negotiate their multilingual identities.

From Experience to Experiment: Toward a Political Strategy in Multilingualism

Over the past twenty years, a shift of interest from *experience* to *experiment* seems to have taken place in transcultural literature.[5] According to Esther Kilchmann "[f]ocus is transferred from the author's lingual biography as well from the sociolinguistic context of the text production to the performed unique dynamic(s) and the constant movement of languages and language in general" (2017, 185). While the interest in communicating the autobiographical *experience* of multiculturalism, migration, marginalization, racism, and social inequality would dominate the early stages of transcultural literature, *experiments* with multilingualism and language increasingly characterize more recent stages of postmigrant literature. I argue that this shift moves the focus away from the autobiographical dimension of the literary works and toward language and style, a move that is symptomatic of the general "linguistic turn" of the period.

According to Kilchmann, the new generation of transcultural authors explores national languages in terms of code switching or code mixing. They play with the syntactic, grammatical, and lexical levels of the language and invent alternative criteria for lingual combination. Kilchmann refers to Austrian author Wolf Haas who, in his novel *Die Verteidigung der Missionarsstellung* (*The Defense of the Missionary Position*) (2012), includes long passages of Chinese in the otherwise German text. She also mentions the Swiss author Heike Fiedler, who writes in German, French, and English, but makes use additionally of Spanish and Cyrillic characters. Material aspects of language such as orthographic and phonological features become a kind of playground for these authors, pointing to the performative potential of this particular mode of multilingual literature. These multilingual experiments, which reveal the *homo ludens* of the authors, are a recurrent feature of avant-garde approaches to public poetry events, as well as of later forms such as *Spoken Word* or intermedial performances such as *Digital Poetry* (Kilchmann 2017, 184–185). However, the apparently playful ways of working with a variety of national languages that are found in multilingual literature differ from these other kinds of experimental art. The aim of mixing together national languages is not solely to mirror the heterogeneity of a standard language by pointing to the existence of sociolects, dialects, and multiethnolects, but to question the monolinguistic and monocultural norms of the social and historical context of the work.

Multilingual literature has existed for many centuries, visible in the mixture of Latin and Roman vernacular languages in so-called macaronic literature. With the increasing globalization and migration of recent decades, however, multicultural and multilingual texts now make up a much larger segment of literary output, and their provocative political effect reaches further than ever. The reasons behind the highly subversive effect of polyglossia are located in a specific historical context, as Yasemin Yildiz points out in her ground-breaking study *Beyond the Mother Tongue: The*

Postmonolingual Condition (2012). Yildiz states that the mere existence of multilingualism challenges the so-called monolingual paradigm, which has prescribed *one* national language and *one* mother tongue since emerging in late eighteenth-century Europe. Yildiz emphasizes that:

> monolingualism is much more than a simple quantitative term designating the presence of just one language. Instead, it constitutes a key structuring principle that organizes the entire range of modern social life, from the construction of individuals and their proper subjectivities to the formation of disciplines and institutions, as well as of imagined collectives such as cultures and nations. According to this paradigm, individuals and social formations are imagined to possess one "true" language only, their "mother tongue," and through this possession to be organically linked to an exclusive, clearly demarcated ethnicity, culture, and nation. (Yildiz 2012, 2)

Here, Yildiz addresses the ways in which a mother tongue was instrumentalized in the service of nation-building and the shaping of a homogeneous and monolingual state. Set against this monolingual status, which remains the dominant paradigm of most European nations, the political function of multilingual writing is clear. Transgressing the ideal of monocultural and monolingual society, it becomes a powerful instrument with which to critique the establishment. As the case studies I will explore demonstrate, autofictional multilingual writing has proven particularly effective as an aesthetic strategy which enables authors to showcase and mobilize their multilingual capacity and to address political discourses on migration, transculturality, and racism.

The claim that multilingualism is a key autofictional strategy in transcultural autobiographical literature raises important questions in terms of genre and narratological description. Given that the explicit multilingual traits act as strong referential signposts, they bear witness to the authors' multilingual and multicultural biographical background. What kind of relationship does this autofictional, multilingual mode thus establish between fiction and fact, author and narrator, in these texts? Acker and Fleig (2018, 19) comment on this issue: "Multilingual narration dissolves the strict distinction between author and narrator, as multilingual texts always refer to the lingual-cultural multiple affiliation, and thus to the lifeworld of its authors. Consequently, the narratological distinction between factual and fictional narration, which goes hand in hand with the distinction between author and narrator, is questioned." As a central aim of the texts I will examine is to spark an extratextual dialogue, how does the autofictional serve in multilingual literature to reshape the relationship between author and reader?

To explore these theoretical questions, I will turn now to works by Zaimoğlu, Khemiri, and Hassan. I will compare the autobiographical backgrounds of the authors before analyzing the different ways in which their multicultural and multilingual backgrounds emerge in aesthetic terms. These texts do not only address transcultural life experience as a theme; their multifocal narrative structure and interweaving of languages also bear witness to the multicultural and multilingual lifeworld of the authors. Finally, I will evaluate the political impact of these three works with specific reference to their reception.

Voices from Germany, Sweden, and Denmark

While Zaimoğlu, Khemiri, and Hassan's multilingual works are situated somewhere between experience and experiment, the autofictional status of these works enables all three authors to privilege the obsessive experimentation with language over the elements of autobiographical experience. The three works differ with respect to national origin, time period, and genre, but what they share is the authors' endeavor to fight with words, by mobilizing multilingualism as an aesthetic strategy. Feridun Zaimoğlu is German-Turkish, born in 1964 in Bolu; Jonas Hassen Khemiri is Swedish-Arabic-French, born in 1978 in Stockholm; and Yahya Hassan, who was Swedish and Danish-Arabic, was born in 1995 in Aarhus and died in 2020, at the age of twenty-four. Zaimoğlu's *Kanak Sprak: 24 Misstöne vom Rande der Gesellschaft* (1995) comprises a collection of interviews with young Turkish migrants who respond to the question: "What is life as a Kanak like in Germany?" Khemiri's *Ett öga rött* (2003) takes the form of a novel in which fifteen-year-old Halim gives an account of his life as the son of Moroccan parents, who migrated to Stockholm, where Halim was later born. Hassan writes a volume of poetry that bears his own name, *Yahya Hassan* (2013), in which he describes the life of a young migrant in the Gellerup ghetto in Denmark. The similarities between the three texts, however, testify to a transcultural mode of multilingual autofiction, which cuts across differences in nation, language, and form. All three authors give an account of the issues they faced first-hand with respect to integration and racism. When Zaimoğlu wrote *Kanak Sprak*, xenophobia had increased dramatically after many years of a relatively liberal migration policy in Germany. In the 1990s, Germany was hit by a wave of violent attacks on so-called foreigners, which provoked mass protests and new social movements. According to Yildiz, "*Kanak Sprak* comes out of this moment and gives literary form to social assertion in the face of exclusion" (Yildiz 2012, 174). Khemiri, for his part, wrote *Ett öga rött* in 2003, almost ten years after Zaimoğlu but in similarly tense conditions. After centuries of a relatively liberal attitude toward immigration in Sweden, the political discourse changed drastically around 2000 and outbursts of xenophobia became a serious problem. Writing his volume of poetry in 2013, Yahya Hassan also confronted an inflamed discourse on marginalization, structural racism, and freedom of speech in Denmark in the wake of the 2005–2006 Cartoon Crisis. The right-wing party, "Dansk Folkeparti," with its overt anti-foreigner policy, was highly influential in the political landscape between 2006 and 2013, an influence which explains at least in part the virtual absence of postmigrant literature in Denmark prior to Hassan's debut. Hassan's was the first major voice of the second generation of migrants in Denmark, and the first to seriously challenge the political discourse.

In these three texts, the "multicultural, autofictional strategy" works in part thematically, through the authors' indignant descriptions of multicultural experience, and in part stylistically, through the ways in which the authors experiment with narrative structures and hybrid language. Each one bears witness to a strong emotional response, primarily anger, and gives voice to the ghetto, the very symbol of failed integration and a typical heterotopia. In this space, a multitude of languages co-exist, but multilingualism is considered a stigmatizing indicator of social and economic inferiority as opposed to a lingual resource. Zaimoğlu, Khemiri, and Hassan, on the other hand, take advantage of their multilingual capacity, drawing on it as cultural capital in the Bourdieusian sense and thus using it as part of a subversive aesthetic strategy.[6] At the heart of this aesthetic strategy is the authors' use of polyphony. In Bakhtin's discussion of polyglossia and heteroglossia, he addresses the subversive energy in marginalized social groups and the potential power of a multi-layered use of language and languages. These concepts provide an important way into understanding the structural choices in these texts, particularly the interrelation of biography and fiction that will now be explored.

Bakhtin's Voices and Languages

According to Bakhtin, literature and life are fundamentally based on a dialogical principle which always leaves space for the other's voice (Bakhtin 1984). This concept is rooted in his ideological and political thinking as a subversive writer under Stalin's totalitarian regime. For Bakhtin, monologue in literature, where the story is told through one dominant voice, is symptomatic of social homogenization, whereas dialogical and polyphonic literature testify to a diversity of opinions. When he argues that the subversive power of literature derives its force from a diversity of voices (Bakhtin 1981, 65), he points to the ability of literature to instigate dialogues through its aesthetic form. It is on this basis that I propose understanding polyglossia as a strategy of particular importance for transcultural authors as they broach social and political issues through their autofictional works.

What form, then, does this dialogical principle take in literary works? On a textual level, the narrative organization is polyphonic, which, in Bakhtin's writing, means that it includes a multitude of voices, making utterances and expressing their points of view (Bakhtin 1981). The substitution of the classical sovereign narrator by this multifocal orchestration not only questions conventional ways of writing but also more generally a monologic attitude to life. Furthermore, the texts also have a strong focus on multilingualism on a linguistic level, in the shape of heteroglossia as well as polyglossia (Clark and Holquist 1984, 289). While the concept of polyglossia refers to "interlanguage differences," heteroglossia covers the concept of "intralanguage differences" (Clark and Holquist 1984, 289). Whereas polyglossia implies "the interaction with other national languages" (Clark and Holquist 1984, 289), heteroglossia implies interaction between all varieties within a national language including regional dialects, social dialects, ethnolects, and styles (König and Pfister 2017, 236). In the case studies on which I focus in this chapter, polyglossia is best understood as a subcategory of heteroglossia and appears as a distinct linguistic manifestation of Bakhtin's idea of polyphony. Starting at the level of narrative, I will consider the different ways in which Zaimoğlu, Khemiri, and Hassan establish a multitude of voices in their texts. I will then analyze the consequences of the play with the multi-layered structure of language in the three texts, with particular reference to polyglossia. Finally, I will turn to the extratextual question as to how far "the subversive power of the diversity of voices" succeeds in having an impact on political discourse. In pursuing this question, I set out to shed light on a largely unexplored dimension of Bakhtin's theory. Other studies on multicultural and multilingual literature based on Bakhtin's ideas include Holdenried (2014) and Acker and Fleig (2018). My investigation intends to draw more attention to the concrete historical and political dimension of the aesthetics of Bakhtin's literary theories than is the case in either of these studies.

Polyphony on the Narrative Level

From its very title, Zaimoğlu's *Kanak Sprak: 24 Misstöne vom Rande der Gesellschaft* indicates the enormous importance of polyphony in this work, positing no less than twenty-four different voices. In the foreword, itself a significant part of the fictional work, the author presents the project of this book in the same vein as a conductor would introduce a piece of music, in this case a choir of twenty-four discordant voices. These voices belong to young men from a German-Turkish background, who live on the margins of society. All the characters are, on the face of it, subversive figures, ranging from rappers, dealers, and hip-hop artists to drug addicts, and together they form a chorus of angry voices from the ghetto. From a Bakhtinian point of view, the text is a piece of polyphonic documentary.

The narrator of Khemiri's *Ett öga rött* is the fifteen-year-old Halim, who is the child of migrants from Morocco. His mother is dead, and Halim is left alone with his father, who insists that they move out of the ghetto into a more socially respectable part of Stockholm. The novel takes the form of a diary, which principally describes the communication between the father and Halim. The father's remarks, as well as those of the other characters, are all spoken through the mouth of Halim. At first glance, Halim thus appears to be an autonomous first-person narrator, who exerts complete control over the narration. How, then, can we refer to Khemiri's *Ett öga rött* as a polyphonic work? First and foremost, because of the characterization of Halim: he is bicultural and bilingual, and constantly seeks to establish his identity between Swedish and Arabic cultures. Furthermore, he is young, very bright, and full of imagination, giving rise to a narrator who thinks both creatively and unorthodoxically. He refers to himself as "Tankesultan," meaning "Sultan of Thoughts," and this neologism concisely conveys the multicultural background of Halim: he performs not only as a European intellectual *à la Sartre* but also proudly refers to his Arabic roots. The construction of this ambiguous and multifaceted character underpins the polyphonic organization of the text, as his narrative perspective straddles various positions and discourses and thereby denies the reader any singular or fixed point of view from which to observe the unfolding of events. What unsettles the position of the reader still further is that at the end of the story, a young author by the name of Khemiri enters the narrative (Khemiri 2003, 184). His appearance calls into question the identity and authority of the narrator, Halim, as this *mise en abyme* reminds the reader that Halim is just a textual construction by the grace of the author. Just as in Zaimoğlu's *Kanak Sprak*, therefore, in *Ett öga rött*, we encounter a polyphonic narrative structure and the emergence of the empirical author inside the fiction.

Hassan's poetry collection, too, is written in the first person. The fact that the collection bears Hassan's name points to a sovereign author and narrator figure, and to fundamentally monological narrative dynamics. But what if this "I" is heterogeneous to the extreme, positioned on the edge of schizophrenia? In a self-reflexive nod to the ongoing discussion around autofiction, Hassan affirmed in an interview with the German magazine *Der Spiegel* that the person speaking in the poem *is* Yahya Hassan himself: "What I write, that's my identity, that's who I am ... But that doesn't mean I am the way my readers think I am. The reading depends on the individual reader, the reader's reality. I am not responsible for the interpretation" (Rapp 2014). Who, then, is Yahya Hassan? Certainly not just *one* person. The collection of poems showcases the multitude of roles and positions of Yahya Hassan: he is at once son, brother, grandchild, schoolboy, psychiatric patient, violent criminal, drug dealer, the lover of a married woman, celebrated author, and the darling of social media. Added to these multiple positions is the fact that Hassan is bicultural and bilingual, with more than one homeland and mother tongue. His poetry broaches numerous polemical discourses in Denmark, including the devastating conditions of the Danish ghettos, the hypocritical way in which Islam is practiced by his family, the weaknesses of the highly praised welfare state, the right-wing populism, and the self-satisfied cultural establishment, all of which are addressed from different roles and positions. The multiple angles from which these issues are addressed in the collection provide strong grounds from which to consider this work to be polyphonic.

Polyglossia on a Linguistic Level

Having established that polyphony is a key structuring principle in each of these works, I will now consider how the multiple voices they present are characterized by language. How does polyglossia manifest itself on a linguistic level in these three texts? In Zaimoğlu's work, at least two languages or varieties of language are spoken: standard German and the so-called Kanak Sprak. Kanak Sprak is spoken by the twenty-four "Kanakters," a pejorative expression for young migrants in Germany of Turkish origin. Standard German is spoken by the apparently empiric author, Zaimoğlu, in the foreword. It is here that he gives an introduction to Kanak Sprak:

> A long time ago, they created an underground-codex and now speak their own jargon, "Kanak-Sprak," a kind of creol or Rotwelsch[7] with secret codes and signs.
> […]
> The Kanake speaks his mother tongue only erroneously, and only masters "alemannisch" to a certain degree. His vocabulary consists of a gibberished glossary and idioms that do not exist in any language.[8]

In this multiethnolect, which could be interpreted as a sociolect on the basis that it is also the language of the precariat, these young German-Turkish men give aggressive expression to their negative experience of Germany, or as they call it, the country of the "Alemannen." This designation, which is just as pejorative as that of the "Kanakster," underlines the tensions between these two social groups. It is important to note, however, that Zaimoğlu's "Kanak Sprak" is not in fact an authentic multiethnolect. Zaimoğlu informs us in the foreword that he has recorded his interviews with these young men, and then re-told their mini-autobiographies in his version of Kanak Sprak, a version which he says should be more intelligible for the intended reader than the original. The text had a significant impact on youth language in Germany in the 1990s, and today Kanak Sprak is a general term for a multiethnolect: the mixture of German, Arabic, and Turkish spoken by young second- and third-generation migrants. For the purposes of this chapter, however, the importance of the fact that Kanak Sprak is a linguistic construction rather than an authentic language of the ghetto cannot be overstated.

Khemiri's work, too, features multiple languages and language varieties. Alongside Swedish, the matrix language, a multiethnolect is spoken in which linguistic features of Arabic and Turkish are mixed with Swedish. The impact of Arabic is visible on a lexical level in Halim's frequent recourse to words like "Walla" (Khemiri 2003, 12) and "Inshallah" (Khemiri 2003, 13), and even more so on a syntactical level, where Halim uses inversions that are atypical in Swedish. Interestingly, Halim also demonstrates from time to time that he can speak perfect Swedish, but much to the regret of his Moroccan father, he opts for the multiethnolect, which is strongly reminiscent of Rinkebysvenska. This hybrid youth language is spoken by young Swedes from migrant backgrounds, a "cool" multiethnolect that has nothing in common with the clumsy, broken Swedish of Halim's father. But the question of authenticity arises once again when we consider the conflict between critical reviews of *Ett öga rött* in 2003, which deemed Halim's narration an "authentic representation of Rinkeby-Swedish" (Behschnitt and Willems 2012, 11), and interviews of Khemiri, in which he maintains that this is a fallacy, arguing instead that Halim speaks his own language. Khemiri insists that he attempted to create a main character who spoke a language that reflected the desperate search for his identity (Behschnitt and Willems 2012, 12). Halim's multiethnolect, in other words, is just as contrived as Zaimoğlu's Kanak Sprak.

In Hassan's volume of poetry, we see the same multilingual pattern: standard Danish is used in conjunction with a multiethnolect, which Hassan dubs "perkerdansk." "Perkerdansk"—another example of pejorative expression—is a hybrid principally composed of elements from Arabic, Turkish, and Danish.[9] The variations of standard Danish are manifest in the presence of Arabic words, mixed metaphors, and the "false" use of genus, as well as in atypical inversions, as was the case in *Ett öga rött*. In addition, Hassan experiments with the phonetic dimension of his texts, by performing his poems in the mesmerizing manner of an imam and thereby indicating the underlying impact of Arabic culture. The orthography of the text also varies from standard Danish in that all letters are capitalized and no punctuation is used, as in the following example:

THEN YOUR FATHER WAS BORN IN A REFUGEE CAMP
AND THEN MY FATHER WAS BORN IN A REFUGEE CAMP
THEN YOUR FATHER FLEES FROM A REFUGEE CAMP
THEN MY FATHER FLEES FROM A REFUGEE CAMP
AND THEN OUR FATHERS THEY CHANGE

DANISH APARTMENT BLOCKS INTO REFUGEE CAMPS
THEY BRING OUR GRANDPARENTS
OUR UNCLES AND AUNTS
AND ALL OF THEM THEY RECEIVE CASH BENEFITS
THEY BRING THEIR COUSINS
AND THEN THEY START THEIR
INBREEDING INDOCTRICATION
FITTING IN INSHA'ALLAH
AND YOU YOU TURN INTO A DONKEY
A WASH GENUINE DONKEY
YOU YOU TURN INTO A HIPHOP AND CRIMINAL AND MUSLIM
YOU YOU TALK A BROKEN DANISH
AND A BROKEN ARABIC[10]

The syntax is characterized throughout by repetition, indicating a limited capability of varying the language, and morphologically, in the original Danish, articles are often left out or the wrong article has been chosen. These lingual strategies together produce a highly expressionistic form, the capitalized writing indicating that the lines should be screamed out in an accusatory manner.

Parts of the collection of poems are written, by contrast, in a high standard Danish that bears the stamp of Yahya Hassan's life outside the ghetto, namely, as an intellectual, a student at the Danish Author's School (Forfatterskolen), and a celebrated writer. It is noteworthy, however, that in the final and explosive thirty-three-page poem "LANGDIGT" ("Long Poem"), the most comprehensive autobiographical account in the collection, Hassan chooses to express himself in the multiethnolect (Hassan 2013, 135–169). In this poem, he compiles events from his life and his opinions, writing in "perkerdansk," and through this multiethnolect immersion he foregrounds the "perkerdansk" version of his existence. As the reader is aware from the earlier poems in the collection that he masters an elegant Danish style perfectly, the "perkerdansk" of the final poem appears to be something of a caricature. As in Khemiri's and Zaimoğlu's texts, the mixture of languages is not simply a matter of multilingualism but also a matter of the deliberate construction of multiethnolects.[11]

By hybridizing language and referring to these languages by their pejorative names, the three authors make their texts a performative act in the sense of Judith Butler's "resignification" (Butler 1990). The conventional power relations between the national matrix languages and the subversive multiethnolects are turned on their head in a way that exposes a *mundus pravus*. This maneuver is perhaps best interpreted in terms of a Bakhtinian carnivalesque scene, in which the very notion of a national language is deconstructed through the use of polyglossia. Khemiri and Hassan both refer explicitly to the immense power of language inside their texts, conceiving of words as a weapon. Halim states that "words are like the most powerful weapons which will never be blunt or run out of bullets" (2003, 89) and Yahya Hassan ends his "LANGDIGT" with the line: "ME, I FIGHT AGAINST YOU WITH WORDS" (2013, 169).

PERFORMATIVITY AND THE AUTHOR IN HIS SOCIAL FIELD

Kanak Sprak: 24 Misstöne vom Rande der Gesellschaft, *Ett öga rött*, and *Yahya Hassan* all comment on the existing discourses on migrant-related matters in their respective historical, cultural, and geographic contexts. They are landmark texts in light of the challenge that they pose to the "monolingual paradigm" (Yildiz 2012, 2), and the ways in which they showcase the subversive power of polyphony. Yildiz comments that Zaimoğlu "almost single-handedly propelled young postmigrants' linguistic practices into the public sphere of post-unification Germany with his book *Kanak Sprak* [...]" (Yildiz 2012, 172). With respect to Khemiri, Yildiz states: "Khemiri's manipulations of Swedish transpose the country's newly globalized linguascape into literature for the first time" (Yildiz 2012, 180). And in 2015, the editorial of the Danish newspaper *Politiken* gave the following account of Yahya Hassan: "There is no reason to underestimate the nineteen-year-old poet. He has already turned upside down what the role of poetry and literature could be in a modern society" (*Politiken* 2015, 1).

In the final section of this chapter, I will move from the abstract conception of subversive power that is typically drawn from Bakhtin's work to the concrete impact of these texts, focusing on their successful intervention in contemporary political and social discourses. All three authors have had a significant influence in this respect: in the wake of *Kanak Sprak*, Zaimoğlu instigated the anti-racist movement "Kanak Attak," which comprises "a community of different people from diverse backgrounds who share a commitment to eradicate racism from German society" (Kanak Attak 1998). Zaimoğlu's highly public profile has played a crucial role in the extratextual impact of his work: he has appeared on talk shows, given book tours, contributed to newspaper and magazine features, and even turned *Kanak Sprak* into a stage production. He uses all of these public appearances to radically call into question conventional interpretations of German society and "to turn the dominant discourse on migration upside down" (Gürsel 2012).

Khemiri is a similarly prominent personality in Swedish culture, a regular participant in talk shows and an active contributor on social media. Yet, while *Ett öga rött* secured him a place in the cultural establishment, he uses this position to interrogate embedded injustice and racism. In 2013, he wrote an open letter to the Swedish Justice Minister, Beatrice Ask, criticizing the policy of the Swedish government with reference to his own experiences of racial prejudice. This letter (Khemiri [2013]), in which he accuses Sweden of "constant, low-intensity oppression," is the most widely read open letter in Swedish public history, and it was re-published in the *New York Times*, thus securing Khemiri's international recognition.

Yahya Hassan, for its part, is the most successful collection of poetry in the history of Danish literature: to date, more than 120,000 copies have been sold and it has been translated into over ten different languages. Hassan was already well known prior to this publication, having first come to prominence when he was interviewed for an article in the Danish newspaper *Politiken* in 2013 entitled "I Am Fucking Angry with My Parents' Generation" (Omar 2013). Right up to his death in 2020, his provocative statements and actions made him a permanent fixture of both social media and public life. His oeuvre is best described as a "total work of art," in which writing is inextricably linked to public performance. It is by way of this fusion that Hassan succeeded in sparking highly influential discussions about political, religious, ethnic, and aesthetic discourses in Denmark, his social impact outstripping that of any other author or politician.

A Genre In-Between

The impact of these three works on the political discourse in their respective countries is indisputable: it demonstrates the successful implementation of Bakhtin's dialogical principle in society. It is on this basis that I propose that these three works exemplify a new autofictional multicultural mode, characterized by: (1) a polyphonic narrative structure; (2) the author's explicit appearance in the fiction; (3) different languages spoken by the various "voices" in play, the dominant one being a constructed multiethnolect; and (4) the author appearing on an extratextual level in a performative capacity. By making a multitude of voices the basis of the narrative structure, the authors mirror the conditions and perceptions of human beings in a modern world, whose perspective is becoming ever more multifocalized as a result of increasing numbers of transcultural crossings. In this way, the works attain a mimetic function, communicating the life experience not only of the multicultural author but of a whole segment of people from transcultural backgrounds. As they strive toward narrative plurality, the authors challenge the singular perspective of traditional autobiography, since the voices represent a collective "we" rather than an "I."[12] By presenting themselves on the same level as the other voices in the texts, the authors posit an anti-hierarchic, dialogical way of thinking. Rather than adopting the sovereign stance of the autobiographer, the in-between position that autofiction affords these writers allows them to invite other voices into the discourse.

Despite positioning themselves in this way as one voice among others, the authors are nonetheless the principal orchestrators in these texts. They use their multilingual capacity to organize language, narration, and dialogue. Author and polyglossia are inextricably linked, as the multilingual author inevitably leaves lingual and thus biographical footprints. But multilingualism is not only a crucial tool for representing the multicultural experience of living in-between; it also functions as a key strategy through which the authors instigate and attempt to reshape extratextual dialogues. By way of their strongly performative dimension, these works aspire unapologetically to effect political and social change.

With respect to the generic categorization of their works, the appearance of the authors inside the fiction and the fusion of fiction and referentiality at the heart of the artificial multiethnolects certainly invites comparison with Doubrovsky's conception of autofiction. Yet, as we have seen, these works diverge palpably from the game of hide-and-seek between author and reader that is also characteristic of autofiction, and which lies at the center of accusations of the genre's lack of social engagement.[13] *Kanak Sprak*, *Ett öga rött*, and *Yahya Hassan* have their playful moments, but these are put in the service of racial and cultural responsibility and testify to the authors' concerns with contemporary social conditions. It is for this reason that I propose the term "multilingual autofiction," which accounts for the powerful role that language plays in enabling these literary works to question social norms and power relations. These examples of a multilingual autofictional mode invite a different theoretical focus, one which gives less attention to the play between author and narrator, fact and fiction, and more to the potential affordances of autofiction beyond the text.

Notes

1. The term is used in my PhD project "Against a Multilingual Autofictional Mode in Literature: Studies of Aesthetic Expressions and Political Impacts in Three Multilingual and Transcultural Literary Works."
2. For research in the field of multilingual literature in general, see Dembeck and Parr (2017), Schmitz-Emans (2004), Arnold Knauth (2004), Radaelli (2011), Yildiz (2012), and Zemanek and Willms (2014).
3. According to their respective websites for national statistics, in 2020, 14% of the Danish population had a migrant background compared to 22% of the Swedish population in 2019 and 26% of the German population in 2020.
4. Unless stated otherwise, translations are my own.
5. For studies on this tendency, see Kilchmann (2017), Richter (2017), and Acker and Fleig (2018).
6. In his work *Language and Symbolic Power* (1991), the French sociologist Pierre Bourdieu suggests that language should be considered as a kind of symbolic capital.
7. Rotwelsch was a secret language, spoken primarily by marginalized groups in Southern Germany or Switzerland in the nineteenth century.
8. "Längst haben sie einen Untergrund-Kodex entwickelt und sprechen einen eigenen Jargon, die 'Kanak-Sprak,' eine Art Creol oder Rotwelsch mit geheimen Codes und Zeichen. [...] Der Kanake spricht seine Muttersprache nur fehlerhaft, auch das 'alemannisch' ist ihm nur bedingt geläufig. Sein Sprachschatz setzt sich aus 'verkauderwelschten' Vokabeln und Redewendungen zusammen, die so in keiner der Sprachen vorkommen" (Zaimoğlu 1995, 13).
9. For studies on bilingualism in Denmark, see Quist and Jørgensen 2009.
10. SÅ DIN FAR BLEV FØDT I FLYGTNINGELEJR
    OG SÅ MIN FAR BLEV FØDT I FLYGTNINGELEJR
    SÅ DIN FAR FLYGTER FRA FLYTNINGELEJR
    SÅ MIN FAR FLYGTER FRA FLYGTNINGELEJR
    OG SÅ VORES FÆDRE DE FORVANDLER
    DANSKE BLOKKE TIL FLYGTNINGELEJRE
    DE HENTER VORES BEDSTEFORÆLDRE
    VORES ONKLER OG TANTER
    OG ALLE SAMMEN FÅR DE KONTANTHJÆLP
    DE HENTER DERES KUSINER OG DERES FÆTRE
    OG SÅ GÅR DE I GANG MED DERES
    INDAVL INDOKTRINERING
    INDPASNING INSHA'ALLAH
    OG DIG DU BLIVER EN ÆSEL

EN VASKEÆGTE ÆSEL
DIG DU BLIVER EN HIPHOP OG KRIMINEL OG MUSLIM
DIG DU TALER EN GEBROKKEN DANSK
OG EN GEBROKKEN ARABISK (2013, 146–147).
11. One of the few Danish critics who pay attention to the effect of multilingualism in Yahya Hassan's work is Lilian Munk-Rösing (2020).
12. Astrid Erll (2005, 187–188) specifically refers to Bakhtin in a paragraph on "Multiperspektivität" in her study on collective memory.
13. Criticism of the insincerity of autofiction has been made by Arnaud Schmitt and Marie Darrieussecq, among others. See Acker and Fleig (2018, 24–26).

Works Cited

Acker, Marion, and Anne Fleig. 2018. Die Aufrichtigkeit der Mehrsprachigkeit: Autofiktion, Autonarration oder das Konzept dialogischer Autorschaft bei Yoko Tawada. In *Sich selbst erzählen: Autobiographie—Autofiktion—Autorschaft*, ed. Sonja Arnold, Stephanie Catani, Anita Gröger, Christoph Jürgensen, Klaus Schenk, and Martina Wagner-Egelhaaf, 19–37. Kiel: Verlag Ludwig.
Bakhtin, Mikhail Mikhailovich. 1981. *The Dialogic Imagination: Four Essays*. Edited by Michael Holquist. Austin, TX: University of Texas Press.
———. 1984. *Problems of Dostoevsky's Poetics*. Translated and edited by Carol Emerson. Minneapolis, MN: University of Minnesota Press.
Behschnitt, Wolfgang, and An Willems. 2012. Jonas Hassen Khemiri and the Post-Monolingual Condition: Or, the Camel with Two Humps. *Multiethnica* 34: 10–14.
Bourdieu, Pierre. 1991. *Language and Symbolic Power*. Translated by Gino Raymond and Matthew Adamson. Cambridge: Polity Press.
Butler, Judith. 1990. *Gender Trouble: Feminism and the Subversion of Identity*. London: Routledge.
Clark, Katerina, and Holquist, Michael. 1984. *Mikhail Bakhtin*. Cambridge, MA: Harvard University Press.
Dembeck, Till, and Rolf Parr. 2017. *Literatur und Mehrsprachigkeit: Ein Handbuch*. Tübingen: Narr France Attempo.
Doubrovsky, Serge. 1977. *Fils*. Paris: Galilée.
Editorial. 2015. Politiken, April 10, 2015.
Erll, Astrid. 2005. *Kollektives Gedächtnis und Erinnerungskulturen*. Stuttgart: Metzler.
Gebauer, Mirjam. 2009. 'Lebensgeschichte einer Zunge': Autobiographisches Schreiben jenseits der Muttersprache bei Yoko Tawada. In *Autobiographisches Schreiben in der deutschen Gegenwartsliteratur. Bd. 3: Entwicklungen, Kontexte, Grenzgänge*, ed. Michael Grote and Beatrice Sandberg, 114–129. München: Iudicium.

Gronemann, Claudia. 2019. Autofiction. In *Handbook of Autobiography / Autofiction*, ed. Martina Wagner-Egelhaaf, 241–246. Berlin: De Gruyter.
Gürsel, Duygu. 2012. Kanak Attak: Discursive Acts of Citizenship in Germany. *Opendemocracy.net*, November 9, 2012. https://www.opendemocracy.net/en/can-europe-make-it/kanak-attak-discursive-acts-of-citizenship-in-germany/. Accessed Apr 6, 2021.
Hassan, Yahya. 2013. *Yahya Hassan*. København: Gyldendal.
Holdenried, Michaela. 2012. Eine Poetik der Interkulturalität? Zur Transgression von Grenzen am Beispiel von Yoko Tawadas Schreibverfahren und Sprachprogrammatik. In *Yoko Tawada. Fremde Wasser: Vorlesungen und wissenschaftliche Beiträge*, ed. Ortrud Gutjahr, 169–185. Tübingen: Konkursbuch.
———. 2014. Zur Poetik des Törlü Gjuvetch Polyglossie im postkolonialen Kontext am Beispiel von Ilija Trojanows Der Weltensammler. In *Polyglotte Texte*, ed. Weertje Willms and Evi Zemanek, 241–255. Special issue, *Komparatistik Online* 2. https://www.komparatistik-online.de/index.php/komparatistik_online/issue/view/9. Accessed Apr 6, 2021.
Iversen, Stefan. 2020. Transgressive Narration: The Case of Autofiction. In *Narrative Factuality: A Handbook*, ed. Monika Fludernik and Marie-Laure Ryan, 555–565. Berlin: De Gruyter.
Kanak, Attak. 1998. "About" page on website. November 1998. https://www.kanak-attak.de/ka/about/manif_eng.html. Accessed Apr 6, 2021.
Khemiri, Jonas Hassen. 2003. *Et öga rött*. Stockholm: Norstedts Förlag.
———. 2013. An Open Letter to Beatrice Ask. n.d. https://www.asymptotejournal.com/nonfiction/jonas-hassen-khemiri-an-open-letter-to-beatrice-ask/. Accessed Apr 6, 2021.
Kilchmann, Esther. 2017. Von der Erfahrung zum Experiment: Literarische Mehrsprachigkeit 2000–2015. In *Gegenwart schreiben: Zur deutschsprachigen Literatur 2000-2015*, ed. Corina Caduff and Ulrike Vedder, 177–186. Paderborn: Wilhelm Fink.
Knauth, Alfons K. 2004. Multilinguale Literatur. In *Literatur und Vielsprachigkeit*, ed. Monika Schmitz-Emans, 265–289. Heidelberg: Synchron.
König, Ekkehard, and Manfred Pfister. 2017. *Literary Analysis and Linguistics*. Berlin: Erich Schmidt.
Munk-Rösing, Lilian. 2020. Der var et særligt drive og en insisterende pulseren i hans poesi. *Politiken*, May 2, 2020.
Omar, Tarek. 2013. Jeg er fucking vred på mine forældres generation. *Politiken*, October 5, 2013.
Quist, Pia, and Normann J. Jørgensen. 2009. Bilingual Children in Monolingual Schools. In *Handbook of Multilingualism and Multilingual Communication*, ed. Peter Auer and Wei Li, 155–173. New York: Mouton de Gruyter.
Radaelli, Giulia. 2011. *Literarische Mehrsprachigkeit: Sprachwechsel bei Elias Canetti und Ingeborg Bachmann*. Berlin: De Gruyter.

Rapp, Tobias. 2014. Literary Sensation: The Rise of a Danish Immigrant Poet. *Der Spiegel*, March 14, 2014.
Richter, Sandra. 2017. *Eine Weltgeschichte der deutschsprachigen Literatur.* München: C. Bertelsmann.
Schmitz-Emans, Monika. 2004. Literatur und Vielsprachigkeit: Aspekte, Themen, Voraussetzungen. In *Literatur und Vielsprachigkeit*, ed. Monika Schmitz-Emans, 11–26. Heidelberg: Synchron.
Wagner-Egelhaaf, Martina. 2006. Autofiktion Oder: Autobiographie nach der Autobiographie. Goethe—Barthes—Özdamar. In *Grenzen der Identität und der Fiktionalitä:. Autobiographisches Schreiben in der deutschsprachigen Gegenwartsliteratur. Band 1*, ed. Ulrich Breuer and Beatrice Sandberg, 353–368. München: Iudicium.
———, ed. 2020. *Handbook of Autobiography / Autofiction.* Berlin: De Gruyter.
Yildiz, Yasemin. 2012. *Beyond the Mother Tongue: The Postmonolingual Condition.* New York: Fordham University Press.
Zaimoğlu, Feridun. 1995. *Kanak Sprak: 24 Misstöne vom Rande der Gesellschaft.* Berlin: Rotbuch Verlag.
Zaimoğlu, Feridun, and Julia Abel. 2005. Migrationsliteratur ist ein toter Kadaver: Ein Gespräch. In *Text + Kritik. Sonderband IX/06. Literatur und Migration*, ed. Heinz Ludwig Arnold, 159–166. München: Richard Boorberg Verlag.
Zemanek, Evi, and Willms, Weertje. 2014. Polyglotte Texte—Einleitung. In *Polyglotte Texte*, ed. Weertje Willms and Evi Zemanek, 1–6. Special issue, *Komparatistik Online* 2. https://www.komparatistik-online.de/index.php/komparatistik_online/issue/view/9. Accessed Apr 6, 2021.

Open Access This chapter is licensed under the terms of the Creative Commons Attribution 4.0 International License (http://creativecommons.org/licenses/by/4.0/), which permits use, sharing, adaptation, distribution and reproduction in any medium or format, as long as you give appropriate credit to the original author(s) and the source, provide a link to the Creative Commons licence and indicate if changes were made.

The images or other third party material in this chapter are included in the chapter's Creative Commons licence, unless indicated otherwise in a credit line to the material. If material is not included in the chapter's Creative Commons licence and your intended use is not permitted by statutory regulation or exceeds the permitted use, you will need to obtain permission directly from the copyright holder.

CHAPTER 9

Visual Autofiction: A Strategy for Cultural Inclusion

Karen Ferreira-Meyers and Bontle Tau

This chapter considers the use of autofiction as a visual storytelling method by contemporary artists, a practice designed to initiate cultural inclusion within a field that has historically favored European visual narratives and excluded many others. Here we consider the autofictional as a literary form that rests in between autobiography and fiction, creating a space in which fact and fiction can coexist within a single testimonial. While it originated as a literary term, autofiction has since been interpreted and integrated, as a concept, into various other creative forms, including the visual arts (de Bloois 2007; Ahmed 2014). One of the dominant issues currently being addressed within the visual arts, a traditionally Western European field of practice, is that of cultural inclusion and decolonization within broader visual narratives. This chapter contends that contemporary artists are tackling this issue through the innovative methods of visual autofiction they employ to represent their experiences through their

K. Ferreira-Meyers (✉)
Institute of Distance Education, University of Eswatini, Kwaluseni, Eswatini

B. Tau
Bloemfontein, South Africa

© The Author(s) 2022
A. Effe, H. Lawlor (eds.), *The Autofictional*, Palgrave Studies in Life Writing, https://doi.org/10.1007/978-3-030-78440-9_9

creative practice. These artists use autofiction as a storytelling strategy in order to construct a multiform and multifaceted narrative that foregrounds the diversity of selves and stories in the visual arts, further supporting the overall aim of cultural inclusion within representations in the field.

One of the key freedoms afforded by autofiction is that of self-narration undertaken from a variety of perspectives. Autofiction challenges the factuality of autobiography, in terms of its concrete and verifiable truth, in combining any such truth with aspects of fiction and fictionalization (Ferreira-Meyers 2012, 2015, 2018). In so doing, it opens up the possibility of a practice of self-narration which can be ever-changing in terms of viewpoint, mode, and its potential reception by an audience. While the fictional maintains its creative freedom, its placement in such close proximity to the perceived factual elements of autobiography persistently critiques the authenticity and stability of the autobiographical. The act of "narrating the self" is revealed instead as taking place in a reality that is created by and particular to the author. As autofictional practice draws attention to the "trickery" behind this narration, it reveals a different kind of truth behind the autobiographical account: the author or artist's subjective desire to present themselves in a certain manner. The foregrounding of the subjective angles from which the self can be viewed and represented is a key focus in visual art, and nowhere more so than in the domain of self-portraiture.

In its most basic definition, a self-portrait is "a representation of oneself made by oneself" (MoMA 2021). Ben Grant mentions, in his chapter in this volume, the importance of recognizing self-portraiture as synonymous in visual and literary practice. He argues that the prerequisite for a self-portrait across mediums is the absence of a continuous narrative, giving the creators of these self-portraits the liberty to present themselves without the usual (autobiographical) constraints such as chronology or logical order (this volume, 288). It is important to recognize, however, that more than a creative practice, the self-portrait posits a metaphysical awareness of what constitutes the "self." The artist is first required to *recognize* the "self," that is, before attempting to *represent* the "self" (Crozier and Greenhalgh 1988). As the MoMA glossary definition implies, artists are given the opportunity to "re-present" themselves in various modes, each time presenting the audience with a new self-narrative. "Truthfulness" in the self-portrait becomes negotiable due to the multiple, differing, and at times contradictory portrayals of the self. As in autofiction, these multiple versions offer a kind of fictionalized account of the "self." Dating back to the early Renaissance, the self-portrait has been a critical component of the formal training and identity of a visual artist (Smith 2001). It is regarded as an essential tool in their arsenal, and, for this reason, the majority of practicing artists will have made a self-portrait in the course of their career.

A long-standing dilemma in the institution of the visual arts has been the need for more inclusive representation of subjects from various cultural backgrounds, as in the "canon" of the Fine Arts, only one cultural group has been broadly and accurately represented. The initial parameters of the Fine Arts or "Beaux Arts," as an institution for recognition, training, and cultural appreciation for the arts, were set in a European context. While prehistoric art originates primarily in the African continent, the formalization of creative visual practice—that is, where art was recognized as a profession—takes place in Europe. As a result, the most influential art institutions are informed by European visual representations. In a twenty-first-century context, while many racial and cultural groups form part of the framework of practicing visual artists, the parameters of cultural representation within the field are too narrow to accommodate the variety of practitioners, and indeed the variety of their works. The multicultural contemporary artist is thus left to subscribe to a predetermined Western narrative and to contend with the notion of the "Old Masters" of the Fine Arts, as well as the visual narratives chosen by them. As recognized "Old Masters" were predominantly European males, their methods of representation operated from a single cultural and gendered perspective, bringing that particular visual perspective to the fore. Contemporary artists who are not part of this former cultural narrative thus face the task of finding innovative methods to include themselves, or individuals of a similar background, within a visual narrative that did not accommodate them previously. In order to figuratively insert themselves into the visual canon, some artists adopt what we refer to as an "autofictional approach" through their various interpretations of what constitutes a self-portrait. The freedom to "fictionalize truths" provides these artists, or "visual storytellers," with the means to highlight social issues and unjust realities, using strategies that are playful, subtle, and layered. It affords non-European artists in particular a space in which to imagine themselves into the "canon" of self-portraiture.

Bontle Tau, a visual artist from South Africa, uses what she refers to as "autofictional practice in self-portraiture" to create a multicultural representational platform, in an effort to encourage the decolonization of the visual art canon, through inserting herself as a representative of an often-excluded subject in the historically recognized Fine Art narrative, the black female. Tau forms part of a large collective of contemporary African artists who address their desire to be represented within this narrative through imaginative visual storytelling strategies. Her primary medium of choice is self-portrait photography, which she perceives to be a deceptive medium. As a photographer, Tau pays mind to the popularized quotation from Richard Avedon, which states: "All photographs are accurate, but none of them tell the truth" (Avedon 1993). In acknowledging the role of the photographer as one who manipulates the content of the image through framing, composition, light, and perspective, Tau is able to operate within an imaginative and fluctuating mode of self-expression.

The Role of Cultural Mimicry in Autofictional Practice

As a polyglot who speaks seven languages, Tau's work focuses on the navigation of a multilingual cultural identity. In her artistic practice, she constantly questions the authenticity of the self as she witnesses the change in her self-expression when moving between languages. French is one of the more recent languages she has acquired and also one of the languages that she has explored most extensively. Her interest in the language lies in its "inaccessibility," as she lives in a non-Francophone nation, as well as in the historical-colonial ties between France and Africa, which still have an important impact on African societies today. As a visual artist and researcher in Fine Arts, Tau recognizes the traceable influence of the French *École des Beaux Arts*, which has shaped the structure and training methods of many contemporary art schools, even in South Africa. Conscious of the former colonial relationships between Africa and France, Tau sees her identity as that of an African artist and the encounter with the French language and culture as an inevitable conversation of cultural exchange.

Tau employs various visual storytelling techniques to project herself, or representations of people like her, into canonical and influential visual narratives. As a point of departure in her oeuvre, Tau considers the work of social linguist M.A.K. Halliday who states that language is something which can be performed and, more specifically, can serve as a medium for social performance in a given social (or cultural) setting. In his book *Language as Social Semiotic: The Social Interpretation of Language and Meaning* (1978), Halliday portrays language as something which exists on a *social field*. By "social field," he refers to any cultural setting such as a classroom, a boardroom, or even a casual social setting such as a restaurant or coffee house. Within this particular social field, Halliday identifies a "role-play" which takes place between those present. This refers to the position each individual takes in a given social field or the "role" that is played in each cultural setting. Halliday further identifies a "mode": the medium through which the language is performed and received, be it speaking, listening, reading, or writing (Halliday 1978, 53). In Tau's *Mirror Series* (2018) of self-portraits, she allows herself the freedom to play a range of linguistic and cultural roles by photographing herself in a mirror with asemic writing (illegible writing or marks that resemble writing but do not have any meaning), a visual symbol of a universal language smokescreen through which she moves in and out of these different roles. The "smokescreen" depicted in Tau's images enables her to adopt different poses, thus representing different cultural gestures.

"The Look of Reading (After Garrett Stewart)" (Fig. 9.1) was created in response to the work of the same name by literary theorist Garrett Stewart which explores the visual representation of the act of reading. In this work, Stewart analyzes the visualization of "thinking" that takes place through reading, paying tribute to the use of the book as a prop in classic or traditional painted portraits in order to portray an enlightened individual. Notably, the subjects who were placed in the role of "reader" and/or that of an enlightened individual were commonly women in a seated posture (Stewart 2009). Tau's response to Stewart's work was to adopt this very position of the "enlightened" woman. In this image, Tau interacts with a series of Larousse books, one of the most widely recognized publishing houses of classic French literature, casting herself in the role of the seated woman who reads to enrich her mind and to pass the time. Second only to nobility, the subject in question—a woman taking on the role of the reading scholar—is one of the most highly esteemed subjects portrayed in portraiture. In imagining herself into the Western tradition of women in portraiture, Tau highlights the absence of representations of black women in the classical canon. Her imaginative autofictional representation inscribes the black female into this esteemed artistic tradition.

In Fig. 9.2, "L'Inscription" (The Inscription) (2018), Tau positions herself behind the smokescreen in order to subscribe to a specific lingual identity, in this case, Francophone, in keeping with the French title of the work. Her gesture of leaning forward and her imitation of the act of writing, together signify the act of "signing up" for this identity. Taken

Fig. 9.1 "The Look of Reading (After Garret Stewart)," 2018. Digital Self-Portrait Photograph

through a mirror, a surface that distorts the presentation as well as the perception of the self, both these images speak to the autofictional representation and reception of the self. The distortion of reality symbolized by the mirror is discussed by Stephen Paul Miller (1993) with reference to the sixteenth-century painter Francesco Parmigianino who, through a convex mirror, attempted to capture everything in his studio in one single view. His objective was to represent everything that appeared on his three-dimensional mirror as truthfully as possible onto a two-dimensional circular canvas. Parmigianino called this his "Self-Portrait in a Convex Mirror" (1524). A flat, conventional mirror, according to Miller, cannot achieve this all-encompassing effect, which is where the affordance of autofiction comes in. While a convex mirror creates images that are obviously distorted, it can capture everything. A flat mirror, on the other hand, does not capture everything before it, but presents a more mimetically "correct" image than the convex one. Tau's use of a flat mirror indicates her wish to be truthful to reality while also recognizing the fact that not "all"

Fig. 9.2 "L'Inscription," 2018. Digital Self-Portrait Photograph

reality can be captured. As autofictional practice grapples with the concepts of truth and factuality or "reality," in this case, in the process of self-narration, Tau's use of the mirror as a vessel to present the "self" constitutes a visual autofictional tool in her own practice of self-narration.

Tau's multiple lingual identities fuse together her self-representation in autofictional practice—which in art necessitates a recognizable reproduction of the self—with an individual who operates or speaks toward a colonial expression through imitation and mimicry. The mirror in this work plays a significant role in this regard, insofar as it also symbolizes a distortion of the self. As mentioned in the case of Miller, we see an incomplete representation of the self and its immediate environment through the flat mirror; simultaneously, the notion of "doubling" is brought to mind, as one is inherently aware of the "original" self that the mirror reflects. The question of authenticity when expressing oneself through different cultural identities comes to the fore as Tau investigates whether or not she will maintain (aspects of) her former cultural identities, after she has acquired new ones. In *The Location of Culture* (1994), Homi Bhabha describes "mimicry" as a response to the African postcolonial movement, a term which he coined to describe the previously colonialized society's adoption of new languages and assimilation of a new cultural identity. Mimicry, according to Bhabha, is "a form of double articulation [which] appropriates the other as it visualizes power" (Bhabha 1994, 86). It allows one to adopt the cultural and lingual tendencies of another ethnic group (which in Bhabha's understanding is a dominant, colonial group) while maintaining and continuing to express the lingual and cultural tendencies they possessed before encountering this foreign culture. Mimicry is the resultant simultaneous expression of two or more cultures that have interacted within an individual. In the act of mimicking colonial discourse, the individual thus becomes layered, and indeed enhanced, in the domain of (visual) language and culture (Bhabha 1994). Far from being left powerless and non-identifiable, the individual has mastered what was previously considered to be the "master's" tongue. The subversive and playful approach to "mimicking" another cultural identity as well as distorting the self or the environment in which one finds oneself, finds an ideal vehicle in autofictional portraiture, in which the artist visualizes a desired alternate self, using a real-life environment or version of the self to do so. It also assists the artist in creatively projecting themselves into a cultural visual narrative that is not their own.

Cultural Assimilation and Language Loss

In her personal quest to authenticate her identity, an identity that is now informed by multiple lingual and cultural perspectives, autobiographical elements become important for Tau's oeuvre as she looks to her heritage for answers in relation to her cultural choices and pursuits in the present. Tau describes herself as having been an "inside child" during her childhood: her family sought to keep her away from the township (in South Africa, a "township" refers to a suburb or city of predominantly black—and often poor or working class—occupation, formerly designated for black occupation by apartheid legislation). They feared that she would be "contaminated" by the culture of these streets, a contamination that would be frowned upon in her future personal and professional pursuits. The "inside" in Tau's case pertains to her grandmother's home in Bochabela, in the Free State, where she was prohibited from participating in township cultural customs and behavior, which included speaking creolized versions of her home language, Sesotho. Instead, Tau explains that she was encouraged to practice Western spoken languages such as English in the home, cut off from the very different cultural and lingual environment that was mere meters away. For many African families like Tau's, access to Western culture and language equates to access to the kind of spaces which will offer success and opportunity. This preoccupation with access, according to Tau, is a prevailing social issue in African households, where assimilation is held in high esteem owing to the cultural domination exercised by a single group in their colonial cultural history.

French postcolonial writers form the framework of Tau's research portfolio, including the acclaimed French Caribbean writer Maryse Condé, who was awarded the Nobel Prize in Literature in 2018 following the publication of her autobiography entitled *La Vie sans fards* (*What Is Africa to Me?*) (2014). In response to Condé's text, Tau created a series of photographic portraits, including two self-portraits which evoke the ways in which her childhood was shaped by the pursuit of cultural assimilation.

The two portraits, "Je t'attends, je t'attends là pendant toute ma vie" (I'll wait for you, I'll wait here for you all my life) (Fig. 9.3) and "En

Fig. 9.3 "Je t'attends là, je t'attends là pendant toute ma vie," 2020. Digital Self-Portrait

regardant mes peuples" (Looking at my peuples) (Fig. 9.4) depict Tau in the backyard of her late grandmother's home in Bochabela. Tau wears her grandmother's nightgown, which was fashioned to emulate a European design, and stands passively in a jungle gym that was placed inside the yard for her to play on during her childhood. In "Je t'attends, je t'attends là pendant toute ma vie," Tau assumes the role of acquiescent prisoner. She describes herself as emulating in this image the ghost of her grandmother in the hope of her return, a figure whom she believes to have been the only authentic reminder of her own Sesotho heritage. In "En regardant mes peuples," by contrast, Tau's position transforms the setting, formerly portrayed as a prison, into a stronghold. Here, Tau takes refuge in the confines of her inside position, adopting a stance in which she looks downward onto any outsider from her confines of assimilation. In this image, perception and point of view become critical, as the shadow of a bar from Tau's confining jungle gym is cast over her eyes, making subject and viewer alike physically and metaphorically "blind" to one another through this particular portrayal of self.

Fig. 9.4 "En regardant mes peuples," 2020. Digital Self-Portrait

Through these images, Tau puts into dialogue the two very different positions that she adopts in the same setting as a comment on assimilation and self-expression within a cultural narrative. Together, the images remind us of the impact of assimilation on identity, in which ties to former cultural "selves" must be relinquished in the adoption of a dominant cultural identity. Tau considers the loss of her Sesotho cultural identity as a prerequisite for mastering English and French. In her endeavor to immerse herself more fully in the cultures that these dominant languages represent, neglecting (parts of) her mother tongue becomes a necessary part of the process. The consequential loss of language is addressed by Joshua A. Fishman in *What Do You Lose When You Lose Your Language?* (1996), where he discusses the intergenerational loss of ethnic languages in favor of a dominant language. Fishman describes a first-generation immigrant who is bilingual, but who sacrifices their ethnic mother tongue for a dominant language. Imparted less and less to each new generation, the mother tongue is eventually lost (80–91). Tau addresses the issue of language loss through this pair of images, which represent the paradoxical nature of language acquisition: the gain of one lingual identity, for the loss of another. Tau grapples with the nostalgia for her Sesotho heritage in these two images by projecting elements of her memory and her imagination onto the artworks. While she visualizes herself in a position of "power" within the stronghold of a European cultural identity, by autofictionally evoking the Eurocentric aspects of her childhood, the images subtly remind us of her longing for the African self that she leaves behind, as she returns to the last memorable location which possessed remnants of her culture.

Imagining the "Self" Through Time and Memory

A common practice in traditional self-portraiture is the depiction of the artist over time. This practice is visible in the canonical work of many of the "Old Masters" such as Caravaggio, Monet, Rembrandt, Da Vinci, and even Van Gogh in their self-portraits at different life stages, portraits which have been permanently etched in the visual narrative of self-portraiture, to be studied and valued for centuries after their creation (Woods-Marsden 1998, 295). In Tau's attempt to expand the parameters of this institutionalized practice, she projects the same narrative onto her self-portraiture as she copies a portrait of herself as a child in "Of Another Time When I Existed" (Fig. 9.5). It is important to note that, while examples of the

Fig. 9.5 "Of Another Time When I Existed," 2020. Self-portrait drawn in smoke and charcoal on paper

"Old Masters" are seen in the context of moving forward in time through different life stages, Tau decides here to move backward in time, and thus operate through the lens of memory. She chooses to use the autofictional approach of imitating a former practice of self-portraiture and subverting this narration by reversing the sequence in which her self-portraits are made, thereby inverting the practice of the "Old Masters" to suit her personal narrative.

Memory operates on two different levels in this image: first, we observe its visual trace in the photograph that Tau uses as her source material, the physical manifestation of the memory, so to speak. Second, Tau stages the act of remembering an event from her childhood in how she recreates the image in a different medium. This self-portrait, unlike many of Tau's other works, is made using candle smoke and charcoal. The image forms part of a series of candle smoke and charcoal drawings for a group exhibition at Galerie L'App'Art in Périgueux, France (2020). In her artist statement to the gallery, Tau explains the creative process behind the series in the following terms:

> The Smoke Drawings are a method of accessing memories through imagery. These are inclusive of cultural memories. Smoke is a tentative, unstable medium, similar to how we access our memories. The fragility involved in the process of accessing memory is the motivation behind incorporating this fragile medium. The elements of charcoal used to reinforce lines in the drawings are symbolic of the methods used to reinforce images in our memories, where we relive and attempt to commemorate moments in our past, attempting to burnish them into our recollection forever. This series is a way of me trying to hold onto and commemorate memories of current happenings and the past.

Here, Tau addresses the tentative nature of autofiction and self-portraiture as she highlights the shared use of memory in self-writing and self-depiction. In making memory the medium through which she narrates the self, Tau highlights that the foundation of such a narrative is inherently unstable and fluctuating. She implies that one can never fully trust the legitimacy of this account, as it will fluctuate and distort just as memories do. The idea that memories are unreliable and distorted can be analyzed further with reference to Freud's notion of the screen memory:

> [T]o fictionalize one's self is essentially an autofictional enterprise. If we are to believe Freud's theory on screen memories, according to which the memories we have of our childhood are only screens that hide repressed contents, autofiction would in Laouyen's terms be a more authentic way. Authenticity is always related to subjectivity, and "lies and fiction can give a truer picture than autobiography." (Sébastien Hubier cited in Ferreira-Meyers 2015, 214)

Below is an example of how Tau uses the autofictional in her work to play with the memory of her "self," and how the fictionalization of an aspect of her childhood points to repressed content.

In "Of Another Time When I Existed" (2020), Tau depicts herself at the age of five. She wears a "Sunday dress" (one that would be based, typically, on a semi-formal European design), which required the five-year-old

Tau to assume a polished and lady-like demeanor. In the image we see a young Tau crouched on a chair, poised to launch herself from it, and thus disregarding the required "decorum" of her dress. Contrary to the elegant and adult-like demeanor that her outfit demands, the rebellious position that Tau depicts shows the child straining against normative expectations of both behavior and appearance, the trappings of which point to European norms. For the child's caretakers, who have sought here to culturally "polish" her, the primary source of shame is her disheveled Afro (ruffled during her playtime), which Tau draws using smoke. Culturally, the young Tau's untidy Afro symbolized a child who was ungroomed, and it is no coincidence that the trappings of the cultural regulations toward which Tau points in this image are European. The purity and innocence in a child's defiance of such regulations is what she seeks to remember of herself and preserve through this image. At the same time, she gives a subtle reminder of the fragility of this memory by representing it through a medium that could very easily disintegrate, just as the memory itself does with time (Wixted and Ebbesen 1991, 409–415). The blurry appearance of the smoke medium visually represents the opacity of autofictional practice. While it gives the impression of translucence or even transparency, upon closer inspection one discovers that it is impossible to see fully through the medium.

The "Trickery" Revealed

As autofiction takes place between autobiography and fiction—whether shifting between the two or situated as a midway point—it has the unique feature of maintaining a sense of transparency about the possible "trickery" which occurs in the process.

"I knew who I was this morning, but I've changed a few times since then" (Fig. 9.6) is a self-portrait that Tau took in Saint-Émilion, France, where she resided in 2020. Saint-Émilion was declared a UNESCO World Heritage site in 1999 due to its viticulture and historic architecture: all the buildings have a limestone structure, which has been a trademark of the village since the eleventh century (UNESCO n.d.). The composition consists of three layers, superimposed onto each other. The first layer is a façade of a limestone building in Saint-Émilion, the second is Tau herself taking the self-portrait, and the third is her artist's studio. The image testifies to Tau's desire to partake in the history of this space and to integrate as a resident during her stay. Revealing her studio space in the third layer

9 VISUAL AUTOFICTION: A STRATEGY FOR CULTURAL INCLUSION   175

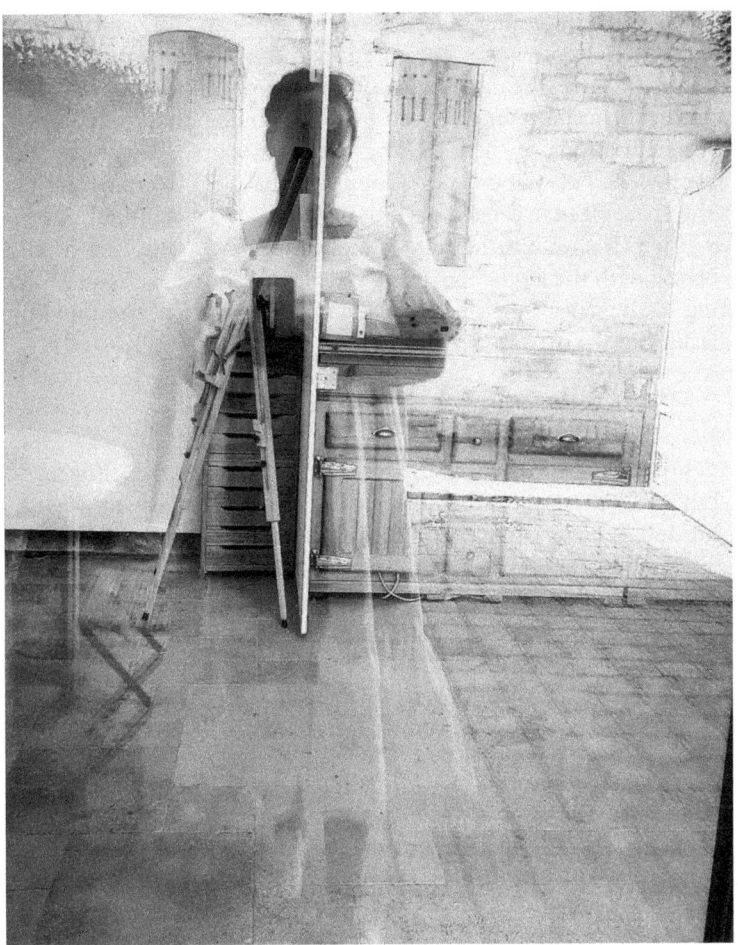

Fig. 9.6 "I knew who I was this morning, but I've changed a few times since then" (After Lewis Carroll), 2020. Digital Self-Portrait

of the image offers a glimpse "behind the curtain" or "through the smoke-screen" that she has placed in the performative space of the self-portrait. Contrary to works like "The Look of Reading (After Garret Stewart)" (Fig. 9.1), Tau adopts the process of layering and superimposition when considering her cultural identity rather than moving between identities.

The fusing of all the apparent layers together in such a translucent manner allows for more depth in the presentation of the cultural "self." Here, Tau can identify as a new Francophone, or one who participates in the historical, cultural space she finds herself in, and simultaneously accommodate her other variations of "self." Using imaginative visual symbols, such as the translucent "smokescreen," as autofictional tools to integrate herself into the space, Tau creates a narrative where she has cultural ties to the space in which she finds herself. She does this by attempting to visually fuse herself with the landscape, using the glass in the image as a translucent binding element for her reflection and the reflection of the buildings in the background.

Unrequited Love

The desire for inclusion in a historical-cultural narrative that runs throughout Tau's oeuvre conjures the notion of an unrequited love between Africa and Europe. It is this same desire that underpins the work of many African artists who, like Tau, do not form part of the cultural and racial group that has been institutionalized in the globally acclaimed visual art narrative, and who use their creative practice to figuratively insert themselves therein. This impulse toward self-inscription illuminates the painful reality of an unreciprocated reverence toward European subjects, as ethnic groups which fall outside of the Eurocentric norm are not given the same institutional value within the visual arts. While the white European body is omnipresent in the acclaimed tradition of self-portraiture, the ethnic body is virtually invisible. We see this in particular in the lack of representations of black protagonists in the canon. American self-portrait photographer Carrie Mae Weems discusses the idea of "unrequited love" in relation to the striking lack of representations of the black body in traditional Western art in her interview with The National Gallery of Art, which preceded her participation in the Diamonstein-Spielvogel Lecture Series in 2015: she speaks of "unrequited love" toward the black body as subject matter in the works of the "Old Masters." The starting point for Weems's discussion is her own relationship as a visual artist to the representation of the black body in traditional Western art. The black body, she argues, serves as a background figure or as decorative to white protagonists in the work of the Old Masters. As a means of exposing and resisting this imbalanced representation, Weems choose to use fictionalized techniques of either inserting the left-out subjects into contemporary visual narratives of the classic paintings, or drawing figures who were originally part of the background into the foreground of the image. Weems describes this practice in the following terms:

> At a certain point you realise that I'm not his [referring to Manet as an example] subject. This historical body [the black body] has not been the subject of these great painters. From the nineteenth century, to the twentieth century, even moving on to the twenty-first century, it is not a part of their imagination. It is not a part of their fantasy … but of course, art has a lot to do with imagining the unimaginable. (Kleinburg 2015)

In Tau's own quest for multicultural representation in the visual art canon, she identifies one painting in which the black female is presented as the main protagonist: "Portrait d'une négresse" (Portrait of a Negress), recently renamed "Portrait de Madeleine" (Portrait of Madeleine), by Marie-Guillemine Benoist. The recent name change of the work points toward an effort to personalize the portrait, to portray its subject as an individual rather than as a generic representative of a racial group. The name change also demonstrates a significant effort to humanize the subject by changing the word "négresse," which was seen as a derogatory term, to the subject's own name. When analyzing the image, as well as its countless reproductions by other artists, it quickly becomes apparent that one of the most identifiable qualities of the portrayed subject is her toplessness. Her bare breasts, for this reason, seem to become the key "qualifying" factor for her appearance as protagonist in this portrait. In her discussion of "Portrait de Madeleine," Cécile Bishop describes two initial reactions to Benoist's controversial work at the time. Created in 1800 between the first abolition of slavery in France and its reinstatement in 1802, responses to this work from art historians and critics were divided between praising the humanizing quality of the image, as a rare example of a portrait which focused on a black woman, and critiquing its objectification of the black body (Bishop 2019, 1).

Perplexed by the seeming prerequisite of toplessness for the entry of the black female body into this visual narrative, Tau participates in the recurring tradition of reinterpreting this painting in her work as many other artists have done before her. "Portrait de Madeleine" is the only representation of a black female as protagonist in the Louvre and, as a result, it has been identified as an important visual reference for black artists when negotiating their relationship with the canon. "Amour non partagé" (Unrequited Love) (Fig. 9.8) is the final self-portrait in Tau's 2020 series. It was taken in the courtyard outside of her residence in Saint-Émilion, as a closing ode to a language and culture that she reveres.

In a similar manner to Carrie Mae Weems, Tau exposes and resists the lack of reciprocity in the affection for Western languages and cultures in this image. She does so by projecting her body onto the sole portrayal of the black female as protagonist in canonical portraiture, playing the role of the "Negress" in Benoist's image. Tau wears her traditional Sesotho "seshweshwe" dress, as a final reminder of home and her Sesotho identity before "stripping bare" to a historical European landscape. Tau demonstrates the dual nature of autofiction in this work by layering the aspects of self-projection onto the French landscape. Throughout her studio

Fig. 9.7 "Portrait de Madeleine" (formerly known as Portrait d'une négresse), Marie-Guillemine Benoist, 1800. Louvre Museum, Paris. Picture in public domain

practice, Tau recognizes the "duality" in autofiction which allows an artist (or writer) to present the self from an imaginative perspective, but which simultaneously exposes a sense of vulnerability as they reveal existing imaginative fantasies using the fictional platform that autofiction implies. Formal elements of art such as framing and composition provide a desired perspective of the captured scene to the viewer, in this case, a perspective where one sees a close-up image of Tau and very little of her surrounding environment. In this way, Tau is able to juxtapose her African cultural roots with the European landscape in which she finds herself. As an ode to Madeleine, who is depicted in Benoist's work, Tau endeavors to re-enact and remind us of the occasion when this European landscape, to which the canon of self-portraiture has long been limited, invited the black female body into its visual narrative. In this image Tau crops her face out of the image to offer her body as a universal representation of a black woman. Contrary to the effect of the personalization of Madeleine in Benoist's work (Fig. 9.7), Tau emphasizes the anonymity or "invisible" nature of the black female in Western presentations. By way of this anonymous posture, she appropriates the objectifying Western gaze onto the black female

Fig. 9.8 "Amour non partagé" (Unrequited Love), 2020. Digital Self-Portrait

body, using the practice of self-portraiture to position herself as at once the subject to be consumed and the voyeur who consumes.

Finally, Tau draws attention to the windowpane through which this self-portrait is taken, a lens reminiscent of the viewfinder of a camera and which reinforces the virtual distance between viewer and subject. She makes subtle reference in this regard to the creation and staging of the image, as well as to the inaccessibility of the subject. By creating a barrier between the viewer and herself as subject, she creates an awareness of the spatiality of the photograph. Two spaces or "positions" become prevalent: the outside, which is represented by the position that Tau occupies in the courtyard, and the inside, which is occupied by the viewer, who is positioned where Tau's camera is on the inside of the residence, looking out toward her as voyeur. Drawing here on the social connotations of being an "insider" versus an "outsider," Tau brings the notion of inclusion to the fore. In this photograph, Tau, in her seshweshwe dress within a European landscape, and placed on the physical exterior, resembles an outsider to Western culture. The viewer, on the other hand, automatically occupies the position on the physical and metaphorical "inside" of the European culture, by way of the perspective provided through the camera's lens. By situating the viewer on the virtual "inside," an uncommon viewpoint, and placing herself on the exterior, Tau implies the power dynamic between viewer and subject, one of socio-cultural position and of authoritative gaze, due to the freedom to look at her body without the opposition of the subject who looks back at the viewer, challenging the voyeur's consumption of her body. Unlike the original portrait by Benoist, Tau removes the face of the subject, making her more vulnerable and accessible to the viewer's consumption. This, in turn, functions as a subversive displacement mechanism, as the "inside" position makes the viewer painfully aware that they are a voyeur to a vulnerable subject.

"RE-PRESENTATION": AN AUTOFICTIONAL STRATEGY FOR ALTERNATE PRESENTATIONS OF THE "SELF"

Tau's oeuvre showcases some of the key ways in which autofictional techniques are used to create an imaginative role-play in which an artist is able to project herself into varying lingual and cultural identities. In visual practice, these autofictional techniques may take the form of a "smokescreen," which blurs the lines between these identities and allows the artist to move between them. Language acquisition and assimilation into dominant cultures pose a potentially significant challenge to those who belong to external cultural groups. The concept of sacrifice comes into view where an aspiring polyglot or master of various cultural identities is left to question whether creating the space to adopt new cultural identities truly requires the erasure of the former identities. The endeavor to combine lingual identities that are on opposing ends of the cultural spectrum, such as Sesotho and French, in a single manifestation of the "self" necessitates an alternative lens through which to view the self. The use of the autofictional in contemporary self-portraiture provides this lens.

The unsettling nature of autofiction, in which truth and fiction are uncomfortably juxtaposed, invites us to question the former association between self-representation and truth, an association that is perhaps even more persistent in visual than in literary depictions of the self. Through the role-play it foregrounds in self-representation, the autofictional undoes former solidified narratives based on the self and illuminates the multiple perspectives and subjective angles from which the self is always seen. Crucially, it creates a space in which alternative narratives of self can coexist. Adopting this autofictional approach is a step toward establishing more cultural inclusion and social cohesion in the tradition of self-portraiture, by challenging the pre-structured and compartmentalized views on self and singular cultural identity.

Works Cited

Ahmed, Maaheen. 2014. The Art of Splicing: Autofiction in Words and Images. *International Journal of Comic Art* 16 (1): 322–338.
Avedon, Richard. 1993. *An Autobiography*. New York: Random House.
Bhabha, Homi. 1994. *The Location of Culture*. London: Routledge.
Bishop, Cécile. 2019. Portraiture, race, and subjectivity: the opacity of Marie-Guillemine Benoist's *Portrait d'une négresse*. In *Word and Image* (35): 1–11.
de Bloois, Joost. 2007. Introduction. The Artists Formerly Known As… Or, the Loose End of Conceptual Art and the Possibilities of 'Visual Autofiction.' *Image and Narrative* 8 (19): n.p.
Condé, Maryse. 2014. *La Vie sans fards*. POCKET Publications.
Crozier, W. Ray., and Paul Greenhalgh. 1988. Self-Portraits as Presentations of Self. *Leonardo* 21 (1): 29–33.
Ferreira-Meyers, Karen. 2012. Autofiction: 'Imaginaire' and Reality, an Interesting Mix Leading to the Illusion of a Genre? *Caietele Echinox* 23: 103–116.

———. 2015. Autobiography and Autofiction: No Need to Fight for a Place in the Limelight, There Is Space Enough for Both of These Concepts. In *Writing the Self: Essays on Autobiography and Autofiction*, ed. Kerstin Shands, Giulia Grillo Mikrut, Dipti R. Pattanaik, and Karen Ferreira-Meyers, 203–218. Huddinge: Södertörns högskola.

———. 2018. Does Autofiction Belong to French or Francophone Authors and Readers Only? In *Autofiction in English*, ed. Hywel Dix, 27–48. Cham: Palgrave Macmillan.

Fishman, Joshua A. 1996. What Do You Lose When You Lose Your Language? In *Stabilizing Indigenous Languages*, ed. Gina Cantoni, 71–81. Flagstaff, AZ: Northern Arizona University.

Halliday, Michael Alexander Kirkwood. 1978. *Language as Social Semiotic: The Social Interpretation of Language and Meaning*. London: Edward Arnold.

Kleinburg, Jerry. 2015. *Diamonstein-Spielvogel Lecture Series: Carrie Mae Weems*. Last updated September 15, 2015. https://www.nga.gov/audio-video/diamonstein-spielvogel/diamonstein-spielvogel-weems.html. Accessed Apr 6, 2021.

Miller, Stephen Paul. 1993. 'Self-Portrait in a Convex Mirror,' the Watergate Affair, and Johns's Crosshatch Paintings: Surveillance and Reality-Testing in the Mid-Seventies. *Boundary 2* 20 (2): 84–115.

Museum of Modern Art Glossary. 2021. *Self-Portraiture*. https://www.moma.org/collection/terms/self-portrait. Accessed March 20, 2021.

Smith, David R. 2001. Renaissance Self-Portraiture: The Visual Construction of Identity and the Social Status of the Artist. *The Art Bulletin* 83 (2): 354–357.

Stewart, Garrett. 2009. *The Look of Reading*. Chicago: University of Chicago Press.

Tau, Bontle. 2018. *Multilingual role-play and authentic self. An autofiction by Bontle Tau*. University of the Free State.

UNESCO. n.d. Jurisdiction of Saint-Emilion. In *World Heritage List*. https://whc.unesco.org/en/list/932. Accessed Apr 6, 2021.

Wixted, John T., and Ebbe B. Ebbesen. 1991. On the Form of Forgetting. *Psychological Science* 2 (6): 409–415.

Woods-Marsden, Joanna. 1998. *Renaissance Self-portraiture: The Visual Construction of Identity and the Social Status of the Artist*. Yale University Press.

Open Access This chapter is licensed under the terms of the Creative Commons Attribution 4.0 International License (http://creativecommons.org/licenses/by/4.0/), which permits use, sharing, adaptation, distribution and reproduction in any medium or format, as long as you give appropriate credit to the original author(s) and the source, provide a link to the Creative Commons licence and indicate if changes were made.

The images or other third party material in this chapter are included in the chapter's Creative Commons licence, unless indicated otherwise in a credit line to the material. If material is not included in the chapter's Creative Commons licence and your intended use is not permitted by statutory regulation or exceeds the permitted use, you will need to obtain permission directly from the copyright holder.

CHAPTER 10

Autofiction, Post-Conflict Narratives, and New Memory Cultures

Hywel Dix

It has now been established that a reaction against the idea of the death of the author provided one of the contexts in which autofiction developed in the 1970s. The autofictional rebuttal of the death of the author has been very noticeable among postcolonial writers, who, because their voices and experiences had been historically marginalized until the very recent past, are unlikely to accept the tacit silencing of those same voices that theories of the death of the author might entail. More specifically, two of the elements of autofictional practice that have been of particular interest to postcolonial writers are its capacity to mediate between individual and collective forms of memory, on the one hand, and, at the same time, to radically destabilize notions of absolute truth and authenticity. Drawing on current research into the relationship between writing and forms of public commemoration, this chapter argues that the tools and techniques afforded by autofictional modes of writing have been taken up by postcolonial writers seeking to draw attention to a number of atrocities that took place during or shortly after the colonial period.

H. Dix (✉)
Bournemouth University, Poole, UK
e-mail: HDix@bournemouth.ac.uk

Through a discussion of Chimamanda Ngozi Adichie's depiction of Nigeria's Biafran War of 1967–1970 in *Half of a Yellow Sun* (2006) and Justin Cartwright's reflection on the massacre of Zulus by Boers in 1838 in *Up Against the Night* (2015), the chapter will show how these writers contribute to new forms of public memory and hence to post-conflict reconciliation. In doing so, their work can be said to make innovative use of some of the techniques associated with autofiction—not so much because the historical stories they tell are exactly their own, but because these authors feel they have a personal stake in them. That is, Cartwright and Adichie use those techniques to draw attention to the fraught nature of the process of remembering and therefore both contribute to and complicate the process by which we collectively remember traumatic events that have been neglected for decades, if not centuries. At the same time, these authors also enrich our understanding of what we mean by the elusive term "autofiction."

Singular Collective Voices

Analysis of autofictional texts has so far focused overwhelmingly on prose fiction, with important theoretical studies by Vincent Colonna (2004), Max Saunders (2010), Lut Missinne (2019), and Marjorie Worthington (2018) treating textual exegesis of the printed novel as the primary objective of autofictional inquiry. Yet, as autofiction presumes a close identification between author and protagonist, the only means by which this identification can be apprehended is through recourse to a range of paratextual material—the consideration of which shifts critical attention away from the bounded text. For this reason, Allira Hanczakowski (2020) has recently argued that works of autofiction need to be discussed in the context of their paratexts. Even the briefest consideration of autofictional paratexts points to a dialogic interplay between intra-textual and extratextual dimensions in Serge Doubrovsky's original definition in the blurb for *Fils* (1977), according to which autofiction is constituted when the protagonist and author share a name and identity in a work which is designated a novel. On the one hand, the concern with the protagonist points inward toward the textual object, in a move orientated toward its interpretation and extrapolation on an aesthetic level. On the other hand, the generic categorization of any given work takes place just outside the limits of the text itself within its epitexts and peritexts, in all those material aspects of the work that are of the text but not in it.

This move from text to paratext has significant implications for how we think about the position of autofiction vis-à-vis contemporary memory cultures. Within the field of autobiography studies, the diminishment of the idea of a sovereign self was one of the occasions for Doubrovsky's development of the concept of autofiction. In effect, it replaced the idea of the authorial self with a multiplicity of different textual selves. As character is a construct and constructs are historically contingent and variable with circumstance, a single ostensible author could evince as many different selves as there are narrative occasions for their expression. This, of course, is the basis of Camille Laurens's unconventional shift in conjugation of the verb "to be," from "I am" to "I are":

> What interests me in particular, undoubtedly because I have seen its effects within myself, is the question of splitting. The ego is not fixed, we do not have a single monolithic identity, we are made up of the tensions between our different personal avatars. 'I are,' we should say. (2016)[1]

Pushing Laurens's idea of the multiplicity of selves a stage further, this chapter proposes that the conjunction of "I" with "we" implicit in the "I are" of autofiction can usefully be articulated in the genesis of new forms of memory culture. This is because, as a mode of writing that involves a dialogic interplay between text and paratext, autofiction has the capacity to recall to public consciousness brutal episodes from the colonial past which have been left to drop out of public memory, giving rise to a collective silence and forgetting which certain authors feel a direct personal responsibility for re-presenting. In the process, they challenge that cultural amnesia at simultaneously an individual and a collective level of discourse, so that autofiction has the capacity to enact an integration of subjective narratives with concerns that are social and historical, or of "I" with "we," and so re-inscribe expressions of collective experience.

In my 2020 paper "Autofiction, Colonial Massacres and the Politics of Memory," I explored how Fred D'Aguiar's *Feeding the Ghosts* (1997), Jackie Kay's "Lament for the Mendi Men" (2011), and Kamila Shamsie's *A God in Every Stone* (2014) engaged in a writing practice that attempts this re-inscription of collective experience in bringing to light a number of incidents from the colonial past that have unjustly been allowed to lapse out of public consciousness (Dix, 2020). Strictly speaking, their work is not autofiction in Doubrovsky's sense. Although based on real historical events, the experiences narrated are not the authors' own, so it is impossible for the authors to appear as protagonists under their own names. This means that, if autofiction is treated as a genre, these works cannot be assimilated to it. But simply debating whether a given text can be defined as autofiction in a categorical sense is a theoretical cul-de-sac, at best a ludic game and at worst a critical distraction from the more important themes and questions that they raise. A more fruitful way of talking about these texts is in terms of autofictional modes of reading they enable. D'Aguiar, Shamsie, and Kay all seem to feel involved in what they portray, creating the impression that although the experiences are not their own, the stories are in some senses theirs.

These works contribute to new forms of memory culture by challenging hegemonic constructions of imperial history and inserting into them the voices of the forgotten, the dispossessed, and the defeated. If they can be considered autofictional in any useful way, it is because of how their paratextual apparatus invokes an authorial "I" that not only supplements but is actively conjoined with the subjective experiences of the different human lives they narrate. This dialogue between text and paratext points to a specific way of deploying autofiction, not necessarily as a categorical definition, but as a mode of writing which flares up at specific points in the text to affirm the connection between author and subject. In what follows, I suggest that in different ways Adichie and Cartwright also apply some of the methods afforded by autofiction to re-inscribe themselves into narratives of the Nigerian Civil War (1967–1970) and the massacre of Zulus at Blood River (1838), in stories which are not just theirs, but more than theirs.

CHIMAMANDA NGOZI ADICHIE'S *HALF OF A YELLOW SUN*

In a comparative study of the diasporic literatures of what he calls the Afro-American and Caribbean traditions, Ndubuisi Martins Aniemeka has argued that thematic preoccupations, especially of a political or historical nature, have received more critical attention than autobiographical writing in each case. Drawing on a model of textual kinesis proposed by Aderemi Raji-Oyelade (2000), according to which character construction and plot trajectory become incorporated into aspects of a physical or metaphorical journey in order to conceptualize and articulate experiences of conflict, he then proposes a model of "characterology" (2019, 11), whereby authors are understood by their readers to have imbued fictional characters with aspects of their own experiences and/or aspirations in order to express "struggle, identity and cultural survival in purposively selected self-fictional text[s]" (10). Examples Aniemeka finds of this purposive self-fictionalization in the literatures of the Afro-American and Caribbean diasporas include Zora Neale Hurston's *Dust Tracks on the Road* (1942), Richard Wright's *Black Boy* (1945), George Lamming's *In the Castle of my Skin* (1953), V.S. Naipaul's *House for Mr Biswas* (1960), Michael Anthony's *The Year in Fernando* (1965), and Maya Angelou's *I Know Why the Caged Bird Sings* (1986). He concludes: "A plot characterology reveals the transmutability of the characters in the texts examined. Apart from such reconstructive ideology couched in the self-writings of these authors, the network of transformation is occasioned by the reader-characters' analytical mapping to awareness" (19–20). These comments suggest that the purpose of restoring a sense of biographical agency to the authors in question is to attempt a degree of social and political transformation through the raising of a new form of critical consciousness that combines individual experience with collective struggle, especially between dominated or marginalized communities and dominant ones. Yet, the awkward term "self-writings" does not quite succeed in elaborating a sense of how these techniques are different from those of straightforwardly autobiographical fiction.

A somewhat different approach to diasporic writing is propounded by Amber Lascelles. In a discussion of Edwidge Danticat's short story "Caroline's Wedding" and Chimamanda Ngozi Adichie's story "Imitation" from the collection *The Thing Around Your Neck* (2009), she suggests that theories of diasporic writing have focused too greatly on the migrant subject's continued attachment to their country of origin, such that it becomes both mythologized, rendered the object of a restorative nostalgia, and cathected as the symbolic repository of both personal and familial value. Lascelles's point is not that these things do not happen, but that too great a concentration on the home country fails to make possible a dynamic conceptualization of the experiences of the migrant subject in the new or host country. This is especially true among second- or third-generation subjects, whose ties to the home country, though tangible in many ways, are likely to be less strong than those of their parents and grandparents. Moreover, since applying for such legal statuses as the right to work, right of residence, and ultimately rights of citizenship is also more prevalent among later generations, the refusal of the category of diasporic writers, in Lascelles's account, enables the expression of a greater degree of equality among second- and third-generation migrants with regard to the population of the host country than was the case for their forebears, who were likely to be extremely marginalized. This realization prompts Lascelles to bring forth the suggestion: "Reading [Danticat and Adichie's] stories comparatively allows me to explore whether new frameworks and terminologies, centrally the emerging term post-diaspora, are useful to capture the complexity of diaspora and its meaning in the twenty-first century" (2020, 227). In the context of her wider argument, the adoption of the term "post-diaspora" by Lascelles seems like a logical choice to refer to the literature she discusses (although it should be noted that she also critiques the accompanying implication that the distinction between diasporic and post-diasporic writings is of a binary nature). Combining Aniemeka's attention to diasporic autobiographies and other forms of self-writing with Lascelles's insight into post-diasporic experience makes it possible to suggest here that autofiction can be considered among the new frameworks and terminologies adumbrated by Lascelles.

Elena Murphy (2017) has shown that in many of the stories in *The Thing Around Your Neck* (2009), Adichie "adeptly queries Western ways of perceiving and defining the African *Other* from the position of different and diverse characters and, at the same time, the distance from Nigeria allows her to reflect upon her culture of origin" (2017, 101). A similar description could be applied to Adichie's novel *Americanah* (2013) in which the main character Ifemelu migrates between Nigeria and the USA and blogs about her experiences. Miriam Pahl has shown that following publication of the novel, Adichie "transfer[ed] this fictional blog into the real world (wide web)" and continued it under the title "The Small Redemptions of Lagos" in order to demonstrate "a strong political and social commitment" (2016, 77). This leads Pahl to conclude that "[a]lthough the experiences depicted in the novel should not be taken as autobiographical information, they do elucidate Adichie's carefully honed public persona" (78).

These insights alone seem like fertile ground for approaching Adichie's work as autofictional, especially in the light of Bran Nicol's suggestion that one of the features of autofiction in North America (where Adichie works) is that it is "best regarded less as a form which interrogates the complex workings of memory and their effect on subjectivity and more as evidence of the preoccupation with the conditions of authorship, especially institutional" (2018, 257). The current chapter, however, takes a slightly different approach, not merely classing Adichie as a writer of autofiction but also expanding our theoretical understanding of the concept itself. It is to

Adichie's novel *Half of a Yellow Sun* (2006) that we can turn for a fuller articulation of this new combination of post-diasporic writing with the collective potential of autofiction as a means of building forms of solidarity with marginalized peoples and achieving alternative forms of collective memory.

Half of a Yellow Sun is a novelistic history of the Biafran War in Nigeria (1967–1970) focusing on five main characters and alternating between their lives in the early 1960s and at the end of the decade, to situate the war in the context of the historical double coup that was the immediate occasion for it. This coup had occurred partly because the artifact now known as Nigeria itself had only been created by British colonizers during the imperial period, so that when its post-independence administration became corrupt there was first a coup to remove it followed by a counter-coup directed against the ethnic Igbo people who were the main protagonists of the first and who were perceived to have become too powerful as a result of it, to the detriment of Nigeria's other ethnic groups, especially the Hausa and Yoruba. Moreover, the federal leader Gowon was thought to have betrayed the Igbo by forming a compromise between them and the central government, and so his counterpart Ujukwu declared Biafran independence.

At the start of the novel the protagonist Odenigbo is an academic in the university town of Nsukka, the town where Adichie was raised and where her father was also a university academic. Although the novel is not written in the first person and so violates Doubrovsky's criteria for autofiction, both setting and profession hint at a close alignment between the family of the author and the historical action depicted in the novel, but places it at a generation's remove from her. Adichie was born seven years after the Biafran War and raised on a university campus, not to mention in a country that had been torn apart by the war. So, although the characters in the novel are an invention, the historical story that her book narrates informs her life to a great degree.

There is a significant metafictional aspect to *Half of a Yellow Sun* because the main plot is interspersed with extracts from a book-within-the-book, a manuscript entitled "The World Was Silent When We Died," which readers assume to be by the British scholar, Richard. This character is a conventional figure of European cultural authority who had already attempted two books: "The Basket of Hands," which gets burned by Kainene when she finds out he slept with Olanna; and "In the Time of Roped Pots," which gets left behind buried in his garden in Port Harcourt by his houseboy Harrison when he evacuates (Adichie 2006, 182, 170). Both are about the ancient art of rope making, how intricate and refined it is and hence how it demonstrates evidence of a sophisticated civilization and culture existing in Nigeria before the arrival of European colonizers (although Richard is rebuked by a guest at one of Odenigbo's soirées for expressing surprise at this). As readers are led to assume that the extracts from "The World Was Silent When We Died" are also by him, it is a surprise when the last line of the novel reveals that they are in fact by Odenigbo's old houseboy, Ugwu. Although the other houseboy, Harrison, has given up writing by then, Ugwu's new critical literacy may be a sign of hope for the future. This metafictional aspect is significant for two reasons. First, it allows Adichie to participate in the form of metafiction that is particular to postcolonial writers struggling to overcome a common inferiority complex with regard to the apparently rich literary traditions of Europe. Second, it enables Adichie to bear witness to historical events which she did not, in fact, experience, but which nevertheless played a strong part in shaping the society in which she was raised and hence in her own life.

Reading *Half of a Yellow Sun* as an autofictional contribution to the building of a post-conflict memory culture makes it possible to extrapolate the novel's retrospective reconstruction of conflict as a form of testimony. The novel follows earlier autobiographical accounts of the Biafran War such as Elechi Amadi's *Sunset in Biafra* (1973), which narrates the author's bitter experiences with the authorities of Biafra during the war. Yet, a key difference is that, as Kalu Wosu points out, Amadi's war narrative "condemns the domineering attitude of the Igbos who, according to the author, dragged other ethnic minorities of the defunct Eastern region into a senseless and brutal war" (2018, 122), whereas Adichie wrote "out of solidarity for the oppressed Igbo people" (129) so that in *Half of a Yellow Sun* "all the characters killed during the war were Igbo, the theatre of war was the Igbo heartland, the refugee crisis affected the Igbo only, the Igbo suffered the Abandoned Property issue, and the pogroms took place only in the Northern parts of Nigeria" (Wosu 2018, 129). Such violence is represented in the novel when Olanna's Aunty Ifeka, Uncle Mbaezi, and cousin Arize are killed in the Northern town of Kano; when Olanna only escapes from Kano on the last train out of the town, on which she meets a woman carrying a calabash containing the severed head of her murdered daughter; when Richard has a similar experience trying to get a flight out of Port Harcourt and witnesses Hausa troops shoot all the Igbo people they find, including a young airport official executed for refusing to recite "Allahu Akbar" at the troops' demand because his accent would have given him away as Igbo (Adichie 2006, 152). It is also conveyed through such details as the doctor who attends the refugee center where Kainene works as a volunteer being spat on by a woman he has come to help because he is not Igbo; through the fact that the poet Okeoma and scientist Ekwenugo, who had been regulars at Odenigbo's salons before the war, both die during it; through the fact that Ugwu's sister Anulika is raped by federal soldiers occupying Biafra and his girlfriend Eberechi is killed on the last day of the war. These details bear witness to the historical experience of the Igbo people during the war because as Wosu points out, although the precise characters are literary inventions, Adichie "relied on historical facts to craft her work of fiction" in a way that "blends historical evidence with literary creativity" (Wosu 2018, 123).

On the other hand, Wosu also emphasizes that the nature of a historical experience like a civil war makes drawing a simple dividing line between aggressors and victims somewhat untenable. In the case of Biafra, this is partly because the Igbo were "part of the failed political leadership of the First Republic which led to the crisis" and partly because it is impossible to imagine that there were "no reprisal killings in the East in response to the pogroms in the North" or "even in the North, by Igbos who resisted the pogroms." Yet, *Half of a Yellow Sun* "is silent on this particular issue" (Wosu 2018, 130). Speculating on potential reasons for this very significant omission leads Wosu to three distinct findings. First, that because Adichie's writing is a medium for both preserving and disseminating the collective cultural memory of the people of Biafra, the overall effect is that the book "makes a strong case for the Igbo nation" (130). Although interpreting Adichie as an advocate of Igbo nationhood is a somewhat extreme and unconventional approach to her work, this bears on the second finding, namely that, because the post-independence nation of Nigeria was defined in a territorial sense by the parameters of the British colony there, the nation itself is in part constituted by its colonial history. This is both why Britain supported the republic against the secessionist Biafran movement during the war, and why its whole history has been constructed according to the logic of what Wosu calls "western logocentrism" (2018, 131). By centering her narrative on the Igbo rather than other Nigerian communities such as the Hausa, Ikwerre, or Yoruba, Adichie rewrites that logocentric history, revealing that the "binary opposition black/white is a western construct which, at the discursive level, seeks to give the European an imaginary ascendancy over the African" (131).

In making this point, Wosu performs a slippage from one form of binary differentiation (between federal Nigerian aggressors and traumatized Igbo secessionists) to another (between European colonizers and African colonized). There is a certain logic that makes this slippage possible, as the territory of independent Nigeria was geographically defined by that of the British colony which preceded it, so that to critique the yoking together of many different peoples and ethnicities on the basis of the shared experience of having been colonized by Britain, is to simultaneously critique both the post-independence state and its prior colonial determinants. Yet, if a refusal of the categorical distinction between black and white or between Africa and Europe is one of the philosophical insights to emerge from Wosu's reading of *Half of a Yellow Sun*, this refusal would presumably apply equally to both the Igbo people and the other ethnic communities in Nigeria. Given that the novel appears to recruit historical understanding for the Igbo in contrast to those other groups, it is difficult to see how this commonality can be envisaged in the text in practice.

A solution to this challenge is suggested by Wosu's third key finding, which is about how Adichie handles the relationship between fact and fiction: "'Fact' still remains for us literally 'a thing done.' And fiction has never lost its meaning of 'a thing made'" (2018, 124). This distinction usefully informs an extrapolation of the potential for reading *Half of a Yellow Sun* as a form of autofiction, revealing that what we encounter in the text is not so much Adichie telling her own story as creating a collective story of the Igbo people (which includes her) and of Nigeria as a whole (which includes the Igbo). This creation is made in the service of forging a new form of reconciliation in the present, based on shared memory and an alternative collective relationship to the Civil War and to the past. Such striving would have been especially necessary a generation after the war because as Wosu shows, the "reconciliation, reconstruction, and rehabilitation which [Nigerian leader] General Gowon promised [after the war] ended up as a hoax" (2018, 131). That is, Adichie uses the novel to attempt a fictional version of the post-war reconciliation that the Nigerian state failed to deliver historically. Elena Murphy notes that Adichie "describes herself as belonging to the Engli-Igbo generation of Nigeria and this shows in her works, where what could be defined as a 'transcultural form of English' is employed" (2017, 99). English as a transcultural tool enables the novel to speak to and for all the different peoples within Nigeria and transcend their differences. This commitment to overcoming enmity, rather than the strictest representation of verifiable, factual truth, enables Adichie to portray the war but also to begin consigning it to the past. Or as Wosu puts it: "Reality is thus relative, and the author tries to reconstruct it in her quest for a new wholesomeness" (2018, 130). The story of the Biafran War is not Adichie's but that of the people to whom she relates, namely, the Igbo. *Half of a Yellow Sun* can thus be seen as autofiction on a collective scale. It not only narrates how Adichie and the Igbo fit into the Nigerian whole but actively works toward such integration.

SHARED HERITAGE IN *UP AGAINST THE NIGHT*

Writing from a different context to Adichie, the South African-born writer Justin Cartwright (1943–2018) was interested in exploring different kinds of truth and investigating how subjective and objective truths complicate each other without easy resolution. For example, his 1993 novel *Masai Dreaming* is about a filmmaker, Kurtiz, traveling to Kenya in the 1990s to make a documentary about a female French Jewish anthropologist who had lived and worked there in the 1930s and 1940s. Her love affair with a Masai farmer, who was subsequently executed, so outraged her English lover that he demanded that she be tested for syphilis and while traveling to Paris to have this test she was arrested by the Nazis and sent to her death. Yet, in the film made about her life in the 1990s, this detail is altered so that she escapes back to Kenya via Cape Town because the filmmaker feels such an ending is a better way of affirming the supposedly universal spirit of the Masai people, whose way of life was in fact on the brink of extinction. Through these plot details, Cartwright shows Kurtiz exploring a series of dilemmas about what a writer owes to art and to truth, and how these things relate to each other, especially with regard to the uncomfortable truth that a number of French people had been complicit in the Nazi roundup of French Jews at Drancy.

Cartwright's narrative exploration of the relationship between truth, art, and meaning continues in his next novel, *In Every Face I Meet* (1995), portraying a South African banker in London who has a powerful childhood memory of watching a tribal Swazi king dance at an annual ceremony of cultural renewal and who pins his hopes for redeeming the failed aspirations of Thatcherism on another tribal Prince, Nelson Mandela. Before he can fly out to watch Mandela's release from political prison he is mugged at gunpoint by a black youth and ends up on trial for murdering the mugger. Although he is acquitted, he feels somewhat morally ambivalent, even guilty, suggesting that his privilege as a white banker compared to the young black attacker might explain the original mugging even if it does not condone it. Interracial violence and questions of both forgiveness and reconciliation—which in South Africa in the year of Mandela's release had very broad and powerful implications for the whole society—are thus revealed to be highly complex and no easy answers are envisaged by the novel.

The role of art in mediating potential responses to the questions "What is truth?" and "What is good?" is even more explicitly the focus of Cartwright's later novel *The Promise of Happiness* (2004) about a London accountant who is pushed out of his own firm during a hostile takeover. The accountant and his wife retire to Cornwall to plan the marriage of their son to a glamorous but unintellectual South American model whom they doubt will make him happy. In turn the son has spent two years visiting his older sister in prison in America, where she was convicted for her role in fencing a Tiffany stained glass window believed to have been stolen from a cemetery years earlier, on behalf of her boyfriend, the British owner of a New York art gallery. She seems to have taken the blame partly to protect him from a longer sentence and partly out of guilt, as she had been too distracted by a love affair with an American writer to notice that the gallery was in financial trouble. Moreover, when she is released, a *New York Times* journalist discovers that the window was never actually stolen. Rather, an ambitious FBI agent eager to improve his clean-up rate for art crimes had orchestrated the affair. There are thus as many "truths" of the event as there are stories about it. As in Umberto Eco's *Prague Cemetery*, the scene in which the valuable window had originally been stolen is different each time it is re-told, and the role played by art and artifice in each re-telling is explicitly foregrounded by the novel.

An idiosyncratic feature of *The Promise of Happiness* is that although for the most part it is narrated in the third person, it frequently shifts into the first to get inside the thoughts of whichever character is thinking at the time. At one specific point during a meditation on the human propensity to imagine angels as a symbol for uncorrupted happiness, the phrase "The author…" is also used in this way:

> Another thing about angels: they are not direct participants in life's struggle: they are above it. And that's why we like them. They are disinterested

observers, impartial do-gooders. They only acquired wings in later centuries. The author thinks that they were a necessary invention, an antidote to the harshness of religion and a comfort in death. (2004, 138)

The technique of dispersed focalization shifting between one character and another appears to have given rise to a situation in which ideas cannot be conceptualized if they are not associated with the particular character experiencing them. So ideas not explicitly owned by a specific character cannot be expressed in any other way than by invoking the author as a briefly active character, and the presence of Cartwright obtrudes.

This sallying forth of the authorial presence is even more detectable in Cartwright's final novel, *Up Against the Night* (2015), in which Cartwright returns to a number of themes that had characterized the works discussed above: the relationship between Britain and a number of African countries; experiences of migration between countries and continents on a global scale; the question of value, what confers it and what confers meaning on it; plus the matter of how art relays these questions to us while also being implicated in the very problematics it raises. Cartwright had already used the metafictional device of having a main character who is a filmmaker in *Masai Dreaming* (1993), and had associated his disillusioned banker's search for transcendental meaning with his own reading of current affairs in *In Every Face I Meet* (1995), so that an interest in the role of the artist in addressing questions of meaning, value, and ethics was already present in these earlier novels but without an explicit use of autofiction. Autofiction then starts to enter his work in *The Promise of Happiness* (2004), though only in a brief and occasional way at this point. In *Up Against the Night* (2015), Cartwright portrays a protagonist who shares a number of his own biographical details, and thereby more explicitly uses the techniques of autofiction to explore the same themes that had interested him all along. In other words, he appears to have been gradually and increasingly attracted to autofictional modes of writing throughout his career and this process reaches its zenith in his final novel, which revisits thematic material that he had already explored in earlier work, with a greater degree of self-awareness and critical self-consciousness than before.

Read alongside the earlier texts, *Up Against the Night* thus reveals a higher degree of autofictional writing in its portrayal of the coming to terms with the uneasy colonial past in South Africa. The protagonist, Frank McAllister, is in his 60s and, having retired from a prosperous career in England, increasingly finds himself feeling out of place and looking to

South Africa, where he was born and where his mother died during his childhood, for a sense of belonging. His sense of not belonging is conveyed through minor details like the fact that he is in the process of separating from his spoiled, fashion-conscious wife Georgina. Frank's feeling of dislocation is also conveyed through the fact that his old friend and colleague Alec has made a fool of himself by allowing a young Latvian pole dancer whom he had promised to put through university to abscond with half a million pounds, has suffered a minor stroke since retiring, and later dies of a second stroke. The sense of alienation is further compounded by the fact that Frank's daughter Lucinda is in a drug rehabilitation clinic in California, and his distant cousin Jaco Retief has been imprisoned by the church of scientology in the USA and needs US$50,000 to bail him out.

This last character is especially relevant in considering the novel as an autofictional contribution to emerging memory cultures in South Africa, as not only are Frank and Jaco both descended from Piet Retief, the nineteenth-century leader of the Boer settlers in the Zulu territories of what is now KwaZulu-Natal in South Africa, but the jacket blurb of *Up Against the Night* tells us that this is also true of the author Justin Cartwright himself. It was noted at the start of this chapter that paratexts have a crucial role in signaling texts as autofictional, since autofictional texts raise truth claims that can be judged only by looking outside the text proper. The paratexts are the pivots between the words of the main body of text and the world to which it relates. In the case of *Up Against the Night*, the paratextual biography given in the blurb, and other paratextual apparatuses, such as Cartwright's obituary in the *Guardian* (Kean 2018), cultivates a strong connection between the protagonist and the author.

Like Cartwright, the aging Frank is portrayed as becoming both conscious of his own mortality and more reflective of his South African origins, causing him to research the killing of Retief and his followers by the Zulu leader Dingane in 1838. The Great Trek across the Eastern Cape that Retief had led is often presented in Boer and Afrikaner folklore as a narrative tantamount to a foundational myth or moment of origin for the culture as a whole. But Frank's research causes him to feel that the truth is both more complicated and more morally ambivalent than this. Although the death of Retief took place in a massacre of Afrikaners by Zulus, which is narrated in the historical passages in *Up Against the Night*, Frank is unable to condemn the Zulu leader Dingane's acts, as it was clear that Retief did not intend to abide by the existing peace treaty, and in fact meant to dispossess the Zulus of their land. On the other hand, the fact that Piet was Frank's ancestor makes him feel a connection with him despite himself. He feels further ambivalence because in retaliation for the killings, the remaining Boers wiped out virtually all the Zulus in the Battle of Blood River, and this is again a history from which Frank cannot distance himself however much he may feel ashamed of it, because in an affective sense it is his own history, so that to deny it would be to deny a part of his own existence. Given that Cartwright has endowed Frank with his own Retief ancestry, although the plot of the novel is invented, Frank's dilemmas can in a meaningful way be described as Cartwright's own.

As often in Cartwright's oeuvre, artistic work is mobilized as a vehicle for exploring these dilemmas. One of the recurring motifs of the novel is a memory Frank has of watching a moving production of *Macbeth* performed in Johannesburg by a Zulu cast. This precise choice of play (about political violence, murder, and revenge) contributes thematic material to the novel's wider exploration of the rights and wrongs of a violent power grab in the historical past and of its long-term historical reverberations in the present. Moreover, the selection of a work by perhaps the most archetypally English dramatist, Shakespeare, being performed by a Zulu cast emphasizes Frank's dual heritage, in which the European and African elements complicate each other.

In his extended reflective engagement with a dubious political past that can be neither fully embraced nor entirely disclaimed, Frank is thus an avatar for Cartwright. Frank's personal implicature in a heritage he deems morally repellent causes him constantly to seek endless alternative ways of belonging. The complexities involved in that attempt are contrasted with the character Jaco, an unreflective privileged white South African who continually laments the state of the nation since the ending of apartheid, criminalizes the black population, and, in an apparently self-fulfilling prophecy, shoots a group of black armed robbers in order to rescue both Frank and Nellie, along with Frank's daughter Lucinda and the baby she has brought with her from America, Isaac.

Through this baby Cartwright brings the disparate relatives together, and in this sense follows a very common trope in postcolonial writing whereby the late arrival of a baby symbolizes uneasy reconciliation with the past and a feeling of hope for the future. In the quite convoluted plot structure—Isaac is the biracial son of Lucinda's ex-boyfriend's ex-girlfriend, causing Frank to wonder if Lucinda is even legally permitted to travel with him as he is not her baby—this trope has an additional effect. The classic fictional plot device of the swapped baby hints simultaneously at a relationship of connection and separation. And this, of course, is what both Frank and Cartwright feel about their shared colonial ancestor, Piet Retief, so that like Adichie's *Half of a Yellow Sun*, *Up Against the Night* produces a feeling of autofiction at one remove. Cartwright's book ends with Frank going to Sotheby's to collect a Howard Hodgkin painting Alec gifted him as a wedding present. Its abstract landscape makes him think first of the descriptions of blood draining into the ground after the massacre of Piet in 1838, and then of the blood soaking his own house in Cape Town after the recent shooting. He realizes that his life, and in some ways the history of his family, has come full circle. There is thus a convergence between the content of the novel, which is entirely fictional, and the family history of the author, which is not.

Autofiction and Memory Cultures

In a discussion of Achmat Dangor's novel *Bitter Fruit* (2001), about a woman who was raped in apartheid-era South Africa and comes face to face with her rapist during the sessions of the Truth and Reconciliation Commission (TRC), through which the post-apartheid nation attempted to heal the wounds of the past, Ronit Frenkel says:

> The inconclusive nature of such archaeological endeavours therefore becomes paramount to understanding the TRC and the construction of histories in South Africa, where the consequences of either recalling or suppressing the past are severe, because ultimately post-colonial pathos shapes all response and history cannot be redeemed. (2008, 84–85)

To a large degree, this comment could be applied to any novel that deals with the politics of memory and reconciliation in post-apartheid South Africa. *Up Against the Night* is distinctive for the way it evokes a sense of Cartwright being personally implicated in the process of coming to terms with the past. Such a feeling is then supported by the paratexts and enforced by the parallel plotlines about Piet Retief in the past and Frank McAllister in the present. To the extent that Frank is constructed as a discernible avatar of Cartwright, the novel can therefore be considered autofictional in its dealing with the politics of memory. It represents a conjunction of personal experience with collective history in its evocation of the difficulties inherent in building new forms of memory culture in a society emerging from historical conflict.

Interpreting Adichie's work as an instance of autofiction elucidates a different form of post-conflict narrative and reconciliation. It was suggested above that there are many grounds on which Adichie's work could be considered autofictional: her application of autobiographical elements to fiction, her careful control of her public persona as author, and the sense her work evinces that the stories she tells are almost, if not quite, her own. This last point is the main argument that has been developed here. The chapter explored how the autofictional dimension of Adichie's work enables an active engagement by the author with questions of public memory with regard to a conflicted past and its reverberations in the present.

Both Cartwright's and Adichie's works create the feeling that the stories they tell in some senses both are and are not their own. They are stories of historical events that unfolded before either of them was born, but which nevertheless have cast shadows over their lives and played a powerful part in determining their subjectivities and those of the people in the societies they come from, in the present. Autofiction in this context can be understood to open a narrative space in which those historical conflicts and their latter-day ramifications can be explored. Thus, the combination of autofiction and post-conflict narratives that has been discussed throughout this chapter provides a powerful means of contributing to new forms of public memory and to affective forms of reconciliation. In turn, this new combination expands and enriches our understanding of autofiction itself.

Note

1. "Ce qui m'intéresse particulièrement, sans doute parce que j'en observe les effets en moi-même, c'est la question du clivage. Le moi n'est pas fixe, nous n'avons pas une identité simple et monolithique, nous sommes faits de tensions entre nos différents avatars intimes. 'Je sommes,' devrions-nous dire."

Works Cited

Adichie, Chimamanda Ngozi. 2006. *Half of a Yellow Sun*. London: 4th Estate.
———. 2009. *The Thing Around Your Neck*. London: 4th Estate.
———. 2013. *Americanah*. London: 4th Estate.

Aniemeka, Ndubuisi Martins. 2019. Ambivalent Identity and Self Repatriation in the Plot Characterisation of Selected Black Auto/Biographical Novels. *International Journal of English and Literature* 10 (2): 9–20.

Cartwright, Justin. 1993. *Masai Dreaming*. London: Sceptre.

———. 1995. *In Every Face I Meet*. London: Sceptre.

———. 2004. *The Promise of Happiness*. London: Bloomsbury.

———. 2015. *Up Against the Night*. London: Bloomsbury.

Colonna, Vincent. 2004. *Autofiction & autres mythomanies littéraires*. Auch: Tristram.

D'Aguiar, Fred. 1997. *Feeding the Ghosts*. London: Chatto & Windus.

Dix, Hywel. 2020. Autofiction, Colonial Massacres and the Politics of Memory. *University of Bucharest Review* 22 (1): 10–22.

Doubrovsky, Serge. 1977. *Fils*. Paris: Galilée.

Frenkel, Ronit. 2008. The Politics of Loss: Post-Colonial Pathos and Current Booker Prize-Nominated Texts from India and South Africa. *Scrutiny 2: Issues in English Studies in Southern Africa* 13 (2): 77–88.

Hanczakowski, Allira. 2020. Uncovering the Unwritten: A Paratextual Analysis of Autofiction. *Life Writing*, published online July 29, 2020. https://doi.org/1 0.1080/14484528.2020.1801132.

Kay, Jackie. 2011. *Fiere*. London: Picador.

Kean, Danuta. 2018. Justin Cartwright Obituary. *The Guardian*, December 20, 2018. https://www.theguardian.com/books/2018/dec/20/justin-cartwright-obituary. Accessed Apr 5, 2021.

Lascelles, Amber. 2020. Locating Black Feminist Resistance through Diaspora and Post-Diaspora in Edwidge Danticat's and Chimamanda Ngozi Adichie's Short Stories. *African and Black Diaspora: An International Journal* 13 (2): 227–240.

Laurens, Camille. 2016. Entretien avec Camille Laurens à propos de son ouvrage *Celle que vous croyez*. *Babelio*, April 7, 2016. https://www.babelio.com/auteur/Camille-Laurens/13674. Accessed Apr 5, 2021.

Missinne, Lut. 2019. Autobiographical Novel. In *Autobiography/Autofiction: An International and Interdisciplinary Handbook*, ed. Martina Wagner-Egelhaaf, 464–472. Berlin: De Gruyter.

Murphy, Elena Rodríguez. 2017. New Transatlantic African Writing: Translation, Transculturation and Diasporic Images in Chimamanda Ngozi Adichie's *The Thing Around Your Neck* and *Americanah*. *Prague Journal of English Studies* 6 (1): 93–104.

Nicol, Bran. 2018. Eye to I: American Autofiction and Its Contexts from Jerzy Kosinski to Dave Eggers. In *Autofiction in English*, ed. Hywel Dix, 255–274. Cham: Palgrave Macmillan.

Pahl, Miriam. 2016. Afropolitanism as Critical Consciousness: Chimamanda Ngozi Adichie's and Teju Cole's Internet Presence. *Journal of African Cultural Studies* 28 (1): 73–87.

Raji-Oyelade, Aderemi. 2000. Character Theory in the Black Novel. In *The Black Novel*, ed. Asha Viswas, 29–40. New Delhi: Bahri Publications.

Saunders, Max. 2010. *Self Impression: Life-Writing, Autobiografiction, and the Forms of Modern Literature*. Oxford: Oxford University Press.

Shamsie, Kamila. 2014. *A God in Every Stone*. London: Bloomsbury.

Worthington, Marjorie. 2018. *The Story of "Me": Contemporary American Autofiction*. Lincoln, NE: University of Nebraska Press.

Wosu, Kalu. 2018. Writing and Discourse: Chimamanda Ngozi Adichie's *Half of a Yellow Sun* as a Civil War Narrative. *Africology: The Journal of Pan African Studies* 12 (2): 121–133.

Open Access This chapter is licensed under the terms of the Creative Commons Attribution 4.0 International License (http://creativecommons.org/licenses/by/4.0/), which permits use, sharing, adaptation, distribution and reproduction in any medium or format, as long as you give appropriate credit to the original author(s) and the source, provide a link to the Creative Commons licence and indicate if changes were made.

The images or other third party material in this chapter are included in the chapter's Creative Commons licence, unless indicated otherwise in a credit line to the material. If material is not included in the chapter's Creative Commons licence and your intended use is not permitted by statutory regulation or exceeds the permitted use, you will need to obtain permission directly from the copyright holder.

CHAPTER 11

Autofiction as a Lens for Reading Contemporary Egyptian Writing

Hala Kamal, Zainab Magdy, and Fatma Massoud

Autobiographical writing and life writing occupy a visible position in Arabic literary history, but they are conventionally situated within biographical and historical studies and sociological/anthropological research. Consequently, Arabic literary studies cannot boast of a critical theory developed around autofiction, which, to the best of our knowledge, has not yet been thoroughly explored as a critical approach to reading Arabic literature.[1] The term "autofiction" itself does not yet have an established equivalent in Arabic literary studies, though a few attempts have been made to translate the term into "al-takhyīl al- dhātî" and "riwāyat al-dhāt."[2] This chapter offers an original autofictional approach to three case studies

H. Kamal (✉)
Department of English Language and Literature, Faculty of Arts, Cairo University, Cairo, Egypt
e-mail: hala.kamal@cu.edu.eg

Z. Magdy
Cairo University, Cairo, Egypt

F. Massoud
The British University in Egypt, Cairo, Egypt

of Arab writing, including one case of Arabic-Anglophone literature. In her study of the Egyptian blogosphere, Teresa Pepe reflects on the history of autobiographical writing in Arabic literature as being characterized by the "mixing of fiction and factual elements in life-writing" (Pepe 2019, 11), where she highlights the critical approaches to Arabic literature as being from an autobiographical rather than autofictional point of view. Pepe suggests using an autofictional lens in the study of Egyptian blogs, arguing that "Arab critics rely heavily on Western literary debate and have not tried to instigate their own critical debate on Arabic autofiction" (10–11). In this chapter, we intend to start this critical conversation, taking an autofictional approach to the work of three writers who have not been recognized as mainstream literary figures. Waguih Ghali is among the very few Egyptian writers of the 1960s generation who wrote and was published in English. It is only recently that his name has been revived through the publication of his diaries and the translation of his work into Arabic. On the other hand, Radwa Ashour's writings in Arabic (occasionally translated) have set her apart from the mainstream writers of her generation, primarily owing to her immense investment in (re)historicization, both in her autobiographical and fictional texts. In a different, but related, manner Miral al-Tahawy has established herself as a distinct voice among a rebellious and innovative new generation of Egyptian writers and artists. It is therefore perhaps only fitting that their three texts be read here from an emerging and original critical approach—namely, through the lens of the autofictional.

We discuss the work of three bicultural Egyptian writers: Waguih Ghali's *Beer in the Snooker Club* (1964), Radwa Ashour's *Specters* (1999), and Miral al-Tahawy's *Brooklyn Heights* (2010). The three authors have written other texts that have been classified as either novels or autobiographical texts, while these three texts have been categorized by publishers as novels, and read by critics as autobiographical novels. Here we read them instead through an autofictional lens and suggest that autofictionality can be identified in them in terms of not only genre but also technique. The first section, on "Autofictional Identity," focuses on the fictional and autobiographical personas in Waguih Ghali's *Beer in the Snooker Club*, which was mostly read as a fictional text until its recent republication and translation into Arabic, after which it has been received increasingly as a representation of its author's life. The second section, "Autofictional Threads," offers a reading of Radwa Ashour's *Atiaf* (published in Arabic in 1999 and translated into English as *Specters* in 2010), with a focus on autofictional engagements with memory and experience. The third section, "Autofictionalizing Experience," addresses the use of personal memory in fictionalizing women's experiences in times of cultural displacement in Miral al-Tahawy's *Brooklyn Heights* (published in Arabic in 2010 and translated into English in 2011). Our reading of the three texts testifies to the affordance of an autofictional lens in reading Arabic literature. It allows new insights into these authors' constructions of identity, memory, and experience at the intersections of reality and the imagination, and in interaction with readers and critics.

WAGUIH GHALI'S AUTOFICTIONAL IDENTITY

Waguih Ghali (192?–1969) was an Egyptian Anglophone essayist and writer known for his one work of fiction, *Beer in the Snooker Club* ([1964] 2010). It was not until 2006 that the first translation of *Beer* appeared in Arabic, followed by another translation in 2012, while selections from his diaries were published still more recently in Cairo, with the title *The Diaries of Waguih Ghali: An Egyptian Writer in the Swinging Sixties* (2017). The online publication in 2013 of his diaries, personal papers, letters, and an unfinished manuscript of a second "novel" has drawn further attention to his work.[3]

We focus on Ghali's *Beer in the Snooker Club*, which tells the story of a young, upper-class, Christian Egyptian man, Ram, who returns to Cairo after having lived in London for a number of years, in the aftermath of the 1952 Egyptian Free Officers' Revolution against the British occupation. In love with a Jewish Egyptian woman and disillusioned with the "revolution" and his English education, while having no money of his own to keep up with his lifestyle or his class, Ram narrates a personal memoir-like story that moves between Cairo in the present and London in the past, creating an antihero with great appeal and charisma. Reading the text in its historical context brings to light the strikingly similar personal, social, and educational backgrounds, as well as the geographical associations, that Ghali and his protagonist share. Ghali chooses to write in English (reflecting his colonial education) about a period in the life of a young bicultural Egyptian man, making reference to real-life locations during a particular socio-historical moment contemporaneous with the author's life.

The autobiographical traces in this work emerge not only in the biographical details that Ghali and Ram share, but in Ghali's utilization of an intimate first-person narrator, in his sense of humor, which is apparent in Ram's witty and cynical comments and reflections, and in the fact that the protagonist of the novel is known only through his nickname, Ram, thus allowing for a play on nomenclature. These three features create a verisimilitude of the autobiographical, as the first-person narration allows for the possibility of reading *Beer* as a memoir despite the genre label (a novel) provided on the back-cover blurb. The fact that the protagonist is known only by his nickname prevents an autobiographical pact from being established, yet allows for the possibility that the protagonist/narrator is the author, as his first name is never mentioned. This possibility is further enhanced by Ghali's humor, which is most apparent in *Beer* through Ram's reflections, commentary, and behavior, thus connecting the author with protagonist and narrator. This humor posits a voice that seems to speak simultaneously for Ram and Ghali as it ridicules both self and society.

Such elements led critics to read *Beer* as "autobiographical fiction" for many years. We propose, however, that *Beer* can be read more productively as an autofictional text. The comparison between autofiction and the autobiographical novel, in generic terms, is significant in this context, because "[a]utofiction follows the autobiographical novel, but transposed to our times in different ways partly because readers' text reception changed" (Shands et al. 2015, 8). Using an autofictional reading strategy makes it possible to move beyond genre labels when reading *Beer* and to closely examine how autobiographical markers pave the way for Ghali's autofictional identity. Reading Ghali via paratextual material serves as the foundation for this autofictional reading: it becomes clear that the reception of the text, when first published and then republished 50 years later, is premised on the playful convergences between Ghali's identity and that of Ram. This chapter shows how autofiction as a reading strategy allows us to see the book in relation to its textual and historical contexts but also to expand our understanding of it, seeing it as a novel about colonial reality for a Cairene of Ghali's/Ram's class. A focus on the autofictional in Ghali's book shows us how Ghali playfully creates dialogue between life and fiction, and between the personal and the general.

Auto/Fictional Gestures

Ghali's text occupies a space between fiction and memoir, manifesting what we call autofictional gestures: hints and clues that prevent the text from being read as just a novel or just a memoir. These autofictional gestures are present in Ghali's use of humor, certain nuances of the self that are internalized in the first-person narrative, and most prominently from its very beginning, in *Beer*'s epigraph. The epigraph is a quote from Dostoevsky's *Notes from Underground* (1864): "Rather, we aim at being personalities of a general ... a fictitious type" (Ghali 2010). Placed at the beginning of the text, the epigraph initiates the readers into a text that lies between the autobiographical and the fictional. The aim to be fictional characters sets the scene for the autofictional play that will take place in the text. The playfulness of Ghali's chosen epigraph gains a certain weight when his protagonist speaks of becoming a character in a book. When Ghali writes, and Ram states, "Gradually, I have lost my natural self. I have become a character in a book or in some other feat of the imagination; my own actor in my own theatre; my own spectator in my own improvised play. Both audience and participant in one—a fictitious character" (60)—the statement connects to and reinforces the epigraph's notion of a possible fictionalization of the self.

As the epigraph indicates the blurred boundaries between the autobiographical and the fictional, when Ram asserts that "[t]hat moment of putting on my coat was the very beginning—the first time in my life that I had felt myself cleave into two entities, the one participating and the other watching and judging" (68), a connection emerges between the "two entities" he describes and the roles of author/narrator and protagonist/character. The echoes of the fictionalized self are clear in the way in which Ram comes to observe himself and reflect on the self he witnesses, and then narrates these reflections. The interconnections between self and life in this act of reflection blend author with narrator and protagonist and thus feel like an echo of the epigraph as an autofictional gesture. Read in conjunction with the above quotation, the epigraph connects the "auto" and the "fictional." It pays homage to the world of fictional writing, to an imaginary world that Ghali is looking to create. The epigraph could refer, on a surface level, to the way Ram feels as he separates into "two entities," but it could also offer insight into how Ghali weaves himself into his own fictive narrative.

Contextual Identifications

Paratextual evidence points clearly to the way in which Ghali fictionalizes himself in the character of Ram. The text's socio-political context, historical background, geographical locations, as well as references to concrete events and places in both London and Cairo, all underline the autofictional identification between author and protagonist. This connection is consolidated by readers, critics, and reviewers who have focused on drawing out the autobiographical in the fictional. In Helen Stuhr-Rommereim's review, for example, she writes that *Beer* "is so clearly autobiographical that not only do the details of Ram's life match Ghali's but the man that Diana Athill, Ghali's editor, describes in her introduction as 'gazelle-like' is immediately recognizable as the narrator who is so immediately disarming" (Stuhr-Rommereim 2011). Based on affective association and known facts about Ghali, the reading process that Stuhr-Rommereim proposes transcends clear-cut differences between text and paratextual material. Assuming that the boundaries between "auto" and "fiction" are being blurred, she writes, "Ghali himself committed suicide only a few years after completing the novel, and because it is so easy to conflate Ram with his creator, learning of Ghali's suicide becomes the novel's tragic epilogue" (Stuhr-Rommereim 2011). Thus, autofiction as a reading strategy shines a spotlight on the subtle convergence of life and fiction in the text.

While reviewers of Ghali's text, when it was published in 1964, read it within its assigned genre (the novel), these reviews nonetheless reveal an early awareness of the intersections of the autobiographical and the fictional in *Beer*. Irving Wardle begins his review with the text's biographical note: "A PUBLISHER'S note describes Waguih Ghali as a young Egyptian now exiled in Germany" (1964). Connecting Ghali's state of exile to Ram's complaints about the "aliens department" and being denied visas, Wardle adds: "Assuming the complaint to be autobiographical, Mr. Ghali seems from his book to have fully recovered from the English curse" (1964). Wardle here uses the publisher's biographical note on Ghali as the basis from which to make an autobiographical assumption that any critique of British racism stems from personal experience. Similarly, when another reviewer, W.L. Webb, writes that "Ram, one guesses, speaks with his master's voice" (Webb 1964), it is evident that he connects Ram to Ghali through the first-person narration. In this way, Webb and Wardle's readings of the text, which precede the development of theories of autofiction, managed to identify the autobiographical in Ghali's "very attractive comic style" (Webb 1964). Despite the lack of strong paratextual material with which to support their claims of the autobiographical, the two reviewers were able to touch upon the playfulness with which Ghali writes his text and allows his "self" to take a place in the narrative through autofictional gestures.

Epilogue of the Self; Epigraph of Fiction

Our reading of *Beer* through an autofictional lens goes beyond trying to find the autobiographical in the fictional. While part of this reading process involves cross-identifying the author with the narrator/protagonist against and/or in the absence of paratextual material, a reading of *Beer* as autofictional is rooted in the playful gesture of the epigraph. If Ghali's suicide is *Beer*'s "tragic epilogue" (Stuhr-Rommereim 2011), then it could be argued that the act of fictionalizing the self comes through in the grand gesture of playing with autofiction. Rather than taking Ghali's tragic suicide to be *Beer*'s epilogue, an autofictional reading allows for the self to exist in a text that resists generic limitations, so that the epigraph takes on full meaning when Ghali's suicide is contemplated, making *Beer* an epilogue to his suicide, as he lives on in his fiction. Reading *Beer* through the lens of autofiction thus intensifies the function of the epigraph as a paratexual interchange between Ram's life and Ghali's text.

RADWA ASHOUR'S AUTOFICTIONAL THREADS

Radwa Ashour's *Specters* (2010) is another example of a text situated at the generic crossroads of memoir and fiction. The autofictional as a critical lens through which to approach the text reveals a mediated space between generic intersections where the author weaves a narrative from threads of her life, intertwined with fictionalized versions of "reality" that she had witnessed. Ashour (1946–2014) was a professor of English language and literature at Ain Shams University in Egypt and an active advocate for academic freedom. In addition to her academic career, Ashour was a prominent writer of fictional and non-fictional works, including novels, short story collections, and autobiographical writings, in addition to her contribution as a literary critic. In most of her writing—both fictional and autobiographical—Ashour infuses layers of factuality and referentiality with imagined environments, settings, and situations, which encourages the reading of her work through an autofictional lens. Here, Pierre Nora's concept of the "site of memory" (1989, 7) will be used to highlight the way in which the autofictional is manifested in Ashour's text, especially with reference to the intersections between authorship, fictionality, and referentiality.

Specters is divided into two parallel lines of action involving two academics: Radwa, a professor of English literature (the author/narrator/protagonist), and Shagar, a professor in the History Department. The story moves between Radwa and Shagar in alternate chapters, first recounting their childhoods, their social backgrounds, and their family histories, before continuing to narrate their interconnected lives as present-day academics. The story is set at Ain Shams University, which is also the place where Ashour herself worked.[4] The chapters in which Radwa is the protagonist are narrated in the first person, while the chapters focusing on Shagar feature an omniscient third-person narrator. Furthermore, Ashour herself remarks in one of her essays that she intended to write Shagar, the second protagonist, as a "Qareen or Ka" (2000, 91). "Qareen" is an Arabic word that means a companion—most likely an imaginary one—and *Ka* is a mythical Ancient Egyptian Hieroglyphic syllable that refers to "the creative energy which accompanies a person from the moment of his or her birth to the afterlife," as Ashour explains (2000, 91). Shagar seems to serve as a complementary fictional creation to Ashour's first protagonist, Radwa, who bears the author's first name, perhaps offering more creative liberties of self-expression not available to the first protagonist (and, by extension, to the author).

Critic Marcia Lynx Qualey describes the text as a "twinned narrative" (2011, 31), one that displays two apparently separate structures which ultimately end up being interspersed and interlinked. Yet, on the whole, *Specters* has not received its due critical attention, mainly owing to its problematization of issues such as the lack of academic autonomy, university politics, and the exposure of corruption, issues that remain sensitive in most academic circles. In *Specters*, the relationship between the author, narrator, and protagonist is complex and layered. Ashour distances herself from her narrator's voice when she steps out of the narrative and enters a metanarrative space, addressing the reader directly in the authorial voice and reflecting self-consciously on the act of writing:

> What happened? Why did I leap so suddenly from Shagar the child to middle-aged Shagar? I reread what I have written, mull it over, stare at the lighted screen, and wonder whether I should continue the story of young Shagar, or return to her great grandmother, or trace the path of her descendants to arrive, once again, at the grandchild. And the ghosts—should I consign them to marginal obscurity, leaving them to hover on the periphery of the text, or admit them fully and elucidate some of their stories? (2010, 15–16)

Ashour's use of metanarration scrutinizes the process of writing Shagar's life, shifting between the narrative that we assume belongs to Ashour and the inner monologues of the protagonists Radwa and Shagar. Sometimes, the line between author and narrator is blurred to such an extent that it is difficult to distinguish who is who. For instance, Radwa refers to the dilemma of her constant immersion in literature and history, and the fact that on occasions she unknowingly interweaves the two, when she says, for example: "Aristotle said something regarding this. He distinguished literature from history, as I well know. I'd better refer to his book" (74), while the readers are left wondering whose voice this is: the author's, the narrator's, or both intertwined. In Chap. 8, Ashour incorporates a memoir of Shagar's grandfather, which he had left on her desk shortly before his death, into the seemingly autobiographical narrative. The chapter is divided into sections with subheadings, each recounting a specific episode in the imagined life of the fictional protagonist's grandfather, written in the first person. This generic interpolation allows Ashour to experiment with the kind of autofictional narrative strategies that are usually used as "a matter of introducing an unknown subject to the audience" (Dix 2018, 4), namely, the historical experiences or narratives presented through the lens of memoir writing.

The University as lieu de mémoire

The two parallel narratives constructed in *Specters* are situated in Ain Shams University, the physical campus where the author had built her own forty-year career. The prominent presence of the university in this text has even led to its classification as an academic novel (Morsy 2009; Zidan 2015). The setting of the university in its physical and metaphorical manifestations can be seen as a "site of memory" as Nora conceives of it, that is, "the embodiment of memory in certain sites where a sense of historical continuity persists" (1989, 7). While Nora does not include universities among his typical sites of memory (1989, 12), the campus in *Specters* seems to fit his description of these sites as being constructed by collective, not merely individual, memory. Representing an authoritarian location, it offers a subversive counter-narrative, where the two protagonists fight to create a better place that would conform to romanticized ideals of the university as a place for intellectual rigor, resistance to the status quo, and the exercise of academic and public freedoms. At the same time, it exposes the existing nationalistic and authoritarian narratives of power politics prevalent within Egyptian academia. Ashour constructs the reality of the university as she lived it as an academic, and then complements the narrative with her own imagined alternative space (or site) of a better university, one which is actively engaged in social and political change. She establishes the university in this way as an extension, if not a microcosm, of society through Shagar's realization that "the university isn't outside society—what happens in society happens in the university, too!" (2010, 91).

Shagar also admits to facing challenges in her acts of remembering, challenges which might be interpreted as a dangerous obstacle to her position as a historian, and to the construction of her version of her life and struggles at the university. This, by extension, jeopardizes the legitimacy of the creation of a "truthful" subversive account of the established *lieu de mémoire* in the text. This process does not only rely on memory and reconstruction but also involves forgetting and states of forgetfulness. Shagar's reflections on forgetfulness are narrated in the third person, opening up a shared space in which the author seems to also reflect on her own fallibility and subjectivity:

> Forgetfulness is a dodgy thing. It seems to a person that she has forgotten: she thinks that some desire, some idea, some reality, has slipped away from her, gone missing; the evidence is its total absence from her consciousness, she gazes at that river and sees upon it a thousand things—[...]. Then one day she realizes that this thing has surfaced all of a sudden, as if it had been preserved there in the depths, submerged in the water, solid as a coral tree or a pearl resting in its oyster. Forgetfulness is a dodgy thing [...]. (63)

Forgetfulness is presented as a potential threat to Shagar's existence, whose life and work, as a history professor, is founded on reviving and commemorating historical moments. Similarly, forgetfulness is an unacceptable loss to Radwa, as a professor of literature who is fascinated by historicization as a conscious process toward remembering and away from forgetting. Author and protagonist alike (re)historicize important eras of Egyptian modern history, while situating the university (both as a physical place and as a metaphor for academia) as a witness—and sometimes instigator and agent of change—to historical events. Ultimately, both protagonists (Radwa and Shagar) fail in enacting the idealized view of the university that they had envisioned. Ashour offers two parallel endings in the narrative: one where Shagar resigns and admits defeat in fighting a corrupt dean, and another where Radwa refuses to admit failure and preaches optimism for a better university. Moreover, Ashour offers a critical reflection upon her own literary practice, highlighting the importance of seeking "originality" in one's writing, noting that "the 'experience of the Self' is a very important aspect in looking at any text […]. Historical reality and the specificity of the experience of the Self are two determinants of how *original* the work is" (2001, 97–98; emphasis added).[5] In relation to *Specters*, she implements her conception of originality in the text by drawing attention to the interaction between personal experience and the author's referentiality both to self and others—to real places, people, and events. She then moves beyond referentiality to depict the university as a physical and metaphorical site of memory, reinforcing remembering, and commemorating the university as a place that infuses reality with imagination, disappointment, hope, defeat, and determination; and finally, fighting the process of forgetting both individual and collective struggles within that site.

Memory is closely connected to the notion of subjective truth, which underpins personal narratives: "autobiographical truth is not a fixed but an evolving content in an intricate process of self-discovery and self-creation" (Eakin 2014, 3). Along similar lines, autofiction "is less concerned with faithfully reporting what its protagonist did, or even how that person thought and felt, and is more concerned with the speculative question of how that subject might respond to new and often imagined environments" (Dix 2018, 6). Ashour, for her part, creates a parallel imagined environment and a protagonist who complements parts of her life and consciousness. As was the case in *Beer*, the autofictional in *Specters* manifests itself through narrative technique as well as referential locations, which are verifiable through paratextual references in Ashour's other writings to her own life experiences. The paratextual layer in this analysis serves to complement the autofictional manifestations within the texts themselves. An autofictional reading of *Specters* allows for emphasis on Ashour's agency as a Middle Eastern female academic, amplifies her voice, in which she expresses her views on many political, social, and academic causes, and stresses her commitment to fighting corruption, participating and/or writing about revolution(s), and fighting for a better Egyptian academia. Autofiction affords a creative space where the author can situate her lifelong struggles within a fictionalized context that moves away from a strict autobiographical frame. In this space, Ashour can create multiple selves and personas that function in parallel and share common struggles that the author witnessed in her real life, a space which provides better access to, and interaction with, a diverse reading audience.

Autofictionalizing Experience in Miral al-Tahawy's Brooklyn Heights

In Miral al-Tahawy's *Brooklyn Heights* (2011), the fictionalization of memory plays a crucial role in grappling with the experience of cultural displacement. The protagonist's process of remembering the past is structured in parallel with the fictional narrative, where memory registers experience in fictional terms. Miral al-Tahawy (1968-) is a contemporary Egyptian writer, belonging to the generation of Egyptian writers who appeared on the cultural scene in the 1990s and who are considered to have created new spaces for artistic expression in literature, theater, and the cinema (see, e.g., Elsadda 2008, 2012; Anishchenkova 2017; Pepe 2019). This generation of writers has produced a distinct body of literature, identified by literary critics and historians as foregrounding personal experience, breaking traditional literary conventions, and writing across generic boundaries, a trend known as "New Writing."[6] Al-Tahawy is one of the foremost female writers of this period, most of whom continue to write today. She published her earliest pieces of writing in a short story collection entitled *Rīm al-barārī al-mustahīla* (*Reem of the Impossible Wilderness*) in 1995, followed by her first novel, *The Tent* (1996), which established her as an original voice in the Egyptian literary scene owing to her portrayal of women belonging to Egyptian Bedouin culture. In addition to its cultural specificity, her writing is marked by the crossing of generic boundaries, where fiction intersects with memoir. In our autofictional reading of *Brooklyn Heights*, we will focus on the specific ways in which al-Tahawy fictionalizes identity, experience, and memory, and on the potential repercussions for the contemporary reception of writing by Egyptian women.

Experiences of Displacement and Self-Representation

Brooklyn Heights opens with the protagonist Hend's arrival in Manhattan with her young son and describes her attempt to settle down as an immigrant in the USA. Rather than striving for assimilation, she focuses on her estrangement from her new community, constantly remembering and being reminded of her past. She intentionally frequents immigrant neighborhoods and seeks the company of other Arabs with whom she can identify, as well as attending English language courses with other minority representatives, foreigners, immigrants, and asylum seekers. The text is structured around a series of shifts in time and place, and her encounters in the present bring to Hend's mind scenes from her recent past in Cairo, as well as childhood memories from her native village in the Egyptian Delta. Geographical, cultural, and personal displacement governs the whole narrative and seems to dominate the protagonist's experience from the opening lines of the text:

> She finds it on a Google map of Brooklyn as she hunts for an apartment, a narrow strip winding its way up to the long arching bridge that connects the two islands. [...] She turns her back on Manhattan and chooses Flatbush Avenue from among all those myriad streets because it becomes her: a woman shouldering her solitude, a couple of suitcases, and a child who leans into her whenever he grows tired of walking. She carries a few manuscripts of unfinished stories in a small backpack along with the other important documents: birth and vaccine certificates, residence papers, copies of degrees, employers' letters of recommendation, bank papers, and a signed rental contract for an apartment she's never seen. (Al-Tahawy 2011, 1)

In these lines, referentiality is established through the protagonist's detailed description of real places, relying on a "Google map of Brooklyn," with specific streets and locations, as she walks in search of her destination. At the same time, al-Tahawy foregrounds Hend's sense of displacement in establishing her identity as an outsider, a foreigner who carries identification documents and "residence papers." Hend is also identified as an aspiring writer, who, along with her documents, keeps with her "manuscripts of unfinished stories," stories through which author, narrator, and protagonist intersect in their identity as writers.

Fictionalizing Personal Memory

Memory is a central focus of *Brooklyn Heights*, both thematically and structurally, and is closely related to various acts of writing. Each chapter opens at a moment in the present in which the protagonist's experience in the USA triggers a memory from the past, and then takes us back to the narrative present.[7] Hend seeks to find her own place in the new surroundings, attempting to set down roots in a place inhabited by people with whom she can identify, and who remind her of her past, as "everything around her invites nostalgia" (2). One of her main concerns becomes her continual attempts to remember, together with her conscious fear of failing to do so, as "she thinks about how she has begun to forget so many things—addresses, events, the whereabouts of documents. She worries that her keen memory is getting moldy" (4). The protagonist's strain to remember can be understood as a kind of equivalent to the author's technique of fictionalizing memory: while Hend is remembering scenes and situations from her past in her village and then in Cairo, al-Tahawy is weaving her narrative using threads from Hend's present and past experiences. The author creates imaginary scenes of the remembered past, foregrounding the connections between the past and the present, memory and experience, author and protagonist. That is to say, Hend's narrative voice as well as her experience, as an aspiring Arab woman writer, intersects with al-Tahawy's (herself an Arab woman writer who had recently moved to the USA); and the descriptions of the setting in New York, the Egyptian Delta, and Cairo are anchored not only in real life but specifically in the life of the author.

In terms of the characterization of Hend, there is a clear convergence between her identity and that of the author, despite the lack of direct correspondence in names. The overlap is maintained when Hend identifies with the fictional character of Lilith, an aging Egyptian immigrant who is presented to us through Hend's eyes: all three are Egyptian/Arab women struggling to fit into the USA. It is the correspondence in experience rather than nomenclature that establishes the autofictional identity. Second, in terms of narrative voice, there is a clear convergence between al-Tahawy's omniscient authorial voice and that of the protagonist in Hend's interior monologues. Toward the end of the text, we read the following: "The notebook meanwhile remained innocent of writing. She sketched one self-portrait after another in charcoal on the white pages, images of a woman with hollow cheeks and a long nose, and curly black hair, hands clasped to her withered breast—a solitary woman on the threshold of winter" (156). More than anywhere else in the text, though not singularly, the protagonist's voice seems here to merge with the author's, their converged identities representing an autofictional narrative technique. Structured within the framework of individual and indirectly collective cultural memory, the fictional merges with the remembered. The whole text thus emerges as an example of a specific form of the autofictional, where the "auto" stands for memory rather than for the self or identity.

Memory additionally carries a generic dimension, most evident in memoirs where the term itself suggests a process of writing/fictionalizing personal memory. The protagonist's identity as an aspiring writer is established from the opening pages of the text when we see her carrying her manuscripts among her documents. Writing, as an identity marker, is extended throughout the text through the connection between Hend and Lilith. Two plot lines focusing on the lives of Hend and Lilith seem to be running in parallel across time, until they unexpectedly converge when Hend introduces Lilith as follows:

> She carries all her important papers with her in the pocket of her coat but she's terrified most of the time that she'll lose them or forget them […] She also keeps a small notebook where she jots down the things she wants to remember […] She writes other things in a clear hand on little snippets of paper and then forgets where she's put them. (146)

This scene, describing Lilith's "important papers" kept in "the pocket of her coat," mirrors the introduction of Hend as carrying "a few manuscripts of unfinished stories in a small backpack along with other important documents" (1). The act of writing can be interpreted as a metaphor for a lost past for both Hend and Lilith as they try to write their memoirs to capture and relive their experiences, as well as for the displaced present, when subtle reference is made to a fragmented process of life writing:

> Back then, she was still capable of living alone, of sitting on a park bench by herself and jotting down in a little notebook the sentences that she hoped would eventually become her memoirs. […] Her memory rebelled against the blank white pages. She was incapable of conjuring all the little details that make up a life. (155)

Hend comes across these papers after Lilith's death, and the connection between the two women is further augmented by Hend's total identification with Lilith's photos and papers: "I know that I've written every word in them myself, she thinks. This is my handwriting, they belong to me" (181). Memory in this situation not only maintains its significance as a thematic element and structural component, but acquires important generic significance, merging identity and experience with writing with reference to a particular genre, namely, memoir. An important metanarrative dimension surfaces here in which the author's writing of *Brooklyn Heights* is subtly represented in Lilith's fragmented memoir, which in turn is appropriated by Hend. Al-Tahawy thus establishes an autofictional effect by connecting Lilith and Hend through their experiences of displacement and their acts of life/writing, a process in which the voices and identities of author, narrator, and protagonist seem to merge.

Autofictional Memoir?

While in its original Arabic edition *Brooklyn Heights* is subtitled and classified as a "novel," the English edition adds the subtitle "An Egyptian Novel," thus situating the text culturally as well as generically. Hend's personal experience is set against an elaborate transnational socio-cultural background. Reading *Brooklyn Heights* through an autofictional lens brings the generic hybridity of the text into view: it presents a fictionalized life-narrative while simultaneously employing one of the main features of memoir writing in its depiction of human experience against a specific socio-historical background, that is, the experience of displacement and immigration from an Egyptian woman's perspective. Her voice, autofictionally echoing the author's, replaces the conventional passive representations of women in Arabic literature with agency, through active self-representation. Yet, by asserting its fictionality, the text destabilizes the tendency to receive women's writing as life writing, and thus affords an alternative space beyond an autobiographical reading.

*

It might seem that we are stretching the concept of the autofictional in our reading of Waguih Ghali's *Beer in the Snooker Club*, Radwa Ashour's *Specters*, and Miral al-Tahawy's *Brooklyn Heights*, but paratextual sources support the viability of such an approach. The current and widely circulating edition of *Beer* is published with an introduction by Ghali's editor, Diana Athill, derived from her memoir *After a Funeral* (1986), in which she writes about the years Ghali spent living in her house. Athill comments on Ghali and his text as follows: "He knew that as a writer he had only one subject, himself, and he saw his life as raw material for a work of literature which he had only begun in his first novel" (2010). Although she identifies the text as a novel, a work of fiction, she also points to Ghali's inscription of himself in his writing. Similarly, Ashour describes *Specters* as "a semi-autobiographical narrative, a partial record of my life intertwined with that of another character of my age and profession" (2000, 91). She further stresses the autobiographical, self-referential elements in her narrative and the integral part they play in shaping her experience (92). Her categorization of the text as a "semi-autobiographical narrative" manifests the absence (at that time) of a critical concept equivalent to her autofictional narrative, where she intentionally combines the autobiographical with the fictional. Al-Tahawy, in turn, remarks in an interview about her book, when reflecting on her life in the USA, that "you're geographically in America, but you really live somewhere else when you close the front door—the place of your memory. I was really thinking about this when I was writing about Hend" (East 2012). In this quotation, as well as in other interviews, al-Tahawy acknowledges the connection between herself as author and her protagonist Hend, while at the same time emphasizing the fictional nature of the narrative. These sources show that, as both Dix's and Schmitt's chapters in the present volume underscore, paratexts can provide a crucial tool in an approach to the autofictional. Dix, moreover, shows that this is of particular importance when extending the concept to texts not typically considered to be autofictional.

The three texts we have examined in this chapter demonstrate the affordances of the autofictional as a literary strategy in negotiating identity, memory, and experience in the writing of Egyptian literature. In the absence of an established tradition of autofiction criticism in Arabic literary studies, this chapter has argued for using autofiction as a critical lens. We would like to end on a note about a potential topic for further discussion. Taking into consideration that we, as critics, enjoy various degrees of proximity to the authors (knowing them personally in the case of Ashour and al-Tahawy; or knowing people who have known them in the case of Ghali), another question emerges, about "autofictional critical practice"[8] and "personal criticism" (Anderson 2011, 127). These author-critic connections raise further questions about the effects of personal communication and interaction between critic and author in real life and, in particular, about how such relations affect or create an autofictional reading of a text.

Acknowledgments This chapter includes two sections derived from the following PhD theses in progress: Zainab Magdy, "Representations of the Self in Works by and on Waguih Ghali," and Fatma Massoud, "'Autofiction' in Selected Works by Radwa Ashour and Doris Lessing," both supervised by Hoda Gindi and Hala Kamal (The Department of English Language and Literature, Faculty of Arts,

Cairo University, Egypt). The chapter combines three presentations originally presented in the panel on "Autofictional Modes in Contemporary Egyptian Writing" at the conference on autofiction held at the University of Oxford in 2019. We wish to express our gratitude to the British Council Egypt Office, and particularly to Ms. Cathy Costain, Head of Arts at the British Council, for supporting our participation in the conference.

Notes

1. In his book *Des autofictions arabes* (2019), Francophone critic Darouèche Hilali Bacar examines three fictional works by Arab authors. He seems to be among the first critics to apply the term autofiction in his reading of Arabic literature.
2. Moroccan novelist and critic Mohamed Berrada translated the term "autofiction" into "al-takhyīl al-dhātī" in his novel *Like a Summer Never to Be Repeated* (originally published in Arabic in 1999 and translated in 2009), which emphasizes autofiction as narrative technique. More recently, in an attempt to encompass both generic and technical aspects of autofiction, Hala Kamal translated the term into "riwāyat al-dhāt" in her article, written in Arabic, entitled "From Autobiography to Life-Writing: Trajectories and Intersections across the Humanities and Social Sciences" (2020).
3. The unpublished papers of Waguih Ghali became available under a Creative Commons License in 2013, in an archive entitled *Waguih Ghali Unpublished Papers: Diaries (1964–1968), Manuscript Fragments and Letters* available at https://ghali.library.cornell.edu/. A selection has been edited recently and published in two volumes: *The Diaries of Waguih Ghali: An Egyptian Writer in the Swinging Sixties* (2017).
4. We are using the author's last name, Ashour, to refer to the text's author, and Radwa to refer to the protagonist, who is the first-person narrator.
5. Translated from Arabic by Fatma Massoud.
6. For more on the "New Writing in the 1990s," see Elsadda 2008, 145–164.
7. The only exception is the last chapter, which begins with reflections on the past and Arab culture in general terms, before the final shift to the present in the last pages of the book. It is at the end that Hend's identification with Lilith is at its fullest, and is manifested in their shared displacement, Hend's sense of aging, and being surrounded by scattered memorabilia from the past.
8. This point was raised by Hywel Dix in an informal conversation, during the conference "Autofiction—Theory, Practices, Cultures—A Comparative Perspective" at the University of Oxford (October 2019).

Works Cited

Al-Tahawy, Miral. 2011. *Brooklyn Heights: An Egyptian Novel*. Translated by Samah Selim. Cairo: American University in Cairo Press.

Anderson, Linda. 2011. *Autobiography*. London: Routledge.

Anishchenkova, Valerie. 2017. "Feminist Voices of the 1990s Generation: A Quest for Identity in Miral al-Tahawy's *Blue Aubergine*. *Journal of Middle East Women's Studies* 13(1): 87–106.

Ashour, Radwa. 2000. Eyewitness, Scribe and Storyteller: My Experience as a Novelist. *The Massachusetts Review* 41 (1): 85–92.

———. 2001. Al-tafā'ul al-thaqāfi wa tiqaniyāt al-kitāba: Namādhij min ibdā' al-mar'a al-arabiya. In *Ṣayyādu al-thākira*, 96–109. Cairo: Dar Al-Shorouk.

———. 2010. *Specters*. Translated by Barbara Romaine. Cairo: American University in Cairo Press.

Athill, Diana. 2010. Introduction by Diana Athill. In *Beer in the Snooker Club*, by Waguih Ghali. London: Serpent's Tail.

Berrada, Mohamed. 2009. *Like a Summer Never to Be Repeated*. Translated by Christina Phillips. Cairo: American University in Cairo Press.

Dix, Hywel. 2018. Introduction: Autofiction in English: The Story so Far. In *Autofiction in English*, ed. Hywel Dix, 1–23. Cham: Palgrave Macmillan.

Eakin, Paul J. 2014. *Fictions in Autobiography: Studies in the Art of Self-Invention*. Princeton, NJ: Princeton University Press.

East, Ben. 2012. Life That Is Neither Here Nor There. *The National News*, December 6, 2012. https://www.thenationalnews.com/arts-culture/books/life-that-is-neither-here-nor-there-1.474198. Accessed Apr 6, 2021.

Elsadda, Hoda. 2008. Egypt. In *Arab Women Writers: A Critical Reference Guide, 1873–1999*, ed. Radwa Ashour, Ferial Jabouri Ghazoul, and Hasna Reda-Mekdashi, 98–161. Cairo: American University in Cairo Press.

———. 2012. *Gender, Nation, and the Arabic Novel: Egypt, 1892–2008*. Edinburgh: Edinburgh University Press.

Ghali, Waguih. 1964. *Beer in the Snooker Club*. London: André Deutsch.

———. 2010. *Beer in the Snooker Club*. London: Serpent's Tail.

———. 2017. *The Diaries of Waguih Ghali: An Egyptian Writer in the Swinging Sixties, Volume 1, 1964–1966* and *Volume 2, 1966–1968*. Edited by May Hawas. Cairo: American University in Cairo Press.

Hilali Bacar, Darouèche. 2019. *Des Autofictions arabes*. Lyon: Presses Universitaires de Lyon.

Kamal, Hala. 2020. "Min al-sīra al-dhātiyya ila kitābat al-hayā" (From Autobiography to Life-Writing). *Alif: Journal of Comparative Poetics* 40: 65–103.

Morsy, Faten. 2009. The University in *The Open Door* and *Atyaf*. *Alif: Journal of Comparative Poetics* 29: 139–152.

Nora, Pierre. 1989. Between Memory and History: Les Lieux de Mémoire. *Representations* 26: 7–24.

Pepe, Teresa. 2019. *Blogging from Egypt: Digital Literature, 2005–2016*. Edinburgh: Edinburgh University Press.

Qualey, Marcia Lynx. 2011. A Twinned Narrative. *The Women's Review of Books* 28 (2): 31–32.

Shands, Kerstin, Giulia Grillo Mikrut, Dipti R. Pattanaik, and Karen Ferreira-Meyers. 2015. Introduction. In *Writing the Self: Essays on Autobiography and Autofiction*, 7–28. Huddinge: Södertörns högskola.

Stuhr-Rommereim, Helen. 2011. Beer in the Snooker Club - Waguih Ghali. *Full Stop*. July 5, 2011. https://www.full-stop.net/2011/07/05/reviews/helen-stuhr-rommereim/beer-in-the-snooker-club-waguih-ghali/. Accessed Apr 6, 2021.

Wardle, Irving. 1964. Anglo-Egyptian Attitudes. *The Observer*, February 16, 1964. https://www.proquest.com/docview/475686628/E0D2127C6DD14815PQ/1. Accessed Apr 6, 2021.

Webb, W.L. 1964. Anger in Egypt: *Beer in the Snooker Club* by Waguih Ghali. *The Guardian*, February 21, 1964. https://www.newspapers.com/clip/35958317/the-guardian/. Accessed Apr 6, 2021.

Zidan, Ashraf. 2015. Reflections of Egyptian Society in the Campus Fiction: A Study of Radwa Ashour's *Specters*. *English Language and Literature Studies* 5 (1): 70–77.

Open Access This chapter is licensed under the terms of the Creative Commons Attribution 4.0 International License (http://creativecommons.org/licenses/by/4.0/), which permits use, sharing, adaptation, distribution and reproduction in any medium or format, as long as you give appropriate credit to the original author(s) and the source, provide a link to the Creative Commons licence and indicate if changes were made.

The images or other third party material in this chapter are included in the chapter's Creative Commons licence, unless indicated otherwise in a credit line to the material. If material is not included in the chapter's Creative Commons licence and your intended use is not permitted by statutory regulation or exceeds the permitted use, you will need to obtain permission directly from the copyright holder.

PART III

Forms

CHAPTER 12

Autofiction and Film: Archival Practices in Post-millennial Documentary Cinema in Argentina and Spain

Anna Forné and Patricia López-Gay

> *What kind of common point can there be among the principal forms of resistance in the current audiovisual scene? I think—basically—the answer is memory.*
> —José Luis Guerín, "Work in Progress"

This chapter discusses some of the theoretical insights on autofiction gained in the context of the international research project "Rethinking the Real: Autofiction and Critical Discourse in Spain and Argentina." Coordinated by Ana Casas (University of Alcalá), the project is currently being conducted by an interdisciplinary group of scholars with the support of a research grant awarded by the Spanish Ministry of Science and Innovation (FFI2017-89870-P).

A. Forné (✉)
Department of Languages and Literature, University of Gothenburg, Gothenburg, Sweden
e-mail: anna.forne@sprak.gu.se

P. López-Gay
Department of Latin American and Iberian Studies, Bard College, Annandale-On-Hudson, NY, USA
e-mail: plopezga@bard.edu

This chapter examines three autofictional documentaries produced in Argentina and Spain in the past decade that share a distinctive "archival impulse" (Foster 2004; Derrida 1995): not a will to totalize so much as a will to relate to, and explore, a misplaced past or present time. These archival cinematic works propose an order and a meaning in a very specific political sense, which will be read here in relation to the contexts of the Iberian financial crisis and to the memories of political violence during the last dictatorship in Argentina (1976–1983). We will address the strategies through which the filmmakers use autofictional modes to "re-stage" the archive, so to speak, by adopting an aesthetics of ambiguity that intermittently destabilizes the evidential paradigm of the modern archive.

In the domain of literature, the autofictional turn that took place in the late 1970s, originating in France, was driven at least in part by the desire to render undecidable conventional dichotomies such as life versus text, historical versus literary discourse, life narration versus the writing body, and autobiographical writing versus the novel (López-Gay 2020, 25–33; 2017).[1] In film studies, several concepts are currently in use when referring to autofictional or autobiographical films, such as "subjective cinema" (Rascaroli 2009), "the cinema of me" (Lebow 2012), and "first-person documentary" (Piedras 2014), to mention just a few. As Matthias Christen suggests, the field of autobiographical film is vast and multifaceted, and cannot easily be outlined:

> It ranges from narratives centered on a filmmaker's life, in an established documentary or diaristic mode, to the display of a personal sensibility in the avant-garde and experimental film and broaches on the hybrid forms of web-based life-writing. The mode of authorship and subjectivity as well as the degrees of temporal coverage and personal presence of the filmmakers vary accordingly. (2019, 451)

Informed by its literary origins, we understand autofiction as a contemporary cinematic mode that challenges, and at times subverts, the generic limits of documentary and fiction film from a self-reflexive position. As a result of its transgeneric status, autofictional cinema creates a space in-between which includes, but cannot be reduced to, documentary and/or fiction cinema. Autofiction is based on what Spanish theorist Manuel Alberca has described as an "ambiguous pact" established between author and audience (2007). Ambiguity not only permeates the form of the films that we will analyze in this chapter; it also suffuses the poetics of memory that they deploy.

The act of archiving the real through the malleable trope of personal memory raises a number of questions that invite the audience to become active interpreters of a historical past or present. The term "archive" refers to both the act of archiving and its product. In autofictional literature and the visual arts, including film, the term evokes the notion of a trace or an ordered ensemble of traces, as well as the repository where such traces are organized and preserved, following an artistic process of selection and aesthetization (López-Gay 2020, 17–23). In this chapter, the notion of the archive will encompass various kinds of objects, records, and documents, and more broadly, recorded images of a given historical reality, in addition to referring to the documentary films themselves.

A decentered conception of the archive as something that is incomplete and thus open to diverse interpretations permeates the production of Argentine director Albertina Carri. In her autofictional documentary trilogy on recent Argentinian history—*Los rubios* (*The Blonds*) (2003), *Restos* (*Remains*) (2010), and *Cuatreros* (*Rustlers*) (2016)—Carri gathers and mobilizes archival documentation in her personal search for her parents, Ana María Caruso and Roberto Carri, who are among the estimated 30,000 people kidnapped and disappeared by the military during the last dictatorship in Argentina. The trials of the members of the military responsible for these crimes against humanity continue today, as does the painful search of many Argentine families for the remains of their relatives. Since the turn of the millennium, the artistic work carried out by the so-called second generation has reshaped the early narratives of the memories of dictatorship in Argentina that were articulated in the 1980s and 1990s. These children of the disappeared have abandoned expectations of certainty in testimonial writing and conventional documentary film in favor of an autofictional mode that experiments with generic boundaries, and thus privileges ambiguity and uncertainty (see, e.g., Blejmar 2016). By means of staging archival material alongside fictional reproductions, meta-reflexive commentaries, and formal experimentation, Carri's oeuvre challenges its viewers to take an active part in the never-ending process of memory construction. Similarly grounded in a sentiment of uncertainty, Mercedes Álvarez's *Mercado de futuros* (*Futures Market*) (2011) and Víctor Erice's *Vidros partidos* (*Broken Windows*) (2012) illuminate the impossibility of documenting absolute origins, be it the origins of capitalism as it was experienced by the first working classes or the origins of the ongoing financial recession. While these two cinematic autofictions are markedly self-referential, by calling obliquely for practices of counter-memory of the crisis that focus on the creative appropriation of space by citizens, Álvarez and Erice draw attention not only to the status of these works as cinematic text, or art, but also to the need to move beyond the text and take political action.

The autofictional sensitivity of documentary cinema that these Argentine and Spanish filmmakers highlight challenges the assumption that Bill Nichols (1991, 154) famously ascribed to the genre, the idea that "what we see is evidence of historical occurrences, not fictional simulations of them." While their autofictional films are documentaries whose propositions, tacit or explicit, target contemporary history, they suggest nevertheless that there can be no direct access to the past, and at times approach history through fictional, scripted simulations of human experiences, overt performances, and personal storytelling. The autofictional mode disrupts one of the fundamental principles in which documentary cinema is grounded: the presumption that each audiovisual trace is the direct, indexical imprint of a spontaneous, tangible reality. The films from Argentina and Spain that we will explore unsettle in distinct, original ways the modern paradigm of the archive as static evidence of a given reality. They revolve instead around a newer conception of the archive as a self-reflective process, as an event that becomes the subject matter in its own right.

"But the Images Are Not There": Archival Excess in Albertina Carri's *Cuatreros*

Albertina Carri's filmic production on political violence in Argentina and her personal search for her disappeared parents expands in a seemingly inconclusive manner, without a clear beginning or an end. Carri's rhizomic cartography of political violence in Argentina began with the groundbreaking documentary *Los rubios* (2003) and continued more recently with *Restos* (2010) and *Cuatreros* (2016). The first film formally and thematically narrates the inquiry that Carri undertakes into the fate of her parents: the story in *Los rubios* is pieced together through the self-reflexive staging and reorganization of a series of archival objects such as photographs, videotaped interviews, and toys. Carri makes the relationship between reality and construction ambiguous by means of metalepsis and reenactment (Forné 2017). In *Restos* she resumes the (re)search initiated in *Los rubios*. However, on this occasion, Carri does not follow the traces of her disappeared parents but undertakes instead to track down the remains of the militant cinema of the 1960s and 1970s in Argentina. The specific film she seeks is *Los Velázquez* (1972), directed by Pablo Szir and based on an essay by Roberto Carri (the director's disappeared father) entitled *Isidro Velázquez: Formas prerrevolucionarias de la violencia* (*Isidro Velázquez: Pre-revolutionary Forms of Violence*) (1968). Like its director, this never-released film disappeared during the dictatorship. The material remnants of the audiovisual archive are incorporated and staged in *Restos*, putting together a spatio-temporally complex narrative on the militant cinema of the 1960s and 1970s and the devastating political violence of the dictatorship. Imaginary vestiges are manufactured to replace the lost pieces in a way that draws attention to the porous boundaries between fact and fiction (Forné 2020).[2] *Cuatreros*, just like *Restos*, revolves around the disappeared film of Pablo Szir, whose script was based on Roberto Carri's abovementioned essay on the mythical figure of the rural bandit to whom these two works owe their name: Isidro Velázquez. Behind the character of Velázquez, and the narrative of the symbolic role he played for militant intellectuals in Argentina in the 1960s and 1970s, is the figure of the film-maker in search of material traces of her disappeared parents.

Cuatreros opens with the voice-over of Albertina Carri, who for three minutes reads from the prologue of *Isidro Velázquez :Formas prerrevolucionarias de la violencia*. Even though its viewers are promptly informed about the origin of the recited text, the initial information on the research conducted by Roberto Carri could also be understood as a comment on Albertina Carri's own archival collection and its staging in *Cuatreros*:

> A small research project in the field, conversations with locals, the reading of newspapers and other periodicals that dealt with the case, exchange of correspondence with friends who live in the area, constitute the "empirical" basis of this work. Obviously, the material used can be questioned by serious researchers, but I have no problem declaring that this is of very little concern to me. The real crux of this problem lies not always in what Velázquez and Gauna did for a long period of their wanderings in the countryside, but what the vast majority understood Velázquez meant to them. (01:04–01:42)[3]

Cuatreros is an investigation into what happened to Szir's film, and much like Roberto Carri's book, it makes use of "empirical" archival material, but does so in a highly fragmented way, dismissing observational, narrative-realist cinema from the start. In *Cuatreros*, Carri does not limit herself to suggesting the inaccessibility of the past and the impossibility of an immediate indexical imprint of "the real," but also formally evokes the unreachability of the real, abandoning conventional documentary ocularcentrism. The rapid pace of the voice-over, the multiple, parallel, and simultaneous screens, which show internally disconnected fragments of found footage, and the asynchronicity between sound and image, turn this film into a highly demanding exercise for the viewer. Moreover, the visual absence of the narrator-protagonist further increases the ambiguity of the film. Whereas in *Los rubios*, (referential) historical material is gathered and staged, albeit in a fragmented way, and in *Restos*, archival material in the form of found footage is manufactured, in *Cuatreros*, referentiality is unequivocally suppressed, foreclosing the possibility of a precise historical record (Fig. 12.1).

Fig. 12.1 Albertina Carri, *Several parallel but thematically disconnected screens of found footage in Cuatreros*

In an interview by Horacio Verbitsky, Albertina Carri describes *Cuatreros* as a frustrated road-movie with no script but with a conventional structure, whose originality lies in its entirely archival and recycled character: "Somehow the script is not original at all, rather it is a genre film with a classical structure. So what makes it original is that not a single new image has been generated for that script to become a film" (Carri 2018). Indeed, in *Cuatreros*, Carri plays with the fact that the audiovisual medium is still more opaque and disruptive than written documents even as it appears, deceptively, to be more tangible as well as more transparent: "They seem 'closer' to the past they represent and are potentially seductive in their seeming transparent textuality: and although every trace, written or otherwise, is open to interpretation, indexical audiovisual recordings are especially resistant to full comprehension or interpretation" (Baron 2014, 4). Despite the excess of audiovisual documents staged in *Cuatreros*, every possible referential anchor vanishes when sound and image present two different narratives and the images are intermittently multiplied and decontextualized. This multiplicity of screens, according to the filmmaker, is not primarily an aesthetic device, but rather an ethical and political one, designed to awaken passive spectators who are accustomed to the grammar and semantics of conservative contemporary cinema (Carri 2018).

Although it is visually fragmented as well as sonorously layered, *Cuatreros* displays a series of discontinuous but recurring storylines—militant cinema, archives, political violence, disappearance—which all connect back to the entangled rhizome of the filmmaker's production. These narratives repeat endlessly, never rounding up to provide certainty or a sense of veracity, as would be expected in a conventional documentary. The sole approximately stable referent to be found in Carri's film is the enunciating "I" of the filmmaker. As a consequence, *Cuatreros* does not seem to present a plurality of viewpoints, nor an opaque figuration of the identity of the director—two of the essential characteristics that Pablo Piedras (2014, 90–94) identifies in contemporary first-person documentary made in Argentina, together with a broken linearity, a fragmented temporality, and narrative distance. Although not visually present in the film, the identity of the filmmaker is clearly articulated in the narrative of *Cuatreros* and the point of view verbally presented is distinctively subjective. Albertina Carri is a central figure in the Argentine cultural landscape and her intellectual lineage (as well as her ancestry) is well known, facts which are inserted into the narrative. Consequently, in *Cuatreros*, the narrator seeks to accurately represent herself, while the ambiguity of the representation, proper to autofiction, lies precisely in the tension created between the personal memory and the public archive. This tension translates aesthetically as the friction between sound and image, that is, between the assertive narrative voice of the filmmaker and the arbitrary montage of film clips found in archives.

In *Cuatreros*, the (hi)story of militant cinema is absorbed into, and then expelled once more from, the filmmaker's "damaged navel" in the sequence where Carri narrates her visit to Cuba. The disappointment she experiences while she is there, when the utopian dream of revolution for which her parents died is shattered, is difficult to accept as a daughter of revolutionaries. In this short episode, Carri tells the story of her visit to the archives of the Cuban Institute of Cinematographic Art and Industry, in search of Szir's film on Velázquez. The various sound levels—Carri's voice, the tick-tock of a clock, the breaking of glass, the clicking noise of an old film projector, the crackling of the fire—which are superimposed onto a series of disconnected archival images of a clock, a crater, fire, and bottles, among other items, accompanies the voice-over narrative on the importance of Enrique Juárez's documentary *Ya es tiempo de violencia* (*Now Is the Time for Violence*) (1969) for Albertina Carri.[4] The separation of images and sound is absolute when Carri informs the attentive viewer that this particular documentary reconciles her with the choices, despite their disastrous consequences, that her parents made:

> Every time I watch it again, I'm reconciled with my dead parents. What's more, every so often I watch it to remember this feeling that made me bitter the first time I saw it. If I had been old enough at that time, I would have done the same as them, as Juárez, as Szir, as Mom and Dad. I would have belonged to a subversive cell, without a doubt. But times are different, and I got this one. It gave me a such a sore belly button that I'm not able to get away. (Carri 2016, 24:32–24:59)

As well as its seemingly redemptive function in Carri's self-figurative narrative, the documentary also has an impact on the fragmented and ambiguous aesthetics of *Cuatreros*. It is as if Carri's formal experimentation draws intertextually on Juárez's documentary—"the best Argentine movie that she had ever seen" (22:35)—which heterogeneously combines expository representation with avant-garde experimentation when staging different kinds of archival material (Luchetti 2015). Notwithstanding the entirely archival nature of *Cuatreros*, which is composed from found footage alone, the pronounced ambiguity and opacity of the film forcefully disrupts the evidential paradigm of the modern archive. As Carri maintains (Carri 2018), the medium of cinema always unsettles time and is hence an "oneiric machinery" which resists any autobiographical truth. Indeed, the autofictional mode that Carri adopts in *Cuatreros* defies the main purpose that Bill Nichols (1991, 30–31) famously assigned to the mainstream documentary genre: the gratification of the viewer's "desire to know." Instead of filling in the voids of history, the staging of the archive in *Cuatreros* engages its viewers by means of its inconclusive narrative and ambiguous aesthetics. In the final sequence of the film, Carri articulates the gaps that not even the material excesses of her archival recollection and staging are able to fill: "But the images are not there, the bodies do not appear, the trial does not arrive, and I cannot forget" (1–20:31–37).

"You Are the One Who Has No Memory!" Autofictional Cinema in Response to the Iberian Crisis

This section puts two autofictional films about the current Iberian crisis into conversation: the long feature *Mercado de futuros* (*Futures Market*) and the short film *Vidros partidos: Testes para um filme em Portugal* (*Broken Windows: Tests for a Film in Portugal*) by Spanish directors Mercedes Álvarez and Víctor Erice, respectively.[5] Álvarez and Erice join a wide range of directors new and old who have explored the crisis in their cinema, including Isaki Lacuesta in *Los pasos dobles* (*The Double Steps*) and *El cuaderno de barro* (*The Clay Diaries*) (2011), Sergio Oksman in *A Story for the Modlins* (2012), José Luis Guerín in *En construcción* (*Under Construction*) (2002), and Joaquim Jordà's entire oeuvre. These filmmakers have experimented at the margins of the Spanish documentary film industry by openly intruding on their object of cinematic inquiry, proposing a self-reflective form of cinema, and showing a careful authorial preoccupation with the aesthetic component of their artistic work. Through the medium of autofictional cinema, presenting their work simultaneously as documentaries and fiction films, these directors break with the illusion that presupposes an unproblematized relation between the visual trace and its origin, personal memory and its referent, what is presented as real and reality itself.

The title *Vidros partidos*, or "broken windows," alludes to the name used by the current residents of Guimarães, in Northern Portugal, to refer to the Vizela River Factory. When it opened its doors in 1845, the factory brought electricity and trains to the region. Half a century later, at the time when Louis and Auguste Lumière in France made the first short motion picture, it had become the second-largest textile manufacturing company in Europe. With their memorable, silent black-and-white documentary, *La Sortie de l'usine à Lyon* (*Workers Leaving the Lumière Factory*) (1895), the Lumière brothers had filmed a group of workers leaving their place of work. When making his documentary in a twenty-first-century context, Erice asked a group of men and women to reoccupy the empty canteen of the Vizela Factory.[6] Erice's documentary is best described as a participatory autofiction: it takes the form of a visual archive of staged testimonies given by former workers who have remained unemployed during the financial crisis. From its subtitle, *Testes para um filme em Portugal*, the film presents itself as an unfinished work, a series of screen tests for a documentary to come. As they pose in front of the camera, the newly converted nonprofessional actors attest to the end of their working lives: "I'd like to work again … They told me I was too old. I'm 56 years old, and it's all over for me" (1:00:38–53). On the canteen wall hangs a large group portrait in which we see hundreds of people who worked at the factory at the end of the nineteenth century (Fig. 12.2).

Fig. 12.2 Víctor Erice, *Workers from the Vizela Factory: Close-up of Photograph in Vidros partidos*

The men and women from *Vidros partidos* look at the large black-and-white photograph, which was taken in the very location where they are being filmed. They perceive it as an archived trace of a world that no longer exists: "I find it difficult to look at these people ... I can't recognize anyone"; "These people trouble me. They're looking at us, and it seems like they want to tell us something. But I'm not sure what it is. I don't know. I don't know" (1:09:40–59, 1:12:10–34). *Mercado de futuros* proposes a similar discourse of memory about a more recent past. Álvarez's voice-over warns us, at the beginning of the film, that "one day all the newspapers began to speak of a great financial crisis [...], they would try to explain the path that had led us here. *But the path had disappeared*" (1:27:09–1:28:24, our emphasis). Through documentary cinema, a cinematic genre that is conventionally associated with the ideas of evidence and truth, Álvarez and Erice illuminate the impossibility of archiving definite origins, be it the origins of capitalism as it was lived by the old working class or the origins of the current financial crisis.

The contemporary subjects of *Vidros partidos* do not only tell us about their relationship with the past. By describing their new relation to the future, they also reveal their connection to a present of crisis: "The factory closed, like many others. That's why the generations of workers from here feel lost now. What are they going to do? Where will they go? Most of them don't know"; "Things are different today ... [In the past, factory workers] had their own ideals, and they also had *some hope for the future*" (Erice 2013b, 1:02:28–48, 1:11:20–35, our emphasis). *Mercado de futuros* and *Vidros partidos* are symptomatic of the prolonged and widespread sentiment of social indeterminacy evoked by the former workers of the Vizela Factory, a sentiment which has grown in the Iberian Peninsula since 2008. In the autofictional cinema they propose, Álvarez and Erice *reflect upon* the ongoing crisis which at times they document openly through the lens of fiction. Additionally, by virtue of the transgeneric mode of filmmaking they adopt, their films also *formally reflect* the sense of ambiguity that orients the social imaginaries of that crisis.

In both documentaries, the urge for temporal anchoring is inseparable from another pressing need, that of spatial anchoring. In *Mercado de futuros*, the discourse on the loss and malleability of memory in the voice-over contrasts with footage which documents the drastic transformation of Barcelona's landscape during the period of the real estate bubble that preceded the 2008 economic crisis in Spain. Many indoor scenes are shot in undistinctive "non-places," that is, spaces which "cannot be defined as relational, or historical, or concerned with identity" (Augé 1995, 77). The scenes shot in malls and international real estate fairs held in Barcelona before the financial crash are markedly ambiguous, insofar as the spectator cannot tell whether these are, or are not, the result of intended performances. By repeatedly showing what Sophie Mayer (2012) has described as "elaborate, life-size promotional photographic backdrops and light-up architectural models [that] implicitly indict mainstream cinema," Álvarez highlights the creative artificiality, and consequently the inevitable fictionality, of documentary cinema.

In his introduction to *Vidros partidos* at Madrid's *Cineteca*, Erice (2013a) recalls that documentary cinema is indeed constituted through fiction, not only because the real must be altered at times in order to be more accurately documented, as has been the case from the very origins of documentary film,[7] but also because the filmmaker's gaze is embedded in every film, albeit visible to varying degrees. Throughout *Mercado de futuros*, the voice-over adopts an intimate, and at times nostalgic, tone which persistently reminds the spectator that the documentary is itself a subjective cinematic construct. In *Vidros partidos*, conversely, the worldview proposed by the filmmaker rests on an equally subjective work of scriptwriting, but one that is collective. After conducting a long series of interviews with former workers of the Vizela Factory, Erice interwove their personal testimonies into the film script. In the second phase, the acting crew—nine people chosen from the larger group of interviewees—collaborated with the director in a process of collective script rewriting (Erice 2013a). Erice asked each of them, and one professional actor who joined the crew, to pose in front of the camera as if reciting a part for a screen test. One by one, each subject in this participatory autofiction directs their gaze toward the director positioned behind the camera, whose ghostly figure thus also infiltrates the film.

Unlike mainstream fiction films, *Vidros partidos* and *Mercado de futuros* treat the real not as an effect to be produced for entertainment but as a territory filled with obscure traces to be explored.[8] As cinematic autofictions, *Vidros partidos* and *Mercado de futuros* are clearly distinct from contemporary comedies and dramas that make the Spanish crisis their principal focus, such as Alejandro Marzoa's *Somos gente honrada* (*We're Honest People*) (2013) and Pedro Almodóvar *Los amantes pasajeros* (*I'm So Excited*) (2013). They also distinguish themselves from the Spanish new wave of overtly political documentaries, like Basilio Martín Patino's *Libre te quiero* (*Free is How We Love You*) (2012) and Stéphane Grueso's

15M: Excelente. Revulsivo. Importante (*15M: Excellent. A Wake-Up Call. Important*) (2012), among many others. Yet, while the autofictional films generated by Álvarez and Erice do not seek to transmit an openly political message, they become political in an oblique fashion as they document, and at times propose, alternative orders of memory that are intrinsically linked to transgressive uses of space.

Notably, in *Mercado de futuros*, a series of scenes serve to record and make visible symbolical practices, tactics by which citizens momentarily occupy public spaces and thereby create memories of, and for, their city, Barcelona. For instance, we see lively interactions in Barcelona's *Els Encants* street market (today relocated to a modern shopping mall), a man taking care of a community garden beneath a noisy highway, or a group of people doing parkour surrounded by graffiti art (Álvarez 2005, 00:39:16–47:45, 1:02:48–1:07:34, 1:27:09–28:24). These outdoor scenes serve to document what Michel De Certeau (1988, 41) famously described as "an art of the weak, [...] a proliferation of aleatory and indeterminable manipulations within an immense framework of socioeconomic constraints and securities: myriads of almost invisible movements, playing on the more and more refined texture of a place that is even, continuous, and constitutes a proper place for all people." In contrast to other scenes shot in "non-places," these images interrupt the visual succession of non-specific spaces (such as newly constructed malls or international real estate fairs), which contribute to the global homogenization of the urban landscape, and the growing assumption that its cultural memory is in decline. In *Vidros partidos*, in turn, the reoccupation of space by former workers of the Vizela Factory was carefully planned and set up in order to be documented. The script incorporated the former workers' personal testimonies and was later submitted to them for revision and approval. Each of the nonprofessional actors did not necessarily recite what would have been their own "real-life" part. This participatory autofiction should be understood, therefore, as the enactment and recording of the creative process by which collective memory was reconstructed for the unemployed community of the Vizela Factory. Additionally, *Vidros partidos* includes a performance by a professional actor, Valdemar Santos. After claiming to know by heart every one of the parts that he has played throughout his career, Santos explains his choice to recite a fragment from *O Capital* (1896), by the Portuguese socialist playwright António Ernesto da Silva:

Memory! You want to know if I have a memory. Of course, I do! Because an actor without memory is nothing (....). And I'm an actor. A real actor. I certainly do have a memory. What I don't have is a job! But I remember every part that I've played in my life. Every one. From the first to the last. I was Carlos Marques in *O Capital*, by the great Ernesto da Silva! I see you don't know what I am talking about. You! You're the ones who have no memories. (1:12:50–13:57)

It was the first socialist known to have defended the potential use of theater as a pedagogical tool, Luís de Figueiredo, who asked Ernesto da Silva to write a play to be performed on May 1, 1895, *O Capital*.[9] In Erice's *Vidros partidos*, a film where "nothing was left to improvisation," as María Filomena Molder (2017, 247) has rightly noted, the reference to *O Capital* serves as a reminder of a forgotten tradition of European workers who used to perform socialist plays in factories and theaters as a way of vindicating their working rights. As Beatriz Peralta García recalls (2011, 37–45), while for Marx, art, including theater, was an instrument of analysis among many others, this was far from being the case in the Portuguese socialist circles at the end of the nineteenth century. Today, through a form of participatory autofictional cinema which is generated collectively, in times of crisis, the unemployed assert their right to be visible. Ultimately, Santos's final performance reminds the audience that *we* are the ones prone to forgetting them. By physically re-occupying the empty space of the factory, sharing their stories with each other and with the viewer, and becoming the actors and thus the agents of this cinematic autofiction, the former workers of the Vizela Factory create a new symbolic space of collaboratively constructed memories.

Víctor Erice's *Vidros partidos* and Mercedes Álvarez's *Mercado de futuros* go beyond lamentations over the loss of memory or the impossibility of determining absolute origins. By displaying their own fictionality at multiple levels, and becoming self-reflective archives of constructed memories, these two documentaries about the crisis counteract the proliferation of "new fictions of globalization" (Morán Rodríguez and Gómez Trueba 2017, 22) whose covert intent lies in the manipulation of beliefs, opinions, social attitudes, and emotions. The full force of the lyrical yet political cinema produced by Álvarez and Erice lies ultimately in the original modes of artistic and social resistance that both autofictions document, and at times enact, within the context of the ongoing Iberian financial crisis.

Post-millennial Autofictional Cinema from Argentina and Spain

Contrary to the tendency to associate autofiction with the narcissism and political apathy of the "culture of the spectacle" of the 1990s, the post-millennial films discussed in this chapter interrogate realities that concern the filmmaker not just as an individual but also as a historical and political subject and a member of a given society. These contemporary filmmakers from Spain and Argentina do not seek to entertain their audience with a mode of escapist fiction, nor do they intend to solely *inform* them of the consequences of political violence, the cause of the current recession, or the social movements of protest to which it has given rise. With *Mercado de futuros* and *Vidros partidos*, Álvarez and Erice abandon the univocal, self-enclosed, "centripetal" model of cinematic autofiction, which foregrounds the psychological soliloquy of the self with the self, as in Erice's *La morte rouge* (*The Red Dead Woman*) (2006), or Pedro Almodóvar's *Dolor y gloria* (*Pain and Glory*) (2019). Instead, these films embrace a model of autofiction that is recurrently "centrifugal." They invite the contemporary spectator to question their own relationship with a historical present of crisis through the interrogation of dark archival traces that do not allow for a stable interpretation on the part of the film's narrator, or indeed on the part of the viewer. Likewise, in *Cuatreros*, the archive is not only the subject matter but also the representational mechanism implemented to involve viewers in mobilization and repurposing as a way of rewriting history. In *Cuatreros*, Carri returns to the self, to *herself*, in a centripetal movement as she arranges the fragmented pieces that make up the film's archival narrative. This narrative does not solely concern her as an individual; it is also the (hi)story of her generation, the children of the disappeared in Argentina. A productive tension between the centripetal and the centrifugal thus occurs, which we propose is a central trait of autofiction as a transgeneric cinematic mode, as it has been articulated in-between documentary and fiction cinema since the beginning of the twenty-first century.

In *Cuatreros, Mercado de futuros*, and *Vidros partidos*, the autofictional functions as a mode of creating and making sense of individual and collective memories. In aesthetic terms, the modes of representation employed in these films run counter to mainstream documentary strategies, in the light of the self-reflexive, ambiguous, and open-ended poetics of memory they stage. As the filmmakers seek to reestablish a commitment with their historical context through cinematic autofiction, they do not necessarily denounce social and historical injustice. In creatively distinct ways, Carri, Álvarez, and Erice assert their commitment to rethinking social practices of memorialization through the audiovisual archive, in relation to the ever-expanding narrative reconfiguration of personal and collective identities. As they organize and reorganize traces of historical realities, each director subscribes to an autofictional cinematic sensitivity that goes well beyond the documentation of past or present times of crisis. Post-millennial films like *Cuatreros, Mercado de futuros*, and *Vidros partidos* propose new possible orders of the documentary genre. Aiming to create a shared historical present through their deployment of autofictional strategies, these films also invite the viewer to believe in the possibility of new social and political orders to come.

Notes

1. Scholars such as Patricia Mamayo, Luz Herrera Zamudio, Francisco Javier Gómez Tarín, Agustín Rubio Alcover, Elios Mendieta Rodríguez, and Mario de la Torre Espinosa have extrapolated the concept of autofiction to the visual arts, including film studies. For more information on the proliferation of theoretical approaches applied to autofiction specifically within Hispanic Studies, across different fields of expertise, see Ana Casas (2014, 7–21). With regard to the growing interest in autofiction beyond France, Latin America, and Iberia, see Hywel Dix, *Autofiction in English* (2018).
2. In a key scene in Los rubios, Analía Couceyro, playing the role of Albertina Carri, reads Roberto Carri's essay on Velázquez. Furthermore, in 2013, Albertina Carri returns to the historical character of Isidro Velázquez and the topic of the political armed militancy of the 1960s and 1970s in the performance *El affaire Velázquez* (*The Velázquez Affair*), included in the series *Mis documentos* (*My documents*) by director Lola Arias. (http://lolaarias.com/proyectos/mis-documentos-2/), as well as in the audiovisual installation *Operación fracaso y el sonido recobrado* (*Operation Defeat and the Recovered Sound*) (2015).
3. Our translation. All quotations originally in a language other than English are our own translations.
4. *Ya es tiempo de violencia* belongs to what Pablo Piedras calls the third stage of Argentinian political documentary made between 1956 and 1974, when "film is understood as a weapon that targets viewers of a certain group or class. The filmmaker is no longer in front of the subjects but with them, participating in the conflict and seeking to change reality" (2013, 30).

5. Erice (b. 1940) is the director of other internationally acclaimed feature films such as *El espíritu de la colmena* (*The Spirit of the Beehive*) (1973), *El Sur* (*The South*) (1983), and *El sol del membrillo* (*The Quince Tree Sun*) (1993). Álvarez (b. 1966) is the director of another long feature, *El cielo gira* (*The Sky Turns*) (2005). The artistic sensitivity and meticulous working methods that both filmmakers share have not gone unnoticed; see, for instance, Octavi Martí (2005) and Erice (2014).
6. Like Erice, who hired jobless men and women to act in *Vidros partidos*, Álvarez and the visual artist Francesc Torres hired unemployed people to take part in their artistic project, "The 25% project," which was the entry from Catalonia at the 2013 Venice Biennale of Art. Curated by Jordi Balló, this initiative was conceived as a reflection on the role of art within the current context of crisis.
7. In his presentation, Erice reminds his audience that when Robert Flaherty made the first feature-length documentary, *Nanook of the North* (1922), he encountered great difficulty in filming indoor scenes owing to spatial limitations and the lack of natural light. As a result, most of the indoor scenes which were to make a significant impression on the history of documentary cinema were shot in a three-walled igloo built specifically for the film. For a discussion of the fictionality of *Nanook of the North*, see also Barnouw (1993, 34–36).
8. When we mention that *Vidros partidos* and *Mercado de futuros* "do *not* treat the real as an effect to be produced," we are following an understanding of fiction cinema based upon Aristotle's concept of fable (Rancière 2006, 158).
9. In addition to six other social plays, da Silva wrote *Teatro Livre e Arte Social* (1902), in which he outlines and analyzes the basic rules with which socialist militant theater should comply.

Works Cited

Alberca, Manuel. 2007. *El pacto ambiguo: De la novela autobiográfica a la autoficción*. Colección Estudios Críticos de Literatura 30. Madrid: Biblioteca Nueva.
Álvarez, Mercedes, dir. 2005. *El cielo gira*. New York: New Yorker Films. DVD.
———, dir. 2011. *Mercado de futuros*. New York: Icarus Films. DVD.
Augé, Marc. 1995. *Non-Places: Introduction to an Anthropology of Supermodernity*. New York: Verso.
Barnouw, Erik. 1993. *Documentary: A History of the Non-Fiction Film*. New York: Oxford University Press.
Baron, Jaimie. 2014. *The Archive Effect: Found Footage and the Audiovisual Experience of History*. London: Routledge.
Blejmar, Jordana. 2016. *Playful Memories: The Autofictional Turn in Post-Dictatorship Argentina*. Cham: Palgrave Macmillan.

Carri, Albertina, dir. 2003. *Los rubios*. Buenos Aires: Barry Ellsworth. DVD.
———, dir. 2010. *Restos*. Buenos Aires: Franco Vilche. Vimeo.
———, dir. 2016. *Cuatreros*. Buenos Aires: Albertina Carri and Diego Schipani. Vimeo.
———, 2018. Una revolución en el cine argentino. Interview by Horacio *Verbitsky*. *El Cohete a la Luna*, March 25, 2018. https://www.elcohetealaluna.com/cuatreros/. Accessed Apr 4, 2021.
Carri, Roberto. 1968. *Isidro Velázquez: Formas prerrevolucionarias de la violencia*. Buenos Aires: Sudestada.
Casas Janices, Ana, ed. 2014. *El yo fabulado: nuevas aproximaciones críticas a la autoficción*. Madrid: Iberoamericana Vervuert.
Christen, Matthias. 2019. Autobiographical/Autofictional Film. In *Handbook of Autobiography / Autofiction*, ed. Martina Wagner-Egelhaaf, 446–455. Berlin: De Gruyter.
Da Silva, António Ernesto. 1896. *O Capital: Drama em quatro actos*. Lisbon: Typografia do Instituto de Artes Graphicas.
———. 1902. *Teatro livre e arte social*. Lisbon: Tipografia do Comercio.
De Certeau, Michel. 1988. *The Practice of Everyday Life*. Berkeley: University of California Press.
Derrida, Jacques. 1995. *Mal d'archive: une impression freudienne*. Paris: Galilée.
Dix, Hywel, ed. 2018. *Autofiction in English*. Cham: Springer International Publishing.
Erice, Víctor. 2005 A propósito de 'El cielo gira.' *El País*, 13 May, 2005. https://elpais.com/diario/2005/05/13/cine/1115935209_850215.html. Accessed Apr 4, 2021.
———, dir. 1983. *El sur*. New York: Criterion Collection. DVD.
———, dir. 1993. *El sol del membrillo*. Chicago: Facets Video. DVD.
———, dir. 2006. *El espíritu de la colmena*. New York: Criterion Collection. DVD.
———. 2013a. Presentación de *Centro Histórico*. Cineteca de Madrid. Private video recording by José Chica.
———. 2013b. *Vidros partidos*. A short film included in *Centro histórico*. The Cinema Guild.
Forné, Anna. 2017. Matters of Memory in *Los rubios* by Albertina Carri. In *Materializing Memory in Art and Popular Culture*, ed. Liedeke Plate, Anneke Smelik, and Laszlo Muntean, 158–172. London: Routledge.
———. 2020. El efecto de archivo en el cortometraje documental autoficcional contemporáneo argentino. Una lectura de *Restos* (2010) de Albertina Carri y *Grito* (2008) de Andrés Denegri. *Bulletin of Hispanic Studies* 97 (7): 749–762.
Foster, Hal. 2004. An Archival Impulse. *October* 110: 3–22.
Lebow, Alisa, ed. 2012. *The Cinema of Me: The Self and Subjectivity in First Person Documentary. Nonfictions*. London: Wallflower Press.

López-Gay, Patricia. 2020. *Ficciones de verdad: Archivo y narrativas de vida*. Madrid: Iberoamericana.

———. 2017. Muertes de autor: De los orígenes de la fotografía a la autoficción. *Impossibilia* 13: 131–148. https://doi.org/10.32112/2174.2464.2017.172.

Luchetti, María Florencia. 2015. Tiempo de violencia: Lenguaje audiovisual, estética y modos de representación de la violencia en la década del 60 en Argentina. *Amérique Latine Histoire et Mémoire. Les Cahiers ALHIM*, 30. https://doi.org/10.4000/alhim.5333.

Mayer, Sophie. 2012. Whose Waste? Mercedes Álvarez's *Futures Market*. BFI Film Forever. October 17, 2012. http://old.bfi.org.uk/sightandsound/newsandviews/festivals/blog/lff-2011-10-17-futures-market.php. Accessed Apr 4, 2021.

Molder, María Filomena. 2017. Green Leaves, Green Sorrows: On Víctor Erice's Broken Glasses. In *Thinking Reality and Time through Film*, ed. Christine Reeh and José Manuel Martins, 244–265. Newcastle upon Tyne: Cambridge Scholars Publishing.

Morán Rodríguez, Carmen, and Teresa Gómez Trueba. 2017. *Hologramas: Realidad y relato del siglo XXI*. Gijón: Trea.

Nichols, Bill. 1991. *Representing Reality: Issues and Concepts in Documentary*. Bloomington, IN: Indiana University Press.

Peralta García, Beatriz. 2011. Literatura y movimiento obrero en Portugal: La cultura política del socialismo en su teatro. *Espacio, tiempo y forma* 23: 37–54.

Piedras, Pablo. 2014. *El cine documental en primera persona. Paidós Comunicación*. Buenos Aires: Paidós.

Piedras, Pablo, and Mariana Ortega Breña. 2013. From Recording to Intervention: History and Documentary Filmmaking in Argentina. *Latin American Perspectives* 40 (1): 23–36.

Rancière, Jacques. 2006. *Film Fables*. New York: Bloomsbury Academic.

Rascaroli, Laura. 2009. *The Personal Camera: Subjective Cinema and the Essay Film*. London: Wallflower.

Open Access This chapter is licensed under the terms of the Creative Commons Attribution 4.0 International License (http://creativecommons.org/licenses/by/4.0/), which permits use, sharing, adaptation, distribution and reproduction in any medium or format, as long as you give appropriate credit to the original author(s) and the source, provide a link to the Creative Commons licence and indicate if changes were made.

The images or other third party material in this chapter are included in the chapter's Creative Commons licence, unless indicated otherwise in a credit line to the material. If material is not included in the chapter's Creative Commons licence and your intended use is not permitted by statutory regulation or exceeds the permitted use, you will need to obtain permission directly from the copyright holder.

CHAPTER 13

Autofiction and *Shishōsetsu*: Women Writers and Reinventing the Self

Justyna Weronika Kasza

> *Henry Miller, Philip Roth, Paul Auster and Milan Kundera have all used themselves as their own aliases. When men do it, it is called metafiction and part of their playful experiment. When women do it, it is called autobiography.*
> —Jeanette Winterson

In this chapter, I set out to consider whether and to what end the Japanese *shishōsetsu* (the I-novel) can be approached as a form of autofictional writing. In so doing, I will propose a model for thinking about autofiction that accommodates the Japanese tradition, which, for various reasons, has remained on the "periphery" of research on autofiction. This model is shaped not only by the need to extend the focus of conversations around autofiction beyond the dominant circle of French or Anglophone literature, but to broaden the frameworks of literary genres in the age of the global novel and to implement, where possible, more wide-ranging

J. W. Kasza (✉)
Department of Foreign Language Studies, Seinan Gakuin University, Fukuoka, Japan

interpretative perspectives. My discussion of the relationship between *shishōsetsu* and autofiction will focus primarily on the role of language, with a particular focus on linguistic structures and the use of pronouns, in the process of creating narratives that center around the self and self-representation. I will consider the ways in which Japanese *shishōsetsu* integrates vocabulary that both reveals and conceals the identity of the writing persona, in an attempt to create a reliable and, at the same time, fictitious testimony of the self. The capacity to "reinvent" the self through the text is an integral feature of both *shishōsetsu* and autofictional writing, as, in turn, is the constant shape-shifting and transformation of the forms themselves.

The lack of a clearly delineated theoretical framework is what allows autofiction to assume or influence a variety of different forms. Exploring *shishōsetsu* as one such form enables us to acknowledge the contribution that such texts make to redefining the status of life narratives not only in national literature but in the context of world literature. Yet, what are the grounds for the comparison between literary genres? What should be the point of departure, the criteria, the merits that enable us to approach *shishōsetsu* and autofiction comparatively, or at least, to suggest parallels and similarities? The review of existing studies in *shishōsetsu* demonstrates how few attempts have been made to extend its scope beyond Japanese literature. The dominant tendency is to treat *shishōsetsu* as a form unique to the Japanese literary tradition, and by doing so, studies often overlook the possible cross-cultural influences. There has, however, been some attempt to investigate the similarities between *shishōsetsu* and autobiography. To position *shishōsetsu* against the background of general theories of "life writings," Irmela Hijiya-Kirschnereit, the author of the most substantial monograph on *shishōsetsu* available in English to date, observes,

> Instead of "autobiography," which is often based, albeit unconsciously, on a European notion of the term, it would be wiser to speak of "autobiographical writing," or even use some of the recent general notions like "life-writing," "life narratives," or "self narratives" in the case of Japan with its large number of different genres potentially falling into this category. A notion like "first person writing" [...] would not be applicable to the Japanese case with its wide range of linguistic possibilities to express agency and subject. For strategical and practical reasons, the term "autobiography" is retained here and is used in the wider sense of autobiographical writing to indicate its function as an umbrella term for a large scale of styles and forms of writing the self in Japan [...] We understand autobiography in the Japanese context as an autonomous text in which a person records his or her

experiences over a larger span of his or her life. (Hijiya-Kirschnereit 2019, 1059)

Donald Keene explores the question I briefly touched upon before, that is, the translatability of *shishōsetsu* and other literary genres representing life-writing narratives in Japan. To illustrate the extent of both linguistic and semantic challenges, he applies the notion of "aporetics of translation," and considers the particular problem posed by the first-person pronoun:

> If we want to translate *shishōsetsu* into English, how should we translate the pronoun "watashi"? In Chinese, we say "wo," in English we only have the pronoun "I" but in Japanese we can use multiple pronouns, like "boku," "watashi" or even "ore" and they all mean "I" (Keene 2014, 40).[1]

Keene explains here how the ambiguity of the grammatical pronouns in Japanese, especially the pronoun "watashi" ("I"), affects the translation process, making it even more difficult for a foreign reader to adequately distinguish the plurality of voices within the narrative. The key feature of *shishōsetsu* to which Keene refers is the difference between "watashi" and "jibun" ("I" and "myself"), which can imply both the first-person singular ("I") and the third-person singular ("he/she," although no clear gender distinction is possible in the Japanese language) or, depending on the context, even the plural ("we").

Through the comparison I will undertake in this chapter, I will explore how Japanese writers expand the frameworks of self-narrations by creating literary forms situated somewhere "in-between" autofiction and *shishōsetsu*. The relationship between these two forms has grown in importance in light of several recent studies in Japan that point to a number of similarities between *shishōsetsu* and autofiction. In the following section, I will briefly outline the characteristics of *shishōsetsu* and its position in the history of Japanese literature in order to show how the specificity of the Japanese language determines the ways in which the self is incorporated in this form.

SHISHŌSETSU AND THE AMBIGUITY OF THE SELF

Shishōsetsu occupies an important place in the history of Japanese literature. Male writers of the early twentieth century were the dominant force behind its development. Early studies conceive *shishōsetsu* as both a literary genre and as a mode of reading fictional texts that accentuates the relationship between language and the process of (re)inventing the self in literature. More recent studies on *shishōsetsu* in Japan have extended the scope of existing scholarship by emphasizing that the form originates in the specificity of the Japanese language: the lack of a fixed and stable pronoun "I" has offered the opportunity for creativeness, originality, and inventiveness in expressing the self. This, in turn, raises further questions as to whether a biographical approach is the only possible cognitive path applicable to *shishōsetsu*. To what extent, we might ask, is the "I" in *shishōsetsu* biographically loaded?[2] Does the "I" refer equally to the narrator, the character, and the writing persona? In order to answer this question, we would need to explore the differences between the Japanese notions of *sakusha* (author) and *sakka* (writer), differences that must be taken into consideration when discussing the specificity of the genre and the problem of authorship in Japanese literature more generally. As the editors of the seminal collection *Shishōsetsu Handobukku* (The Shishōsetsu Handbook) observe:

> Without shishōsetsu, we would not be able to talk about Japanese literature anymore. Shishōsetsu was proudly created by the Japanese people. It developed from and through the characteristics of the Japanese language and culture, becoming a tool we use to express human nature and seize the moment through words. It occupies the most secure position in Japanese culture. (Akiyama and Katsumata 2014, 1)

The above statement exemplifies the direction that recent studies have taken, that is, searching for the origin and sources of *shishōsetsu* in the language itself, instead of perceiving it either as the individual choice of the author or as a literary trend. To a certain degree, these studies argue that the characteristics of the Japanese language determine and condition the narrating process. This line of thinking also underpins the analysis I undertake in this chapter, because, as I argue, the linguistic conditions (both its possibilities and limitations) shape the ways in which the writers on which I will focus reinvent their selfhood within the narrative.

Another noteworthy view is represented by Umezawa Ayumi in her study *Shishōsetsu no gihō: Watashi katari no hyakunen shi* (The Structures of *Shishōsetsu*: 100 Years of Narrating the "I", 2017), where she differentiates between six types of "selves" (the "I") explored by the authors of *shishōsetsu*. Umezawa focuses on literary examples from the beginning of the twentieth century up to the present day and discusses the flexibility of the Japanese language to modify, create, recreate, alter, adjust, and transform the self in the narrative, which require our attention in the process of studying *shishōsetsu*. Umezawa emphasizes the diversity of *shishōsetsu* writing by suggesting that just as there is no one figure of the "I" in Japanese (I shall return to this discussion in the section below), there is no one established and dominant pattern of *shishōsetsu* writing.

Attention has been drawn in recent studies on *shishōsetsu* to various literary genres, styles, and conventions, including graphic novels (manga), protest songs, and even poetry. This, in turn, has paved the way for a more inclusive, comparative, and cross-cultural reading of *shishōsetsu*, which is no longer limited to prose narrative, as its traces are detectable in other literary forms. The authors of *Shishōsetsu Handobukku* suggest that in the age of the global novel, it is paramount to approach literature cross-culturally, beyond one's own mother tongue or literary traditions. This might be perceived as contradictory to the approaches discussed above, which accentuate the interconnection between the Japanese language and *shishōsetsu* style. Nonetheless, by expanding the scope of the analyses into other forms of life-writing narratives, including autofiction, Japanese researchers have also pointed to the aspect of "untranslatability," or more precisely "untransferability," that emerges as a result of comparative analysis. The question is: what happens with the narrating subject, the "I" (watashi), when it is translated into foreign languages? As most researchers suggest, neither the English "I," the French "je," nor the German "Ich" are the direct and accurate translations of the Japanese "watashi." The issue of "untranslatability" was the rationale behind Mizumura Minae's bilingual novel, discussed later in the chapter, which, by incorporating both Japanese and English into the narrative, emphasizes the ambiguity of the self.

Ōhara Norisaki, who attempts to redefine *shishōsetsu* in the context of global literature by way of extensive references to European fiction, deems autofictional writing the most compatible with the *shishōsetsu* style. With reference to Serge Doubrovsky's reinvention of Lejeune's autobiographical pact, Ōhara draws out the points of convergence between the Japanese *shishōsetsu* and French autofiction. Focusing on the flexible treatment of personal experiences in both forms and on the playful relationship between the narrator, character, and the writing persona, Ōhara observes that the fictionalization of the self is an essential element of both genres and reminds us that neither *shishōsetsu* nor autofiction needs to be narrated in the first person.

The three contemporary Japanese women writers I will discuss are not straightforwardly aligned with the *shishōsetsu* tradition, by which I mean the form it took during its boom in the 1920s and 1930s, when its popularity and practice were at their peak, and when it was regarded as a confessional form (close to autobiography or the autobiographical novel) that assumes coherence between the author, narrator, and character, with biographical references within the narratives. As I intend to demonstrate in the sections that follow, the female writers in question break with this conventional pattern of *shishōsetsu* in how they reinvent the self (or to be more precise, incorporate the image of the self) in their stories by using the potential of the Japanese language to reveal and conceal, to cover and discover, the multiple forms of selfhood.

I argue that these writers extend the *shishōsetsu* form into other literary genres, including autofictional writing. I set out to re-examine *shishōsetsu* cross-textually, that is, to trace the supposed elements of life-writing narrative and (auto)biographical motifs across texts by Kanai Mieko, Sagisawa Megumu, and Mizumura Minae.[3] Kanai's narratives oscillate between reality and fantasy, with frequent references to the Japanese imaginary and folktales. Sagisawa, affiliated with the underground movement of the 1980s, crosses the boundaries of national identity as a Japanese woman who discovers her Korean heritage, but she can do so only by writing from the perspective of the male narrator who, as she reveals in her stories, resembles the figure of her father. Mizumura, for her part, reflects on the notion of the translatability and untranslatability of the self as it is experienced by a bilingual writer, one whose constant transitions between English and Japanese cause her to lose the sense of her mother tongue.

Before proceeding with my analysis, I will summarize the key premises of *shishōsetsu* writing in order to reconsider the extent to which these works might be compatible or comparable with autofiction. A concise definition of *shishōsetsu* is provided by Edward Fowler, who explains:

The *shishōsetsu*, narrated in the first or third person in such a way as to represent with utter conviction the author's personal experience, is riddled with paradoxes. Supposedly a fictional narrative, it often reads more like a private journal. It has a reputation of being true, to a fault, to "real life"; yet it frequently strays from the author's experience it allegedly portrays so faithfully. Its personal orientation makes it a thoroughly modern form; yet it is the product of an indigenous intellectual tradition quite disparate from western individualism. (Fowler 1988, 6)

Tomi Suzuki, on the other hand, states that "the 'I-novel' is not a given form of text that can be objectively identified, but a historically constructed reading mode and cultural paradigm that not only regulated the production and reception of literary texts but also defined cultural identity and national tradition" (Suzuki 1997, 24).

Despite its prominent position within the literary tradition of Japan, a number of contemporary writers express a distinctly ambivalent attitude toward *shishōsetsu*. A further parallel emerges here with autofiction, which is also often rejected as a label by the authors to whom it is applied. An interesting example in the case of *shishōsetsu* is Murakami Haruki, who in the Introduction to *The Penguin Book of Japanese Short Stories*, published in 2018, bluntly expressed his attitude toward Japanese literature in the following terms: "In my case, my only allergy is to Japan's so-called 'I -novel'—the form of autobiographical writing that has been at the forefront of Japan's modern fiction since the turn of the twentieth century [...] My 'I-novel allergy' was also quite strong back then [...] and since you can't hope either to make your way through or to understand modern Japanese literature if you're going to avoid its constitutional predisposition to producing 'I-novels', I made a conscious effort while young to avoid going anywhere near Japanese literature" (Murakami 2018, xi). Polarized views on *shishōsetsu* and its impact on Japan's literary landscape continue not only with the new names being "added" to the *shishōsetsu* canon but also through new interpretative pathways and more inclusive and cross-cultural approaches to the genre. Despite its polemical status, *shishōsetsu* is nevertheless considered by leading Japanese scholars as one of the most remarkable literary genres in Japanese literature, and for many years has been perceived as the least translatable or transferable into another cultural sphere. As Fowler has noted, "*shishōsetsu* will always occupy the heartland of language and literature in Japan" (Fowler 1988, 298).

Perhaps the most important aspect of *shishōsetsu*, when considering its relation to autofiction, is the ambiguous treatment of the first-person pronoun in Japanese, a complexity that is lost in the translation process. The self in Japanese language is relational, context-dependent, unstable, and defined by the situation. On the level of a sentence, the subject is usually omitted and only the context (with the application of proper grammar structures) will notify the listener or the reader of the identity of the speaker, as well as the latter's number (either singular or plural), and, in some cases, their gender. There are two words in Japanese that designate the notion of "I": "watashi" and "jibun." While the first means the public self and is emotionally neutral, the latter is often regarded as the intimate self, and as emotionally loaded. Of particular importance is the fact that Japanese grammar does not require pronouns in the sentence: the context and appropriate verb form reveal the identity of the speaker or the person to whom they refer. How, then, are "watashi" and "jibun" deployed in the narratives, and how do they affect our reading of texts as possibly autofictional? I will explore this specifically in relation to Sagisawa Megumu's work, considering how she differentiates "watashi" from "jibun" in her texts.

What needs to be reiterated here is that *shishōsetsu* is not the reflection of the self (subjectivity) in the writing. In Japanese, the third-person pronoun could be (and is) in many instances read as "I." As much as the discovery of the confessional literary form was a turning point for Japanese literature in the second half of the nineteenth century (*shishōsetsu* scholar Akiyama Shun considers Jean-Jacques Rousseau's *Confessions* as the key text in this transformation), and would ultimately transport it onto the platform of world literature, most scholars agree that *shishōsetsu* is an indigenous convention in Japanese literature which derives directly from the language. The linguistic context and the characteristics of a language are also the focal point of Barbara Cassin's monumental study *Dictionary of Untranslatables*, where she distinguishes between "I," "me," and "myself," and refers to these as follows: "Having an I, being a person" (Cassin 2017, 463). Referring predominantly to French language (with some reference to other languages, including Japanese), she discusses the "path" from "moi" to the "self" and from "self" to "soi." The focus on semantic levels of "selfhood" in Cassin's method is the result of her background in philosophy of language, which determines her definition of "selfhood" as being anchored, first and foremost, in language itself.

Cassin's methodology, in treating language (and the question of translatability) as the point of departure in discussing the notion of "selfhood," to a certain degree resembles my own line of interpretation of works by Kanai, Sagisawa, and Mizumura.

The application of Cassin's method, that is, a focus on the tools offered by language in the expression of the self, clearly reveals that the very concepts of selfhood in modern and postmodern thought have produced a number of conceptual terms and ideals that overlap but also frequently contradict each other. One area of this confusion is the blurred distinction between "self" and "identity," concepts which are often used interchangeably. Anthony Elliott, the author of *Concepts of the Self*, observes that it was the interference of language (or the linguistic approach to selfhood) that led to the confusion between selfhood and identity, whereas, as he argues, these two notions need to be clearly separated and defined based on their different cognitive premises (Elliott 2006, 18). The following parts of the chapter deal with select examples of the treatment of the "self" in works by three Japanese women writers. I propose that three patterns of self-representation emerge in these texts: the metamorphosed self (Kanai Mieko), the transgender self (Sagisawa Megumu), and the bilingual self (Mizumura Minae).

The Metamorphosed Self: Kanai Mieko

Kanai's 1973 story *Usagi* (Rabbits) is inspired by Lewis Carroll's novel *Alice in Wonderland*. There are clear references to this classic novel but the entire narrative is supplemented by a number of metaphorical expressions and by Kanai's boundless imagination. *Usagi* is not the only work by Kanai that epitomizes her creativeness and brave attempt to challenge literary conventions. Her departure from realistic narrative toward fantasy, with recourse to myths and folktales, has become the hallmark for a younger generation of Japanese female writers, including Tawada Yōko, Kawakami Mieko, and Kawakami Hiromi. Much of Kanai's literary criticism and reflections on Japanese literature makes comparisons between women's writing in Japan and in Western literature, principally in French writing. Her affiliation with the *shishōsetsu* tradition remains problematic, as is true of most post-war Japanese authors. She never labels her writing *shishōsetsu*, yet she constantly uses the terms "jiko hyōgen" (the expression of the ego) or "jiko kakunin" (the confirmation of the ego), thus positioning her writing somewhere in-between fiction and autobiography. Both in her fiction and in her critical texts, Kanai demonstrates a keen attention to word choice: she understands that in order to showcase the full capacity of her imagination and writing skills, she needs to offer a new picture of the writing self. As she confessed in one of her interviews: "I want to be read without being seen as a female writer" (cited in Hijiya-Kirschnereit 2018, 259).

It is by reading her fiction alongside her non-fiction texts that Kanai's intentions become clear. While she wants to distance herself from "gender-based" interpretations of her works, she is nonetheless aware that female writers in Japan of her generation need a new space, and possibly new linguistic tools. In one of her essays, "Onna ni totte onna to wa nani ka?" (What Are Women to a Woman?), published in 1972, she draws out the different expectations for female- and male-authored works:

> For men, behaviour such as delving into and narrating one's life experiences is at once considered tantamount to the work of a novelist. I, however, have been told that it is important for me to write about being "a woman" while listening to others' experiences of being "women"—probably because it is thought that the problems faced by being "a woman" become clearer when "women" delve into them together. Although male novelists who write about the experience of the self are not at all interesting, at least their perspective in writing is not narrowed to probing into what it means to be "a man." Why is it that only women must continue to write about being "a woman"? (cited in Osborne 2019, 95)

Representing a new wave in Japanese post-war literature that emerged in the middle of the 1970s, Kanai goes beyond the tradition of realistic, reliable narrative. By putting the ambiguous "watashi" at the center of her narration, she calls for constant redefinition of "josei no jibun," "the female self." In her interviews and commentary, she uses the Japanese term "jiko" ("ego"), which, more than "watashi" and "jibun," indicates the singularity of the self. However, as Kanai mentioned in one of her most recent interviews (2019), literature should not only serve as the confirmation of "selfhood"; the inventive, creative, and original potential of literature cannot be overlooked in the attempt to be a truthful storyteller. *Usagi*, alongside her other short stories, represents first and foremost the testimony of the writing self and the ongoing examination of the self as a writing persona.

Usagi is, on the one hand, an exploration of what it means to be an author, and on the other, an exposition of the figure of the writing persona. The story touches upon the issue of identity with an openness rarely seen in Japanese literature. As we read in the opening, and probably the most telling part, of the story:

> Writing (also not writing, since that is part of the whole process) means putting pen on paper and this I can do no longer. To write would seem to be my fate … I wrote these words in my diary the day I pretty much forced myself to go out for a walk near my house [...]. Moving myself seemed a far more pleasant alternative than sitting inside and facing my diary, or all those pages of manuscript in my depressing room where the furniture still had to be put in place.
> I was anyway in quite a foul mood. Even when wide awake, I felt as if I were in the midst of a bad dream [...]. Something undefinable, something like an illusion followed me wherever I went…. (Kanai in Birnbaum, 1982, 2)

The main axis of the plot is transformation, or more precisely, the transition from the real to the imagined, from human to animal, to the rabbits of the title. An important and constantly recurring motif is the moment the narrator attempts to envision and understand her bizarre transformation into a rabbit. As she tries to recall the instant of the transformation, the line between humanity and being an animal becomes blurred. The metamorphosis of the self, is, as we find out over the course of the story, the consequence of her father's killing and cooking rabbits. Although the reasons behind his cruelty are not revealed, or, as the narrator states, "not remembered," we can interpret the story as a metaphor for the peculiar relationships within the family, namely, the relations between the narrator and her father and the absence of other members of the family. Though the entire story is full of understatements and at times the narrative seems to lack consistency, the following passage captures the moment of the narrator's metamorphosis:

> Every day since then I have been haunted by the ghosts of the dead rabbits and have behaved like a large, one eyed rabbit. In short, I have clearly confirmed that I can never again return to the world of human beings. Looking back on it, I see that I had lived like a normal human being until the fourteenth of that month several years back. Up to that time, I had been like any normal school girl and had kept hidden my from my classmates everything

about my father's strange tastes—that he killed rabbits and cooked them. (Kanai in Birnbaum, 1982, 14–15)

Kanai frequently uses the words "lost" and "found," which may suggest that, as the writer, the narrator, and possibly the protagonist of the story, she sees literature as a tool for regaining the self; her imagination and the eerie world that crosses the boundaries of rationality effect a shift from the inexpressive "watashi" (neutral "I") toward the more tangible, real, and truthful "jiko" ("ego"). Kanai's writing is an example of a playful approach to the question of subjectivity in contemporary literature. The intertwining of the worlds of animals and people, the role of the writer, and the collision of reality and imagination have become the trademark concerns of many contemporary women writers who seek to go beyond the conventional canon of *shishōsetsu* as a typical narrative of the self.

THE (MIS)GENDERED SELF: SAGISAWA MEGUMU

Two major novels by Sagisawa Megumu, *Kakeru shōnen* (The Boy Who Runs), published in 1992, and her last fictional work *Watashi no hanashi* (My Story), first published in 2002, just two years before her death by suicide, not only complement each other in terms of plot—the figure of the missing father and the (un)reliability of one's memory—but, more importantly, both indicate a subtle line between "the self" and "the other." As in the case of Kanai Mieko, Sagisawa never confirmed the truthfulness and reliability of her stories, and despite the unequivocal title of her last novel, "My Story," her works have only recently been explored as a variation of *shishōsetsu* and as unique examples of referentiality in modern Japanese fiction. Most scholars and critics have focused on other issues which shaped and defined her writing, especially the manifestation of her ethnic background, being of Korean descent in post-war Japan. For this reason, most research to date has overlooked those features of Sagisawa's writing that challenge conventional *shishōsetsu* and exemplify a unique understanding of the problem of the self in her fiction.

Again, similarly to Kanai, central to Sagisawa's reflection and literary sensitivity is the notion of "jibun," the intimate and true self, as opposed to "tasha," the other. She elaborates this issue in a thought-provoking interview which she conducts with herself: *Sagisawa Megumu jishin ni yoru Sagisaw Megumu* (Last interview by herself) (2004), where she explains how writing helped her uncover multiple layers of internal otherness: from the choice of her pen name, which sounds like a male name (her real name was Matsuo Megumi), to the otherness of her background, and finally the otherness that manifests itself in her fiction. As much as Kanai Mieko's works constitute the search for an authentic self through the power of imagination, Sagisawa seems to suppress the notion of selfhood and considers otherness to be the only truthful image of the self. We see this most clearly in the *The Boy Who Runs*, a seemingly simple story that belongs to the subgenre in Japanese literature called *katei shōsetsu* (the domestic novel).

Owing to the principal subject matter of these texts, that is, the author's discovery of her ethnic background—which, as we find out in both stories, had been concealed from Sagisawa until she reached adulthood—critics suggest that they should be read together as Sagisawa's testimony on coming to terms with her complex identity, toward which she assumes a rather ambiguous attitude (see, e.g., Umezawa, Ihara, and Oki 2018, 454–455). In both novels, the narrator assumes a multi-layered and multiform subjectivity, shifting from "watashi" to "jibun," from male narrator to female character. Within this first-person narrative, the "I" remains unthinkable without "the other" (literally "you"—"anata" in Japanese—which appears and reappears in the story). This process can be described as the constant oscillation between "I-the other" and "I-you." "Watashi" ("I") used in the narrative does not refer to Sagisawa (the writing persona), even though it tells the story of the writer Sagisawa Megumu who, upon discovering the truth about her Korean origins, struggles to get some purchase on her experience through the narrative process. The deliberate (mis)gendering of her character indicates the necessity of "writing in disguise," which, for Sagisawa, is the sole means of achieving authenticity and truthfulness in fiction.

Watashi no hanashi is considered to be a *shishōsetsu*, despite the author's explicit assertion that she abhors *shishōsetsu* writing. The narrative is divided into three parts and spans from 1992 to 2005. The final part reveals Sagisawa's understanding of the self but also the notions that she sees as determining the perception of selfhood more broadly, namely, the question of literary truth. Sagisawa explained why she had decided to narrate her story from a male perspective in the following terms: "To make the main character a female would bring me too close to myself [*jibun*]. Thanks to male character, I could keep *jibun* and *watashi* parallel in my fiction" (Sagisawa 2015, 5). Moreover, Sagisawa is conscious of the challenges imposed by the Japanese language and explores these issues in her essay "Watashi to iu Jibun" (The I as the Self):

> What does it mean to live in accordance with the self [*Jibun rashiku ikiru*]. What is "I" [watashi]? How can I live as "I"? I believe there are many people who face the same dilemma. With regard to myself, Sagisawa Megumu, as a writing persona, I refer the self to the relation with the other. This is what I understand as "living in accordance with the self." But why do we need the other in order to reconsider our selfhood?
> [...] I am convinced that the world is made of the "I" and the "other that exists beyond myself" [*Jibun igai no tasha*]. In other words, no matter how solid and stable our "I" may seem, it always needs to be confirmed by the existence of the "other." If there is no other, the ego [*jiko*] cannot exist. What I mean here is that the "I" that becomes *jibun* can only live through the life of the other. (Sagisawa 2015, 5)

The critic Takemoto Toshio distinguishes three stages in Sagisawa's writing—"the strong-self confirmation," "the I determined by others," and "the ever-changing self" (2015, 182)—whereby identity is never fixed. Takemoto approaches her stories through Paul Ricœur's concept of narrative identity, who stated: "To answer the question 'who?' [...] is to tell the story of a life. The story told tells about the action of the 'who.' And the identity of this 'who' therefore itself must be a narrative identity" (Ricœur 1988, 246).

It might be argued that, as in the case of Doubrovsky's *Fils* (1977) or Annie Ernaux's *Les Années* (2008), Sagisawa's texts exemplify the therapeutic effect of autofictional writing: it is not a faithful account or a testimony of life, but rather stands against conventional autobiography, the story of life narrated in an orderly manner. But paradoxically, it is still "my story," retold, reimagined, reinvented through fiction. "I don't really know that myself," says the character of Sagisawa's story (Sagisawa 2005, 9). This uncertainty about her Korean identity is amplified by the metaphor of the character moving around Japan. Japanese, Korean, *Zainichi* (the Korean living in Japan): the simultaneous senses of belonging and alienation evoked throughout the text testify to the impossibility of Sagisawa's identity emerging in relation to just one of these three groups. We might expect the process of writing to bring some kind of consolation or resolution for Sagisawa in dealing with the otherness within the self. Instead, it brings the opposite: it signifies the moment when the narrator discovers that the integrity of the self does not exist. Writing initiates the process of breaking apart selfhood, creating what Paul Ricœur identified as the "shattered cogito" (Ricœur 1990, 11).

The Bilingual Self: Mizumura Minae

Published in 1993, Mizumura's *Shishōsetsu from Left to Right* interweaves English and Japanese. We follow the story of Minae, a Japanese girl, who moved to America at the age of 12. In the form of a conversation with her sister Nanae, Minae endeavors to come to grips with a "self" trapped in a bilingual reality. *Shishōsetsu from Left to Right* is not a conventional life story. Read alongside Mizumura Minae's other works, including her extensive non-fiction works and interviews, this text is a treatise on the anthropology of the self. With an academic background in literary studies, not only does Mizumura recreate her life in narrative form, but she also attempts to explore to what extent "the self" is determined by language. In so doing, she seeks to determine whether *shishōsetsu*—to which she refers directly in the title—has the potential to cross the boundaries of national literature and be written or read beyond the Japanese context. For Mizumura, the self is inseparable from the language that one speaks. She argues that language remodels the self and affects interpersonal relations. The text is often compared with works by other bilingual and translingual writers in Japan: Tawada Yōko, a Japanese writing in German, and Hideo Levy, an American writing in Japanese. These works form what has been termed "ekkyō bungaku," border-crossing literature, that is, literature written outside of the author's mother tongue, and they have contributed to the changing paradigm of thinking about national literature in Japan.

In numerous interviews, Mizumura has explained that the rationale behind her experimental narrative was to challenge the notion that the Japanese language is an integral part, if not a condition, of *shishōsetsu*. Her approach is something of a paradox: while she crosses the boundaries of so-called national literature by writing in two languages, she seems simultaneously to emphasize the unbreakable bond between the Japanese language and *shishōsetsu*. The entire text serves as a re-evaluation of one's national heritage. Attempting to define her literary self, Mizumura moves constantly between what she considers to be her "own" cultural background and what she deems foreign. The following quotation, which I deliberately leave untranslated, illustrates how the two languages are used in the narrative. It is also an important turning point in the story: in a conversation with her sister, Minae, struggling with her identity (her Japanese "watashi" and the English "I") finally realizes that only writing in her native language, Japanese, can bring some kind of reconciliation, a similar remedy to the one that Sagisawa sought in her fiction when concealing her identity and writing as a male character.

> I want to be a novelist. Oh yes? Are you going to write in English or in Japanese? こういう会話は幾度か英語では繰り返したことがあったが、奈苗に同じ質問をされるとは思わなかった。
> ——もちろん日本語でよ。
> ——そりゃあなたが日本が好きになったのは分かるわよ。Boy, that's been your passion … or rather your obsession for, oh, I don't how many years. Japanese this and Japanese that and I never hear the end of it. だけど日本語を書くとなると、話は別じゃない。(Mizumura 1995, 112–113)

The novel's uniqueness lies in the use of Japanese characters in the parts that refer to the author's own self, while the rest of the text appears to be a random juxtaposition of English and Japanese. It can be described as "translating the self," that is, putting forward the "watashi" ("I") in Japanese rather than in English. Mizumura highlights the ambiguity of the self in the Japanese language and claims:

> I did not lose my "Japanese" self and, so far as I used the Japanese language, that self continued to exist; I thought that the "I" in the Japanese language was what I was truly, and continued to live with the belief that I could easily retrieve it once I went back to Japan, because the "I" in the English language was something which hardly seems to me what I am. (cited in Nakai 2005, 25)

Summarizing the text, Mizumura reveals, "It is a how-I-became-a-Japanese-writer story and that story necessarily runs parallel to the story of how I failed to become a writer in the English language" (Mizumura 2004).

SHISHŌSETSU, AUTOFICTION, AND A NEW MODEL OF NATIONAL LITERATURE

Owing to the issues that surround both *shishōsetsu* and autofiction (questions of origin, scope, terminology, definition, translation), the comparison between the two genres may, unsurprisingly, produce a number of methodological challenges and problems. The question that has accompanied me while preparing this chapter is whether we can indeed discern a specifically Japanese form of autofiction. The current state of research in Japan indicates the growing importance of new perspectives and more inclusive, wide-ranging, cross-disciplinary approaches. Attempts made by some Japanese scholars to read *shishōsetsu* "autofictionally" testify to possible new directions not only in cross-cultural but also in cross-textual interpretations. Whether we conceive of *shishōsetsu* as a literary genre, or as a mode of reading, new voices from outside Japan and the Japanese language are playing a key role in recreating the notion of Japanese literature, expanding its borders toward world or global literature.[4] It is not the purpose of this chapter to define the boundaries of *shishōsetsu*, nor to indicate whether a given literary work is or is not an example of *shishōsetsu* or autofiction. The texts discussed demonstrate that we are dealing with a type of writing whose criteria remain flexible, thus encouraging further solutions to the problem of subjectivity in a broad approach. The objective was rather to put *shishōsetsu* and autofiction into dialogue in order to enrich our understanding of both forms.

My comparative reading sheds new light on *shishōsetsu* as a form of writing and as a literary genre, one that exceeds the borders of Japanese literature. In the writings of contemporary French and Francophone writers such as Amélie Nothomb, Eric Fay, Philippe Forest, and Dany Laferrière, for example, we see an interesting attempt to integrate the features of autofiction with the aesthetics of Japanese literature or to include Japanese themes in their narrative (Kasza 2021, 217–235). Establishing the extent to which their works can be considered as autofiction or *shishōsetsu* remains problematic, as, in both forms, textual evidence and literary patterns are flexible and rely mostly on our "mode of reading." The writings of Kanai, Sagisawa, and Mizumura constitute important voices in further discussions on the state of life-writing narratives in Japan. Whether we refer to them as *shishōsetsu*, autofiction, biofiction, or egofiction, they also demonstrate the multi-layered process of exploring the enigma of the self in literature when the Japanese language does not offer a fixed or stable sense of selfhood. But crucially, it is the deviation from patterns of conventional *shishōsetsu* that has become the trademark of these women writers. The way in which all three female writers cross cultural, literary, and linguistic boundaries makes the untranslatable notion of *shishōsetsu* transferable to the realm of world literature.

Notes

1. Unless otherwise stated, all translations from the Japanese are the author's own.
2. It is important to note that "shi" is a Chinese reading of the character 私 and means "I." The Japanese reading of the same character is "watashi/ watakushi." For that reason, there are two possible ways of reading 私小説 as "shishōsetsu" or "watakushi shōsetsu."
3. Throughout the text, I follow the Japanese pattern: family name followed by first name.
4. I explore this topic in my latest monograph, *The I in the Making: Rethinking the Japanese Shishōsetsu in a Global Age* (2021).

Works Cited

Akiyama, Shun, and Hiroshi Katsumata. 2014. *Shishōsetsu Handobukku* [The Handbook of Shishōsetsu]. Tokyo: Bensei Shuppan.
Birnbaum, Phyllis, ed. 1982. *Rabbits, Crabs, Etc.: Stories by Japanese Women.* Honolulu, HI: University of Hawai'i Press.
Cassin, Barbara. 2017. *Dictionary of Untranslatables: A Philosophical Lexicon.* Translated by Emily Apter and Jacques Lezra, Michael Wood. Princeton: Princeton University Press.
Elliott, Anthony. 2006. *Concepts of the Self.* Cambridge: Polity Press.
Fowler, Edward. 1988. *The Rhetoric of Confession Shishōsetsu in Early Twentieth-Century Japanese Fiction.* Oakland, CA: University of California Press.
Hijiya-Kirschnereit, Irmela. 2019. Japan. In *Handbook of Autobiography / Autofiction*, ed. Martina Wagner-Egelhaaf, 1059–1086. Berlin: De Gruyter.
Kanai, Mieko. 1973. *Usagi [Rabbits].* Tokyo: Shinchōsha.
———. 1982. *Rabbits, Crabs, Etc.: Stories by Japanese Women.* Edited by Phyllis Birnbaum. Honolulu, HI: University of Hawai'i Press.
———. 2018. "Joseisakka dato iu ishiki nashide yonde moraitai" [I want to be read not as a female writer]. Interview by Irmela Hijiya-Kirschnereit. In *Joryū hōdan: Shōwa o ikita joseisakka tachi* [The conversations on women's style: Japanese female writers who lived in Shōwa period], 259–285. Tokyo: Iwanami Shōten.
Kasza, Justyna Weronika. 2021. *The "I" in the Making: Rethinking the Japanese Shishōsetsu in a Global Age.* Berlin: Peter Lang.
Keene, Donald. 2014. "Shishōsetsu wa mirai no tameni" [The future of shishōsetsu]. In *Shishōsetsu Handobukku [The Handbook of Shishōsetsu]*, ed. Akiyama Shun and Hiroshi Katsumata, 32–43. Tokyo: Bensei Shuppan.
Mizumura, Minae. 1995. *Shishōsetsu from Left to Right.* Tokyo: Chikuma bunkō.

———. 2004. Authoring Shishōsetsu from Left to Right. *91st Meridian* 3 (2). https://iwp.uiowa.edu/91st/vol3-num2/authoring-shishosetsu-from-left-to-right/. Accessed Apr 7, 2021.

Murakami, Haruki. 2018. Introduction: From Seppuku to Meltdown. In *The Penguin Book of Japanese Short Stories*, ed. Jay Rubin, XI–XXXII. London: Penguin.

Nakai, Atsushi. 2005. Hybridity and Contemporary Japanese-Language Literature. *Hitotsubashi Journal of Arts and Science* 46 (1): 19–29.

Osborne, Hannah. 2019. The *Ai*-Novel: *Ai no seikatsu* and Its Challenge to the Japanese Literary Establishment. *Japanese Language and Literature Journal of the American Association of Teachers of Japanese* 53 (1): 95–121.

Ricœur, Paul. 1988. *Time and Narrative: Volume 3*. Translated and edited by Kathleen. Blamey and David Pellauer. Chicago: University of Chicago Press.

———. 1990. *Oneself as Another*. Translated by Kathleen Blamey. Chicago: The University of Chicago Press.

Sagisawa, Megumu. 1992. *Kakeru shōnen* [The Boy who Runs]. Tokyo: Bungeishunnju.

———. 2004. Sagisawa Megumu jishin ni yoru Sagisawa Megumu [Sagisawa Megumu by herself]. *Bungei* Autumn, 109–119.

———. 2005. *Watashi no hanashi* [My story]. Tokyo: Kawade Bunkō.

———. 2015. Watashi to iu jibun [The I as the Self]. In *NKH Rajio Gakushū memo*. Issue 3 and 4.

Suzuki, Tomi. 1997. *Narrating the Self: Fictions of Japanese Modernity*. Stanford, CA: Stanford University Press.

Takemoto, Toshio. 2015. Constructing the Self in Megumu Sagisawa's and Miri Yu's Travelogues: A Case Study of Two Japan-Based Female Writers of Korean Origin. *Contemporary Japan* 27 (2): 169–188.

Umezawa, Ayumi. 2017. *Shishōsetsu no gihō: "Watashi" katari no hyaku nen shi* [The Structure of Shishōsetsu: 100 Years of Narrating the "I"]. Tokyo: Bensei Shuppan.

Umezawa, Ayumi., A. Aya Ihara, and Shimon Ok, eds. 2018. *Watakushi kara kan'gaeru bungaku shi: Shishōsetsu to iu shiza* [Literary History of the "I." The Shishōsetsu Perspective]. Tokyo: Bensei Shuppan.

Open Access This chapter is licensed under the terms of the Creative Commons Attribution 4.0 International License (http://creativecommons.org/licenses/by/4.0/), which permits use, sharing, adaptation, distribution and reproduction in any medium or format, as long as you give appropriate credit to the original author(s) and the source, provide a link to the Creative Commons licence and indicate if changes were made.

The images or other third party material in this chapter are included in the chapter's Creative Commons licence, unless indicated otherwise in a credit line to the material. If material is not included in the chapter's Creative Commons licence and your intended use is not permitted by statutory regulation or exceeds the permitted use, you will need to obtain permission directly from the copyright holder.

CHAPTER 14

Autofiction and the Diary: The Radicalization of Autofiction in Works by Hervé Guibert and Christine Angot

Sam Ferguson

I recently had the chance to take an overview of the development of autofiction in French writing when I contributed a chapter on autofiction to the *Cambridge History of the Novel in French* (Ferguson 2021). Without elaborating any new theories or definitions (there are too many already), I took stock of how this part of literary history has been told: among other things, I found that Serge Doubrovsky's role in the creation of autofiction has been exaggerated, partly because of the need to keep telling the story of how he invented the word "autofiction" itself; that Roland Barthes' role in this history has been underplayed; and that autofictional writing in French is divided between two general approaches undertaken by two generations, respectively—one born before the Second World War, the other born after it—with Hervé Guibert (1955–1991) playing a pivotal role in the shift from one generation of autofictional writers to another. In the present chapter, I shall supplement these findings with a single broad claim: that autofiction moved from having an orientation toward

S. Ferguson (✉)
Slyne, UK

autobiography in the work of the earlier generation to having an orientation toward the diary in the work of the later generation, who came to prominence in the 1990s, and that this change can be seen as a radicalization of the practices and desires of autofiction. This claim notably runs counter to the common assumption that, "mimicking the chronological progression of traditional autobiographical form, autofiction is normally retrospective, an older self remembering or revisiting their past life" (Arnaud Schmitt, this volume, 92). This is not just a question of whether autofictional works use the *form* of an autobiography or a diary, but rather of whether they use autobiographical modes of writing or diaristic modes of writing, each of them with their own practices, values, and preconceptions about truth and the sort of life that is worth writing. These two modes can result in many different written forms, and even co-exist in a single work.

To illustrate this reorientation of autofiction toward diaristic modes of writing, I shall examine works by two authors: Hervé Guibert, who seems to inaugurate the second generation of autofictional writers with his hugely successful work *À l'ami qui ne m'a pas sauvé la vie* (*To the Friend Who Did Not Save My Life*, [1990b] 1999), and Christine Angot, who became an emblematic figure of autofiction following the publication of *L'Inceste* (*Incest*, 1999). However, while I would argue that the two landmark works mentioned above demonstrate a diaristic orientation in their mode of autofictional writing (without using a strictly dated diaristic form), for each of these writers it will be more revealing to examine an earlier work in which they use the diary far more explicitly as part of an experimentation that leads them to their own individual approach to autofiction. In Guibert's case, the diary is an important element for many works in his overall project to reveal himself as fully possible (Genon 2014, 52–57), but his relatively early work *Voyage avec deux enfants* (*Journey with Two Children*, 1982) has been identified by critics as one in which a complex use of diary writing allows him to carry out his own characteristic type of autofiction for the first time (Genon 2014, 69; Sarkonak 2000, 116). Angot's career path was quite different, moving from primarily fictional novels toward autofiction, but again a work in diary form, *Léonore, toujours* (*Léonore, Always*, 1993) was crucial for working toward her own, equally distinctive form of autofictional writing (Huet 2018, 199–200; Picard-Drillien 2010, 22). Guibert and Angot, in these two radically different works, find in the diary the resources to challenge established literary forms, change their own practice as writers, and forge new approaches to writing the self.

Before discussing these two works in turn, it will be useful to situate them more broadly in the context of a change from one generation of autofictional writers to another, and to engage with some critical reflections which have come to almost the opposite conclusion to my own. In articles on this very question, Michel Braud and Philippe Lejeune have found that the diary, far from being an important element in autofictional writing, is difficult to reconcile with a combination of truth and fiction, and is even fundamentally opposed to fiction itself.

THE TWO GENERATIONS

Our perception of the literary history of autofiction depends on the extension that we give to the phenomenon "autofiction" as an object of study, ranging from, at one extreme, the history of the word itself (necessarily beginning in 1977 with Doubrovsky's *Fils* and including only those writers who positively embraced the term, which would therefore exclude both Guibert and Angot), to the other extreme, where it becomes a "prodigious tool for reading" (Colonna 2004, 13–14),[1] a concept used to examine the permutations of truth and fiction in writing going back to ancient literature. Without implying any judgment of these two positions or the many "affordances" in between (to use a term from the title of the present collection), my own interest is in a phenomenon that lies between these two extremes: a nebulous but identifiable trend connected to both autobiography and the novel from the 1970s onward, and which has become a major part of contemporary literature. From this perspective, despite the diversity of the works that are included within this phenomenon (some of which are labeled as autofiction by critics but not by the authors themselves), it divides into two quite distinct generations, each marked by a series of family resemblances.

The earlier generation consists of writers born before the Second World War, including Roland Barthes, Alain Robbe-Grillet, Marguerite Duras, and Serge Doubrovsky. These writers participated in the general exclusion of the psychological and writing subject in the 1960s, and then the return of the subject in the 1970s and 1980s through various innovative forms. A common theme is a recognition of the inherent fictionality of autobiography's retrospective narrative account of the past, and an exploration of the implications of assuming this fictionality, using resources drawn from the novel. For this generation, the combination of truth and fiction was always paradoxical and a fascinating theoretical problem to be explored.

For the generation born after the war, including Guibert, Angot, Philippe Forest, Nina Bouraoui, Camille Laurens, and Chloé Delaume, the combination of real life and fiction is less of a theoretical problem. Interweaving the two comes more naturally to them, they are more likely to perceive life itself as being suffused with fiction in tangible ways (such as the role of phantasies in our everyday lives), and they are more personally implicated in the process and results of their writing, whether through the imbrication of their public, private, and written personas (as is notably the case for Angot) or through the demanding experiments to which they subject themselves (especially for Delaume). I am also proposing here that the work of this later generation involves more diaristic writing, without necessarily adopting a strictly dated diary form: this would include, for example, works that give an ongoing account of some sort of personal project or experiment with an unforeseeable outcome, and where the writing process over a period of time is itself a significant part of the experience. Whereas the findings of the earlier generation of writers regarding the fictional nature of autobiographical retrospection can now be taken for granted, the second generation makes more extensive use of diaristic writing practices that, owing to their grounding in everyday life, retain a strong connection to reality and give rise to new modalities of truth and fiction.

But the chronology of these two generations is complex: Guibert, who was born in 1955 and died in 1991 from complications related to AIDS and a suicide attempt, now appears as an autofictional writer in keeping with the later generation, with diaries featuring heavily throughout his work, yet his literary experimentation with truth and fiction goes back to his collection *La Mort propagande* (*Propaganda Death*) published in 1977, the very same year as the creation of the word "autofiction" by Doubrovsky. There is considerable overlap between the work of these two groups, which is why it is more appropriate to speak of generations of writers than of clusters of works limited to a certain period of time. Another reason for this complicated chronology is that autofiction was not just created once and then imitated, but was invented over and over again by different writers in the course of their own experimentation. The works that I shall discuss, *Voyage avec deux enfants* and *Léonore, toujours*, offer two distinct examples of these individual inventions of autofiction.

Diaries and Autofiction

My claim that the second generation of autofictional writers had a strong orientation toward the diary is in sharp contrast to the reflection that critics have devoted thus far to the relation between the diary and autofiction, and while I disagree with those critics' overall conclusion that the diary is fundamentally inimical to fiction, they make some valuable distinctions. The two foremost critics to have addressed this question—Michel Braud and Philippe Lejeune—approach the matter with certain preconceptions and even a certain ideology that is common in the academic study of life-writing.

This ideology is most obvious in Lejeune's article "The Diary as 'Antifiction'" (2009, first published in French in 2007). He admits that he created the word "antifiction" to characterize the diary because of his "irritation" with autofiction itself (201). His perspective is typical of a certain hostility toward fiction in general from certain parts of the study of life-writing, a sense that it threatens the continued existence of nonfictional forms. Lejeune considers that writers of autobiography have been tempted to brand their work as autofiction in order to gain some of the literary prestige associated with fiction and the novel (Marie Darrieussecq has also made this claim, as discussed by Alison James in the present volume, 46–47), thereby undermining the pedigree of autobiography itself (Lejeune [2007] 2009, 203). He also concedes that autobiography tends toward fiction because of the need to create a structured narrative of past events and to impose a coherent form on one's personality, but sees the diary as resisting this tendency. As he puts it, "autobiography lives under the spell of fiction; the diary is hooked on truth" (201). His argument regarding the diary runs as follows: given that the diary is written in ignorance of how events will eventually turn out, it is impossible to mix fiction with truth because the untruths would quickly become unsustainable. The only exception would be for cases of "insanity," or more specifically a pathological delusion (205).

Braud's article "'Le Texte d'un roman': Journal intime et fictionnalisation de soi" ("The Text of a Novel": Diary and Self-Fictionalization, 2002) is similarly limited by a narrow conception of fiction. Braud identifies two apparently autofictional diaries, but in both cases these were not "genuinely" written in an autofictional mode as diaries of present events (79). One of these, by Jean-Bênoit Puech, takes an existing, truthful diary and rewrites it, semi-fictionally, for publication. Another work, by

Christophe Deshoulières, was written in diary form but actually covers a period of one year in the past rather than the present. In both cases, the fictionalization has been applied to past events whose development and conclusion is already known to the author. Using these two works as examples, Braud assumes that the creation of a fictional, or even semi-fictional, work requires that the author have an overview of the structure and conclusion of events, which precludes the composition of an autofictional diary in the present. Braud arrives at a similar conclusion to Lejeune: the diary is not only poorly matched with fiction, but positively antifictional, and especially opposed to the perceived threat of autofiction, as the diary "asserts that a literature based on the relation to reality is possible after all" (83).

Essentially, these critics are excellent readers of conventional diaries but poor readers of autofiction. They are right that, overall, the vast majority of diaries maintain a close adherence to the truth, or at least, the subjective truth of the diarist at that moment. They are also right that the diary, much like photography, maintains a strong symbolic connection to the truth, which is grounded in the everyday practices that produce it. But diaries can still be incorporated in autofictional texts precisely to make use of this symbolic attachment to truth (as indeed photographs can). Admittedly, these two critics focus on a more specific question than my own, not just whether autofiction might be broadly diaristic, but specifically whether a diary can be written in a fictional mode in the first instance rather than reworked at a later time (as Guibert often did). It is certainly difficult to write a diary that is partly fictional, but it is evidently possible, especially if we allow fiction to mean things other than the fabrication of a counterfactual sequence of events. But it is this very plurality of types of fiction that the two critics overlook, and which autofiction tends to reveal. This plurality includes, but is not limited to: the fictionality imposed on our lives by competing narratives in our cultural environment; the fictionality of our individual phantasies; and the fictionality inherent in the distancing and transformations of the literary writing process itself. All of these can be explored in the diary, without the need for the narrative coherence and closure of a novel, and perhaps all the more successfully, as the diary reveals the presence of these fictions in the fabric of our everyday lives. Furthermore, whatever the practicalities of the initial composition of these works may have been (we are given no firm assurances), both Guibert's *Voyage avec deux enfants* and Angot's *Léonore, toujours* are interested in the same question as Braud and Lejeune, but without coming to the same negative conclusion: they present their own experimentation with a diary written autofictionally in the first instance and explore the implications of such a possibility.

Hervé Guibert's Diaristic Writing

Guibert found fame and commercial success in 1990 when he published his book *À l'ami qui ne m'a pas sauvé la vie*, which relates his experience of living with AIDS. He is probably still best known for his books on this subject from the final years of his life, and these works are important for the development of his own practices of autofictional writing. Indeed, he claimed that writing about AIDS allowed him to "radicalize a little further still certain systems of narration, of [his] relation to the truth, and the exposition of [his] self" (Guibert 1990a, 19; translation modified). This is where I took the idea of a "radicalization" of autofiction from for the title of this chapter, as this term seems to characterize the general movement toward the second generation of autofictional writing, with a fundamental shift in its orientation. Yet, Guibert's overall aim to reveal himself completely, through a complex play of truth and fiction, goes back to his first book publication in 1977 (Genon 2010, 187). Several of his works use diaries or are adapted from his principal diary, which was published posthumously in 2001 under the title *Le Mausolée des amants* (*The Mausoleum of Lovers*). He refers to this diary as the "spinal column" of his project, and the other books as "appendices" to it (Guibert 1992). The 1982 work *Voyage avec deux enfants* is structured around a complex diary-writing project, and it appears to have allowed Guibert, for the first time in his career, to achieve just the sort of ongoing fictionalization of himself that Lejeune and Braud considered impossible.

The central experience related in *Voyage avec deux enfants* is a trip to Morocco taken by Guibert, another young man, and two adolescent boys aged around 16. Guibert takes a sexual interest in one of the boys, Vincent, with whom he would later have a relationship, and who also features in several other works, including the 1989 book *Fou de Vincent* (*Crazy for Vincent*), which is largely composed of excerpts from Guibert's principal diary presented in reverse chronological order. Guibert exaggerates the youth of the boys, and pedophilia is presented provocatively as one of the book's themes. The ethics of Guibert's attitude toward pedophilia, and of his uncritical use of North Africa as a sexualized oriental setting, are important questions that would warrant a discussion in themselves, but which I shall only indicate here in passing.

Voyage avec deux enfants consists of three parts. Part 1 contains diary entries written before the trip. Part 2 is the diary of the trip itself. Part 3 is a single, undated passage which acts as a kind of epilogue. But the book's chronology is more complicated than this division into three parts suggests. Part 1 has the most eclectic contents, made up of diary entries covering the period when the idea of the trip was conceived and when various preparations were being made. These entries are not printed in strictly chronological order, but have been re-arranged slightly to support the artistic coherence of the book. Some comments from the author in parentheses help to explain these editorial decisions: for example, the second entry printed in the book is introduced with the words "*Samedi 13 mars* (car je recherche des antécédents)" (Guibert 1982, 14). There are also two undated (or rather, ambiguously dated) entries copied from a more distant period in the past, which are included for their thematic relevance (24–26, 28–31).

When the author is just eight days away from the start of the trip, he decides to start writing a diary (still within Part 1) of how he imagines it could go. He takes eight sheets of paper, marks them with the dates of the eight days of the trip, and writes as if he were already there. This "diary of anticipation" gives free rein to his imagination, and develops into a sort of fantastical story: one of the boys has been bitten by a dead man and develops a fever, a witch doctor conducts a strange and erotic ritual involving a two-headed snake, the boy wanders off in a delirium, and is eventually found in the desert. This is presented as a fiction, although it is also a phantasy (in the psychoanalytic sense) that reveals something about Guibert himself.

In Part 2 we find the diary of the real trip. The actual chronology of the entries in this diary is simpler than in Part 1, but as we shall see, its complexity lies instead in the relation to truth and fiction. The single, undated passage in Part 3 relates how Guibert returned home to find himself now obsessed with Vincent. He asks Vincent to send him a letter. The letter that Vincent sends back to him relates an aimless trip that he made to the Paris suburbs, but Guibert describes this letter in a way that clearly functions as a *mise en abyme*, effectively a summary of his own book:

> He himself didn't know why he had left, to what end. And then, suddenly, he knew, and he wrote it down: it was just to be able to write, to be able to

write to me that he had left, so that this letter could be written and posted before the dawn, [...] as it was impossible for him to write to me from his home. (122)

This passage, standing as a description of Guibert's book, certainly does not answer all the questions we might have about it: why is it structured in this complicated way, and what is its overall relation to truth or fiction? But it does give us several indications: the journey and writing project were undertaken without a clear understanding of their nature and in ignorance of their eventual form and conclusion. These things (the project's nature, form, and conclusion) are discovered only in the course of the project itself, and notably through the writing process. One of these conclusions—both for Vincent's trip to the suburbs and for Guibert's trip to Morocco—is that the details of the journey are inconsequential, but that the journey was still necessary for allowing writing to happen and the literary work to appear. And it could not take place at home, both literally and figuratively: the book requires the real travel diary found in Part 2, but Guibert also needed to strike out from his familiar mode of writing to find something new. So, taking our prompt from this *mise en abyme*, let us return to the start of the book and look more closely at the various indications that the text provides regarding Guibert's experience of the writing project.

A note tells us that the plan for the journey dates back to the 14th of March (13), but the entries are not in strict chronological order, and so the first entry is from the 19th. This entry provides a description of his initial, very general imagination of the trip: it depicts a scene "between the desert and the sea" (13), where he watches the boys playing, and feels at ease in his body, which is normally a source of anxiety for him. From the outset, this places his phantasies at the center of the project, phantasies that reveal his desires and fears. Several further entries relate his preparations for the trip: these include some banal, practical steps, but also the gathering of books about travelers, explorers, flora and fauna, as a spur for his imagination, and passages in which he elaborates his phantasies in greater detail.

After a few pages, we find the entry for the 14th of March, when Guibert's friend first invited him on the trip. Guibert writes: "I was so grateful that I could have kissed him. This invitation was a gift: although I didn't know it, he was also offering me a book, which had not yet been written" (23). It is strange to find this comment in a diary entry, that the author did not yet know that he was being offered a book, this book that we are reading, and it suggests that some subsequent editing of the entries has taken place. We later find out that Guibert's friend had invited him because he had discovered a lost fragment of Guibert's diary, containing the following words: "Have the impression of always cutting myself off a little more from the world, whereas the aim of any creative enterprise must be to get closer to the world" (50). The trip was therefore a creative enterprise even before Guibert knew about it, and its aim is to "get closer to the world," which clearly makes his use of fiction paradoxical.

The project is also threatened with failure at various points. In one entry, Guibert is concerned to find that he has no desire for the boys and declares: "I felt all the scaffolding of the trip collapse, and therefore all the novelistic scaffolding" (31). As the writing project seems to depend on his investment in a related set of desires—for travel, for the boys, and for a new sort of book—he makes a concerted effort to nourish and develop his desires, and this leads us up to the "diary of anticipation." With eight days to go, he begins a first, imaginary diary of the trip, and describes his plans as follows:

> This will be the first part of the book: a first trip will take place here, in this quiet study [...], among my books, my files, in my tranquility, my isolation. The second part of the book will be the diary of the real trip, this palinode will take place in the intermittences of harsh light and shadow, among noise, and close to the boys, their laughter [...]. It will be shorter than the first one, more breathless and contrite, perhaps less enchanted as it will be affected by exhaustion and soreness from travel, sleepless nights, disgust or hunger [...]. (33)

Evidently, the finished book contains more than these two parts, the two diaries of the trip, yet this double structure lies at its center. The first diary is manifestly fictional, in a way that extends Guibert's phantasies into a kind of short diary novel. This is in itself a breakthrough for Guibert, as he comments, "for the first time I'm inventing, making up stories, I'm not just relating a recent event or new feeling" (50). But at the end of this diary, on the cusp of embarking on the real trip, the project is threatened once again, as Guibert feels that he has already exhausted his desires in writing, and he is "afraid to continue to be immersed in fiction, as if in madness" (62). But he does continue.

The second diary is concerned with the real trip, yet as it turns out, we are not faced with a contrast between a fictional diary and a real diary. Instead, Guibert now attempts that "madness" (as he puts it, as well as Lejeune) of writing an autofictional diary. The opening passages of the second diary, relating the tedium of the wait at the airport and the petty misbehavior of the boys, presents a banal realism that contrasts sharply with the fantastical world of the "diary of anticipation," and while we cannot determine precisely what is true and false (any banal detail could be present merely to provide a "reality effect"), there is little doubt that Guibert's final sense of being changed by the trip and his infatuation with Vincent, as related in the epilogue, are real. But we also soon see signs of fiction, or conflicting indications of the text's truth status, and we become aware of the subtle transitions where Guibert's imagination seems to take flight. Without pausing here to document those instances, I shall observe only that the work's particular combination of truth and fiction—a fiction that is manifestly present yet impossible to localize or delimit—makes it unsettling to read in a manner that is now familiar (but no less *unheimlich*) from later autofictional works by Guibert and other writers of the second generation.

The important point, with regard to the relation between autofiction and the diary, is that this form of writing did not come easily to Guibert. The writing of an autofictional diary is the culmination of all his preparations in Part 1 (including the "diary of anticipation"), and crucially, in light of Lejeune's comments that such a diary could not be sustained, it lasts for only eight days. Nonetheless, it marks a breakthrough in Guibert's overall project of self-revelation and anticipates the autofictional writing that he continued to develop over his career.

Christine Angot's Diaristic Writing

The action and themes of *Léonore, toujours* are very different from those of *Voyage avec deux enfants*: the narrator relates her everyday experience of looking after her eight-month-old baby, named Léonore, leading up to the latter's sudden death, and she also frequently evokes the theme of incest. However, there are certain parallels between the two texts, both in the broad way in which they act as pivotal works in the authors' respective careers and in the specific way in which an experimental diaristic writing project is used to change the author's relation to writing.

Like Guibert, from the start of her career Angot took an interest in the relation between life and literature, truth and fiction, the author and the textual "Christine" found within her works (Havercroft 2014, Section 2; Sadoux 2002, 171). Despite this, her first two works are manifestly fictional in their overall conception: *Vu du ciel* (Seen from the Sky, 1990) is partly narrated by a murdered girl who is now in Heaven, while *Not to be* (1991), which does not feature the textual "Christine," is narrated by a man speaking deliriously from a hospital bed. Following the emergence of a certain autofictional posture in *Léonore, toujours*, Angot's work continued to explore the permutations of truth and fiction. It was only with the publication of *L'Inceste* in 1999 that she enjoyed considerable commercial success for the first time, and became a leading figure in the new generation of autofictional writers (Ferguson 2021, 680). She continued to equivocate about applying the term "autofiction" to her work (Huet 2018, 203), but this can itself be interpreted as part of an autofictional strategy of ambiguity. Between the clear fiction of the early works and the clear autofiction (however paradoxical this might sound) of the later works, *Léonore, toujours* forms a bridge. It is labeled on the cover as a *roman* (novel), but from the beginning the narrator rejects her former novelistic writing and commits instead to a form of private, diaristic writing rooted in her (apparently) real everyday experience. Yet, the narrator's commitment to truth is undermined throughout the book, and the final section relating the death of the child is revealed to be a pure fabrication (there are signs of its fictionality within this work, and Angot's later books continued to be dedicated to her daughter, the real, living Léonore). Critics have mainly approached *Léonore, toujours* through its principal themes of maternity and incest, which are recurrent in Angot's work and closely connected to the nature of her writing.[2] These themes are undoubtedly connected to the pivotal role of *Léonore, toujours* in Angot's career, but I shall focus here exclusively on the way in which an experiment in diaristic writing is used in Angot's own, individual invention of an autofictional writing practice.

The first indication of Angot's project is found in the epigraph, taken from a letter written by Mme de Sévigné dated February 25, 1671: "It seems to me that I betray my sentiments in wanting to explain them in words; if only you could see what happens within my heart when I think of you" (Angot 1993, 9). Whereas the generic label on the front cover has told us to expect a novel, we are now faced with a form of everyday, private writing, addressed from a mother to a daughter, which expresses the classic topos of the inability of writing—or of explanation through established forms of discourse—to reveal the truth of our interior experience. Immediately after this epigraph, the opening of the main text, which is made up of 24 dated diary entries, sets out with remarkable concision the circumstances for Angot's own attempt to find some new form of expression:

> I gave life. It killed me, I only had one. I'm no longer writing. Since today. This isn't called writing [*écrire*], it's called marking [*marquer*]. I'll mark something about her every day, at least a line. There's only her. Only that. That. Which killed me. / She's called Léonore. It's not yet seven o'clock, she's still sleeping. Because this girl, this little girl, is a dream. (11)

The narrator's experience of maternity, presented here as a traumatic loss of self and subjectivity, as one "life" is now being shared between both mother and daughter, has made her former writing practice untenable, and she resolves to replace this writing with something else, a diaristic practice that she calls "marking." It is worth dwelling on the two terms in this opposition that frames the new project, between the rejected *écriture* and the new "marking."

The concept of *écriture* is variously associated with the public role of an *écrivain* (writer) who writes books related to contemporary social issues (she had previously been working on "something on Iraq" [12]), the practice of writing as the "hard labor" (13) of producing the "composition" and generalization of a work intended for others (150), and above all the prospect of the novel as an end product.[3] Whereas the narrator of *Léonore, toujours* used to feel desire for the novel, it now inspires feelings of disillusionment, and even shame (45–46). Writing a novel is not only practically incompatible with the constant distractions of motherhood (19–20), but it is also "an activity for people without children, who could commit suicide"; in other words, she now finds herself fundamentally more attached to life. Conversely, the new strategy of "marking" is initially based on a simple writing practice suggested by another parent: "Claudine asked me 'are you marking?,' making a writing gesture, today first tooth, today first smile, first proper sounds" (13). However, drawing on certain longstanding mythic ideals of authenticity and immediacy associated with the diary,[4] the narrator elaborates a broader conception of this diaristic practice that responds to every negative aspect of *écriture* mentioned above. It is supposedly a form of private writing intended only for herself

(49), produced "spontaneously" (48), as a material trace of details of her and her daughter's life (13), or as a sort of bodily secretion that preserves her feelings, thoughts, and love (54).[5] The privacy of her marking gives her the right to say what she likes and acts as a proof of her sincerity (20–21), while this "direct" writing in the present moment (26) allows a close contact with the banal reality of her everyday life with Léonore ("I can taste the monotony of the days," 46). This initial opposition between the rejection of *écriture* and the commitment to a diaristic ideal of "marking" tells us a great deal about the author's autobiographical desires, but it also seems to be an impossible goal, and indeed to be contradicted by the fact that, as readers, we hold in our hand a published literary work that is labeled a novel. In practice, the interest of the writing project found in the book lies in the evolution of these terms as the diary progresses toward the final reversal that brings the project to an end with the fictional death of the narrator's child.

We can see this evolution first as a series of compromises that seem to abandon the ideals of "marking," and then as the narrator's return to a revised concept of *écriture*. The idea that she is writing the diary completely privately and spontaneously is steadily eroded: the narrator evokes a series of readers, including Léonore and the narrator's partner Claude (16–17), but also as an *écrivain* she cannot help writing for a general reader (14, 47–48). There are also "others" upstream of her writing process: just as Guibert's writing was inhabited by the influence of Thomas Bernhard (Guibert [1990b] 1999, 233), Angot's writing is inhabited by Guibert and accommodates another narrative voice by including excerpts from Claude's earlier diary which trace their lives together in the years leading up to Léonore's birth. It soon becomes apparent that this "marking" is not a passive record of the narrator's experience, but rather a part of this experience with consequences of its own, such as when she takes actions while anticipating how she will write about them (e.g., she inserts her daughter's fingers in her own mouth while thinking of the effect this will have when it is recorded in the diary, 17).

The narrator eventually acknowledges that the "marking," as it was initially conceived, had lasted for only a few days, and has since been replaced by a form of *écriture* (123). This change is partly manifested in the presence of some of the same types of fictionality that we saw in Guibert's work: she relates a series of phantasies connected to her complex feelings toward Léonore—several scenes of a grown-up Léonore having sex (29–31), the adult Léonore sadistically murdering the narrator's abusive father (53), or a vision of Léonore's corpse in a rubbish bin (90)—and she also reveals her own deception of the reader, such as when she transcribes a poem that she claims to have written, then later admits that she copied this poem from elsewhere (50–51, 79–80).

As it gradually becomes apparent that the passive recording of "marking" has transitioned to the hard labor or "torture" of writing (129), the diary-narrative reflects on the possibility for this text to become a *livre* (book), or even a novel. This includes the practicalities of accumulating a sufficient number of pages, sending a sample to her publisher, and the discussion to which this sample gives rise (115, 119, 132). It also involves increasingly detailed reflections on the apparent contradictions of her project: that the apparently truthful diary itself is a world built of its own conventions and fictions, by which she aims to depict the real Léonore, to "imagine a whole life, her life, in a book" (122), and that, despite her decision to publish, "it's still true" (137). These reflections eventually conclude with the following claim, suggesting that a complete reversal has taken place relative to her previous writing practice:

> In [Claude's] view, since I've finished with novels, there's no *écriture*. It's exactly the opposite. It's now beginning. Since Léonore it's beginning, on a real being. […] There's before her and after her. Since she appeared, composition is ridiculous. (150)

This affirmation, that her *écriture* is really only beginning now that it is grounded in reality, in a real person, and written in a diaristic mode rather than in a mode of novelistic "composition," immediately precedes the final passage, fictionally depicting Léonore's imagined death.

Unlike the phantasies related earlier in the text, this passage is not explicitly presented as nonfactual, although there is an abundance of more oblique signs that this passage is a fictional creation, which is required by the logic of this text in order to provide a conclusion that inaugurates its existence as a *livre*. Quite implausibly (in light of the parents' evident devotion to their child), the narrator and Claude feel a "strange joy" and "solemn tenderness" (153) as they allow Léonore to die from an accidental head injury instead of seeking emergency care, and the text's final words, "Léonore, toujours," produce a sort of literary transcendence for this sacrificed, textual Léonore (155). Indeed, a series of earlier passages in the book portend Léonore's death in terms that suggest that it is linked, on a metatextual level, to this final transformation (69, 78, 123). Huet

(2018, 236–237) summarizes a range of interpretations that critics have made of this ending, in connection to the themes of incest, maternity, and as a response to the narrator's initial sense of having to give up her life to Huet, but with regard to the role of this passage as a resolution to the diaristic writing project, two general viewpoints are possible. On the one hand, the ending can be viewed as marking the failure of the diaristic project, as the only way for the diary to be concluded and so become a book—generalizable and consumable by others—is by imposing a conclusion that is a complete fiction, alien to the diary's adherence to truth and its ongoing, monotonous temporality. From this perspective, the ending is a vindication of the position that an autofictional diary is simply not possible. But this privileging of the conclusion amounts to treating the text as an argumentative essay rather than a literary work. Alternatively, we can consider that the text begins and ends with modes of writing that are equally impossible for the diary, but between the two of them they create the textual space and time (24 days) for this writing experiment to take place, where the modalities and limits of this hybrid form—the autofictional diary, or a diaristic autofictional writing—can be explored. A brief look forward to later works by Angot and other autofictional writers can leave us in little doubt that this second interpretation is to be preferred.

*

Guibert's and Angot's individual inventions of their own forms of autofiction provide us with several responses to that critical position that views the diary as essentially "antifictional." First, in practical terms, it is indeed difficult to write a diary that is both truthful and fictional, but this is mitigated when the dimensions of the diary project are defined and structured in advance, including its duration (just eight days in Guibert's case), its main topic (Guibert's trip and Angot's experience of maternity), and its themes. For Guibert, these themes include the fictive aspects of his own life, the nature of his writing (with the prospect of drawing him into a closer engagement with the world), and the goal of producing a literary work from his life. Alongside Angot's focus on the themes of maternity and incest, she too is focused on developing a new writing practice that would be adequate to the changed relationship between herself, her writing, and the world. And this shared search for new forms leads us to the question of the appeal of the diary for writers of autofiction and why they are willing to engage in this "madness": compared with an autobiographical mode of writing, the diary allows a writer to be more directly invested in an ongoing writing process that has high stakes for their relation to the world and to others. It is a dangerous undertaking, which was only a theoretical possibility, or even impossibility, for the earlier generation, but which has become a reality from Guibert's generation onward.

Notes

1. All translations from French are my own except when indicated otherwise.
2. On the relation between maternity and writing in *Léonore, toujours*, see Marie-Noelle Huet (2018, 193–237), who also summarizes the approach of other critics. Arnaud Genon explains that, for Angot, "writing is an impulse that tries to fill the original fissure constituted by incest, which is omnipresent in her work before the novel entitled *L'Inceste*" (2013, 16).
3. The rejection of a certain stereotype of the novel has become a topos of autofictional writing. For example, see Chloé Delaume's rejection of "the neo-realist novel" or formally straightforward books devoted to "a neat little social problem" (2010, 111).
4. I have discussed elsewhere these mythic ideals of the diary and the impossibility of realizing them in any absolute way (Ferguson 2018, 4–8, 12, 25–26).
5. Camille Laurens emphasizes the origins of autofictional writing in the body, drawing an etymological link between "secrets" and "secretions" (2010, 28–29).

Works Cited

Angot, Christine. 1993. *Léonore, toujours*. Paris: Gallimard.
Braud, Michel. 2002. 'Le Texte d'un roman': Journal intime et fictionnalisation de soi. *L'Esprit créateur* 42 (4): 76–84.
Colonna, Vincent. 2004. *Autofiction et autres mythomanies littéraires*. Paris: Tristram.
Delaume, Chloé. 2010. S'Écrire mode d'emploi. In *Autofiction(s): colloque de Cerisy*, ed. Claude Burgelin, Isabelle Grell, and Roger-Yves Roches, 109–126. Lyon: Presses universitaires de Lyon.
Ferguson, Sam. 2018. *Diaries Real and Fictional in Twentieth-Century French Writing*. Oxford: Oxford University Press.
———. 2021. Autofiction: Writing Lives. In *The Cambridge History of the Novel in French*, ed. Adam Watt, 671–687. Cambridge: Cambridge University Press.
Genon, Arnaud. 2010. Hervé Guibert: Fracture autobiographique et écriture du sida. In *Autofiction(s): Colloque de Cerisy*, ed. Claude Burgelin, Isabelle Grell, and Roger-Yves Roches, 187–206. Lyon: Presses universitaires de Lyon.
———. 2013. *Autofiction: Pratiques et théories*. Paris: Mon Petit Éditeur.

———. 2014. *Roman, journal, autofiction: Hervé Guibert en ses genres*. Paris: Mon Petit Éditeur.
Guibert, Hervé. 1982. *Voyage avec deux enfants*. Paris: Minuit.
———. 1990a. "La vie sida." Interview by Antoine de Gaudemar. *Libération*, March 1, 1990. Cited in Jean-Pierre Boulé, *Hervé Guibert: Voices of the Self* (Liverpool: Liverpool University Press, 1999), 196.
———. 1992. "Je disparaîtrai et je n'aurai rien caché...." Interview by François Jonquet. *Globe*, February. Cited in Arnaud Genon, *Roman, journal, autofiction: Hervé Guibert en ses genres* (Paris: Mon Petit Éditeur, 2014), 52.
———. (1990b) 1999. *À l'ami qui ne m'a pas sauvé la vie*. Paris: Gallimard.
Havercroft, Barbara. 2014. Le Refus du romanesque? Hybridité générique et l'écriture de l'inceste chez Christine Angot. *Temps zéro* 8.
Huet, Marie-Noelle. 2018. Maternité, identité, écriture: Discours de mères dans la littérature des femmes de l'extrême contemporain en France. PhD diss., Université de Québec à Montréal.
Laurens, Camille. 2010. Qui dit ça? In *Autofiction(s): Colloque de Cerisy*, ed. Claude Burgelin, Isabelle Grell, and Roger-Yves Roches, 25–34. Lyon: Presses universitaires de Lyon.
Lejeune, Philippe. (2007) 2009. The Diary as 'Antifiction.' In *On Diary*, ed. Jeremy Popkin and Julie Rak, trans. Katherine Durnin, 201–210. Manoa: University of Hawai'i Press.
Picard-Drillien, Anne-Marie. 2010. Martyres de la cause du moi: Écriture et inconscient de l'autofiction. In *Autofiction(s): colloque de Cerisy*, ed. Claude Burgelin, Isabelle Grell, and Roger-Yves Roches. Lyon: Presses universitaires de Lyon. Supplementary article published online. https://doi.org/10.13140/RG.2.1.2456.5203.
Sadoux, Marion. 2002. Christine Angot's *Autofictions*: Literature and/or Reality? In *Women's Writing in Contemporary France: New Writers, New Literatures in the 1990s*, ed. Gill Rye and Michael Worton, 171–181. Manchester: Manchester University Press.
Sarkonak, Ralph. 2000. *Angelic Echoes: Hervé Guibert and Company*. Toronto: University of Toronto Press.

Open Access This chapter is licensed under the terms of the Creative Commons Attribution 4.0 International License (http://creativecommons.org/licenses/by/4.0/), which permits use, sharing, adaptation, distribution and reproduction in any medium or format, as long as you give appropriate credit to the original author(s) and the source, provide a link to the Creative Commons licence and indicate if changes were made.

The images or other third party material in this chapter are included in the chapter's Creative Commons licence, unless indicated otherwise in a credit line to the material. If material is not included in the chapter's Creative Commons licence and your intended use is not permitted by statutory regulation or exceeds the permitted use, you will need to obtain permission directly from the copyright holder.

CHAPTER 15

Autofiction and Self-Portraiture: Jenny Diski and Claude Cahun

Ben Grant

Jenny Diski (1947–2016) was a British writer, principally of novels, memoirs, and essays, all of which drew upon her own life in some way. As she said in her final book, *In Gratitude* (2016), "I write fiction and nonfiction, but it's almost always personal. I start with me, and often enough end with me" (2016, 10–11). Claude Cahun (1894–1954), a French writer and photographer, is best known for the many photographic self-portraits she produced with her partner Marcel Moore, and she has been described as "the first example of a specialist, career self-portraitist" (Hall 2014, 243). In this chapter, I will argue that Cahun and Diski alike can be seen first and foremost as self-portraitists. In using this term, I have in mind not, in the first instance, the genre of visual art, but the literary self-portrait, as it has been defined by Michel Beaujour in his *Miroirs d'encre* (1980, published in English translation as *Poetics of the Literary Self-Portrait* [1991]; subsequent references are to the latter edition). I will focus primarily on Diski's novel *The Dream Mistress* (1996a) and Cahun's most substantial written work, *Aveux non avenus* (1930), translated into

B. Grant (✉)
Oxford, UK
e-mail: benjamin.grant@conted.ox.ac.uk

English as *Disavowals; or Cancelled Confessions* (2007). While these two texts most obviously belong to the genre of the self-portrait, they also exhibit some features of autofiction, as this genre has been defined by Serge Doubrovsky, who coined the word in 1977, and others. It is my contention that self-portraiture and autofiction represent two poles in life-writing, which correspond to two different conceptions of the self.

The distinction between self-portraiture and autofiction has already been implicitly made by Philippe Gasparini in his essay "Autofiction vs. autobiographie," in which he describes "two main tendencies which share the field of contemporary self-writing," both of which arise from the recognition that "any autobiographical narrative tends to develop like a novel." The approach of autofiction to this recognition is to "assume and amplify the fictional compulsion of the narrative of the self." The other tendency is to "be careful, wherever possible, not to fall into the narrative" (2011, 18).[1] Gasparini's essay is most concerned with autofiction, and he does not name this second tendency. However, in its avoidance of a narrative, it corresponds to what Beaujour calls the literary self-portrait, of which he says: "The *absence* of a continuous narrative in the self-portrait distinguishes it from autobiography" (1991, 2). In contrast, then, to autobiography, which gives us the continuous narrative of a self developing through time, the self-portrait is fragmentary in form, and its structure is spatial rather than temporal (105). This largely unacknowledged tradition of life-writing begins with Michel de Montaigne's sixteenth-century *Essais* (*Essays*) and includes Friedrich Nietzsche's *Ecce Homo* (1908), Michel Leiris's *L'Age d'homme* (*Manhood*) (1939), and Roland Barthes's *Roland Barthes par Roland Barthes* (*Roland Barthes by Roland Barthes*) (1975). Incorporating Beaujour's term into Gasparini's scheme, we can say that both self-portraiture and autofiction oppose autobiography's claim to present a truthful account of its subject, but whereas autofiction does so by foregrounding the fictionality of the self, self-portraiture highlights its fragmentariness and lack of a coherent narrative.

In its form, Cahun's *Aveux non avenus* is exemplary of the literary self-portrait, as it refuses to present a continuous narrative of its author's life. It comprises, instead, short texts and aphorisms, which move between the first and third person and in which Cahun assumes a range of personae. Furthermore, each section of the book begins with a photomontage—attributed to Cahun's partner and collaborator Marcel Moore—which brings together multiple self-portraits of Cahun. The fragmentary form of the text is echoed in the montaging of cut-up images. In her contribution to this volume, Laura Marcus points out that, in the early twentieth century, "autobiographical texts, like biographies, began to incorporate a sequence of photographic images, providing visual representations of the writing 'I' and a visual narrative of the life being recorded" (311). Cahun's book subversively occupies this new, hybrid form to fragment and montage autobiography's continuous narrative, in both its textual and its visual elements. *Aveux non avenus*, therefore, looks like a literary self-portrait. However, it and Cahun's other work can also be read as autofiction, particularly in the way in which they challenge stereotypes of gender, sexuality, and race through Cahun's serial performances of her own identity. This performativity recalls autofiction's tendency to "assume and amplify the fictional compulsion of the narrative of the self." Doubrovsky defines autofiction as "Text/life: the text, in turn, operates in a life, not in the void" (1980, 90). Thus, another key characteristic of autofiction is that the self is reimagined not only in the text but also in the author or artist's "real life." We find this in the work of Cahun, whose self-construction is a process undertaken not only in the text, whether that be written or visual, but also in the real world which she and her readers inhabit. Elements of self-portraiture and autofiction are therefore co-present in Cahun's work.

The same can be said of Diski's writings. As these take the form of memoirs, and of novels which incorporate episodes from her own life, our first impulse is to read them as autofiction, as opposed to self-portraiture. However, while Diski does combine fiction and non-fiction, her texts do not take their charge from the boundary between the two, as Doubrovsky argues is the case with autofiction when he defines it as "text/life." Diski declares, by contrast, "I think it's a pity that the fiction/non-fiction dichotomy exists" (2020, 60), and she prefers to see herself as "a writer. Period" (Diski 2006, 1). Moreover, although Diski resembles an autofictionalist in writing fictional narratives, she does this only reluctantly, as she makes clear when she says, "I hate writing stories. I hate plot, I hate characters. I just know that I have to have them, or I think I have to have them, but they're not really what I want to be writing about" (1999, 47). What she really wants to write are "abstract shapes" (47). This phrase brings to mind the self-portrait, with its spatial structure, rather than autofiction, which embraces chronological narrative. It also recalls Cahun and Moore's photomontages, which take photographic images out of their temporal context, and relocate them in a new spatial arrangement.

The abstract shape of *The Dream Mistress*, Diski tells us, is that of "Chinese boxes," or "Patterns coming out of other patterns" (1999, 47).

In my discussion of Diski's work, I have chosen to focus on this novel in particular because it is an excellent example of a literary self-portrait and because it is the book in which I believe Diski explores most profoundly her own identity as a life-writer. We might call it a self-portrait of the self-portraitist as a self-portraitist. This self-representation is bound up with the importance of narcissism in *The Dream Mistress*. Narcissism is a central theme in Cahun's *Aveux non avenus* too, and Diski's and Cahun's explorations of this topic are similar. They also correspond to those of the French philosopher and psychoanalyst Julia Kristeva, and in looking at Diski and Cahun alongside Kristeva, I will argue that self-portraiture arises from a different relationship between narcissism and creativity than the one which underpins straightforward autobiographical writing. This argument will then lead me to speculate further on the relationship between self-portraiture and autofiction.

Facelessness and Masquerade

Masks feature frequently in Cahun's photographic self-portraits; in one she is wearing a black cloak with many carnival masks pinned to it, and in another she places her own head behind a display of masks in the British Museum. She also dwells at length on the topic of masks in her writing. It is the subject of an essay entitled "Carnaval en chambre" (Bedroom Carnival) (1926), and in a passage of that essay reproduced in *Aveux non avenus*, Cahun speaks of "disguising my soul" with "masks [...] so perfect that when their paths crossed in the grand square of my consciousness they didn't recognise each other." But then, she continues: "the make-up I had used seemed indelible. I rubbed so hard to remove it that I took off all the skin. And my soul, like a flayed face, naked, no longer had a human form" (2007, 14). The vivid image of Cahun's consciousness as a carnivalesque masquerade points toward a conception of her identity as both multiple and performative. Furthermore, the removal of her face with her mask undermines the very notion of the human self, which is insistently identified, in the Western tradition at least, with the face.

Cahun's linking of facelessness to masquerade is echoed in Diski's *The Dream Mistress*, in which a flayed face literally appears. At the beginning of the novel, the central protagonist Mimi encounters an unconscious, elderly female tramp behind a London cinema and calls an ambulance for her. One of the paramedics who arrives on the scene ironically names the tramp Bella (Italian for "beautiful") before she is taken to a hospital, where two nurses cut away her filthy clothes, and then, in a surreal twist, proceed to remove the outer layers of her body, as Bella herself looks on from a disembodied point of view. Bella is entranced by what she sees and particularly by the tracery of nerves and blood vessels beneath her face. However, "[a] face without features offered no story, and above all else it was a story that Bella ached for. She closed her eyes on her anatomy and searched the darkness for something with a narrative. Something fit for a Bella without a past or future" (Diski 1996a, 17). There then follows, like a pattern coming out of a pattern, a story entitled "Mask," about another woman named Bella, who is also lying in a hospital bed. She, too, has lost her face, having been seriously injured in a terrorist bomb blast, and she is visited daily by the unnamed stranger who gave her the kiss of life, and who has fallen in love with her.

It is, above all, the centrality of facelessness in *The Dream Mistress* which makes it a self-portrait of a self-portraitist, for, according to Beaujour, "the self-portraitist's inaugural experience is one of emptiness, of absence unto himself" (1991, 4). Bella's facelessness is such an experience, which leads her to yearn for a narrative to fill the void. The story that performs this role is a fictional self-portrait, which serves as a mask for the tramp. This is not a mask which disguises a presence, but one which supplements an absence, just as Beaujour speaks of the self-portraitist as "[a]n awareness without a *self*, without a person. No sooner does a *person* appear than he is replaced by another mask among a host of possible masks: ancestors, contemporaries, fictitious characters whom I or others have created" (1991, 33, emphasis in original). In the self-portrait, the self can be presented only as a series of masks, so it is not surprising that a mask also features in the story entitled "Mask." When she leaves the hospital, the other Bella and the man who loves her move into a house from which all reflective surfaces have been removed because Bella refuses to confront the reflection of her disfigured face. The only mirror in the house is locked away in a cabinet, for use by the man when shaving, and Bella finally looks at herself in it when wearing a Pierrot mask she has been given by the man. If, as Diski says, the structure of *The Dream Mistress* is that of Chinese boxes, or boxes within boxes, then we can think of this cabinet containing a mirror as the central box, in which the self can be seen only as a mask.

In *The Dream Mistress*, the self-portraitist's inaugural experience of emptiness is figured not only as facelessness but also in Mimi's lack of knowledge of the tramp's life story. We are told: "The unknown distance trod between the tramp's conclusion and her absent story gave Mimi a vertiginous sense that she might, for all Mimi could fathom, have been someone she had once known. Storyless spaces, like black holes, suck ferociously on whatever comes into their orbit in their need to be occupied" (Diski 1996a, 33). Specifically, the storyless space which the tramp represents for Mimi prompts her to recall her mother, Leah, who abandoned her when she was a child, and about whom she has heard nothing since. This recollection leads, like another pattern emerging out of a pattern, into the story of Leah after she left Mimi: following a nervous breakdown, she took the name Bella, and became a heretical nun. Bella's story ends with her as the tramp behind the cinema where Mimi found her at the beginning of the novel.

To complicate matters further, the author, Diski herself, is drawn into the masquerade which constitutes *The Dream Mistress*, for Mimi's childhood memories of her mother are, to a large extent, Diski's own. We know this because they are repeated in her memoir, *Skating to Antarctica* (1997), which was published a year after *The Dream Mistress*. In both the novel and the memoir, which Diski has described as "companion volumes" (2020, 60), the memories are accompanied by reflections on the nature of memory itself. For Mimi, memory is unreliable because it is "a contrivance, a picture created after the event, and with no more verisimilitude than any other fiction" (Diski 1996a, 34). There is thus a complete discontinuity between Mimi's remembering self and her childhood self: "It was not even that the child was *no longer* her. The divorce was more profound than that. She allowed that the child had existed, and even that she continued to exist in her own right, in the past, lodged inside Mimi's mind, but there was no umbilical connection between them" (34). This idea of memory accords with Beaujour's statement: "*A memory without a person*—do not all self-portraits tend towards the paradoxical status that clearly opposes them to autobiographies?" (1991, 33, emphasis in original). In the self-portrait, a memory is nothing but a mask supplementing the absence of that continuous person upon which autobiography depends. In this way, self-portraiture contrasts with autofiction, in which the fictional self as mask calls into question the identity of the self, but is not predicated on absence. In *The Dream Mistress*, a blank page is inserted before Mimi's memories to indicate that they, like Bella's story, are founded upon an absence and provide a narrative for a self "without a past or a future." In *Skating to Antarctica*, Diski reflects upon memory in similar terms to Mimi, and remarks that her attribution of events from her own life to her characters produces "proliferated mes; mes with their own autonomy—at least within the confines of their story" (1997, 87). This description perfectly captures the driving force of self-portraiture: in the absence of a self, autonomous mes are endlessly proliferated, so a self-portrait is necessarily multiple, and essentially fictional. This proliferation of mes is brilliantly expressed in the name Mimi (pronounced "Me me"), which tells us, among other things, that this character is one of Diski's many masks.

This proliferation takes the shape of Chinese boxes because "no sooner does a *person* appear," in the form of a mask supplementing an absence, than it must be replaced by another mask, leading to a structure of one mask emerging from another. This same motif appears in Cahun's *Aveux non avenus*. In the text, Cahun writes, "[e]very living being—Russian doll, nest of tables—is expected to contain all the others" (2007, 103), and this nested structure is then represented visually in the final photomontage of the book (Fig. 15.1). The photomontage includes both a series of Russian dolls, in each of which is a fetus at a different stage of development, and an image which Lee-Von Kim describes as "two columns of overlapping faces—all Cahun, but some masked—sprouting from a single neck. Beneath each face lies another, a seemingly endless proliferation of selves" (2014, 118). Around this image are written the words, "Under this mask another mask. I will never be done taking off all these faces" (quoted in Kim 2014, 118). Cahun's performativity must be understood in relation to this structure: it is not simply a performance of identity, but a serial self-representation based on the understanding that, in the final analysis, the self is absent. Self-representation therefore always goes by way of self-cancelation. This distinguishes it from autobiography, which, in the genre of photography, would involve a faithful representation of oneself at different moments in one's life, and from autofiction, which does not foreground this structural relationship between self-fictionalization and self-erasure.

In the introduction to her book *Claude Cahun: A Sensual Politics of Photography*, Gen Doy writes:

> I began to consider whether Cahun's famous self-portrait photographs were not just about staging the self, or theatrical tableaux of femininity (as many writers have discussed) but embodiments of something much more fundamental to human beings: the possibility that the image is only a tantalising bait, to trick us—even Cahun—into thinking that we can represent ourselves. (2007, 12)

Fig. 15.1 Photomontage at the beginning of chapter IX, entitled I.O.U., of Cahun's *Aveux non avenus*. Courtesy of the Jersey Heritage Collections

It is precisely this way of apprehending the photographic image which makes Cahun's self-portraits (literary) self-portraits, in Beaujour's sense. According to Beaujour, "The presence of a Self, unto oneself, which one could naively think of as constituting the illusory subject of the self-portrait, is but a lure, or its reverse side" (1991, 7). This suggests that the absence of the self unto itself is the real subject of the self-portrait. In Cahun's case, though, while her self-portrait photographs do embody this fundamental truth as their condition of possibility, it would be more accurate to say that the negation of self is their reverse side, while the image as lure or bait is the uppermost side. This accords with Kim's comparison of Cahun's work with Barthes's *Roland Barthes par Roland Barthes*, which Beaujour identifies as a literary self-portrait, and which begins with a series of photographs of Barthes at different stages of his life. Kim argues that "Cahun does not share Barthes's anxiety to rid himself of the image-repertoire. She sees in photography the potential to constantly revision herself" (2014, 124). In other words, while Barthes is an exemplary self-portraitist in his desire to avoid falling into the life-narrative which the image-repertoire produces, Cahun finds in the contingency of this repertoire the basis for her performative self-revision.

In Cahun's work and Diski's *The Dream Mistress*, the "image-repertoire" is figured as a masquerade, though Diski would seem to differ from Cahun in finding in these masks not so much the potential for constant revision, as a necessity which she cannot do without. The tramp Bella's yearning for a story to fill the void indicates that the need for a life-narrative is a psychological one as well as a technical one for Diski as a writer. Despite this difference of emphasis, both Cahun and Diski add a new dimension to self-portraiture by placing its reverse side, the "illusory subject," uppermost. In this way, the genre is broadened to include serial photographic self-portraits, and fictional and non-fictional life-narratives. These works remain self-portraits because they are founded on facelessness, or an absence of self. Despite their apparent continuity, therefore, Cahun's photographs and Diski's writings are radically discontinuous, just as Diski's memories, which we might be inclined to read as moments in the continuous story of a life, take the form instead of a proliferation of selves, each autonomous within the confines of her own story.

Self-Portraiture and Narcissism

The Narcissus myth first began to be used to describe a state of mind in the late nineteenth century, and, especially after the publication of Sigmund Freud's essay "On Narcissism" in 1914, quickly gained widespread currency, so much so that in *Aveux non avenus* (1930) Cahun could write, "[t]he myth of Narcissus is everywhere. It haunts us" (2007, 32). The aspect of this myth which we most associate with narcissism is Narcissus's falling in love with his reflection in a pool of water and drowning when he tries to kiss his image. In *Aveux non avenus*, Cahun remarks of this fate: "The death of Narcissus has always seemed totally incomprehensible to me. Only one explanation seems plausible: Narcissus did not love himself. He allowed himself to be deceived by an image. He didn't know how to go beyond appearances" (31). In this reading of the myth, Narcissus's fixation on his reflection detracts from what is most essential to his self-love: "Oh Narcissus, you could love yourself in everything […]. Can Narcissus die withered, he whose self-love is fulfilled in an egoism for two, for many, for all, in the universal orgy?" (31–32). For Cahun, true narcissism is a going beyond the image in the mirror, so that one loves oneself in everything; thus she writes, "'Mirror,' 'fix,' these are words that have no place here" (33). If we relate this interpretation of Narcissus to the practice of self-portraiture, we can say that Narcissus's deception by an image is equivalent to his capture by the image-repertoire, or his falling into a life-narrative. By avoiding fixation on a single mirror image, Cahun embarks, instead, on a continuous revisioning of the self through an interaction with others in "a universal orgy" within the image-repertoire. Cahun's self-portraiture is therefore of a piece with her articulation of a new form of narcissism, which she describes as "the neo-narcissism of a practical humanity" (32).

Tirza True Latimer notes that when Cahun and Moore published *Aveux non avenus*, "the thematic of narcissistic femininity" (2005, 87) was being widely deployed to denigrate female sexuality, in general, and lesbian desire, in particular. The re-envisaging of narcissism in *Aveux non avenus* is therefore a way of reclaiming it "as both a feminist and a homophile signifier" (92). According to Latimer, Cahun's photographic self-portraits achieve this by "pictur[ing] a particular collaborative mode of authorship" (96), in which Moore, who likely took the photographs, played an essential role. Latimer summarizes the nature of this collaboration as follows:

Cahun's restaging of the narcissistic scene—the simultaneous evocation of both likeness and difference, the triangulation of a doubled internal image with an external point of self-regard (that of her lover's camera)—offers an alternative to representations of the same-sex partnership as a self-enclosed unit deficient in social or cultural meaning. (90)

Moore's involvement in the production of Cahun's self-portraits is crucial to their innovativeness because it introduces difference and multiplicity into a genre which is traditionally conceived primarily in terms of solipsism and self-regard. In so doing, the photographs perform a radical reconceptualization of narcissism, of which self-portraiture is taken to be a manifestation.

The "triangulation of a doubled internal image with an external point of self-regard," which characterizes Cahun and Moore's collaborative process, is echoed in Julia Kristeva's theory of narcissism. This theory challenges the commonly held view that narcissism is a state in which the subject enjoys a sense of plenitude and self-sufficiency, recalling the newborn child's blissful union with its mother. Kristeva contends that narcissism is, instead, a psychic structure which involves a "third party" who interrupts the "autoeroticism of the mother-child dyad" (Kristeva 1987, 22). The narcissistic subject is not a fully-fledged ego, but a pre-ego, and the mother is not an object, but an abject (Kristeva's word for that which is rejected or cast out in order for a self to come into being). Kristeva calls the "third party" the "imaginary father" (41) but because narcissism predates an awareness of sexual difference, this figure is not to be identified with the father as such. In Latimer's description of Cahun's "restaging of the narcissistic scene," this third party corresponds to the triangulating "external point of self-regard" occupied by Moore's camera. Like Kristeva, then, Cahun substitutes a tripartite structure for the mother-child dyad, upon which "representations of the same-sex partnership as a self-enclosed unit" are based.

According to Kristeva's theory, the act of separation of the child from the abjected mother, brought about by identification with the imaginary father, creates an "emptiness" which is essential not only for the child's sense of difference from the mother but also for all the other distinctions upon which symbolization is based. Without this emptiness, there can be no conceptualization of the world and no language. Kristeva then posits that narcissism arises as "a means for protecting that emptiness" (24). Following this logic, at the very origin of the self, there is a "zone where *emptiness* and *narcissism*, the one upholding the other, constitute the zero degree of imagination" (24, emphasis in original). This "zero degree of imagination" is, I suggest, what Beaujour calls the self-portraitist's inaugural experience of emptiness. The self-portrait therefore emerges out of an elementary structure of the psyche, a "space of imagination," which, Pleshette DeArmitt explains in her commentary on Kristeva, "gives rise to necessary fictions that will form the core of an individual's identity" (2014, 59). In contrast, then, to the author of autofiction, who inhabits the boundary between fictional and non-fictional selves, the self-portraitist operates in a space where fictions of the self proliferate. Cahun, who seems to inhabit this "zone," is able to exploit its potential for continuous self-fashioning. However, this is also a place where identity is always on the point of falling into an abyss of emptiness. Thus, Cahun laments: "Why does God force me to change faces? […] Why am I unravelled the minute I close my eyes?" (2007, 34).

The separation of the child from the mother which forms the basis of Kristeva's structure of narcissism is also central to Diski's *The Dream Mistress*. In the novel, the tramp, the encounter with whom prompts Mimi to recall her mother, could not be more abject: she is "a diseased and broken specimen to which a healthy creature would give wide berth, refusing to recognize any semblance of connection with itself" (1996a, 5). In Kristeva's scheme, it is the child who must move away from the mother in order to identify with the imaginary father. In the child's imaginary, this is perceived as its having killed the mother in an act of "[m]atricide" (1989, 27). In *The Dream Mistress*, Diski posits a fundamentally different model of the mother-child relationship and therefore of subject formation, as Mimi does not leave her mother, but is left by her. Diski underlines the importance of this when she says that her "abandonment is absolutely essential to who Mimi is and what she can achieve" (1999, 46), and Mimi's memory of having been abandoned by her mother is crucial to her later sense of identity as someone who "did not think of herself as one who leaves, but as one who was left" (Diski 1996a, 48). Furthermore, Mimi does not mind being left on her own; indeed, she cherishes the space around her as "[a] cultivated void that required silence and inactivity to satisfy its emptiness" (93). The absences of those who have left her then become more "storyless spaces," which are a spur to Mimi's imagination. Her mother's absence coincides with that of the tramp and prompts her to spin the story of Leah changing her name to Bella and becoming a nun given to deeply metaphysical speculation about the nature of God and language.

Leah's story is Mimi's, and, we presume, Diski's, fantasy portrait of her mother. In Diski's case, her mother Rene did not leave suddenly, as Mimi's did, but Diski went to live with the famous writer Doris Lessing when she was 15 and lost all contact with her mother at the age of 19. The details of this mother-daughter relationship are given in *Skating to Antarctica* and create many points of intersection between that book and *The Dream Mistress*. As well as being a story about the absent mother, Mimi's story of Leah is also a self-portrait, of both Mimi and Diski, the personal element of which is most evident in Leah's depression, which is manifested in an interior landscape "[u]nbounded and without signposts," an "empty panorama" (72). This landscape echoes, without being identical to, Mimi's cherished "void." Fittingly for a self-portrait of a self-portraitist as a self-portraitist, what the proliferated mes in *The Dream Mistress* share is an inaugural experience of emptiness. In Leah's case, this results in a form of depression resembling Diski's own, which she movingly describes in an essay on the subject as an inescapable space of "negative upon negative. Blackness ever blackening" (2014). In *The Dream Mistress*, then, there is no clear distinction between the story of the self and that of the mother. This confusion of selves reflects Kristeva's narcissistic structure, in which identity is expressed not as a unified ego, but in the interplay between three points, "enacted around the central emptiness of that transference [to the imaginary father]" (1987, 42).

Kristeva writes: "Depression is the hidden face of Narcissus, the face that is to bear him away into death, but of which he is unaware while he admires himself in a mirage" (1989, 5). This depression occurs because the origin of the self in matricide results in overwhelming feelings of guilt and mourning. These feelings are only overcome when the subject is able to negate the loss of the mother by finding substitutes for her in the signifying system of language (43). The depressed narcissist cannot achieve this because he or she is unable to get over the loss and remains in a state of perpetual mourning in which life lacks all meaning. The depression which the characters in *The Dream Mistress* experience is somewhat different. Because the emptiness at the heart of the novel is the consequence of abandonment by an unloved and unloving mother, rather than matricide, it lacks the affective burden of guilt and mourning which Kristeva sees as essential to the constitution of the subject. Quite the contrary, for Mimi, the absence of the mother comes as a welcome relief. Diski's female characters are always in danger of falling into an abyss of loneliness and isolation, but they also have the potential to find in the void images and stories which satisfy their desire for narrative and self-representation. Their deployment of signs is a way of living with lack of meaning rather than a means of exorcising it, and so their creativity has an entirely different basis than the one envisaged by Kristeva. This origin of self-portraiture in a preoedipal conception of the self distinguishes it from autofiction, which can better be understood as foregrounding the relationship between the self and its reflection in the Lacanian mirror stage.

The difference between Kristeva's and Diski's understandings of the connection between narcissism and language comes into sharp focus in the final section of *The Dream Mistress*, which narrates the first dream Mimi has ever recollected. The dream is presented to us in the second person and the "you" addressed by the narrator travels across a vast ocean in a ferry, which stops at a brick tower in the middle of the sea. You and the other passengers then file through this tower, a kind of toll booth, in which you see a woman lying in a bed in a windowed alcove, writing in a notebook. When you ask the conductor if she is not distracted by all the people, he replies, "No [...] That's the price for being in a room with such a view" (Diski 1996a, 186). This woman is the Dream Mistress of the novel's title. It is significant that she is a writer, for, as Beaujour says, "There is no self-portrait that is not of a writer *qua* writer" (1991, 9–10), and it is reasonable to assume that it is she who is writing the novel we are reading. We can compare this woman writer with Kristeva's description of the "negative narcissist," who creates within herself an "oceanic void": "In the midst of its lethal ocean, the melancholy woman is the dead one that has always been abandoned within herself and can never kill outside herself" (1989, 29). The Dream Mistress has much in common with this melancholy woman, but, for her, the oceanic void ceases to be lethal nothingness and becomes instead a mesmerizing view. It is then that writing, or the entry into language, can begin.

Diski has said of *The Dream Mistress*: "It's about pre-fiction in a sense [...] It's daydreams spinning around in someone's head at that stage before I as it were take them and turn them into a nice neat novel with a definite story" (1996b). This pre-fiction corresponds to Kristeva's "zero degree of imagination," which involves not only separation from the mother but also primary identification with the imaginary father. Kelly Oliver, in her reading of Kristeva, describes this as "the originary identification that sets up all subsequent identifications, including the ego's identification with itself" (1993, 77). At this early stage of the ego's development, "It is not one being imitating another, the child imitating its object. Rather, it is a reduplication of a pattern" (72). It is in this preoedipal space that the narcissism and self-portraiture of Cahun and Diski have their origin. In Cahun's photographic self-portraits, the reduplication of a pattern, by which the self is constantly formed and reformed, emerges in the complex interplay of self and other, as Cahun's self-representation is mediated through the gaze of her collaborator and lover, Moore. In *The Dream Mistress*, the reduplication of a pattern is perfectly figured by the sea, with its endless waves, upon which the Dream Mistress gazes as she writes. It is then no wonder that *The Dream Mistress* and *Aveux non avenus*, as self-portraits of narcissistic writers, both prominently feature the motif of Chinese boxes, or "[p]atterns coming out of other patterns," for it is this shape which most aptly captures the structure of a narcissistic subjectivity.

Naming: Self-Portraiture and Autofiction

According to Doubrovsky, "[w]hat characterizes autofiction is—Philippe Lejeune has posited this as a rule of autobiography—the identity of name between author, narrator, and character. This seems essential to me" (2005, loc. 2193). Autofiction is therefore the same as autobiography as Lejeune defines it in his influential book *Le Pacte autobiographique* (*The Autobiographical Pact*) (1975), but differs from it in declaring itself to be fiction, not fact. Consequently, whereas in autobiography the identity of name serves as a guarantor of the veracity of the narrative, in autofiction it functions instead to draw attention to the boundary between fact and fiction. The subject to which the name is attached is then posited as both real and fictional at the same time. One writer who has exploited this fundamental characteristic of the genre is Chloé Delaume, who, in her book *La Règle du Je: Autofiction: un essai* (which can be loosely translated as *The Rule of I: Autofiction: An Essay*, but which plays in addition on the French homophone je/jeu, I/game), accepts the identity of name posited by Doubrovsky as "the base rule, the constraint" of autofiction ([2010] 2015, loc. 151). Yet, in her case, the name "Chloé Delaume"—shared by author, narrator, and character—is a fictional one, which the writer adopted in place of her birth name, Nathalie Dalain. Delaume writes of her autofictional practice: "I reinvent my personality and my existence through literature, while reconstructing my real identity on the basis of a change of name" (loc. 507). Autofiction then extends into Delaume's lived reality, as a "self-fictionalization" (loc. 477), which she declares to be "an act of resistance [...] to collective fictions" (loc. 477–478) that impose narratives of the self upon us. In her hands, the tendency of autofiction to amplify the fictional compulsion of autobiographical narrative is politically inflected to become a form of "literary mythomania to counter collective fiction" (loc. 432).

Claude Cahun and Marcel Moore also changed their names from Lucy Schwob and Suzanne Malherbe, respectively. Furthermore, Cahun, like Delaume, used her self-portraits to challenge prevailing constructions of gender, sexuality, and race. However, the manner in which this is achieved is different from Delaume's autofiction, in that, rather than creating an alternative fiction of the self, Cahun and Moore's photographs counter collective fictions by drawing attention to their constructedness and by producing a proliferation of selves. We see this in their chosen names. As Latimer says, "In the case of both Cahun and Moore, the alliterative initials C.C. and M.M. reproduce *themselves* (initiating self-generation, as it were) while investing each name with the character of a pair, a double pair—pair of lovers, pair of sisters" (2005, 74, emphasis in original). Their names therefore perform the doubling and redoubling which is fundamental to their collaborative artistic practice. The constructedness of the names is also highlighted in the fact that Claude and Marcel are traditionally men's names, adopted by these women as a challenge to fixed gender identities and roles. In their playfulness and artificiality, these "false signatures" (81) are as much an undercutting of the signifying power of the name as an act of self-fictionalization, and Latimer argues that "[r]enaming, unnaming, and refusing to be named or labeled afforded Cahun and Moore a symbolic means to unravel the familial and cultural nets that enmeshed them" (2006, 201). In line with the genre of the self-portrait, their adopted names are used to avoid falling into narratives of the self, rather than as a means of amplifying their fictionality.

In a masterpiece of economy befitting a dream, the self-generation and redoubling performed by the names Claude Cahun and Marcel Moore are perfectly encapsulated in the single name Mimi (Me me) of the main protagonist of Diski's *The Dream Mistress*. There are many other ways in which names and naming are central themes of both *The Dream Mistress* and *Skating to Antarctica*. We have already seen that Leah changed her name to Bella, and we are told that, from Bella's point of view, "Leah

Feldman was an *intimate* stranger whose summoning-up at the sound of her name came complete with a life of her own. Not Bella's, for Bella's life was relatively recent" (Diski 1996a, 71–72, emphasis in original). This difference between Leah and Bella echoes the discontinuity between Mimi's remembering self and her childhood self, which is itself reinforced by a difference of name, albeit more subtle, because as a child Mimi was known by her full name, Miriam. In *Skating to Antarctica*, we find that the author's name "Jenny Diski" is also an adopted one: as well as her first name being short for "Jennifer," which she was called as a child, "Diski" was a new name taken by Jenny and her husband Roger when they married. In reflecting on the appearance of versions of Jennifer in her novels, Diski says, "I'm free to play around with who Jennifer was, might have been, never could have been. Sometimes it seems that I can get closer to her, or an essence of her precisely because of the distance between us" (1997, 86). Diski's writing is not, therefore, an act of self-fictionalization, but the fictionalization of another (self), who can best be described as an "*intimate* stranger." The same doubling of self and other is apparent in the relationship between Cahun and Moore, and it is different from the autofictional performance of a self which simultaneously occupies both sides of the boundary between fiction and non-fiction, thereby allowing an interchange between these two domains.

Although Doubrovsky is credited with coining "autofiction," the word is, as a contraction of "autobiography" and "fiction," to all intents and purposes the same as "autobiografiction," which, Max Saunders points out, was coined by Stephen Reynolds in 1906. When Saunders revives this term in his book *Self Impression* (2010), he claims that "autobiografiction is not a minor form at all, but [...] is a very widespread and diverse practice" (179), which produced numerous innovations in life-writing and autobiographical fiction in the Modernist period. Many of the features which Saunders identifies as characteristic of this genre are also features of literary self-portraiture. These include multiplicity and masquerade. However, autobiografiction is more akin to autofiction in drawing its energy from the boundary between autobiography and fiction, as Saunders suggests when he writes: "autobiografiction can be seen not so much as a separate genre or hybrid of two genres, as an expression of the structuration of genres: a relationship between the fictional and the autobiographic that defines them as different from each other by means of a moving between them" (524). Autofiction is not the same as autobiografiction, particularly in its positing of an identity of names, but, as "an expression of a structuration of genres," it might be thought of as its successor. Self-portraiture, by contrast, arises within a pre-fictional zone of the imagination which precedes the distinction between fact and fiction upon which autofiction depends and, while it exhibits similar characteristics to autofiction, these are expressions of a very different structure: Chinese boxes, as opposed to a boundary between genres. Autofiction and self-portraiture may co-exist within a single work, just as the different conceptions of the self upon which they depend co-exist within the psyche, but they will do so with varying degrees of visibility. In the case of Diski and Cahun, self-portraiture is very much to the fore and goes hand-in-hand with their characterization of a preoedipal form of narcissism.

If autobiografiction was a widespread and diverse practice in the early twentieth century, Cahun's *Aveux non avenus* gives us a hint that we can also find a figuring of self-portraiture in the Modernist imaginary. In the second photomontage of that book (Fig. 15.2), at the bottom center of the page, as though all the other self-portraits are emerging from it, there is a photograph of Cahun as a young girl, and she is wearing a Pierrot costume. Pierrot is a character who recurs repeatedly in Modernist writing and art. As a masked clown, s/he (androgyny is one of Pierrot's characteristics) is unique, both in that the mask is virtually featureless—a white surface, often with a single tear—and in that it is painted onto the face, from which it is indistinguishable. As Robert Storey says, "Pierrot's pathetic white face cannot be unmasked: creator and role are fused into a single character" (1978, 31). Jean Starobinski comments on the "virtual facelessness" (192) of these sad clowns: "It is only at the price of this *vacancy*, of this initial *void* that they can *pass over* into the meaning that we have discovered in them. They have need of an immense reserve of nonsense in order to pass over into sense" (Starobinski, quoted in Storey 1978, 192, emphasis in original). In this way, Pierrot perfectly figures and names self-portraiture, as a genre of self-writing which originates in emptiness, and is dependent upon the absence of the very self it sets out to describe. No wonder, then, that in the center of the nest of boxes within boxes which constitutes Diski's *The Dream Mistress*, what we find, in yet another echoing or redoubling of Cahun's *Aveux non avenus*, is a woman looking at herself in a mirror, wearing a Pierrot mask.

15 AUTOFICTION AND SELF-PORTRAITURE: JENNY DISKI AND CLAUDE...   305

Fig. 15.2 Photomontage at the beginning of chapter I, entitled R.C.S., of Cahun's *Aveux non avenus*. Courtesy of the Jersey Heritage Collections

NOTE

1. Translations from Delaume 2010, Doubrovsky 1980, 2005, and Gasparini 2011 are my own.

WORKS CITED

Beaujour, Michel. 1991. *Poetics of the Literary Self-Portrait*. Translated by Yara Milos. New York: New York University Press. Originally published in French as *Miroirs d'encre* (Paris: Éditions du Seuil, 1980).
Cahun, Claude. 2007. *Disavowals: or Cancelled Confessions*. Translated by Susan de Muth. London: Tate Publishing.
DeArmitt, Pleshette. 2014. *The Right to Narcissism: A Case for an Im-Possible Self-Love*. New York: Fordham University Press.
Delaume, Chloé. (2010) 2015. *La Règle du Je: Autofiction: Un essai*. Paris: Presses Universitaires de France. Kindle.
Diski, Jenny. 1996a. *The Dream Mistress*. London: Phoenix.
———. 1996b. *Meridian*. 16 July. Audio. BBC iPlayer. https://www.bbc.co.uk/sounds/play/p03m0wwh. Accessed Apr 4, 2021.
———. 1997. *Skating to Antarctica*. London: Granta.
———. 1999. Jenny Diski. Interview by Frederic Tuten. *Bomb* 66: 42–47. https://www.jstor.org/stable/40425913.
———. 2006. *On Trying to Keep Still*. London: Little, Brown.
———. 2014. Blackness Ever Blackening: My Lifetime of Depression. *Mosaic*, May 12, 2014. https://mosaicscience.com/story/blackness-ever-blackening-my-lifetime-depression/. Accessed Apr 4, 2021.
———. 2016. *In Gratitude*. London: Bloomsbury.
———. 2020. Jenny Diski. Interview by Derek Neale. *Writing Talk: Interviews with Writers about the Creative Process*, ed. by Derek Neale. London: Routledge.
Doubrovsky, Serge. 1980. Autobiographie/Vérité/Psychanalyse. *L'Esprit Créateur* 20 (3): 87–97. www.jstor.org/stable/26283821.
———. 2005. L'autofiction selon Doubrovsky. Interview by Philippe Vilain. In *Défense de Narcisse*, by Philippe Vilain. Paris: Grasset. Kindle.
Doy, Gen. 2007. *Claude Cahun: A Sensual Politics of Photography*. London: I.B. Taurus.
Gasparini, Philippe. 2011. Autofiction vs Autobiographie. *Tangence* 97: 11–24. https://doi.org/10.7202/1009126ar.
Hall, James. 2014. *The Self-Portrait: A Cultural History*. London: Thames and Hudson.
Kim, Lee-Von. 2014. Autobiographical Revisions: Photography in *Roland Barthes by Roland Barthes* and Claude Cahun's *Disavowals*. *a/b: Auto/Biography Studies* 29 (1): 107–126. https://doi.org/10.1080/08989575.2014.921986.

Kristeva, Julia. 1987. *Tales of Love*. Translated by Leon S. Roudiez. New York: Columbia University Press.
———. 1989. *Black Sun: Depression and Melancholia*. Translated by Leon S. Roudiez. New York: Columbia University Press.
Latimer, Tirza True. 2005. *Women Together/Women Apart: Portraits of Lesbian Paris*. New Brunswick, NJ: Rutgers University Press. ProQuest Ebook Central.
———. 2006. Entre Nous: Between Claude Cahun and Marcel Moore. *GLQ: A Journal of Lesbian and Gay Studies* 12 (2): 197–216. https://doi.org/10.1215/10642684-12-2-197.
Oliver, Kelly. 1993. *Reading Kristeva: Unraveling the Double-Bind*. Bloomington and Indianapolis, IN: Indiana University Press.
Saunders, Max. 2010. *Self Impression: Life-Writing, Autobiografiction, and the Forms of Modern Literature*. Oxford: Oxford University Press.
Storey, Robert F. 1978. *Pierrot: A Critical History of a Mask*. Princeton, NJ: Princeton University Press.

Open Access This chapter is licensed under the terms of the Creative Commons Attribution 4.0 International License (http://creativecommons.org/licenses/by/4.0/), which permits use, sharing, adaptation, distribution and reproduction in any medium or format, as long as you give appropriate credit to the original author(s) and the source, provide a link to the Creative Commons licence and indicate if changes were made.

The images or other third party material in this chapter are included in the chapter's Creative Commons licence, unless indicated otherwise in a credit line to the material. If material is not included in the chapter's Creative Commons licence and your intended use is not permitted by statutory regulation or exceeds the permitted use, you will need to obtain permission directly from the copyright holder.

CHAPTER 16

Autofiction and Photography: "The Split of the Mirror"

Laura Marcus

A starting point when we trace the long history of the connection between life writing and the visual image is the relationship between the visual and the literary self-portrait, and this now includes the literary genre which has recently come to be called autofiction. A significant number of autofictional texts make substantial use of photography, and the interchange between image and text, the visual and the verbal, photography and narrative, creates and crosses a borderline which has a charged relationship to autofiction's own hybridity. The referential dimensions of the photograph—its testimony to, in Roland Barthes's terms, what has been—frequently become, in the autofictional work, less certain: subject to manipulation, technical or interpretative. In some instances, as in Annie Ernaux's *Les Années* (2008; translated as *The Years* [2017]), which is discussed more fully below, descriptions of photographs shape the chronology of the narrative but the actual visual image is never shown. Hervé Guibert's *L'Image fantôme* (*Ghost Image*)—a collection of fragments of memory, mediations, and prose poems—is a text

---

Laura Marcus sadly passed away prior to the publication of *The Autofictional*. We were privileged to have the opportunity to work with Laura, whose leading expertise and great generosity of spirit have enhanced the writing of this volume.

about photography which also includes no photographic images; writing of his decision not to include "favourite photographs" in the text, he notes that his story "is really becoming a negative of photography. It speaks of photography in negative terms, it speaks only of ghost images, images that have not yet issued, or rather of latent images, images that are so intimate that they become invisible" ([1981] 1996, 113–114).[1]

From classical antiquity onward, with the philosopher Plotinus's essay on self-portraiture, the suggestion has been that the visual artist, like the literary autobiographer, turns inward to find his or her self-image, rather than merely representing the mirrored self. "Withdraw into yourself and look," Plotinus writes ([250] n.d.: 1.6.9). For the artist and art critic Julian Bell: "Self-portraiture is a singular, in-turned art. Something eerie lurks in its fingering of the edge between seer and seen" (2000, 5). Images of seeing and mirroring are central to autobiographical writing, while numerous autobiographers have used the language of the artist in describing their acts of autobiography. Life writing (biography and autobiography) has, throughout its history, been defined in visual terms: portrait, picture, sketch, impression. The term "self-portraiture" arises at around the same time (the beginning of the nineteenth century) as "autobiography." Before this, the term used for what we now call the self-portrait—"a likeness of the artist by his own hand"—paralleled that of autobiography as "the life of a man told by himself." We have seen in Ben Grant's and Karen Ferreira-Meyers and Bontle Tau's chapters in this volume that self-portraiture in both literature and in the visual arts can be reimagined through autofictional modes and vice versa. This chapter turns to a specific mode of "capturing" or "picturing" the self in life writing, the photograph, and considers its role within autobiographical and autofictional modes of self-representation.

Self-Representation and the Advent of the Photographic Image

With the advent of photography in the early nineteenth century (Niépce in 1825), a new and heightened relationship between text and visual image emerged. In conceptual terms, as Douwe Draiisma has noted, "photographic metaphors of all kinds appeared in papers on the visual memory, gradually changing the human brain into a light-sensitive plate, the memory into an album full of silent snapshots, consciousness into a gallery, its walls covered with long rows of daguerrotypes and talbottypes [...]. Until the invention of cinematography, in 1895, photography was the dominant metaphor in the para-optics [Gilbert Ryle] of the mind" (2000, 104). The relationship between photography and memory was, however, contested, while in more specifically literary contexts it was by no means without anxiety. A repeated theme was that photography, with its inability to select from the details that come into view, was having a negative effect on literary and artistic representation, pushing toward both an "inartistic" and an unselective realism or naturalism. We also see an increasing concern, particularly relevant to autobiographical contexts, about the ways in which photography might be replacing memory: what we think we recall may not in fact be a "memory image" but a "photographic image."

The use of photography in biography—and the perception of the relationship between the two modes of representation—has been linked to the Romantic cult of the author, which developed from the nineteenth century onward, and to the rise of celebrity culture in the same period. The habitual presence of photographs in autobiographies seems to have come rather later—perhaps in the early decades of the twentieth century—when autobiographical texts, like biographies, began to incorporate a sequence of photographic images, providing visual representations of the writing "I" and a visual narrative of the life being recorded. A photographic series depicting the author from early to later life represents the evolving, changing, aging body and the different life-stages of the authorial self, as a counterpart to the chronological narratives of many autobiographical texts. There are, of course, differences: photography provides a record of the self at a particular moment, or moments, in time, by contrast with the retrospective narrative mode of most autobiographical texts. Autobiography and photography are perceived to share, however, a "referential" quality, a "truth to life," which is perceived to differ from that of fiction or painting.

The emergence of photography as a technology followed closely upon the "naming" of autobiography as a genre distinct from biography. Photography also came to be used as a way of documenting identity. As the listing of the autobiographer's name as the author of the book was taken (as theorized by Philippe Lejeune [1975]) to secure the identity of the writer and the subject, so the conjuncture of a photograph and an officially registered name was taken as a proof of identity. Photographic identity documents were issued to exhibitors and employees at the 1876 Centennial Exposition in Philadelphia, though passports and other identity documents with photographs did not come into general use until around the First World War. The possibility of "seeing yourself as others see you" in the early decades of the photographic medium (the claim that would later be made for film in its first years) almost certainly played its part in shaping literary self-representations. On one hand, photography could be said to have produced a new form of self-consciousness and hence a sharper divide between biography and autobiography: the representation of the self is perceived to differ radically from the depiction of another. On the other, it may in fact have blurred this divide, precisely because the self in the photograph is seen as another, as if from the outside.[2]

If photography—or its metaphors—has raised particular questions about identity, it has also become inseparable from questions of memory. Photographs may bring back the past or they may stand in for, and hence replace, memory images. Is it events, places, and people that we recall, or photographs of them, in addition to the stories we are told about the past and which we adopt as our own memories? As Freud wrote: "Our childhood memories show us our earliest years not as they were but as they appeared at the later periods when the memories were aroused" ([1899] 1953, 322). Public figures aside, childhood is likely to have been the period when an individual is most fully photographed. The adult autobiographer's relationship to these images of a childhood self may reinforce the sense of childhood as a lost world, distinct and separate from everything that came after it. There would seem to be significant connections not only between photography and autobiography in general but also between the advent of photography and the autobiography of childhood, which intensified throughout the nineteenth century and beyond. The relationship between the photographic image and the memory image was explored in depth by the German critical theorist Siegfried Kracauer. In a 1927 essay, "Photography," Kracauer argued that "memory images are at odds with photographic representation" because photography "grasps what is given as a spatial or temporal continuum," while "memory's records are full of gaps." "An individual," he writes, "retains memories because they are personally significant," though there is a "truth" to the authentic memory image which transcends individual circumstance. "In a photograph," by contrast, "a person's history is buried as if under a layer of snow" ([1927] 1995, 50–51).

Russian Album, the Canadian writer and politician Michael Ignatieff's account of his grandparents' lives (split between pre-revolutionary Russia and post-revolutionary exile) opens with a meditation on photography, memory, identity, and history. "Photographs," he writes, "are the freeze frames that remind us how discontinuous our lives actually are." By contrast, it is in "a tight weave of forgetting and selective remembering that a continual self is knitted together." Photographs are not adequate, he suggests, to a living history: "photographs only document the distance that time has travelled; they cannot bind past and present together with meaning" ([1987] 1997, 5). Ignatieff takes up some of the arguments of early twentieth-century theorists of photography: "Photography stops time and serves it back to us in disjunctive fragments. Memory integrates the visual within a weave of myth […]. Memory heals the scars of time. Photography documents the wounds" (6–7). These are assertions with which we might wish to argue, but they indicate the extent to which photographs have become bound up with trauma theory as wound theory.

Changing Reflections: Photography in Transsexual Life Writing

Writing about photography is frequently tinged by the melancholic and the elegiac. As Susan Sontag writes, in *On Photography*: "All photographs are *memento mori* […]. Precisely by slicing out this moment and freezing it, all photographs testify to time's relentless melt" (1997, 15). For Roland Barthes, the tense of the photograph is "that-has-been": "it has been here, and yet immediately separated; it has been absolutely, irrefutably present, and yet already deferred" (1980, 120–121). The suggestion I would now like to explore is that the relationship between life writing and photography, and the incidence of photographs (actual or described) in life-writing texts, are at their most prominent in works which possess a particular generic hybridity, autofiction paramount among them, or represent identity itself in hybrid terms. Virginia Woolf's *Orlando* ([1928] 1993) is an early twentieth-century example of this relationship: both and neither biography and fiction, the photographs use the construction of simile ("like a"/"as a") which is also the central trope of the text as a whole. Thus, the photographs and their captions point to Orlando "as a boy"; Orlando "as Ambassador"; instead of anchoring identity in biographical and historical reality, the photographs (and painted portraits) point to its theatricality. Images of veiling and unveiling in the text become metaphors for its "strangest transformation"—Orlando's change from a man to a woman—but the work is in its entirety built around oscillations and vacillations, as in the identity shifts in autofiction.

Gertrude Stein's *Autobiography of Alice B. Toklas* (1933), in which self and other, biography and autobiography, swap places, with Stein ventriloquizing her own autobiography as if it were her partner Toklas's "biography" of her life, contains photographs (usually not included in later editions), as does Stein's *Everybody's Autobiography* which includes photographs of herself and Alice taken by Carl Van Vechten. It returns repeatedly to questions of picturing, portraiture, and "likeness" or "resemblance" and to the relationship between the visual and verbal "portrait."

Orlando's "strangest transformation"—from man into woman—has been taken up as an early indication of interest in transsexualism as sex change. Jumping forward by some four decades, we find the narrative of the travel writer, Jan Morris, who, born as James Morris, undertook sex-change surgery in his/her 40s. At the start of her memoir *Conundrum*, Morris (as Jan Morris) writes: "I was three or perhaps four years old when I realized that I had been born into the wrong body, and should really be a girl. I remember the moment well [of sitting under his mother's piano as she played Sibelius] and it is the earliest memory of my life" (2002, 1). Morris's account of the surgery undergone in Casablanca comes toward the end of the memoir, and she uses both the terms of "transformation"— "man into woman"—that we find in *Orlando*, as well as a mirror-scene— "the split of the mirror" (Prosser 1998, 50–55)—which is the nodal point of the text, as it is in a striking number of transsexual autobiographies published over the last few decades.

In *Orlando*, we hear that, subsequent to the mysterious process by which Orlando has "become a woman"—"Orlando looked himself up and down in a long looking-glass, without showing any signs of discomposure, and went, presumably, to his bath"—the text's only "sign of discomposure" is that it, after this point, shifts the pronoun from "he" and "his" to "she" and "her" ([1928] 1993, 98). Jan Morris writes, of the hours immediately preceding surgery: "I got out of bed rather shakily, for the drug was beginning to work, and went to say goodbye to myself in the mirror. We would never meet again, and I wanted to give that other self a long last look in the eye, and a wink for luck" (2002, 122). Considering her choice, Morris writes: "Thirty-five years as a male, I thought, ten in between, and the rest of my life as me. I liked the shape of it" (128). The "shape" here is both the life-course and its narrative construction: Morris recalls the surgeon in Casablanca, after the operation, admiring his own handiwork—"*Très, très bons*, you would nevair get surgery like that in England—you see, now you will be able to *write!*" (124).

There is, as critics have noted, an intimate relationship between autobiography and transsexualism. Jay Prosser has argued that "whether s/he publishes an autobiography or not [...] every transsexual, as transsexual, as a transsexual, is originally an autobiographer" (1998, 116). By this, Prosser (himself a female to male transsexual) is pointing to the requirement that, in order to be permitted treatment and surgery, the transsexual person produce an "autobiography" for the clinician, a narrative account of (gender) identity and identifications: "Narrative composes the self." In this sense, "the conventions of transsexuality are thoroughly entangled with those of autobiography, this body thoroughly enabled by narrative" (116). Autobiographies and memoirs of sex-change acts, as Patricia Gherovici has argued, are testimonies to stories of transformation: "Writing a sex-change memoir does not just aim at passing from one side to the other; it has the function of tying together body and text [...] the writing of the memoir can bring the author home to the body transformed" (2010, 262). This might also serve as one explanation for the striking incidence of photographs in transsexual autobiography. These photographs serve, however, complex functions. They exist not only on the axes of continuity and change (which is perhaps true of all photographs in autobiography) but also, as Prosser suggests, "on a tension between revealing and concealing transsexuality. Their primary function is to expose the transsexual body: yet how to achieve this when transsexuality on the body is that which by definition is to be concealed" (1998, 209). Narrative and image work both together and apart in this interplay between revelation and concealment.

The relationship between absence and presence is also fundamental to the photographic, as to the cinematic, medium. From the early days of film, commentators pointed to the ways in which it produced "the presence of an absence"—the illusion of an embodied and substantial reality. For the writer John Berger, photography "finds its proper meaning" between "the poles of absence and presence" (2013, 19–20). The elegiac and melancholic nature of much photography theory of the last decades—as in writings by Roland Barthes, Susan Sontag, and many others—continues the parsing of the medium in the mode of loss. In every photograph, Barthes writes, there is "the return of the dead" (1980, 23). He wrote these words in his book on photography, *La Chambre claire* (translated as *Camera Lucida*), which is also a work of mourning: in particular, for his deceased mother, a photograph which he talks about but does not reproduce for the reader: he says of this "Winter Garden Photograph" that "[i]t exists only for me" (1980, 115).

The use of photography—or the metaphor of photography—to represent ontological and emotional presence and absence recurs in many autobiographical writings. In *The Invention of Solitude* (1982), written in the week after his father's death, Paul Auster gives an account of emptying out his deceased father's house, the family home before his parents' divorce. He finds an expensively bound photograph album, with the lettering "This is Our Life: The Austers." It was "totally blank inside" (14). In the memoir, Auster describes a number of family photographs, but includes only two as actual images. It has, as its front cover, a trick "multiplicity photograph" of his evasive and emotionally absent father, whose multiplied image seems to embody the disappearing act which was his life: "It is a picture of death, a portrait of an invisible man" (33). Autofiction might be said to operate with similar transformations. The silence surrounding a scandal in the family appears in visual form through a torn and patched-together photograph, from which the figure of his grandfather (the subsequent perpetrator of a violent crime) has been cut out, so that only his fingertips remain (36). The torn photograph becomes an image not only of family secrets but also of the "wound" Auster experiences in relation to his father's death—and his life.

The American author and journalist Susan Faludi's memoir *In the Darkroom* (2016) is an account of her journey to visit her estranged father who, after returning to his native Hungary has had, in his 70s, a sex-change operation—Steven (his adopted American name) is now Stefánie. The photograph in transsexual autobiographies, as I have suggested, exists in a complex negotiation with old and new identities. In Faludi's text, there is a different take on the medium and its metaphors. At the start of the book, in which she includes no actual photographs, she uses her father's professional work as a "trick photographer" (before the age of digital photography)—"dodging" (making dark areas look light), "masking" (concealing unwanted parts of the picture), and making a perfect copy from a print—as a metaphor for the secrets, evasions, and assumed identities by and through which he lived. "He made the story come out the way he wanted it to" (34). As she travels further back in search of her father's and his family's past—during the war years in particular—photographs take on more fully evidentiary status, which they share with the investigative journalism which is Faludi's professional practice (and which is set up in the book's early pages in contrast to photography's manipulations of reality). At the very end of the book, Faludi writes of the immediate aftermath of her father's death: "I studied my father's face, averted as it had so often been in life. All the years she was alive, she'd sought to settle the question of who she was. Jew or Christian? Hungarian or American? Woman or man? So many oppositions. But as I gazed upon her still body, I thought: there is in the universe only one true divide, one real binary, life and death. Either you are living or you are not. Everything else is molten, malleable" (417).

PHOTOGRAPHY AND THE AUTOFICTIONAL IN ANNIE ERNAUX'S OEUVRE

A different take on photography and/as absence structures the autofictional work of Annie Ernaux, in particular, two companion works from the early 2000s—*Les Années* (2008) and, co-written with Marc Marie, *L'Usage de la photo* (The Uses of Photography) (2005a). In *Les Années*, which is written as a form of "collective autobiography," charting the passing of historical as well as personal time, Ernaux opens each new section with a lengthy and detailed description of a photograph of a woman at different stages of her life. The text opens, however, with a sequence of free-floating "images"—those of memory rather than photography—alerting us to the (complex, irresolvable) question of the relationship between the "memory image" and the "photographic image." "Our memory is outside us, in a rainy breath of time" (2017, 12/2008, 17) reads one fragment, but another refers to "[a]n intimate memory, impossible to share" (2017, 15/2008, 19). After this initial sequence of memory images, the narrative "proper" opens with a description of a photograph, beginning a sequence of verbal descriptions of photographs of a child, girl, and then woman whose descriptions punctuate the text. We infer that these are photographs of Ernaux, but she writes of the images as radically other to herself, and as speaking only of the time and place in which they were taken. When describing the images, Ernaux tends to point to discontinuities rather than to continuities. She writes of a school photograph "[i]t is difficult to see in her the girl with the provocative pose from the previous photo, taken scarcely two years earlier." (2017, 73–74/2008, 76) The external quality of the photograph to the photographed subject is "mirrored" (Ernaux's term) in the use of the pronoun "she" (and not "I") throughout the text.

Ernaux writes, "The distance that separates past from present can be measured, perhaps, by the light that spills across the ground between shadows, slips over faces, outlines the folds of a dress—by the twilight clarity of a black-and-white photo, no matter what time it is taken" (2017, 64/2008, 65). For the Turkish writer Orhan Pamuk, the black-and-white image is the medium of memory and of nostalgia. This does not appear to be Ernaux's message, though she does suggest that the light and shadow of the black-and-white photograph trace the lineaments of an irrecoverable past. Later, she writes of her aspiration for the book she had hoped to write (the imagined, idealized version of the one we are reading), that it should leave the impression of "an image of light and shadow streaming over faces. But she hasn't yet discovered how to do this" (2017, 170/2008, 179). This ideal work (and Ernaux instances Proust's *À la recherche du temps perdu* [*In Search of Lost Time*] and Vassily Grossman's *Life and Fate* as exemplars) is, then, envisaged in relation to a photograph or, at least, to a visual image in which individuals ("faces") are contoured by the processes of time itself.

Does Ernaux's decision to withhold the actual photographs she describes—there are no visual images in *Les Années*—indicate "an ethics of photographic abstention" (to borrow François Brunet's phrase) in the face of the contemporary image saturation of culture? We could discuss the motives underlying, and the effects of, the "pursuit of photographic absence" in a text so bound up with photographic imaging, and think about it alongside Ernaux's *L'Usage de la photo*, in which the text is structured around a series of actual photographs, but ones in which no human subject is depicted. The photographs depict the clothes, scattered on the floor, which she and her partner, Marc Marie, had removed before making love. This gave them the idea of producing a series of photos from 2003 to 2004, which they subsequently (and separately) began to write about. They agreed not to move the clothes before photographing them, nor to change the texts (2005a, 10). As she said in an interview, "The rule of the game was to stick to the truth with both the photos and the writing" (2005b, n.p.).

Ernaux declares: "I don't expect life to bring me *subjects* for but *unknown organisations* of writing" (2005a, 56; original emphasis).[3] Previously, photos had been objects of discussion in her writing; now, she says, they are the starting point. She aims to describe the photos from both a past and a present angle, focusing not on context but on the objects and their placing. "It's my imagination which deciphers the photo, not my memory" (24), Ernaux asserts. It is only a little later that the memories return, "in a sort of deferred remembering." This is one of the differences between her commentaries on the photos and those by her partner, Marc Marie, who tends to describe the immediate contexts of the images. The theme of absence and presence is constantly addressed by Ernaux: "For an outsider, they are only traces, whereas we see precisely what is *not* represented: what happened before, during and just afterwards" (2005a, 95). This model of the trace—which in other contexts might be linked to the anticipation of a future absence (the end of the affair, the end of life)—is a dominant trope in much writing about photography, and in contemporary photo-texts.

Ernaux has resisted the label of "autofiction," in part because she believes it to be a way of ghettoizing women writers (to whom the category, with its implication of narcissism, is, she states, more often applied than it is to men). She has written of her work that the facts are true, and that the events she describes actually happened, but that the result is a "fiction." Autofiction includes two contracts, Ernaux writes, "which I think are opposed: to tell the truth and to invent. I am the character in a history but that history is structured [*arrangé*]." She prefers the term "autosociobiographer" (see Snauwaert 2012). Nonetheless, Ernaux concedes that autofiction arouses passions "because it obliges readers to examine themselves, to say 'me too' or 'not me'" (*Le Monde*, February 3, 2011).

Despite Ernaux's reservations, her work lies, for many commentators on her work, in the category of the "autofictional," in which we find a significant number of texts which use photography (or the motif of photography) in their play with the porous boundary between autobiography and fiction. The French writer Hervé Guibert is another significant example here—and also one in which there is a particularly marked play with absence—as is the artist and writer Sophie Calle, who has worked with both photography and film to record the narrative events, encounters, and pursuits which she has constructed and staged in various cities: she has been described as a "first-person artist." There would thus, as I suggested at the beginning of this chapter, seem to be a significant link between the crossings of photography/narrative and those of the autofictional mode and these seem to be more prominent in French than in British literature, perhaps following the example of Barthes's *La Chambre claire*.

Ernaux has stated in interview: "I do not really consider myself as a unique being, in the sense of absolutely singular, but [more] as a sum of experiences and also determinations which are social, historical, sexual, linguistic, and continually in dialogue with the world (past and present). All this does, necessarily, form a unique subjectivity" (2003, 43–44). It is this focus on the collective framework for the autobiographical project—enabled, we could argue, by the photograph's interface between private and public context and meaning—that connects her projects with the rather different explorations of photography and life writing in British contexts. There are also strong links to work in the US—including that of Marianne Hirsch (1997), as well as explorations of history, race, and ethnicity through visual anthropology and of the complex and often fraught terms of photographic ethnography.[4]

Arising out of the developments in cultural studies in Britain in the 1970s and beyond, the "democratization" of life writing (especially autobiography) was linked not only to developments in social, feminist, and oral history—"history from below," as it came to be known—but also to interest in photography as a medium. Photography, while not entirely outside the parameters of what defines "art," was perceived, by some academics and intellectuals on the Left, to be free of the "contamination" of the fine arts by commercial considerations (see Berger 2013). The understanding of the photograph, defined in relation to its "social function," can be placed in parallel with the move in (what we now call) life-writing practices and studies toward the view that all human lives possess the value of their experiences and their place in, and passage through, historical circumstances. "The task of an alternative photography," John Berger wrote in his essay "Uses of Photography" (a response to Susan Sontag's *On Photography*), "is to incorporate photography into social and political memory, instead of using it as a substitute which encourages the atrophy of any memory" (2013, 57). This task is, he suggests, to create an adequate context for the photograph—and to replace it in "narrated time": "Narrated time becomes historic time when it is assumed by social memory and social action" (60). For Berger, it is the "phenomenon and faculty" of memory that should shape photographic construction; memory is not linear, he argues, but radial and the printed photograph should be situated in a way that is faithful to the multiplicity of associations and contexts attached to any given memory: "The aim must be to construct a context for a photograph, to construct it with words, to construct it with other photographs, to construct it by its place in an ongoing text of photographs and images" (59).

Berger's model of an "alternative photographic practice" was developed not only in his own writing and photographic projects but also in the "memory-work" advocated and advanced by women theorists, artists, and writers in recent decades, in which reversals and transgressions of the traditional direction of the "look" or "gaze" were paramount. The project also became one of cutting across the divide between the "private" and the "public" photograph (see Berger 2013, 53). The British film theorist and cultural historian Annette Kuhn, in particular, has developed a method of analysis which she calls "memory-work" and which is centered on the forms of private and public memory attached to photographic images. Her book *Family Secrets: Acts of Memory and Imagination* (1995) (which she defines not as an autobiography or confession but as a memory-text) is structured around photographs from her childhood, as well as films that have particular resonance for her. Her title refers to her belief that families are repositories of secrets: "From the involuntary amnesias of repression to the willful forgetting of matters it might be less than convenient to recall, secrets inhabit the borderlands of memory" (1995, 2). Kuhn shares the widely held view that narration and storytelling are fundamental aspects of identity-construction, but adds to this the idea that "such narratives of identity are shaped as much by what is left out of the account—whether forgotten or repressed—as by what is actually told." The past, she writes, "is like the scene of a crime: if the deed itself is irrecoverable, its traces may still remain" (1995, 4)—the words echoing those of Freud's (though without his sense of the precarity of the enterprise) when he describes "our method of concluding from faint traces, exploiting trifling signs. The same as in criminal cases, where the murderer has forgotten to relinquish his *carte de visite* and full address on the *Tatort*" [the scene of the crime] ([1921] 1993, 408–409).

For Kuhn, the "traces" (her use of the term and concept bearing interesting comparison to that of Ernaux) which are the starting point of her "memory-work" are images and the memories associated with them—both "private" (family photographs) and "public" (such as films, news photographs), though, as she notes, "private" and "public," "inner" and "outer," are porous categories. In exploring her own family photographs, she will always seek to situate them in broader cultural contexts: the cultural conventions of photographing babies and children; the commemorative occasions on which the photographs were taken (such as the Queen's coronation), which give them both private/individual and public/collective meanings. In all "memory texts," Kuhn insists, personal and collective remembering are continuous with each other (1995, 5). *Family Secrets* is a personal memoir of kinds, but it is also offered as a guide to the "memory work" which Kuhn understands to be an important cultural and political practice. There is also a strongly psycho-therapeutic dimension to Kuhn's account, which follows the "phototherapy" and "family album" work of artists and photographers Rosy Martin and Jo Spence: Spence is perhaps best known for her self-images during the treatment (and refusal of treatment) of the breast cancer from which she died in 1992. For Kuhn, "bringing the secrets and the shadows into the open, allows the deeper meanings of the family drama's mythic aspects to be reflected upon, confronted, understood" (1995, 6).

When Kuhn turns to her "family album"—more particularly, photographs of herself as a child, either alone or with a parent—she opens up her family's dynamics and, in particular, the increasingly conflictual relationship between herself and her mother. Photographs are "evidence," she writes, in that they offer "material for interpretation—evidence in that sense [...]. Evidence [...] though, can conceal, even as it purports to reveal, what it is evidence of [...]" (1995, 11–12). Kuhn finds, in almost all the photographs she discusses in the book, evidence of her mother's need for control (as figured, for instance, in the inscriptions she made on the back of her photographs or in her cutting down of the images), "involvement with her daughter's appearance"—mothers finding in their girl-children an opportunity for self-love—and the increasing exclusion of her father from the family scene (though his is the eye behind the camera).

The image of the family album—the family frame—has also been central to the work of Marianne Hirsch, whose concept of "postmemory" is closely tied to the forms of remembering, forgetting, and imagining associated with post-Holocaust, exilic, and intergenerational memory. Photographs, she argues, "are precisely the medium connecting first- and second-generation remembrance, memory and postmemory" (1999, 10); as Michael Ignatieff has suggested, they are "often the only artefacts to survive the passage through exile, migration or the pawnshop" (1997, 2). Hirsch proposes, like Annette Kuhn, an approach to family pictures through "a multi-layered reading practice that pierces through the photograph's flat surface" (1999, xvi).[5] The terms echo Ernaux's name for the overlapping of past and present, "where, it seems, she flickers in and out of all the shapes of being she has been" which she calls "the palimpsest sensation" (2017, 194/2008, 213). Hirsch's is also a spatialized model of memory, linked to W.J.T. Mitchell's model of "imagetext, a double-coded system of mental storage and retrieval." Here we see the ways in which the metaphors of mind, memory, historical process, and visual technologies continue to be rethought, now in the service of practices of historical and future-oriented interpretation and understanding.

*

When John Berger wrote, in 1968, of the photograph's ability to "bear witness to a human choice being exercised in a given situation," he was referring to a principle of selectivity: "A photograph is a result of the photographer's decision that it is worth recording that this particular event or this particular object has been seen. If everything that existed were continually being photographed, every photograph would become meaningless" (2013, 18). We are now in an age in which the concept of what is "worth recording" seems to have radically altered, as Ernaux suggests at the close of *Les Années*, when she considers digital technology—through which, in the recording of existence as we lived it, "we drained reality dry"—and the media, which took charge of "the process of memory and forgetting" (2017, 213–214/2008, 223–224). However we feel about this image-saturation in the digital age and the age of social media, there are undoubtedly interesting and important questions to ask about how it might alter and shape the modes of life writing—and of self-representation more generally, including autofiction—in the future. The broad conception of the autofictional that this volume has adopted, and the flexibility it affords to consider self-representation from multiple different angles, offers a potential avenue for such exploration.

Notes

1. All texts cited from languages other than English are translated by me, unless indicated otherwise.
2. "For the Photograph," Roland Barthes wrote, "is the advent of myself as other: a cunning dissociation of consciousness from identity." "Car la Photographie, c'est l'avènement de moi-même comme autre: une dissociation retorse de la conscience d'identité" (Barthes 1980, 28).
3. "Je n'attends pas de la vie qu'elle m'apporte des *sujets* mais des *organisations inconnues* d'écriture."
4. See the work of Hertha Sweet Young, most recently *Picturing Identity: Contemporary American Autobiography in Image and Text* (2018).
5. The image is from Barthes, at the end of section 10 of *La Chambre claire* (1980, 49).

Works Cited

Auster, Paul. 1982. *The Invention of Solitude*. New York: Penguin.
Barthes, Roland. 1980. *La Chambre claire: Note sur la photographie*. Paris: Cahiers du cinema.
Bell, Julian. 2000. *500 Self-Portraits*. London: Phaidon.
Berger, John. 2013. *Understanding a Photograph*. London: Penguin Classics.
Draiisma, Douwe. 2000. *Metaphors of Memory: A History of Ideas about the Mind*. Cambridge: Cambridge University Press.
Ernaux, Annie. 2003. *L'écriture comme un couteau: Entretien avec Frédéric-Yves Jeannet*. Paris: Stock.
———. 2017. *The Years*. Translated by Alison L. Strayer. New York, NY: Seven Stories Press. First published as *Les Années* (Paris: Gallimard, 2008).
Ernaux, Annie, and Marc Marie. 2005a. *L'Usage de la photo*. Paris: Gallimard.
———. 2005b. *L'Usage de la photo* d'Annie Ernaux et Marc Marie. Entretien. February 2005. http://www.gallimard.fr/Media/Gallimard/Entretien-ecrit/Entretien-Annie-Ernaux-Marc-Marie.-L-Usage-de-la-photo/. Accessed Apr 7 2021.
Faludi, Susan. 2016. *In the Darkroom*. London: William Collins.
Freud, Sigmund. (1899) 1953. Screen Memories. In *The Standard Edition of the Complete Psychological Works of Sigmund Freud*, vol. 3, 301–322. London: Hogarth Press.
———. 1993. *The Complete Correspondence of Sigmund Freud and Ernest Jones, 1908–1939*. Edited by Andrew R. Paskauskas. Cambridge, MA: Harvard University Press.
Gherovici, Patricia. 2010. *Please Select Your Gender: From the Invention of Hysteria to the Democratizing of Transgenderism*. New York: Routledge.
Guibert, Hervé. (1981) 1996. *Ghost Image*. Translated by Robert Bononno. Chicago: University of Chicago Press.
Hirsch, Marianne. 1997. *Family Frames: Photography, Narrative, and Postmemory*. Cambridge, MA: Harvard University Press.
———. 1999. *The Familial Gaze*. Hanover, NH: University Press of New England.
Ignatieff, Michael. (1987) 1997. *Russian Album*. New York: Picador.
Kracauer, Siegfried. (1927) 1995. *The Mass Ornament: Weimar Essays*. Translated by Thomas Y. Levin. Cambridge, MA: Harvard University Press.
Kuhn, Annette. 1995. *Family Secrets: Acts of Memory and Imagination*. London: Verso.
Lejeune, Philippe. 1975. *Le Pacte autobiographique*. Paris: Éditions du Seuil.
Morris, Jan. 2002. *Conundrum*. London: Faber & Faber.
Plotinus. (250) n.d. *The Six Enneads*. Translated by Stephen Mackenna and B. S. Page. http://classics.mit.edu/Plotinus/enneads.1.first.html. Accessed Apr 6, 2021.

Prosser, Jay. 1998. *Second Skins: The Body Narratives of Transsexuality*. New York: Columbia University Press.
Snauwaert, Maïté. 2012. Les Années d'Annie Ernaux: la forme d'une vie de femme. *Revue critique de fixxion française contemporaine*, 4, 102–113. http://www.revue-critique-de-fixxion-francaise-contemporaine.org/rcffc/article/view/fx04.10/0/. Accessed Apr 7 2021.
Sontag, Susan. 1997. *On Photography*. London: Penguin.
Stein, Gertrude. 1933. *Autobiography of Alice B. Toklas*. London: John Lane.
Woolf, Virginia. 1993. *Orlando: A Biography*. London: Penguin.
Young, Hertha Sweet. 2018. *Picturing Identity: Contemporary American Autobiography in Image and Text*. Chapel Hill, NC: The University of North Carolina Press.

Open Access This chapter is licensed under the terms of the Creative Commons Attribution 4.0 International License (http://creativecommons.org/licenses/by/4.0/), which permits use, sharing, adaptation, distribution and reproduction in any medium or format, as long as you give appropriate credit to the original author(s) and the source, provide a link to the Creative Commons licence and indicate if changes were made.

The images or other third party material in this chapter are included in the chapter's Creative Commons licence, unless indicated otherwise in a credit line to the material. If material is not included in the chapter's Creative Commons licence and your intended use is not permitted by statutory regulation or exceeds the permitted use, you will need to obtain permission directly from the copyright holder.

Index[1]

A

Absence, 11, 15, 115, 127, 147, 162, 165, 211, 214, 221, 232, 257, 288, 291–293, 295, 298, 299, 304, 315–319
Acker, Kathy, 52, 63, 68, 72–74
Adichie, Chimamanda Ngozi, 4, 11, 186, 188–195, 200, 201
  Half of a Yellow Sun, 11, 186, 188–195, 200
  The Thing Around Your Neck, 189, 190
Aesthetization, 229
Africa, 5, 110, 111, 164, 176, 194
Agency, 10, 70, 122–125, 128, 132, 134, 136, 137, 189, 196, 214, 215, 220, 240, 248
Alienation, 198, 260
Almodóvar, Pedro, 238, 241
  Dolor y gloria, 241
  Los amantes pasajeros, 238
Al-Tahawy, Miral, 12, 206, 207, 216
  Brooklyn Heights, 12, 206, 207, 216
  Rīm al-barārī al-mustahīla, 216
  The Tent, 216
Álvarez, Mercedes, 13, 229, 230, 235, 237–242, 243n5, 243n6
  Mercado de futuros, 13, 229, 235, 237–242
Ambiguity, 9, 13, 33, 42, 44, 47, 49–51, 53–55, 65, 66, 70, 72, 78n5, 84, 93, 95, 96, 116, 128, 133, 135, 142, 149, 151, 187, 228, 229, 231–235, 237, 238, 241, 249–256, 259, 260, 262, 278, 315
Angelou, Maya, 189
  I Know Why the Caged Bird Sings, 189
Angot, Christine, 4, 5, 14, 96, 267–283
  Léonore, toujours, 14, 268, 270, 272, 277–279, 281, 283n2
  L'Inceste, 268, 278, 283n2
Anthony, Michael, 189
  The Year in Fernando, 189

[1] Note: Page numbers followed by 'n' refer to notes.

Apartheid, 168, 199
Aphorism, 288
Apostrophe, 95–97
Appropriation, 72, 128, 230
Archive, 12, 54, 222n3, 228–242
Argentina, 12, 13, 228–242
Artefact, 322
Ashour, Radwa, 12, 206, 211–213, 220, 221, 222n4
  Atiaf, 12, 206
Assimilation, 168–171, 181, 216
Authenticity, 97, 128–133, 137, 138n6, 143, 151, 152, 162, 164, 167, 170, 173, 185, 259, 279, 312
Author
  authorial alter ego, 67, 70, 77, 78n1, 84, 110, 112, 116, 187, 199, 200
  authorship, 107, 111, 190, 211, 228, 250, 296
  death of the author, 185
Authority, 94, 115, 130, 137n3, 150, 180, 191, 192, 213
Autobiografiction, 41, 84, 189, 208, 303, 304
Autobiography
  autobiographical novel, 26, 83, 84, 86, 206, 208, 252
  autobiographical pact, 32, 33, 36–37n8, 43, 46, 47, 50, 66, 96, 208, 251
Autofiction
  autofictional dimension/gesture/lens/practice/mode/strategy, 4, 5, 7–11, 15–17, 25, 48, 63, 64, 66, 68–73, 76, 77, 78n5, 103, 108, 116, 126, 137n1, 141, 142, 145, 147, 156, 162–168, 174, 180–181, 185, 188, 197, 201, 206–211, 220, 228–230, 235, 242, 271, 278, 301, 310, 319
  autofictionality, 4, 28, 69, 206

autofictionalization, 8, 9, 22, 44, 47, 66, 69–71, 74, 77, 87, 189, 293, 302, 303
autofiction as genre, 1–17, 21–35, 41–56, 61–65, 68, 69, 72, 77, 83–97, 102–105, 107, 109, 110, 114–116, 121–137, 141–156, 161–181, 185–201, 205–221, 228–242, 247–263, 267–283, 287–305, 309–323
speculative autofiction, 215
Autonomy, 41, 56, 149, 212, 248, 293, 295

B
Bakhtin, M. M., 141, 147–149, 154, 155, 158n12
  See also Heteroglossia; Polyglossia
Barthes, Roland, 13, 27, 52, 55, 267, 269, 288, 295, 309, 313, 315, 319, 323n2, 323n5
  La Chambre claire, 315, 319, 323n5
  Roland Barthes par Roland Barthes, 288, 295
Beaujour, Michel, 14, 287, 288, 291, 292, 295, 298, 300
Beckett, Samuel, 103
Benoist, Marie-Guillemine, 177–180
  "Portrait de Madeleine," 177, 178
Biography, 27, 34, 87, 106, 112, 143, 147, 198, 289, 310–314
Boltanski, Christophe, 7, 53, 54

C
Cahun, Claude, 4, 14, 287–305
  Aveux non avenus, 287–290, 293, 294, 296, 301, 304, 305
  "Carnaval en chambre," 290
Canon, 11, 103, 163, 165, 176, 177, 179, 253, 258

Capitalism, 230, 237
  See also Socialism; Working class
Carri, Albertina, 13, 229–235, 241, 242, 242n2
  Cuatreros, 12, 229–235, 241, 242
  Los rubios, 12, 229–232, 242n2
  Restos, 12, 229–232
Carri, Roberto, 229, 231, 232
  Isidro Velázquez: Formas Prerrevolucionarias de La Violencia, 231
Cartwright, Justin, 4, 11, 186, 188, 195–201
  In Every Face I Meet, 195, 197
  Masai Dreaming, 195, 197
  Up Against the Night, 11, 186, 195–200
Character, 1, 8, 9, 27–29, 33, 43, 44, 50–52, 54, 55, 57n2, 63, 65, 67, 68, 70, 74, 75, 78n1, 84, 88, 90, 91, 95, 112, 115, 136, 142, 144, 149, 152, 187–193, 196–199, 209, 218, 221, 231, 233, 242n2, 250, 252, 259, 260, 262, 264n2, 289, 291–293, 300–302, 304, 319
  See also Persona
Chronology, 25, 27, 92, 93, 110, 111, 113, 162, 268, 270, 273–275, 289, 309, 311
Cinema, 4, 12, 13, 17, 127, 195, 228–242, 312, 315, 319, 321
  documentary, 6, 16, 228–242
  fiction film, 228, 235
Citizenship, 189
Climate change, 76, 77
Coetzee, J. M., 105
Cognitive approaches, 16, 62
Collaboration, 91, 108, 136, 296, 297, 302
Colonialism, 164, 167–169, 185, 187, 191–194, 197, 200, 207, 208
  See also Postcolonialism
Colonna, Vincent, 22, 44, 47, 86, 186, 269

Communication, 34, 46, 65, 78n3, 96, 97, 132, 149, 221
Community, 78n5, 123, 131, 132, 154, 189, 193, 194, 216, 239
Confession, 33, 34, 51, 86, 103, 321
Conflict, 53, 54, 68, 125, 134, 142, 152, 188, 191–195, 200, 201, 242n4, 270, 316
  Battle of Blood River, 199
  Biafran War, 11, 186, 191, 192, 195
  Civil War, 188, 193, 194
  post-conflict narrative, 11, 185–201
Consciousness representation, 5, 7, 25, 26, 31, 34, 51, 54, 64, 67, 86, 92, 101, 105, 107–110, 123, 127, 155, 166, 170, 191, 196, 215, 255, 256, 259, 262, 269, 280, 304, 311, 314, 317
Counterfactuality, 52, 72, 112, 272
Creativity, 11, 14, 23, 62, 66, 77, 103, 108, 116, 161–163, 173, 176, 193, 212, 215, 230, 238, 239, 256, 276, 290, 300
Critic, 1–5, 8, 12, 15, 16, 21–23, 28, 30, 32, 36n8, 57n2, 62, 85, 103, 104, 106, 107, 142, 158n11, 158n13, 177, 206–208, 210, 211, 216, 221, 222n1, 222n2, 255, 258–260, 268, 269, 271, 272, 278, 282, 283n2, 310, 315
Culture, 5, 6, 10–13, 15, 23, 74, 77, 121, 124, 136, 141, 145, 149, 152, 155, 161–181, 185–201, 216, 241, 248, 250, 251, 253, 263, 311, 318
Cusk, Rachel, 2, 4, 7, 9, 50, 51, 53, 57n3, 104, 105, 113–116
  Aftermath, 113
  Kudos, 50, 51, 113
  The Last Supper, 113
  A Life's Work, 113
  Outline, 9, 50, 57n3, 105, 113–116
  Transit, 50, 113

D
D'Aguiar, Fred, 187, 188
Dangor, Achmat, 200
Danticat, Edwidge, 189, 190
de Man, Paul, 31, 32
Death, 29, 30, 36n4, 52, 71, 127, 129, 135, 136, 155, 185, 195, 197, 198, 213, 219, 258, 277, 278, 280, 281, 296, 299, 316, 317
Deception, 49, 66, 68, 70, 71, 129, 156, 162, 164, 173, 209, 231, 233, 234, 240, 262, 269, 274, 276, 280, 281, 293, 296, 319
Decolonization, 161, 163
  See also Postcolonialism
Deixis, 49, 56
  See also Pronoun
Delaume, Chloé, 270, 301, 302
Dialogicality, 123, 132, 133, 135, 136, 148, 155, 156
Diary, 4, 6, 12–15, 71, 89, 91, 94, 134, 149, 206, 207, 253, 257, 267–283, 283n4
Diaspora
  Jewish diaspora, 54
Dictatorship, 13, 228, 229, 231
Discourse, 5, 10, 12, 16, 21, 27, 42–44, 46, 48, 52, 55, 57n2, 63, 70, 73, 103, 104, 109, 145, 147, 148, 150, 154–156, 168, 187, 228, 237, 279
Diski, Jenny, 4, 14, 287–305
  The Dream Mistress, 289–292, 295, 298–302, 304
  In Gratitude, 287
  Skating to Antarctica, 292, 299, 302, 303
Displacement, 52, 68, 108, 180, 207, 216–217, 220
Distortion, 70, 166, 167

Doubrovsky, Serge, 2, 4, 7, 9, 13, 16, 21–23, 27, 28, 30–32, 36n4, 36n5, 41–44, 47, 57n1, 66, 102, 142, 156, 186, 187, 191, 251, 260, 267, 269, 270, 288, 289, 301, 303
  Fils, 2, 21, 41, 43, 186, 260, 269
  Le livre brisé, 30, 36n4
Dream, 27, 126, 127, 234, 257, 279, 300, 302

E
Eco, Umberto, 196
Egypt, 211
Ellis, Bret Easton, 87, 88, 90
  American Psycho, 90
  Lunar Park, 87, 88, 90
Embedded narrative, 50, 95, 115, 150, 191, 274, 275, 289, 291, 293, 301, 304
Emotion, 7, 33, 50, 52, 65, 76, 77, 123, 125, 127, 134–137, 147, 197–201, 210, 221, 234, 240, 249, 254, 261, 276, 279, 280, 299, 316
Empirical approaches, 63–66
Epistolarity, 24, 43, 63, 67, 70, 71, 85, 91, 127, 152, 155, 207, 217, 274, 275, 278
Epitext, 186
  See also Paratext; Peritext
Erice, Víctor, 13, 229, 230, 235–242, 243n5, 243n6, 243n7
  La morte rouge, 241
  Vidros partidos, 13, 229, 235–242, 243n6, 243n8
Ernaux, Annie, 4, 7, 10, 15, 26, 49, 50, 124–128, 137n2, 137n4, 260, 309, 317–323
  La place, 49

Les Années, 10, 26, 49, 124–128, 137n3, 260, 309, 317, 318, 323
L'usage de la photo, 127, 317, 318
Escher, E. M., 31
Essay, 2, 22, 212, 231, 242n2, 256, 260, 282, 287, 288, 290, 296, 299, 310, 312, 320
Ethics, 131, 133, 197, 233, 273, 318
Europe, 5, 54, 131, 145, 163, 176, 192, 194, 236

F
Fact, 7, 9, 13, 21–23, 25–27, 30–35, 41–45, 47, 48, 50, 52, 55, 56, 64, 65, 67–71, 86–88, 90, 91, 93, 94, 97n1, 129, 133, 143, 145, 150, 151, 156, 161, 162, 166, 167, 192–195, 198, 208, 210, 211, 213, 231, 233, 254, 280, 301, 302, 304, 311, 312, 319
Fairytale, 133
Feminism, 105, 134, 296, 320
Fiction
 fictionality, 2, 7, 16, 22, 26, 32–35, 42, 44–48, 53, 55, 56, 62–67, 103, 104, 108, 122, 211, 220, 238, 240, 243n7, 269, 272, 278, 280, 288, 302
 fictionalization, 7, 16, 42, 50, 52–56, 57n4, 67, 69, 102, 103, 105, 108, 109, 116, 162, 173, 209, 216, 252, 272, 273, 303
 fiction and nonfiction/reality, boundary between, 7, 22, 23, 33, 41, 42, 44, 46, 48, 62, 68, 76, 88, 96, 97n1, 133, 143, 156, 161, 194, 231, 301, 303, 304, 319
 fiction, theories of, 7, 41, 42, 44, 47, 56, 90

Film, *see* Cinema
Financial crisis, 13, 228, 230, 236, 237, 240, 241
Focalization, 107, 197
 See also Point of view
Foer, Jonathan Safran, 34
Form, 2, 4–15, 22, 23, 25, 26, 28, 32, 42, 43, 45–49, 51, 52, 54–56, 69, 71, 74, 77, 83, 84, 86, 87, 90, 92, 96, 102–104, 106–108, 110–113, 115, 116, 121, 123–125, 127–129, 131, 132, 134, 137, 144, 146–149, 153, 161, 163, 164, 168, 169, 173, 176, 179, 180, 185–192, 194, 200, 201, 218, 228, 229, 232, 234–236, 240, 247–254, 261, 263, 268–272, 275, 277–280, 282, 288–290, 293, 295, 296, 298, 299, 302–304, 312, 316, 317, 320–322
 See also Style/stylistics
Foucault, Michel, 21, 36n6
France, 2, 3, 5, 6, 13–15, 22, 44, 49, 53, 57n4, 84, 85, 96, 97n1, 144, 164, 165, 169, 171, 173, 174, 177, 178, 181, 195, 228, 236, 242n1, 247, 251, 252, 254, 255, 263, 267, 271, 283n1, 287, 290, 301, 319
Freud, Sigmund, 173, 296, 312, 321
 See also Psychoanalysis
Future, 5, 55, 76, 77, 92, 126–129, 134, 135, 137, 168, 192, 199, 237, 291, 292, 319, 323

G
Gasparini, Philippe, 22, 32, 43, 56, 84, 86–88, 94, 288
Gaze, 179, 180, 214, 238, 301, 321

Gender, 13, 49, 85, 103–105, 109, 115, 130, 132, 163–165, 177–179, 195, 215, 216, 249, 250, 252, 254–256, 259, 262, 263, 289, 290, 296, 299, 302, 304, 314, 315

Generation, 13, 22, 33, 85, 124, 125, 127, 128, 144, 147, 171, 189, 191, 194, 206, 216, 229, 237, 241, 255, 256, 267–271, 273, 277, 278, 283, 322

Genre, 2–6, 13, 17, 21, 23, 24, 26, 27, 30, 32, 34, 35, 37n9, 42, 43, 47, 48, 53, 55, 56, 61, 63, 64, 69, 72, 76, 83–85, 90, 103, 105, 110, 111, 133, 143, 145, 146, 155–156, 177, 186, 188, 206, 208, 210, 211, 213, 216, 219, 220, 222n2, 228–230, 233, 235, 237, 242, 247–253, 262, 263, 278, 287, 288, 293, 295, 297, 301–304, 309, 311, 313

Ghali, Waguih, 12, 206–208, 220, 221, 222n3
  Beer in the Snooker Club, 12, 206, 207, 220
  The Diaries of Waguih Ghali: An Egyptian Writer in the Swinging Sixties, 207, 222n3

Glavinic, Thomas, 27, 33

Goethe, Johann Wolfgang von, 4, 7, 24–27, 30

Grueso, Stéphane, 238

Guerín, José Luis, 235

Guibert, Hervé, 4, 14, 96, 267–283, 309, 319
  À l'ami qui ne m'a pas sauvé la vie, 268, 273
  Le Mausolée des amants, 273
  Voyage avec deux enfants, 14, 268, 270, 272–274, 277

H

Hassan, Yahya, 142, 146–148, 150, 152–155, 158n11

Health, 136
  See also Illness

Heteroglossia, 147, 148
  See also Polyglossia

Heti, Sheila, 2, 104

History, 3, 63, 74, 94, 102, 103, 126, 135, 155, 169, 174, 188, 191, 193, 199, 200, 205, 206, 212–214, 229, 230, 235, 241, 243n7, 249, 250, 267, 269, 309, 310, 312, 313, 319, 320

Hoppe, Felicitas, 4, 5, 7, 26, 27, 34, 35, 37n11

Hurston, Zora Neale, 189

Hustvedt, Siri, 4, 8, 85, 86, 89–95
  The Blindfold, 89
  Memories of the Future, 8, 85, 86, 89, 91–93, 95
  The Shaking Woman or A History of My Nerves, 86, 94
  The Sorrows of an American, 86

Hybrid, 2, 9, 33, 42, 44–48, 55, 56, 65, 68, 83, 105, 142, 147, 152, 220, 228, 282, 289, 303, 309, 313

I

Identification, 8, 25, 26, 42, 43, 45, 51, 88, 143, 165, 176, 177, 186, 209–210, 217–220, 233, 271, 295, 297, 298, 300, 301, 303, 315

Identity, 10, 12–14, 43–47, 49, 51–53, 68, 74, 87, 95, 115, 143, 149, 150, 152, 163–165, 167, 168, 171, 175, 178, 180, 181, 186–188, 207–208, 216–221, 233, 238, 242, 248, 252–255,

257, 259, 260, 262, 289, 290, 292, 293, 298, 299, 301, 302, 304, 311–313, 315, 316, 321
See also Self
Illness, 10, 67, 124, 125, 127, 133–137, 270, 273, 278, 290, 291, 299, 322
See also Health
Imaginary, 92, 132, 193, 209, 218, 231, 237, 252, 276, 297–300, 304
Imagination, 10, 12, 24–30, 35, 42, 51, 66, 70, 71, 122–128, 131, 134–137, 149, 171, 177, 207, 209, 212, 215, 255, 256, 258, 259, 274, 275, 277, 298, 304, 318
Intertextuality, 3, 6, 11, 16, 28, 74, 88, 90, 111

J
Japan, 6, 12, 13, 15, 247–263, 264n1, 264n2, 264n3
Jordà, Joaquim, 137n3, 235
Joyce, James, 108
Juárez, Enrique, 234

K
Kanai Mieko, 13, 252, 255–259
Usagi, 255–257
Kay, Jackie, 187, 188
Kehlmann, Daniel, 33
Khemiri, Jonas Hassen, 142, 146–150, 152–155
Knausgaard, Karl Ove, 4, 5, 7, 10, 22, 28–30, 55, 64, 104, 105, 114, 128–133, 137n2, 137n4, 138n9
Knowledge
 indirect knowledge, 66
 real-world knowledge, 65
Kristeva, Julia, 290, 297–300

L
Lacan, Jacques, 300
Lacuesta, Isaki, 235
 El cuaderno de barro, 235
 Los pasos dobles, 235
Laing, Olivia, 4, 7–9, 51–53, 63, 66, 68, 69, 72–74, 78n3, 104
Lamming, George, 189
Language, 1, 9, 13, 15, 16, 23, 27, 28, 30, 32, 37n8, 41–46, 48, 53, 56, 83–97, 107, 132, 141–156, 164, 165, 167–171, 178, 180, 181, 193, 211, 217, 233, 242n3, 248–256, 260–263, 297, 299, 300, 310, 320, 323n1
Laurens, Camille, 7, 55, 57n4, 187, 270, 283n5
Lejeune, Philippe, 22, 26, 32, 33, 36–37n8, 42, 43, 45, 46, 62, 66, 92, 96, 251, 269, 271–273, 277, 301, 311
Lerner, Ben, 4, 8, 9, 55, 63, 66, 68, 69, 75–77, 85–88, 90–93, 95, 96
 "The Golden Vanity," 88, 91
 Leaving the Atocha Station, 75, 85, 88
 10: 04, 8, 9, 63, 67, 75, 76, 85–88, 91, 93, 95
Lessing, Doris, 4, 9, 104, 105, 110–113, 116, 299
 African Laughter, 110, 112
 Alfred & Emily, 110, 112
 Children of Violence, 110, 113
 Going Home, 110, 112
 The Golden Notebook, 105, 110
 Under My Skin, 110, 112
 Walking in the Shade, 110–112
Letters, *see* Epistolarity
Lieu de mémoire, 211, 213–216

Life writing, 2, 5, 6, 12, 14–16, 22, 25, 30, 66, 103, 104, 113, 128, 205, 206, 219, 220, 228, 248, 249, 251, 252, 263, 271, 288, 290, 303, 309, 310, 313–317, 320, 323
Literariness, 12, 14, 15, 33, 44, 103, 104, 108, 133, 143, 144, 253, 269, 271, 272, 275, 287, 288, 309, 310
Lorde, Audre, 134
Louis, Édouard, 50, 53, 236
Lumière, Louis and Auguste, 236

M
Mandela, Nelson, 195, 196
Marzoa, Alejandro, 238
Masculinity, 10, 129, 130
  See also Gender
Mask, 70, 122, 290–295, 303, 304
Media, 4, 6, 12, 15, 17, 61, 68, 73, 77, 112, 125, 129, 130, 150, 154, 155, 231, 237, 323
Memoir, 93, 94, 96, 98n9, 102, 110–114, 133, 208, 211, 213, 216, 219, 220, 287, 289, 292, 314–316, 321
Memory, 8, 11–14, 28, 55, 66, 70–72, 93, 94, 124–128, 137, 171–174, 185–201, 207, 213–219, 221, 229, 234–240, 242, 258, 292, 298, 309–314, 317–323
  collective memory, 158n12, 191, 239
  individual memory, 126, 213
  memory culture, 187, 188, 192, 198, 200–201
  poetics of memory, 229, 241
  politics of memory, 187, 200
Mental representation, 64, 77
Metafiction, 6, 33, 90–92, 95, 121, 191, 192, 197
Metalepsis, 95, 231

Metanarration, 10, 51, 75, 121–137, 212, 213, 220
Metaphysics, 162, 299
Metatextuality, 76, 90, 91, 110, 115, 281
Migration, 10, 126, 142, 144–147, 149, 151, 152, 155, 157n3, 171, 189, 197, 216–218, 322
  refugee crisis, 192
  See also Diaspora
Mimicry, 164–168
Mirror, 3, 13, 24, 27, 33, 47, 51, 68, 69, 77, 109, 111, 121, 122, 126, 133, 134, 176, 186, 208, 209, 214, 215, 243n6, 254, 255, 258, 269, 271, 281, 291, 292, 296, 300, 313–317
  mirror stage, 300 (*see also* Lacan, Jacques)
Mizumura Minae, 13, 251, 252, 255, 261–262
  Shishōsetsu from Left to Right, 261
Modernism, 105, 107, 108, 110, 303, 304
Montaigne, Michel de, 288
Moore, Marcel, 287–289, 296, 297, 301–303
Mother tongue, 143, 145, 150, 151, 171, 251, 252, 261
  See also Language
Movie, *see* Cinema
Multiculturalism, 144
Multilingualism, 141–150, 153, 156, 158n11, 171, 251, 252, 255, 261–262

N
Naipaul, V.S., 189
Narcissism, 21, 241, 290, 296–301, 304, 319
  See also Freud, Sigmund; Kristeva, Julia; Psychoanalysis

Narrative
  narrative structure, 112, 146, 147, 150, 155 (*see also* Form)
  narrative turn, 121
  narrative voice, 48, 89, 91, 218, 234, 280
  open-ended narrative, 103
Narratology, 7, 42, 122, 145
National literature, 13, 248, 261–263
Nazism, 131, 195
Nietzsche, Friedrich, 288
Nigeria, 186, 190–195
Nomenclature, *see* Onomastics
Nora, Pierre, 211, 213
Norm, 2, 10, 50, 103, 104, 123, 130–132, 134, 144, 156, 174, 176
North Korea, 73
Novel, 2, 23, 26, 27, 32, 34, 42, 43, 47, 50–56, 68, 69, 72–76, 78n2, 78n3, 83–86, 88–92, 96, 104–106, 108, 110–113, 143, 144, 146, 149, 186, 190–192, 194–200, 206–208, 210, 211, 213, 216, 220, 222n2, 228, 247, 251, 252, 255, 258, 259, 268–272, 276, 278–281, 283n2, 283n3, 287–290, 292, 298–300, 303

O

Ocularcentrism, 232
Oksman, Sergio, 235
Onomastics, 1, 8, 11, 44, 50, 51, 75, 86–88, 90, 208, 218
Ontology, 44, 57n2, 65
Opacity, 174, 233, 235
Origin, 45, 53, 90, 91, 146, 151, 189, 190, 198, 228–231, 235, 237, 238, 240, 250, 259, 262, 283n5, 297, 299–301

P

Paratext, 34, 89, 186–188, 198, 200, 221
  See also Epitext; Peritext
Patino, Basilio Martín, 238
Pattern, 31, 65, 103, 152, 251, 252, 255, 263, 264n3, 291, 292, 301
Performativity, 7, 30–32, 104, 144, 153–156, 164, 175, 230, 238–240, 242n2, 289, 290, 293, 295, 303
Peritext, 186
  See also Epitext; Paratext
Persona, 52, 73, 150, 190, 191, 201, 212, 213, 248, 250, 252, 256, 257, 259, 260
  See also Character
Philosophy, 44, 45, 143, 194, 254, 290, 310
Photography, 4, 6, 11, 12, 14, 15, 17, 76, 109, 164, 166, 167, 172, 176, 180, 230, 237, 272, 287–289, 293–297, 302, 304, 305, 309–323, 323n2
Plot, 189, 191, 195, 199, 219, 258, 289
  See also Narrative
Poetry, 24–26, 75, 76, 87, 88, 144, 146, 147, 150, 152–155, 251, 281, 309
Point of view, 5, 7, 9, 10, 16, 36–37n8, 45, 51, 61–77, 96, 107–109, 114, 115, 122, 123, 132, 133, 136, 137, 149, 150, 156, 162–164, 168, 170, 179–181, 206, 220, 233, 248, 252, 256, 259, 263, 269, 271, 282, 291, 302
  See also Gaze; Focalization
Polyglossia, 10, 141, 142, 144, 147, 148, 151–154, 156
Portugal, 235, 236, 239, 240

Postcolonialism, 9, 11, 16, 168, 169, 185, 192, 199
  See also Colonialism
Pronoun, 36n2, 36n3, 36n5, 36n8, 45, 49, 52, 89, 94, 97, 97n5, 115, 124, 150, 169, 170, 187, 188, 201n1, 233, 248–251, 254, 256, 258–260, 262, 274, 301, 311, 314, 317, 323n3
  See also Deixis
Proust, Marcel, 104, 318
Psychoanalysis, 105, 106, 108, 110, 112, 114, 116, 187, 255, 256, 258, 260, 297, 299
  See also Freud, Sigmund; Kristeva, Julia; Lacan, Jacques
Psychology, 8, 64, 77, 241, 269, 295
Publishing industry
  marketing, 61
  self-publishing, 61

R

Race, 11, 29, 93, 103, 155, 156, 163–165, 168, 176–179, 193, 194, 196, 199, 218, 219, 237, 289, 290, 292, 302, 304, 320
Realism, 277, 311
Reality, 12, 25, 28, 29, 33, 44–47, 49, 61, 68, 72, 74, 77, 87, 88, 112, 129, 131, 150, 162, 163, 166, 167, 176, 195, 207, 208, 211, 214, 215, 229–231, 235, 241, 242, 242n4, 252, 258, 261, 270, 272, 280, 281, 283, 302, 313, 315, 317, 323
Reception, 1, 2, 4, 6, 8–12, 14–16, 21, 26–28, 30, 32–35, 37n8, 42, 44, 46–48, 50–56, 61–77, 78n3, 78n5, 85–91, 93–96, 105–108, 111, 115, 146, 150, 151, 153, 156, 162, 165, 166, 188, 191, 192, 194, 197, 205–221, 228, 229, 231, 233, 238, 240, 241, 243n7, 249–251, 253, 254, 256, 263, 264n2, 272, 276, 280, 281, 289, 296, 300, 316, 318, 319, 322
Reconciliation, 11, 97, 186, 194, 196, 199–201, 234, 262, 269
Referentiality, 34, 156, 211, 215, 217, 232, 258
Relationality, 132, 135, 136
Relevance, 16, 35, 65, 76, 77, 274
Religion, 54, 78n5, 135, 150, 193, 195, 197, 207, 292, 298, 299, 317
Representation, 11, 46, 51, 63, 64, 68, 73, 76, 77, 94, 103, 104, 107–110, 112, 162–167, 176, 177, 179, 195, 206, 220, 229, 233, 234, 241, 289, 293, 297, 311, 312
Retief, Piet, 198–200
Richardson, Dorothy, 4, 9, 91, 101, 104–111, 116
Ricœur, Paul, 121, 260, 261
Roth, Philip, 4, 8, 63, 66, 67, 69–72, 74, 78n4, 78n5, 105
Rousseau, Jean-Jacques, 28, 43, 103, 254
Rushdie, Salman, 26

S

Sagisawa, Megumu, 13, 252, 254, 255, 258–263
  Kakeru shōnen, 258
  Sagisawa Megumu jishin ni yoru Sagisaw Megumu, 258
  Watashi no hanashi, 258, 259
  "Watashi to iu Jibun," 260
Schema, 43, 63–65, 69, 71, 72, 74, 75
Searle, John, 45, 46

Self
  self-fashioning, 111, 298
  self-inscription, 176
  self-projection, 178
  See also Identity
Self-awareness, 197
Self-portraiture, 4, 6, 11, 12, 14, 15, 31, 78n4, 162–165, 169, 171–176, 178–181, 218, 287–305, 309, 310
Seriality, 6, 9, 15, 28, 101–116, 116n1, 289, 293, 295
Shakespeare, William, 199
Shame, 50, 133, 134, 136, 174, 279
Shamsie, Kamila, 187, 188
Shishōsetsu, 13, 15, 247–263
Silence, 108, 127, 187, 298, 316
Silva, António Ernesto da, 239, 240, 243n9
Socialism, 240, 243n9
  See also Capitalism; Working class
Society, 10–12, 16, 49, 50, 68, 75, 77, 121, 123, 126, 127, 130, 137, 144, 145, 147–151, 154–156, 163–165, 168, 169, 180, 181, 187, 189, 190, 192, 196, 200, 201, 207, 208, 212, 214, 215, 237, 240–242, 243n9, 279, 283n3, 297, 319, 320, 323
Solipsism, 297
Sontag, Susan, 134, 313, 315, 320
South Africa, 163, 164, 168, 196–198, 200
Space, 45, 47, 49, 53, 54, 66, 102, 124–127, 133, 137, 143, 147, 148, 161, 163, 169, 174–176, 180, 181, 201, 208, 211, 212, 214–216, 220, 228, 230, 237, 239, 240, 243n7, 256, 282, 288, 289, 292, 298, 299, 301, 312
St. Augustine, 103
Sterne, Laurence, 95

Stream-of-consciousness, 105, 107, 110, 213
Style/stylistics, 1, 44, 84, 97, 105, 107, 108, 111, 114–116, 129, 131, 144, 148, 153, 248, 251
  See also Form; Language
Subjectivity, 14, 31, 45, 46, 50, 51, 57n3, 62, 72, 102–105, 113–116, 123, 125, 145, 162–165, 170, 173, 176, 177, 180, 181, 187–190, 195, 201, 213–215, 220, 228, 230, 233, 237, 238, 241, 242n4, 248, 251, 254, 258, 259, 263, 269, 270, 272, 273, 279, 288, 290, 295, 297–299, 301, 309, 311, 317, 318, 320
Swan, Astrid, 10, 133–137, 137n2, 138n10
Symbolism, 15, 24, 36n7, 147, 157n6, 165, 173, 176, 189, 196, 231, 239, 240, 272, 302
Szir, Pablo, 231, 232, 234

T
Tau, Bontle, 11, 15, 161, 310
  "Amour non partagé," 177
  "En regardant mes peuples," 170
  "I Knew Who I Was This Morning, But I've Changed a Few Times Since Then," 174, 175
  "Je t'attends, je t'attends là pendant toute ma vie," 169, 170
  "L'inscription," 165, 167
  "The Look of Reading (After Garrett Stewart)," 165
  "Of Another Time When I Existed," 171–173
Testimony, 192, 236, 238, 239, 248, 256, 259, 260, 309, 315
  See also Witness

Therapy, 66, 260
Translatability, 33, 249, 251–253, 255, 263
Transparency, 3, 44, 174, 176, 233
Trauma, 135, 313
Truth, 14, 15, 24–27, 30, 42, 44, 45, 66, 70, 71, 97n1, 102, 103, 109–111, 131–133, 162, 164, 167, 181, 185, 195, 196, 198, 215, 233, 235, 237, 259, 268–275, 277–279, 282, 295, 301, 312, 318, 319

V
Viewer, 170, 179, 180, 229, 231, 232, 234, 235, 240–242, 242n4
Visual art, 11, 17, 161–164, 168, 171, 176, 177, 179, 229, 242n1, 287, 289, 310, 311, 320

W
War, *see* Conflict
Western, 11, 103, 163, 165, 169, 176, 178–180, 190, 193, 206, 253, 255, 290
Witness, 145–147, 164, 192, 193, 209, 214, 323
  See also Testimony
Woolf, Virginia, 4, 108, 313
Working class, 29, 93, 230, 236–240
  See also Capitalism; Socialism
World literature, 97n1, 248, 251, 254, 263
Wright, Richard, 189

Z
Zaimoglu, Feridun, 142, 146–154

Ingram Content Group UK Ltd.
Milton Keynes UK
UKHW020104150623
423463UK00011B/285